EXCEL 2003
PERSONAL TRAINER

CustomGuide, Inc.

O'REILLY®

Beijing • Cambridge • Farnham • Köln • Paris • Sebastopol • Taipei • Tokyo

Excel 2003 Personal Trainer
by CustomGuide, Inc.

Copyright © 2005 O'Reilly Media, Inc. All rights reserved.
Printed in the United States of America.

Cover illustration © 2005 Lou Brooks.

Published by O'Reilly Media, Inc., 1005 Gravenstein Highway
North, Sebastopol, CA 95472.

O'Reilly books may be purchased for educational, business, or
sales promotional use. Online editions are also available for
most titles (*safari.oreilly.com*). For more information, contact
our corporate/institutional sales department: (800) 998-9938
or *corporate@oreilly.com*.

Editors	Tatiana Apandi Diaz and Nathan Torkington
Production Editor	Mary Brady
Art Director	Michele Wetherbee
Cover Designer	Emma Colby
Cover Illustrator	Lou Brooks
Interior Designer	Melanie Wang

Printing History

November 2004:	First Edition.

RepKover™ This book uses RepKover,™ a durable and flexible lay-flat binding.

ISBN: 0-596-00853-8
[C]

CONTENTS

Contents

INTRODUCTION

About the Personal Trainer Series

Most software manuals are as hard to navigate as the programs they describe. They assume that you're going to read all 500 pages from start to finish, and that you can gain intimate familiarity with the program simply by reading about it. Some books give you sample files to practice on, but when you're finding your way around a new set of skills, it's all too easy to mess up program settings or delete data files and not know how to recover. Even if William Shakespeare and Bill Gates teamed up to write a book about Microsoft Excel, their book would be frustrating to read because most people learn by doing the task.

While we don't claim to be rivals to either Bill, we think we have a winning formula in the Personal Trainer series. We've created a set of workouts that reflect the tasks you really want to do, whether as simple as resizing or as complex as integrating multimedia components. Each workout breaks a task into a series of simple steps, showing you exactly what to do to accomplish the task.

And instead of leaving you hanging, the interactive CD in the back of this book recreates the application for you to experiment in. In our unique simulator, there's no worry about permanently damaging your preferences, turning all your documents purple, losing data, or any of the other things that can go wrong when you're testing your new skills in the unforgiving world of the real application. It's fully interactive, giving you feedback and guidance as you work through the exercises—just like a real trainer!

Our friendly gym-themed guides can buff up your skills in record time. You'll learn the secrets of the professionals in a safe environment, with exercises and homework for those of you who really want to break the pain barrier. You'll have your Excel 2003 skills in shape in no time!

About This Book

We've aimed this book at Excel 2003. Some features may look different or simply not exist if you're using another version of the program. If our simulator doesn't match your application, check the version number to make sure you're using the right version.

Since this is a hands-on course, each lesson contains an exercise with step-by-step instructions for you to follow.

To make learning easier, every exercise follows certain conventions:

- This book never assumes you know where (or what) something is. The first time you're told to click something, a picture of what you're supposed to click appears in the illustrations in the lesson.

- When you see a keyboard instruction like "press Ctrl + B," you should press and hold the first key ("Ctrl" in this example) while you press the second key ("B" in this example). Then, after you've pressed both keys, you can release them.

Our exclusive Quick Reference box appears at the end of every lesson. You can use it to review the skills you've learned in the lesson and as a handy reference—when you need to know how to do something fast and don't need to step through the sample exercises.

Conventions Used in This Book

The following is a list of typographical conventions used in this book:

Italic

Shows important terms the first time they are presented.

Constant Width

Shows anything you're actually supposed to type.

Color

Shows anything you're supposed to click, drag, or press.

NOTE *Warns you of pitfalls that you could encounter if you're not careful.*

TIP *Indicates a suggestion or supplementary information to the topic at hand.*

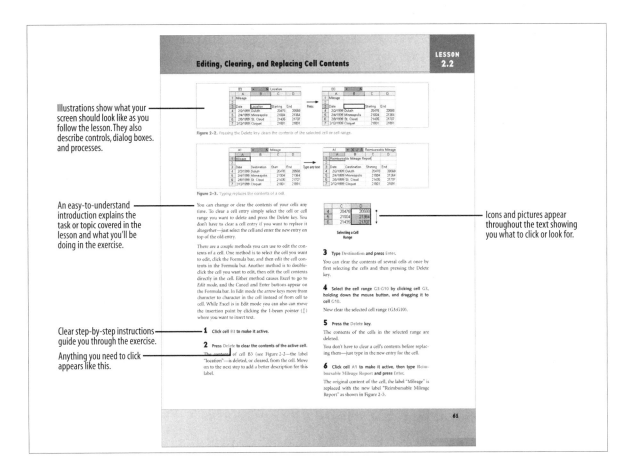

Illustrations show what your screen should look like as you follow the lesson. They also describe controls, dialog boxes, and processes.

An easy-to-understand introduction explains the task or topic covered in the lesson and what you'll be doing in the exercise.

Clear step-by-step instructions guide you through the exercise.

Anything you need to click appears like this.

Icons and pictures appear throughout the text showing you what to click or look for.

Using the Interactive Environment

Minimum Specs

- Windows 98 or better
- 64 MB RAM
- 150 MB Disk Space

Installation Instructions

Insert disc into CD-ROM drive. Click the Install button at the prompt. The installer will give you the option of installing the Interactive Content and the Practice Files. These are both installed by default. Practice files are also included on the CD in a directory called "Practice Files," which can be accessed without installing anything. If you select the installation item, the installer will then create a shortcut in your Start menu under the title "Personal Trainer," which you can use to access your installation selections.

Use of Interactive Content

Once you've installed the interactive content, placing the disc in your drive will cause the program to launch automatically. Then, once it has launched, just make your lesson selections and learn away!

How to Contact Us

We have tested and verified the information in this book to the best of our ability, but you might find that features have changed (or even that we have made mistakes!). As a reader of this book, you can help us to improve future editions by sending us your feedback. Please let us know about any errors, inaccuracies, bugs, misleading or confusing statements, and typos that you find anywhere in this book.

Please also let us know what we can do to make this book more useful to you. We take your comments seriously and will try to incorporate reasonable suggestions into future editions. You can write to us at:

O'Reilly Media, Inc.
1005 Gravenstein Highway North
Sebastopol, CA 95472
(800) 998-9938 (in the U.S. or Canada)
(707) 829-0515 (international or local)
(707) 829-0104 (fax)

To ask technical questions or to comment on the book, send e-mail to:

bookquestions@oreilly.com

The web site for *Excel 2003 Personal Trainer* lists examples, errata, and plans for future editions. You can find this page at:

http://www.oreilly.com/catalog/excelpt/

For more information about this book and others, see the O'Reilly web site at:

http://www.oreilly.com

CHAPTER 1
THE FUNDAMENTALS

CHAPTER OBJECTIVES:

Starting Microsoft Excel

Giving commands to Excel

Entering labels and values into a workbook

Navigating a workbook

Naming and saving a workbook

Previewing and printing a workbook

Closing a workbook and exiting Excel

CHAPTER TASK: CREATE A SIMPLE INCOME AND EXPENSE REPORT

Prerequisites

- **A computer with Windows 2000 or XP and Excel 2003 installed**
- **An understanding of basic computer functions (how to use the mouse and keyboard)**

Welcome to your first lesson of Microsoft Excel 2003. Excel is a powerful spreadsheet software program that allows you to make quick and accurate numerical calculations. Entering data onto a spreadsheet (or *worksheet*, as they are called in Excel) is quick and easy. Once data has been entered in a worksheet, Excel can instantly perform any type of calculation on it. Excel can also make your information look sharp and professional. The uses for Excel are limitless: businesses use Excel for creating financial reports, scientists use Excel for statistical analysis, and families use Excel to help manage their investment portfolios. Microsoft Excel is by far the most widely used and, according to most reviews, the most powerful and user-friendly spreadsheet program available. You've made a great choice by deciding to learn Microsoft Excel 2003.

This chapter will introduce you to the Excel "basics"—what you need to know to create, print, and save a worksheet. If you've seen the Microsoft Excel program screen before, you know that it is filled with cryptic-looking buttons, menus, and icons. By the time you have finished this chapter, you will know what most of those buttons, menus, and icons are used for.

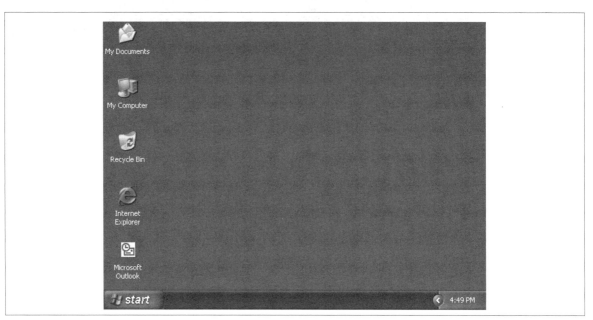

Figure 1-1. The Windows Desktop.

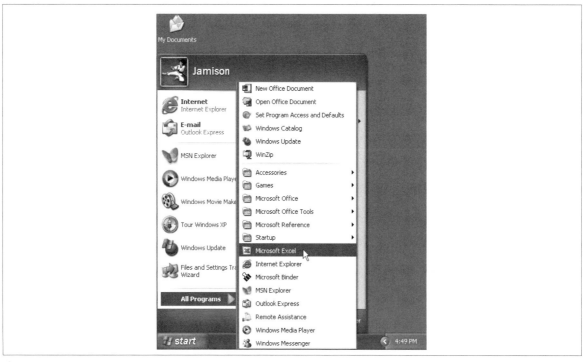

Figure 1-2. Programs located under the Windows Start button.

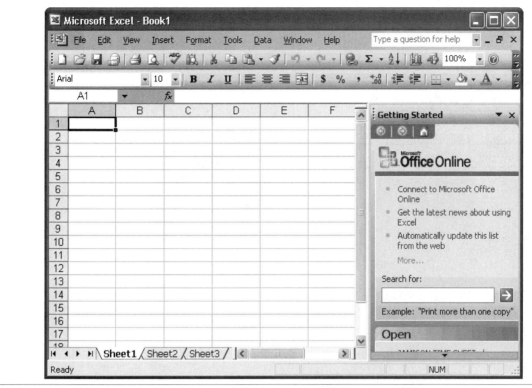

Figure 1-3. The Microsoft Excel program screen.

Before starting Microsoft Excel 2003, you have to make sure your computer is on—if it's not, turn it on! Start Excel 2003 the same as you would start any other Windows program on your computer—with the Start button. Because every computer is set up differently (some people like to rearrange and reorder their program menu), the procedure for starting Excel on your computer may be slightly different from the one listed here.

Start Button

1 Make sure your computer is on and the Windows desktop is open.

Your computer screen should look similar to the one shown in Figure 1-1.

2 Use your mouse to point to and click the Start Button, located at the bottom-left corner of the screen.

The Windows Start menu pops up.

3 Use the mouse to move the pointer over the word All Programs.

A menu similar to the one shown in Figure 1-2 pops out to the right of Programs. The programs and menus listed will depend on the programs installed on your computer, so your menu will probably look somewhat different from the illustration.

4 Select Microsoft Office from the menu.

Almost there.

5 Select Microsoft Office Excel 2003 from the menu.

Depending on how many programs are installed on your computer and how they are organized, it might be a little difficult to find the Microsoft Excel program. Once you click the Microsoft Excel program, your computer's hard drive will whir for a moment while it loads Excel. The Excel program screen appears, as shown in Figure 1-3.

That's it! You are ready to start creating spreadsheets with Microsoft Excel. In the next lesson, you will learn what all those funny-looking objects on your screen are.

QUICK REFERENCE

TO START MICROSOFT EXCEL:

1. CLICK THE WINDOWS START BUTTON.

2. SELECT ALL PROGRAMS → MICROSOFT OFFICE → MICROSOFT OFFICE EXCEL 2003.

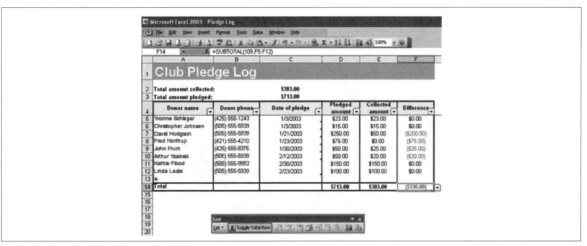

Figure 1-4. Improved lists let you work with the related data outside of the list.

If you're upgrading from Excel 2000 or 2002 to Excel 2003 you're in luck—in most respects, Excel 2003 looks and works *almost* the same as earlier versions of Excel. Table 1-1 lists what's new in Excel 2003.

Table 1-1. What's New in 2003

New Feature	Description
XML Support	Excel 2003 offers industry-standard XML support, which allows you to take structured data and place it in a file that follows standard guidelines and can be read by multiple applications.
Smart Documents	Smart Documents help you reuse existing information and make it easier to share content by responding to your actions within a workbook. They can interact with numerous databases and other Microsoft Office programs.
Person Names Smart Tag Menu	The Person Names Smart Tag menu allows you to rapidly find contact information and complete scheduling tasks. This option is available any time a person's name appears.
Enhanced List Functionality	Enhancements in list functionality include: the ability to create a list from existing information or from an empty range; the capacity to manipulate list data without affecting the non-list data; new user interface and corresponding set of functionality; AutoFilter is enabled by default; dark blue list borders outline the cells designated as a list; insert rows; total rows; and resize handles.
Enhanced Statistical Functions	Microsoft has debugged many of the functions that were problematic in Excel 2002. Other enhancements to statistical functions include more rapid results and better accuracy.
Document Workspaces	Document Workspaces are Windows SharePoint sites that allow multiple people to cowrite, edit, and review documents simultaneously.
Information Rights Management (IRM)	IRM is a method used to create or view documents and e-mail messages with restricted permission. This prevents the printing, forwarding, and copying of sensitive documents by unauthorized people.
Compare Side by Side Command	Save time and effort by scrolling through two workbooks side by side and simultaneously. The Compare Side by Side command eliminates the need to merge workbooks together in order to see the changes.
Research Task Pan	Paired with an Internet connection, the new Research Task Pane gives you access to various types of reference and research sources including an encyclopedia, dictionary, thesaurus, translation services, Web searches, and company profile and stock quote services.

Table 1-1. What's New in 2003 (Continued)

New Feature	Description
Support for Ink Devices	To make working on the Tablet PC or any other ink device easier, view your task panes horizontally. In addition, add your handwriting to Excel Documents using Tablet PC.
Smart Tags (new in 2002)	Context-sensitive Smart Tags are a set of buttons that provide speedy access to relevant information by alerting you to important actions—such as formatting options for pasted information, formula error correction, and more.
Speech Playback (new in 2002)	An option to have a computer voice play back data after every cell entry or after a range of cells has been entered makes verifying data entry convenient and practical. You can even choose the voice the computer uses to read back your data.
Expanded AutoSum Functionality (new in 2002)	The practical functionality of AutoSum has expanded to include a drop-down list of the most common functions. For example, you can click Average from the list to calculate the average of a selected range, or connect to the Function Wizard for more options.
Recommended Functions in the Function Wizard (new in 2002)	Type a natural language query, such as "How do I determine the monthly payment for a car loan," and the Function Wizard returns a list of recommended functions you can use to accomplish your task.
Formula Error Checking (new in 2002)	Like a grammar or spell checker; Excel uses certain rules to check for problems in formulas. These rules can help find common mistakes. You can turn these rules on or off individually.
Multiple Cut, Copy, and Paste Clipboard	An improved Office clipboard lets you copy up to 24 pieces of information at once across all the Office applications and store them on the Task Pane. The Task Pane gives you a visual representation of the copied so you can easily distinguish between items as they transfer them to other documents

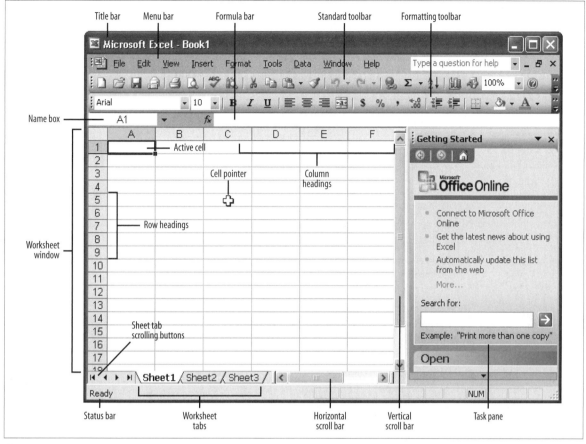

Figure 1-5. Elements of the Excel program screen.

You might find the Excel 2003 program screen a bit confusing and overwhelming the first time you see it. What are all those buttons, icons, menus, and arrows for? This lesson will help you become familiar with the Excel program screen. There are no step-by-step instructions in this lesson. All you have to do is look at Figure 1-5 then refer to Table 1-2 to see what everything you're looking at means. And, most of all, relax! This lesson is only meant to help you get acquainted with the Excel screen; you don't have to memorize anything.

Table 1-2. The Excel Program Screen

Element	Description
Title bar	Displays the name of the program you are currently using (in this case, Microsoft Excel) and the name of the workbook on which you are working. The title bar appears at the top of all Windows programs.
Menu Bar	Displays a list of menus you use to give commands to Excel. Clicking a menu name displays a list of commands. For example, clicking the Format menu name displays different formatting commands.
Standard toolbar	Toolbars are shortcuts containing buttons for the most commonly used commands (instead of having to wade through several menus). The Standard toolbar contains buttons for the Excel commands you use the most, such as saving, opening, and printing workbooks.
Formatting toolbar	Contains buttons for the most commonly used formatting commands, such as making text bold or italicized.

Table 1-2. The Excel Program Screen (Continued)

Element	Description
Task pane	Lists commands that are relevant to whatever you're doing in Excel. You can easily hide the task pane if you want to have more room to view a workbook. Simply click the close button in the upper-right corner of the task pane.
Worksheet window	Where you enter data and work on your worksheets. You can have more than one worksheet window open at a time.
Cell pointer and active cell	Highlights the cell you are working on. The current cell in Figure 1-5 is located at A1. To make another cell active just click the cell with the mouse or press the arrow keys on the keyboard to move the cell pointer to a new location.
Formula bar	Allows you to view, enter, and edit data in the current cell. The Formula bar displays any formulas a cell might contain.
Name box	Displays the active cell address. In Figure 1-5, "A1" appears in the name box, indicating that the active cell is A1.
Worksheet tabs	You can keep multiple worksheets together in a group called a workbook. You can move quickly from one worksheet to another by clicking the worksheet tabs. You can give worksheets your own meaningful names, such as "Budget" instead of "Sheet1." Excel workbooks contain three worksheets by default.
Scroll bars	There are both vertical and horizontal scroll bars; you use them to view and move around your spreadsheet. The scroll box shows where you are in the workbook. For example, if the scroll box is near the top of the scroll bar, you're at the beginning of a workbook.
Status bar	Displays messages and feedback.

Don't worry if you find some of these elements of the Excel program screen confusing at first. They will make more sense after you've actually used them, which you will get a chance to do in the next lesson.

Using Menus

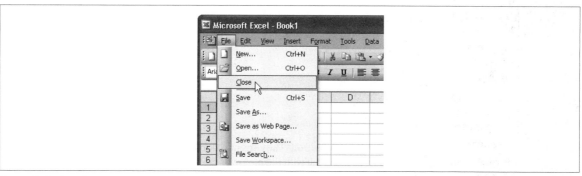

Figure 1-6. The File menu.

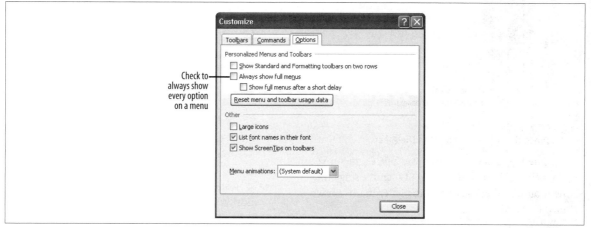

Check to
always show
every option
on a menu

Figure 1-7. The Customize dialog box.

This lesson explains one way to give commands to Excel—by using the *menus*. Menus for all Windows programs can be found at the top of a window, just beneath the program's title bar. In Figure 1-6, notice the words File, Edit, View, Insert, Tools, and Data. The next steps will show you why they're there.

1 Click the word File on the menu bar.

A menu drops down from the word File, as shown in Figure 1-6. The File menu contains a list of file-related commands such as New, which creates a new file; Open, which opens or loads a saved file; Save, which saves the currently opened file; and Close, which closes the currently opened file. Move on to the next step to try selecting a command from the File menu.

2 Click the word Close in the File menu.

The workbook window disappears—you have just closed the current workbook. Notice that each of the words in the menu has an underlined letter somewhere in it. For example, the "F" in the File menu is underlined. Holding down the Alt key and pressing the underlined letter in a menu does the same thing as clicking it. So, pressing the Alt key and then the F key would open the File menu. Move on to the next step and try it for yourself.

The Tools Menu
with less frequently used commands hidden

The Tools menu will display less frequently used commands
after clicking the downward-pointing arrow ⥥ at the
bottom of the menu.

3 Press the Alt key then press the F key.

The File menu appears. Once you open a menu you can navigate through the different menus using either the mouse or the Alt key and the letter that is underlined in the menu name.

4 Press the Right Arrow Key (→).

The next menu to the right, the Edit menu, appears. If you open a menu and then change your mind, it's easy to close it without selecting any commands. Just click anywhere *outside* the menu or press the Esc key.

5 Click anywhere outside the menu to close the menu without issuing any commands.

The menus in Excel 2003 work quite a bit differently than in other Windows programs—even than previous versions of Excel. Microsoft Excel 2003 displays its menu commands on the screen in three different ways:

- By displaying every command possible, just like most Windows programs, including earlier versions of Excel.

- By hiding the commands you don't use as frequently (the more advanced commands) from view.

- By displaying the hidden commands by clicking the downward-pointing arrows (⥥) at the bottom of the menu or after waiting a couple of seconds.

6 Click the word Tools in the menu.

The most common menu commands appear first in the Tools menu. Some people feel intimidated by being confronted with so many menu options, so the menus in Office 2003 don't display the more advanced commands at first. To display a menu's advanced commands either click the downward-pointing arrows (⥥) at the bottom of the menu or keep the menu open a few seconds.

7 Click the downward-pointing arrows (ⓥ) at the bottom of the Tools menu.

The more advanced commands appear shaded on the Tools menu.

If you're accustomed to working with earlier versions of Microsoft Office you may find that hiding the more advanced commands is disconcerting. If so, you can easily change how Excel's menus work. Here's how:

8 Select View → Toolbars → Customize from the menu.

Make sure you select the Options tab. The Customize dialog box appears, as shown in Figure 1-7. This is where you can change how Excel's menus work. There are two check boxes here that are important:

- **Always show full menus:** Uncheck this check box if you want to show all the commands on the menus, instead of hiding the advanced commands.

- **Show full menus after a short delay:** If checked, this option waits a few seconds before displaying the more advanced commands on a menu.

9 Click Close.

Table 1-3. Menus found in Microsoft Excel

File	Description
File	File-related commands to open, save, close, print, and create new files.
Edit	Commands to copy, cut, paste, find, and replace text.
View	Commands to change how the workbook is displayed on the screen.
Insert	Lists items that you can insert into a workbook, such as graphics and charts.
Format	Commands to format fonts, cell alignment, and borders.
Tools	Lists tools such the spell checker and macros. You can also change Excel's default options here.
Data	Commands to analyze and work with data information.
Window	Commands to display and arrange multiple windows (if you have more than one file open).
Help	Get help on using the program.

QUICK REFERENCE

TO OPEN A MENU:

• CLICK THE MENU NAME WITH THE MOUSE.

   OR...

• PRESS ALT AND THEN THE UNDERLINED LETTER IN MENU.

TO DISPLAY A MENU'S HIDDEN COMMANDS:

• CLICK THE DOWNWARD-POINTING ARROW () AT THE BOTTOM OF THE MENU.

   OR...

• OPEN THE MENU AND WAIT A FEW SECONDS.

TO CHANGE HOW MENUS WORK:

1. SELECT VIEW → TOOLBARS → CUSTOMIZE FROM THE MENU.

2. CHECK OR CLEAR EITHER THE ALWAYS SHOW FULL MENUS AND/OR SHOW FULL MENUS AFTER A SHORT DELAY OPTIONS, THEN CLICK CLOSE.

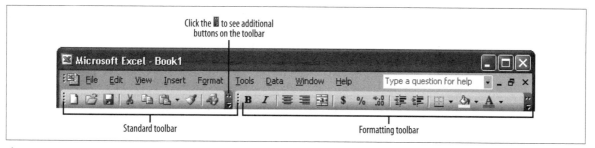

Figure 1-8. The Standard and Formatting toolbars squished together on the same bar.

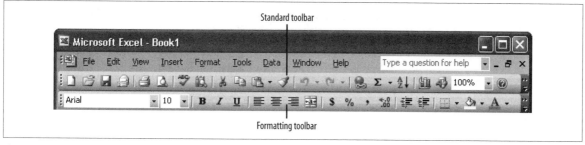

Figure 1-9. The Standard and Formatting toolbars stacked as separate toolbars.

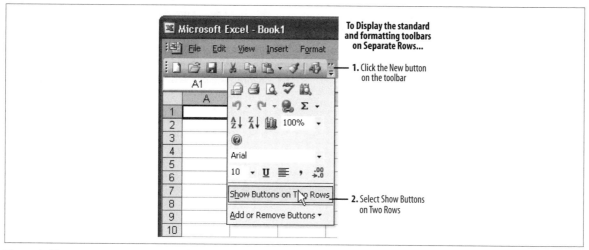

Figure 1-10. The Customize dialog box.

In this lesson, we move on to another common way of giving commands to Excel—using toolbars. Toolbars are shortcuts—they contain buttons for the most commonly used commands. Instead of wading through several menus to access a command, you can click a single button on a toolbar. Two toolbars appear when you start Excel by default:

- **Standard toolbar:** Located either to the left or above the Formatting toolbar, the Standard toolbar contains buttons for the commands you'll use most frequently in Excel, such as Save and Print.

- **Formatting toolbar:** Located either to the right of or below the Standard toolbar, the Formatting toolbar and contains buttons for quickly formatting fonts and paragraphs.

Screen Tip

1 Position the mouse pointer over the New button on the Standard toolbar (but don't click the mouse yet!).

A Screen Tip appears over the button briefly identifying what the button is, in this case "New". If you don't know what a button on a toolbar does, simply move the pointer over it, wait a second, and a ScreenTip will appear over the button, telling you what it does.

New Button
Other Ways to Create a New Worksheet
• Select **File→New** from the menu.

2 Click the New button on the Standard toolbar.

A new, blank workbook appears—not only have you learned how to use Microsoft Excel's toolbars, but you've also learned how to create a new, blank workbook.

Excel's toolbars also have "show more" arrows, just like menus do. When you click a "show more" button, it displays a drop-down menu of the remaining buttons on the toolbar, as well as several toolbar-related options.

3 Click the button on the far-right side of the Standard toolbar.

A list of the remaining buttons on the Standard toolbar appear, as shown in Figure 1-10. Just like personalized menus, Excel remembers which toolbar buttons you use most often and displays them in a more prominent position on the toolbar.

4 Click anywhere outside the toolbar list to close the list without selecting any of its options.

Today, many computers have larger monitors, so Microsoft decided to save space on the screen and squished both the Standard and Formatting toolbars together on the same bar, as shown in Figure 1-8. While squishing two toolbars together on the same bar gives you more space on the screen, it also makes the two toolbars look confusing—especially if you're used to working with a previous version of Microsoft Office. If you find both toolbars sharing the same bar confusing, you can "un-squish" the Standard and Formatting toolbars and stack them on top of each other, as illustrated in Figure 1-9. Here's how…

5 Click the button on either the Standard or Formatting toolbar.

A list of more buttons and options appears, as shown in Figure 1-10. To stack the Standard and Formatting toolbars on top of one another, select the Show Buttons on Two Rows option.

6 Select Show Buttons on Two Rows from the list.

Microsoft Excel displays the Standard and Formatting toolbars on two separate rows. You can display the Standard and Formatting toolbars on the same row using the same procedure.

7 Click the button on either the Standard or Formatting toolbar and select Show Buttons on One Row from the list.

Excel once again displays the Standard and Formatting toolbars on the same row.

So should you display the Standard and Formatting toolbars on the same row or should you give each toolbar its own row? That's a question that depends on the size and resolution of your computer's display and your own personal preference. If you have a large 17-inch monitor, you might want to display both toolbars on the same row. On the other hand, if you have a smaller monitor or are constantly clicking the "show more" buttons to access hidden toolbar buttons, you may want to display the Standard and Formatting toolbar on separate rows.

QUICK REFERENCE

TO USE A TOOLBAR BUTTON:

• CLICK THE BUTTON YOU WANT TO USE.

TO DISPLAY A TOOLBAR BUTTON'S DESCRIPTION:

• POSITION THE POINTER OVER THE TOOLBAR BUTTON AND WAIT A SECOND. A SCREENTIP WILL APPEAR ABOVE THE BUTTON.

TO CREATE A NEW WORKBOOK:

• CLICK THE NEW BUTTON ON THE STANDARD TOOLBAR.

OR...

• SELECT FILE → NEW FROM THE MENU.

TO STACK THE STANDARD AND FORMATTING TOOLBARS IN TWO SEPARATE ROWS:

• CLICK THE ▫ BUTTON ON EITHER TOOLBAR AND SELECT SHOW BUTTONS ON TWO ROWS FROM THE LIST.

Filling Out Dialog Boxes

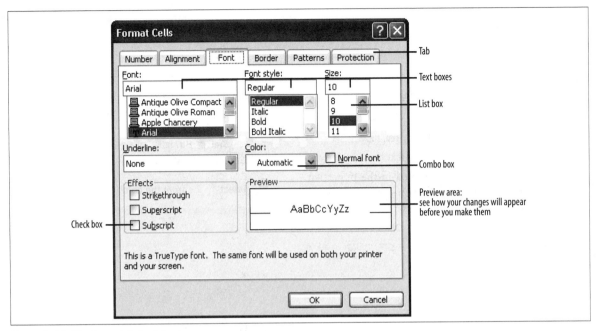

Figure 1-11. The Format Cells dialog box.

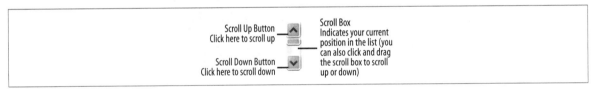

Figure 1-12. Using a scroll bar.

Some commands are more complicated than others. Saving a file is a simple process—just select File → Save from the menu or click the Save button on the Standard toolbar. Other commands are more complex. For example, suppose you want to change the top margin of the current workbook to a half-inch. Whenever you want to do something relatively complicated, you must fill out a *dialog box*. Filling out a dialog box is usually quite easy—if you've worked at all with Windows, you've undoubtedly filled out hundreds of dialog boxes. Dialog boxes usually contain several types of controls, including:

- Text boxes
- List boxes
- Check boxes
- Combo boxes (also called drop-down lists)

It's important that you know the names of these controls, because this book will refer to them in just about every lesson. This lesson gives you a tour of a dialog box and

explains each of these controls, so you will know what they are and how to use them.

1 Click the word Format from the menu bar.

The Format menu appears. Notice that the items listed in the Format menu are followed by ellipses (...). The ellipses indicate that there is a dialog box behind the menu.

2 Select Cells from the Format menu.

The Format Cells dialog box appears. The Format Cells dialog box is actually one of the most complex dialog boxes in Microsoft Excel, and it contains several different components you can fill out.

First, let's look at the tabs in the Format Cells dialog box. Some dialog boxes have so many options that they can't all fit on the same screen. When this happens, Windows divides the dialog box into several related *tabs,* or sections. To view a different tab, simply click it.

3 **Click the** Alignment tab.

The Alignment tab appears in front.

4 **Click the** Font tab.

The Font tab of the Format Cells dialog box appears, as shown in Figure 1-11. Remember: the purpose of this lesson is to learn about dialog boxes, not how to format fonts (we'll cover that later). The next destination on our dialog box tour is the text box.

Look at the Font text box, located in the upper left corner of the dialog box. Text boxes are the most common component of a dialog box and are nothing more than the old fill-in-the-blank that you're already familiar with if you've filled out any type of form. To use a text box, click the text box or press the Tab key until the insertion point appears in the text box, then simply type what you want to appear in the text box.

5 **Make sure the Font text box is selected and type** Arial.

You've just filled out the text box—nothing to it. The next stop in our dialog box tour is the *list box*. There's a list box located directly below the Font text box. A list box is a way of listing several (or many) options into a small box. Sometimes list boxes contain so many options that they can't all be displayed at once, and you must use the list box's *scroll bar*, as shown in Figure 1-12, to move up or down the list.

6 **Click and hold the Font list box's** Scroll Down button **until** Times New Roman **appears in the list, then click the** Times New Roman **option to select it.**

Our next destination is the *combo box*, or drop-down list. The combo box is the cousin of the list box—it also displays a list of options. The only difference is that you must click the combo box's downward pointing arrow to display its options.

7 **Click the** Underline combo box **down arrow.**

A list of underlining options appears below the combo box.

8 **Select** Single **from the combo box.**

Sometimes you need to select more than one item from a dialog box. For example, what if you want to add Shadow formatting *and* Small Caps formatting to the selected font? You use the *check box* control when you're presented with multiple choices.

9 **In the Effects section, click the** Strikethrough **check box and click the** Superscript **check box.**

The last destination on our dialog box tour is the *button*. Buttons found in dialog boxes are used to execute or cancel commands. Two buttons are in just about every dialog box:

- **OK:** Applies and saves any changes you have made and then closes this dialog box. Pressing the Enter key is usually the same as clicking the OK button.
- **Cancel:** Closes the dialog box without applying and saving any changes. Pressing the Esc key is the same as clicking the Cancel button.

10 **Click the** Cancel button **to cancel the changes and close the dialog box.**

QUICK REFERENCE

TO USE A TEXT BOX:

- SIMPLY TYPE THE INFORMATION DIRECTLY INTO THE TEXT BOX.

TO USE A LIST BOX:

- CLICK THE OPTION YOU WANT FROM THE LIST BOX. USE THE SCROLL BAR TO MOVE UP AND DOWN THROUGH THE LIST BOX'S OPTIONS.

TO USE A COMBO BOX:

- CLICK THE DOWN ARROW TO LIST THE COMBO BOX'S OPTIONS. CLICK AN OPTION FROM THE LIST TO SELECT IT.

TO CHECK OR UNCHECK A CHECK BOX:

- CLICK THE CHECK BOX.

TO VIEW A DIALOG BOX TAB:

- CLICK THE TAB YOU WANT TO VIEW.

TO SAVE YOUR CHANGES AND CLOSE A DIALOG BOX:

- CLICK THE OK BUTTON OR PRESS ENTER.

TO CLOSE A DIALOG BOX WITHOUT SAVING YOUR CHANGES:

- CLICK THE CANCEL BUTTON OR PRESS ESC.

Keystroke and Right Mouse Button Shortcuts

Figure 1-13. Hold down the Ctrl key and press another key to execute a keystroke shortcut.

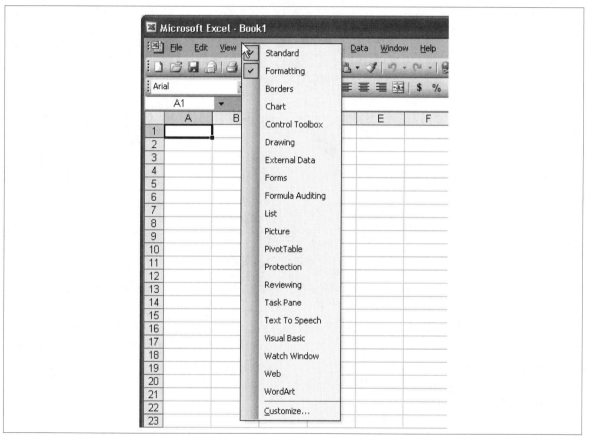

Figure 1-14. Opening a shortcut menu for toolbars.

You are probably starting to realize that there are several methods to do the same thing in Excel. For example, to save a file, you can use the menu (select File → Save) or the toolbar (click the Save button). This lesson introduces you to two more methods of executing commands: right mouse button shortcut menus and keystroke shortcuts.

You know that the left mouse button is the primary mouse button, used for clicking and double-clicking, and it's the mouse button you will use over 95% of the time when you work with Excel. So what's the right mouse button for? Whenever you *right-click* something, it brings up a shortcut menu that lists everything you can do to the object. Whenever you're unsure or curious about what you can do with an object, click it with the right mouse button. A shortcut menu will appear with a list of commands related to the object or area you right-clicked.

Right mouse button shortcut menus are a great way to give commands to Excel because you don't have to wade through several levels of unfamiliar menus when you want to do something.

Shortcut Menu
Right-click an object to open a shortcut menu that lists
everything you can do to the object.

3 Position the pointer over either the Standard or Formatting toolbar and click the right mouse button.

A shortcut menu appears listing all the toolbars you can view, as shown in Figure 1-14.

4 Move the mouse button anywhere outside the menu in the workbook window and click the left mouse button to close the shortcut menu.

On to keystroke shortcuts. Without a doubt, keystroke shortcuts are the fastest way to give commands to Excel, even if they are a little hard to remember. They're great timesavers for issuing common commands you do all the time. To issue a keystroke shortcut, press and hold the Ctrl key, press the shortcut key, and release both buttons.

1 Click the right mouse button while the cursor is anywhere inside the workbook window.

A shortcut menu appears where you clicked the mouse. Notice one of the items listed on the shortcut menu is Format Cells. This is the same Format Cells command you can select from the menu (clicking Format → Format Cells). Using the right mouse button shortcut method is slightly faster and usually easier to remember than Excel's menus. If you open a shortcut menu and then change your mind, you can close it without selecting anything. Here's how:

2 Move the mouse button anywhere outside the menu and click the left mouse button to close the shortcut menu.

Remember that the options listed in the shortcut menu will be different, depending on what or where you right-clicked.

5 Press Ctrl + I (the Ctrl and I keys at the same time).

This is the keystroke shortcut for italics. Note that the *Italics button* on the Formatting toolbar becomes depressed.

6 Type Italics.

The text appears in italics formatting.

NOTE *Although we won't discuss it in this lesson, Excel's default keystroke shortcuts can be changed or remapped to execute other commands.*

Table 1-4 lists the shortcut keystrokes you're likely to use the most in Excel.

Table 1-4. Common Keystroke Shortcuts

Keystroke	Description
Ctrl + B	Toggles bold font formatting
Ctrl + I	Toggles italics font formatting
Ctrl + U	Toggles underline font formatting
Ctrl + Spacebar	Returns the font formatting to the default setting
Ctrl + O	Opens a workbook

Table 1-4. Common Keystroke Shortcuts (Continued)

Keystroke	Description
Ctrl + S	Saves the current workbook
Ctrl + P	Prints the current workbook to the default printer
Ctrl + C	Copies the selected text or object to the Windows clipboard
Ctrl + X	Cuts the selected text or object from its current location to the Windows clipboard
Ctrl + V	Pastes any copied or cut text or object in the Windows clipboard to the current location
Ctrl + Home	Moves the insertion point to the beginning of the workbook
Ctrl + End	Moves the insertion point to the end of the workbook

QUICK REFERENCE

TO OPEN A CONTEXT-SENSITIVE SHORTCUT MENU:

- RIGHT-CLICK THE OBJECT.

TO USE A KEYSTROKE SHORTCUT:

- PRESS CTRL + THE LETTER OF THE KEYSTROKE SHORTCUT YOU WANT TO EXECUTE.

Opening a Workbook

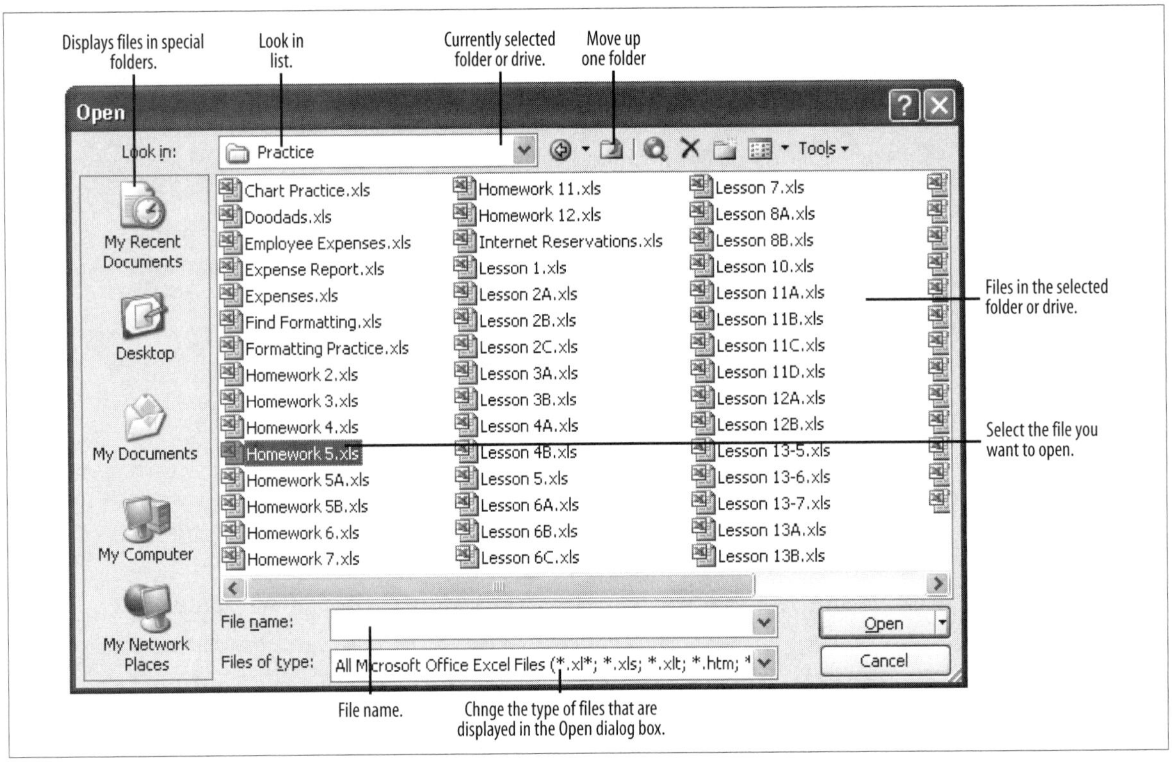

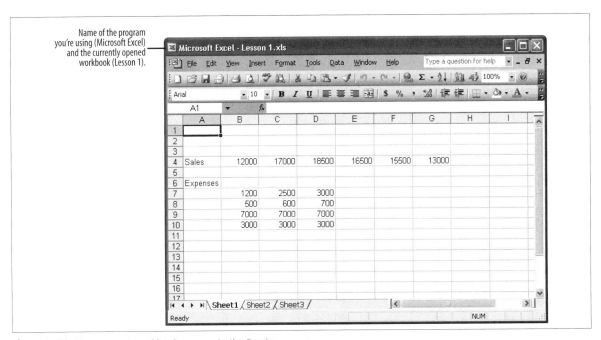

Figure 1-15. The Open dialog box.

Figure 1-16. The Lesson 1 workbook appears in the Excel program.

Open button
Other Ways to Open a File:
• Select **File→Open** from the menu.
• Press <**CTRL**> + <**O**>

When you work with Excel, you will sometimes need to create a new workbook from scratch (something you hopefully learned how to do when we talked about toolbars in a previous lesson) but more often, you'll want to work on an existing workbook that you or someone else has previously saved. This lesson explains how to open or retrieve a saved workbook.

1 Click the Open button on the Standard toolbar.

The Open dialog box appears.

2 Navigate to and open your practice folder or floppy disk.

Your computer stores information in files and folders, just like you store information in a filing cabinet. To open a file, you must first find and open the folder where it's saved. Normally new files are saved in a folder named "My Documents" but sometimes you will want to save or open files in another folder.

The Open and Save dialog boxes both have their own toolbars that make it easy to browse through your

computer's drives and folders. Two controls on this toolbar are particularly helpful:

Look in list

• My Documents **Look In List:** Click to list the drives on your computer and the current folder, then select the drive and/or folder's contents you want to display.

• Up One Level button: Click to move up one folder.

3 Click the document named Lesson 1A in the file list box and click Open.

Excel opens the Lesson 1A workbook and displays it in the window, as shown in Figure 1-16.

Table 1-5 describes the special folders that are located in the Open and Save As dialog boxes.

Table 1-5. Special Folders in the Open and Save As Dialog Boxes

Folder Icon	Folder Name	Description
	My Recent Documents	Displays a list of files on which you've recently worked.
	My Documents	Displays all the files in the My Document folder—the default location where Microsoft Office programs save their files.
	Desktop	Displays all the files and folders saved on your desktop.
	My Computer	Displays a list of the different drives on your computer.
	My Network Places	Lets you browse through the computers in your workgroup and the computers on the network.

QUICK REFERENCE

TO OPEN A WORKBOOK:

- CLICK THE OPEN BUTTON ON THE STANDARD TOOLBAR.

  OR...

- SELECT FILE → OPEN FROM THE MENU.

  OR...

- PRESS CTRL + O.

Specify where you want to save the workbook
(which drive and folder).

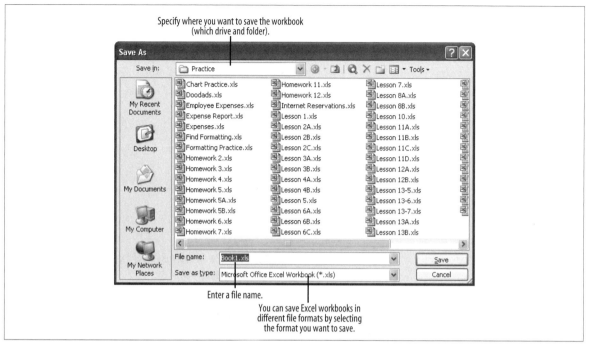

Enter a file name.

You can save Excel workbooks in
different file formats by selecting
the format you want to save.

Figure 1-17. The Save As dialog box.

After you've created a worksheet, you need to save it if you intend on using it ever again. *Saving* a worksheet stores it in a file on your computer's hard disk—similar to putting a file away in a filing cabinet so you can later retrieve it. Once you have saved a worksheet the first time, it's a good idea to save it again from time to time as you work on it. You don't want to lose all your work if the power suddenly goes out, or if your computer crashes! In this lesson, you will learn how to save an existing workbook with a different name without changing the original workbook. It's often easier and more efficient to create a workbook by modifying one that already exists, instead of having to retype a lot of information.

You want to use the information in the Lesson 1A workbook that we opened in the previous lesson to create a new workbook. Since you don't want to modify the original workbook, save it as a new workbook named Income and Expenses.

1 Select File → Save As from the menu.

The Save As dialog box appears (see Figure 1-17). Here is where you can save the workbook with a new, different name. If you only want to save any changes

you've made to a workbook—instead of saving them in a new file—click the Save button on the Standard toolbar, or select File → Save from the menu, or press Ctrl + S.

First you have to tell Excel where to save your workbook.

2 If necessary, navigate to and open your practice folder or floppy disk.

Next you need to specify a new name that you want to save the document under.

3 In the File name text box, type Income and Expenses and click Save.

The Lesson 1A workbook is saved with the new name, Income and Expenses. Now you can work on our new workbook, Income and Expenses, without changing the original workbook, Lesson 1A.

When you make changes to your workbook, you simply save your changes in the same file. Go ahead and try it.

4 Type Income **in the first cell and press the** Enter **key.**

Now save your changes.

Save Button
Other Ways to Save:
• Select **File**→**Save** from the menu
• Press <**CTRL**> + <**S**>

5 **Click the** Save button **on the Standard toolbar.**

Excel saves the changes you've made to the Income and Expenses workbook.

Congratulations! You've just saved your first Excel workbook.

QUICK REFERENCE

TO SAVE A WORKBOOK:

• CLICK THE SAVE BUTTON ON THE STANDARD TOOLBAR.

  OR...

• SELECT FILE → SAVE FROM THE MENU.

  OR...

• PRESS CTRL + S.

TO SAVE A WORKBOOK IN A NEW FILE WITH A DIFFERENT NAME:

1. SELECT FILE → SAVE AS FROM THE MENU.

2. TYPE A NEW NAME FOR THE WORKSHEET AND CLICK SAVE.

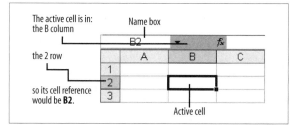

Figure 1-18. Cells are referenced as A1, A2, B1, B2, and so on, with the letter representing a column and the number representing a row.

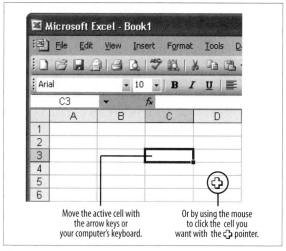

Figure 1-19. The cell reference for the active cell in this example would be B2.

Figure 1-20. Use the keyboard or the mouse to move the cell pointer.

Before you start entering data into a worksheet, you need to learn one very important task: how to move around in a worksheet. This lesson will teach you how to do just that. You must first make a cell *active* before you can enter information in it. You can make a cell active using:

- **The Mouse:** You can click any cell with the white cross pointer (✛).
- **The Keyboard:** You can move the cell pointer using the keyboard's arrow keys.

Worksheets can be confusing places for many people. To help you know where you are in a worksheet, Excel displays row headings, identified by numbers on the left side of the worksheet, and column headings, identified with letters on the top of the worksheet (see Figure 1-18). Each cell in a worksheet is given its own unique *cell address* made from its column letter and row number, such as cell A1, A2, B1, B2, etc. You can immediately find the address of a cell by looking at the *name box*, which shows the current cell address.

Name Box

1 Click cell C3 (located in column C and Row 3) with the ✛ pointer to make it active.

Once you click C3, it becomes the active cell, and its cell address (C3) appears in the name box.

2 Make cell E9 active by clicking it.

Now that you're familiar with the mouse, try using the keyboard.

3 Make cell D5 active, moving the cell pointer by pressing the ← arrow key once and the ↑ arrow key four times.

As you press the arrow keys, watch the name box. Notice it is updated to display the current cell address.

4 Press the Enter key once.

Pressing Enter causes the cell pointer to move down to the next cell. The Enter key is a real timesaver when you're entering data.

5 Press the Tab key twice.

Pressing Tab causes the cell pointer to move to the right, the same as pressing the → key.

6 Press and hold the Shift key as you press the Tab key.

Pressing the Shift and Tab keys at the same time is the same as pressing the ← key. This may seem like an unusual, hard-to-remember keystroke, but it is actually used in many other Windows-based programs.

You have probably already guessed that the worksheet is larger than what you can currently see in the worksheet window. Actually, it is *much, much* larger: there are 256 columns and 65,536 rows in a worksheet! To view the portions of the worksheet that are currently located off-screen, you can use the horizontal and vertical scroll bars, which are located at the bottom and far right of the worksheet screen.

7 Click and hold the right-arrow scroll button on the horizontal scroll bar, until you can see columns X, Y, Z, and AA on your screen.

If you accidently go too far, you can easily move back by clicking the left-arrow scroll button.

When you arrive at the AA column, notice that the cell pointer is not currently located on this screen. Let's see if you remember how to make cell Z4 the active cell.

8 Make cell Z4 active by clicking it with the mouse.

Scrolling up and down in a worksheet is just as easy as scrolling to the right and left. Try it!

9 Click the down-arrow scroll button on the vertical scroll bar several times.

You don't have to use the scroll button to move to worksheet areas that are hidden off-screen—you can do the same thing with the keyboard.

10 Press and hold down the ← key until you reach cell A4.

Congratulations! In one brief lesson, you've become familiar with moving the cell pointer around in a worksheet. Turn the page to go on to the next lesson, where you will learn how to become an expert on getting around in Excel.

QUICK REFERENCE

TO MOVE THE CELL POINTER:

- CLICK ANY CELL WITH THE CROSSHAIR POINTER (⊕) TO MAKE IT ACTIVE.

- USE THE ARROWS KEYS TO MOVE THE ACTIVE CELL AND TO NAVIGATE THE WORKSHEET.

- PRESSING ENTER MOVES THE ACTIVE CELL DOWN.

- PRESSING TAB MOVES THE ACTIVE CELL TO THE RIGHT.

- PRESSING SHIFT + TAB MOVES THE ACTIVE CELL TO THE LEFT.

TO SCROLL THE WORKSHEET:

- CLICK THE LEFT AND RIGHT SCROLL BUTTON ARROWS ON THE HORIZONTAL SCROLL BAR TO SCROLL THE WORKSHEET TO THE LEFT OR RIGHT.

- CLICK THE UP AND DOWN SCROLL BUTTON ARROWS ON THE VERTICAL SCROLL BAR TO SCROLL THE WORKSHEET UP OR DOWN.

Navigating a Worksheet

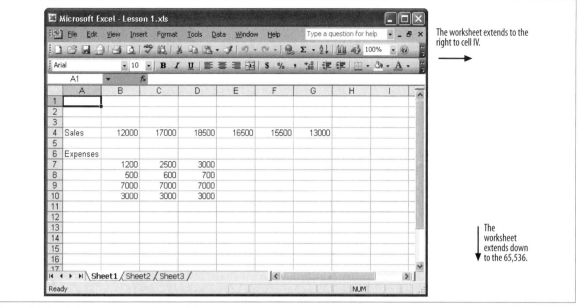

Figure 1-21. Worksheets are actually much larger than what you can see on the screen at one time.

The previous lesson introduced you to the basics of getting around in an Excel worksheet. As workbooks get larger, it gets more difficult to find your way around them. In large worksheets, the simple navigation commands you learned in the previous lesson may take you longer to get to a destination than you would like. This lesson covers the more advanced methods of getting around in Excel.

1 Click cell C15.

You can quickly move up to the first occupied cell in the table by pressing End and then the ↑.

2 Press the end Ctrl key, then press the ↑ key.

The cell pointer moves to the first cell that contains information—C10. Try another shortcut navigation keystroke: the Home key, which moves to column A of the current row.

3 Press Home.

Viola! You're in the A column in the current row.

Table 1-6 displays all the more advanced navigational keystrokes you can use to quickly get around a worksheet.

NOTE *When you refer to the shortcuts in the following table, remember the plus (+) sign between two keys (Ctrl + Home) means you press both keys at the same time. A comma (,) between two keys (End, →) means you must first press and release one key, then press and release the other key.*

Table 1-6. Keyboard Shortcuts for Moving Around in a Worksheet

Press	To Move
→ or Tab	One cell to the right
← or Shift + Tab	One cell to the left
↑	Up one row
↓	Down one row
Home	Jump to the cell in column A in the current row

Table 1-6. Keyboard Shortcuts for Moving Around in a Worksheet (Continued)

Press	To Move
Ctrl + Home	To the first cell (A1) in the worksheet
Ctrl + End	To the last cell with data in a worksheet
Page Up	Up one screen
Page Down	Down one screen
F5	Opens the Go To dialog box where you can go to a specified cell address.
End, → or Ctrl + →	First occupied cell to the right that is either preceded or followed by a blank cell
End, ← or Ctrl + ←	First occupied cell to the left that is either preceded or followed by a blank cell
End, ↑ or Ctrl + ↑	First occupied cell to the top that is either preceded or followed by a blank cell
End, ↓ or Ctrl + ↓	First occupied cell to the bottom that is either preceded or followed by a blank cell

QUICK REFERENCE

TO USE KEYSTROKE SHORTCUTS TO NAVIGATE IN A WORKSHEET:

• REFER TO TABLE 1-6 FOR MOVING AROUND IN A WORKSHEET.

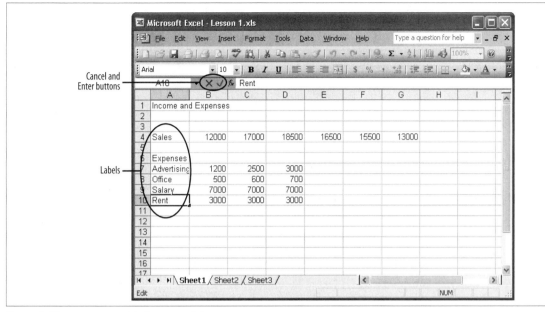

Figure 1-22. Entering text labels in a worksheet.

Now that you are an expert on getting around in Excel, you're ready to start entering data. There are two basic types of information you can enter in a cell:

- **Labels:** Any type of text or information not used in any calculations.
- **Values:** Any type of numerical data, such as numbers, percentages, fractions, currencies, dates, or times, usually used in formulas or calculations.

This lesson focuses on labels. Labels are used for worksheet headings and make your worksheets easy to read and understand. Labels usually contain text, but can also consist of numerical information not used in any calculations, such as serial numbers and dates. Excel treats information beginning with a letter as a label and automatically left-aligns it inside the cell.

1 If necessary, open the workbook named Lesson 1B and save it as Income and Expenses.

2 Click cell A1 to make it the active cell.

This is where you want to add a title for your worksheet. Don't worry if the cell already contains text—anything you type will replace the old cell contents.

Formula bar

3 Type Income and Expenses.

If you make a mistake while you're typing a cell entry, you can press the Backspace key to delete any characters, one at a time.

Notice that as you start typing the text appears in both the cell *and* in the Formula bar. Also, look at the Formula bar—three new buttons have appeared: the Cancel button (the red X), the Enter button (the green check mark), and the Edit Formula button (the = sign), as shown in Figure 1-22. You can click the Enter button when you've finished typing to confirm the cell entry, or click the Cancel button to cancel the entry and return the cell to its previous state.

Enter Button
Other Ways to Enter:
Press the <**Enter**>key.
Press the <**Tab**>key.
Press any of the arrow keys.

4 Click the Enter button on the Formula bar (see Figure 1-22 if you can't find it).

Clicking the Enter button on the Formula bar confirms the cell entry. There are several other, more efficient methods for entering and confirming data; we'll take a look at these methods in the next steps. Notice the text label is too large to fit in the current cell and the text spills into the empty adjacent cells to the right. Excel will use adjacent cells to display labels that are too long to fit in a single cell, so long as they are empty. If the adjacent cells aren't empty, Excel truncates the text—everything's still there, but you just can't see all of it!

Next, you need to add some labels to make the worksheet more meaningful.

5 Click cell A7 to make it the active cell.

The series of numbers located directly to the right of the current cell are the basic monthly expenses for North Shore Travel. Go ahead and enter the labels for the expenses.

6 Type Advertising and press the Enter key.

Excel confirms your entry and moves down to the next cell, A8. You can also complete an entry by pressing any of the arrow keys or Tab, or as you've already learned, by clicking the Enter button on the formula toolbar. Notice the label Advertising doesn't quite fit into the cell. Add the remaining expense labels.

7 Type Office and press Enter.

The cell pointer moves down to the next cell, A9. This row contains the monthly payroll expenses.

8 Type Payroll but don't press Enter this time.

You decide you would rather use the label "Salary" instead of "Payroll" so cancel the change and return the cell to its empty state.

Cancel Button
Other Ways to Cancel:
Press the <**Esc**> key.

9 Click the Cancel button on the Formula bar.

The Payroll label does not disappear, but will disappear once you begin typing in the cell. Go on to the next step to enter the new correct label as well as for this cell and the remaining labels.

10 Type Salary and press Enter, type Rent and press Enter, and then type Totals and press Enter.

NOTE *Excel normally treats any information beginning with a letter as a label and any information beginning with a number as a value. If you want to create a label that starts with a number, type an ' (apostrophe) before typing the number to prevent Excel from recognizing it as a value.*

Congratulations! You've finished entering the expense labels for the worksheet. Move to the next lesson to enter values into the worksheet.

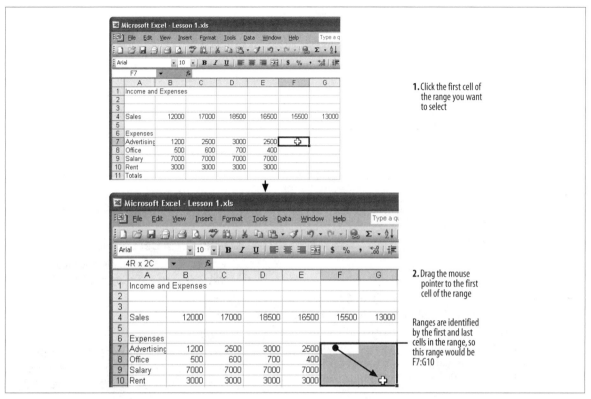

Figure 1-23. Entering values in a worksheet and selecting a range.

In the previous lesson, you learned how to enter labels in a worksheet. In this lesson, you will be working with the other basic type of worksheet information: *values*. Values are the numbers, dates, and other numerical information in a worksheet that are usually used in calculations. A value can be any type of numerical data: numbers, percentages, fractions, currencies, dates, and times. Excel treats information that contains numbers, dates, or times, and certain numerical punctuation as a value and automatically right-aligns it in the cell. Values don't have to contain only numbers. You can also use numerical punctuation including: the period (.) for a decimal point, the hyphen (-) for negative values, the dollar sign ($) for currencies, the percent sign (%) for percentages, and the comma (,) for separating numbers like 1,000.

Entering values in a worksheet is no different from entering labels: you simply type the value and confirm the entry by clicking the Enter button or pressing Enter, Tab, or any of the arrow keys. One more important thing to know about entering values: You can use the numeric keypad on your keyboard to key in values, which for most people is a very fast method to enter data once you're familiar with it.

1 Click cell E7 to make it the active cell, type 2500, and press Enter to complete the entry and move the cell pointer to cell E8.

2 Type 400, press Enter, type 7000, press Enter, type 3000, and press Enter.

Up until now, you have only worked with a single cell. In order to be proficient at Excel you need to know how to select and work with multiple cells.

3 Move the pointer over cell F7, click and hold down the mouse button, drag the pointer over cell G10, then release the mouse button.

You have just selected a *range* of cells. A range consists of two or more selected cells and is identified by the first and last cells in the range; for example, F7:G10. To select a range all you have to do is position the pointer over the first cell, click and hold the mouse button, drag the pointer to the last cell you want in the range, then release the mouse button, as shown in Figure 1-23.

Whenever you see that you're going to have to enter data in a block or range of cells, it is sometimes a good idea to select the range to make data entry easier and faster. Selecting a range of cells restricts the cell pointer so it can only move inside the selected range.

4 Type 1500, **press** Enter, **type** 400, **press** Enter, **type** 7000, **press** Enter, **and then type** 3000. *Do not press Enter after typing 3000.*

By now, you know that pressing Enter normally completes the cell entry and moves the cell pointer down to the next cell. Remember, however, that right now you are working in a selected cell range. Go on to the next step and see what happens when you press the Enter key.

5 Press Enter.

Instead of moving down to the next cell, F11, the cell pointer moves to the next cell in the selected range, cell G7. By selecting a range, you restrict where the cell pointer can move and can therefore concentrate on your data entry instead of worrying about where the cell pointer is. Go ahead and enter the remaining numbers.

6 Enter the following numbers, making sure to press Enter **after you enter each number, except after the last number, 3000.** *Do not press Enter after typing 3000.*

1200
500
7000
3000

You're at G10, the last cell in the selected range. So, what will happen if you press the Enter key now? Go on to the next step and find out.

7 Press Enter.

The cell pointer moves back to the first cell in the selected range, F7. Once you're finished working on a selected range, you can deselect the range by clicking any cell in the worksheet.

8 Click any cell in the worksheet to deselect the range.

QUICK REFERENCE

TO SELECT A CELL RANGE:

• CLICK THE FIRST CELL OF THE RANGE, AND THEN DRAG THE MOUSE POINTER TO THE LAST CELL.

OR...

• MAKE SURE THE ACTIVE CELL IS THE FIRST CELL OF THE CELL RANGE, THEN PRESS AND HOLD THE SHIFT KEY WHILE MOVING THE CELL POINTER TO THE LAST CELL.

TO DESELECT A CELL RANGE:

• CLICK ANY CELL OUTSIDE OF THE SELECTED CELL RANGE.

Calculating Value Totals with AutoSum

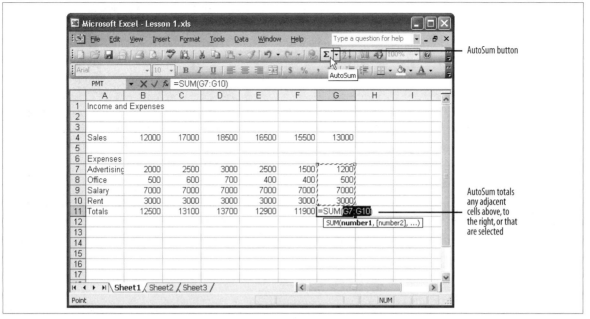

Figure 1-24. Use the AutoSum function to find the column totals.

This lesson introduces what spreadsheet programs are really all about: formulas. A *formula* performs calculations, such as adding, subtracting, and multiplying. Formulas are actually a type of value, like the numerical values you worked with in the previous lesson. Unlike the values in the previous lesson that contained only numbers, formulas contain information to perform a numerical calculation, such as adding, subtracting, multiplying, or even finding an average. A cell with the formula =5+3 will display the result of the calculation: 8.

> **TIP** *All formulas in Excel must begin with an equal sign (=).*

All formulas must start with an equal sign (=). The equal sign tells Excel you want to perform a calculation. Once you have entered an equal sign, you must specify two more types of information: the values you want to calculate and the arithmetic operator(s) or function name(s) you want to use to calculate the values. Formulas can contain explicit values, such as the numbers 5 or 8, but more often will reference the values contained in other cells. For example, the formula =A5+A6 would add together whatever values were in the cells A5 and A6. You're already familiar with some of the arithmetic operators used in Excel formulas: they include math symbols, such as the plus sign (+), to perform addition between

values, and the minus sign (-), to perform subtraction. *Functions* are used in formulas to perform calculations that are more complicated. For example, the SUM function adds together a range of cells, and the PMT function calculates the loan payments based on an interest rate, the length of the loan, and the principal amount of the loan. In this lesson, you will learn how to use one of the most commonly used functions in Excel, the SUM function, which finds the total of a block of cells.

Formulas may sound terribly confusing, but they are usually not much more difficult to work with than a calculator.

1 Click cell B11 to make it the active cell.

This is where you want to enter a formula to total the expenses in B column. The easiest way to add together several number values in a cell range is to use the AutoSum button. The AutoSum button inserts the SUM function (which adds all the values in a range of cells) and selects the range of cells Excel thinks you want totaled.

AutoSum button

2 Click the AutoSum button **on the Standard toolbar.**

Excel enters =SUM(B7:B10) in cell B11. Notice that the cells included in the formula range—B7, B8, B9, and B10—are surrounded by what looks like a line of marching ants. The AutoSum function is quite good at guessing which cells you want to total, but sometimes you will want to modify the cell selection. In our case, AutoSum has correctly selected the cells.

NOTE *Excel is usually smart enough to determine which cells you want to total; however, if the suggested range is incorrect, select the range you want using the technique you learned in the previous lesson and press Enter.*

Enter button

3 Click the Enter button **on the Formula bar.**

Excel instantly calculates the totals of the values in the cell range B7:B10 and displays the result, 11700, in the cell. Look at the Formula bar—notice the formula

=SUM(B7:B10), appears instead of the result of the calculation.

4 Click cell B7, **enter** 2000, **and press** Enter.

You've just made two very important discoveries! The first is that entering data in a cell replaces or overwrites whatever information was currently there. The second discovery is what is more relevant to this lesson: look at cell B11, where you just entered the SUM formula. Cell B11 now reads 12500—it has automatically recalculated the total for the cell range. Go ahead and find the total for the expenses in the C column.

5 Click cell C11, **click the** AutoSum button, **and press** Enter.

Excel totals the expenses in the C column. Finish entering totals for the remaining expense columns.

6 Repeat Step 5 **and enter SUM formulas for the remaining columns (D through G).**

Compare your worksheet with the one in Figure 1-24 when you're finished.

QUICK REFERENCE

TO USE THE AUTOSUM FUNCTION TO FIND THE TOTALS OF A CELL RANGE:

1. CLICK THE CELL WHERE YOU WANT TO INSERT THE TOTAL.

2. CLICK THE AUTOSUM BUTTON ON THE STANDARD TOOLBAR.

3. VERIFY THE CELL RANGE SELECTED BY AUTOSUM IS CORRECT. IF IT ISN'T, SELECT THE CELL RANGE YOU WANT TO TOTAL.

4. COMPLETE THE FORMULA BY PRESSING ENTER.

Entering Formulas

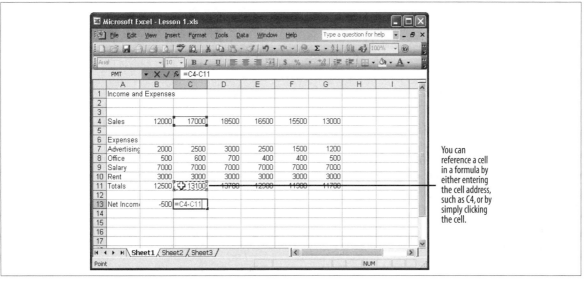

Figure 1-25. Entering a Formula in Excel to find the Net Income.

The previous lesson introduced you to formulas and how you can use the AutoSum button to total a cell range. This lesson takes a closer look at formulas, and instead of using the AutoSum function, you'll get a chance to enter a formula yourself.

Before you start the exercise, let's review. A *formula* is a value that performs calculations, such as adding, subtracting, and multiplying. Formulas start with the equal sign (=), which tells Excel you want to perform a calculation. After the equal sign, you must specify two more types of information: the values you want to calculate and the arithmetic operator(s) or function name(s) you want to use to calculate the values. Formulas can contain explicit values, such as the numbers 4 or 5, but more often will reference the values contained in other cells. For example, the formula =A3+A4 would add together whatever values were in the cells A3 and A4. Look at Table 1-7 to see a variety of formulas that contain different operators, references, and values.

1 If necessary, open the workbook named Lesson 1C and save it as Income and Expenses.

2 Click cell A13, type Net Income, and press Tab.

This row will contain the net income, which you can find by subtracting the total expense values from the sales value.

3 Type = (the equal sign) in cell B13.

Typing an equal sign at the beginning of a cell entry tells Excel you want to enter a formula rather than a value or label.

4 Type B4-B11.

This will subtract the value in cell B11 (12,500) from the value in B4 (12,000).

5 Press Enter.

Excel displays the result of the formula, -500, in cell B13. Notice, however, that the cell's formula still appears in the Formula bar. Instead of manually typing cell references, like you did in Step 3, you can specify cell references in a formula by clicking and selecting the cell or cell ranges with the mouse.

6 Click cell C13.

This is where you will enter the formula to find the net income for the C column.

7 Type =.

Excel is now ready to accept the formula for this cell. Instead of typing in the cell references this time, enter them using the mouse.

8 Click cell C4.

A line of marching ants appears around the cell C4, indicating the cell range. Look back at cell C13. Notice that Excel inserts the cell reference C4 in the formula. The next step is entering the arithmetic operator to the formula.

9 Type – (the minus sign or hyphen).

To complete the formula you must specify the cell reference for the total expenses, C11.

10 Click cell C11.

Excel enters the cell reference, C11, in the formula.

11 Press Enter to complete the formula.

The result of the formula (3,900) appears in cell C13.

Use Table 1-7 as a reference when you start creating your own formulas. Not only does it contain examples of formulas, but also the most common operators and functions used in formulas.

Table 1-7. Examples of Operators, References, and Formulas

Operator or Function Name	Example	Purpose
=		All formulas must start with an equal sign
+	=4+3	Performs addition between values
-	=A1-B1	Performs subtraction between values
*	=B1*2	Performs multiplication between values
/	=A1/C2	Performs division between values
SUM	=SUM(A1:A3)	Adds all the numbers in a range
AVERAGE	=AVERAGE(A2,B1,C3)	Calculates the average of all the numbers in a range
COUNT	=COUNT(A2:C3)	Counts the number of items in a range

QUICK REFERENCE

TO ENTER A FORMULA:

1. CLICK THE CELL WHERE YOU WANT TO INSERT THE FORMULA.

2. PRESS = (THE EQUALS SIGN) TO BEGIN ANY FORMULA.

3. ENTER THE FORMULA.

4. PRESS ENTER.

TO REFERENCE A CELL IN A FORMULA:

• TYPE THE CELL'S ADDRESS–FOR EXAMPLE, A3.
  OR...

• CLICK THE CELL YOU WANT TO REFERENCE.

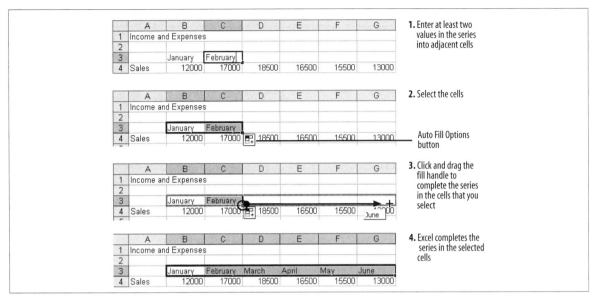

Figure 1-26. Use Auto Fill to enter a series of incremental dates.

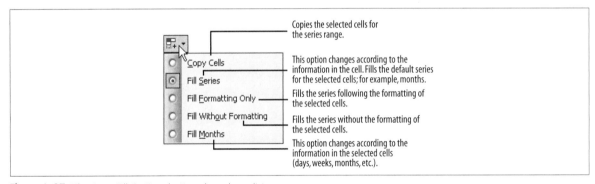

Figure 1-27. The Auto Fill Options button drop-down list.

AutoFill is the best time saving feature for data entry in Excel. AutoFill automatically enters a series of values in any cells you select. For example, imagine you're entering all 12 months as labels in a worksheet. With AutoFill you have to enter a couple of months only and let AutoFill enter the rest for you! Excel can't read your mind (Microsoft's still a few versions away from *that* feature), so the first cell or cells you select must contain the values and increment you want AutoFill to use when it automatically enters values. AutoFill makes a lot more sense when you see it in action, so let's start this lesson…

Enter button

1 Click cell B3, type January, and then click the Enter button on the Formula bar.

Here's how to use the AutoFill feature:

2 With the cell pointer still in cell B3, position the mouse pointer over the fill handle—the tiny box in the cell's lower-right corner—until the pointer changes to a +.

Fill Handle

3 Click and hold the fill handle and drag the mouse pointer to the right until the cell range is extended to include cell G3, then release the mouse button.

When you release the mouse button, Excel enters the months February through June in cells C3 through G3, as shown in Figure 1-26.

If you're working with a more complex data series, such as one that increases by increments other than one (such as every other day or month), you need to enter both the first and second entries to show Excel which increments to use when filling the data series.

4 Click cell C3, type March, and press Enter.

5 Select the cell range B3:C3.

By selecting the cell range B3:C3, you show Excel how you want to increment the data series. Now that Excel knows, use AutoFill to recreate the series.

Notice that the Auto Fill Options button appears on the screen after selecting the two cells. This offers a list of different ways you can Auto Fill the series.

6 Click the Auto Fill Options button, as shown in Figure 1-27. Select Fill Formatting Only from the menu.

This option allows you to change the series to the format you entered in the first two cells, January and March.

7 With the cell range B3:C3 still selected, click and drag the fill handle to the right until you select cell G3 and then release the mouse button.

When you release the mouse button, Excel follows your selected example and completes the data series with cell entries that contain every other month.

AutoFill has another very useful purpose; you can use it to quickly copy data (labels, values, or formulas) from one cell to other cells. You are going to use Auto-Fill to copy the net income formula you created in cell C13 in the previous lesson to the remaining cells in the worksheet.

8 Click cell C13 to make it active.

Cell C13 contains the formula you want to copy.

9 Drag the fill handle to the right until you reach cell G13, then release the mouse button.

When you release the mouse button, Excel copies the formula in cell C13 to the cells D13, E13, F13, and G13.

See Table 1-8 for examples of using AutoFill.

Table 1-8. Examples of AutoFill

First Cell Entry	AutoFill Entries Created in the Next Three Cells
January	February, March, April
Jan	Feb, Mar, Apr
1/10/98	1/11/98, 1/12/98, 1/13/98
5:00	6:00, 7:00, 8:00
Quarter 1	Quarter 2, Quarter 3, Quarter 4

QUICK REFERENCE

TO USE AUTOFILL TO ENTER A SERIES OF INCREMENTAL VALUES:

1. ENTER AT LEAST TWO VALUES INTO ADJACENT CELLS.

2. SELECT THE CELLS YOU USED IN STEP 1.

3. CLICK AND DRAG THE FILL HANDLE TO COMPLETE THE SERIES IN THE CELLS YOU SELECT.

NOTE: USE THE AUTO FILL OPTIONS BUTTON TO FILL THE SERIES WITH THE FORMAT OF YOUR PREFERENCE.

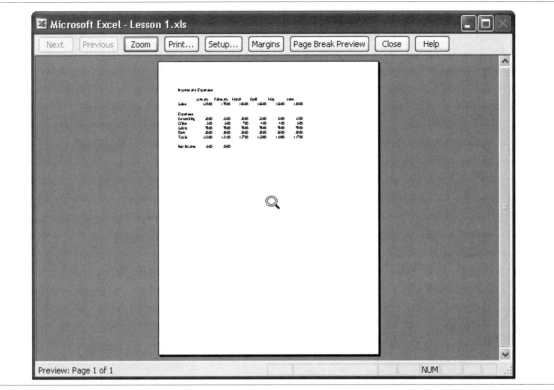

Figure 1-28. The Print Preview screen.

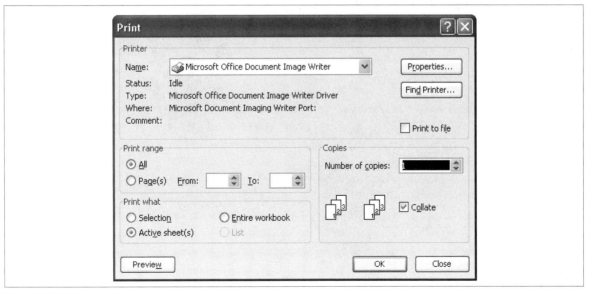

Figure 1-29. The Print dialog box.

Once you have created a worksheet, you can create a printed copy of it (if your computer is connected to a printer.) Sometimes, it is a good idea to preview a document on your screen to see if something needs to be changed before sending it to the printer. You can preview a document using Excel's Print Preview feature.

Print Preview button
Other Ways to Preview:
• Select **File**→**Print Preview** from the menu

1 Click the Print Preview button on the Standard toolbar.

The worksheet is previewed on the screen, as shown in Figure 1-28. You can enlarge the spreadsheet by clicking the area of the worksheet you want to magnify with the 🔍 pointer.

2 Move the 🔍 pointer over an area of the spreadsheet that contains data and click the mouse button.

Excel magnifies the selected area. Once you have seen an enlarged area, you can zoom back out to see the overall page again.

3 Move the 🔍 pointer over any area of the spreadsheet and click the mouse button.

Excel returns to the previous preview size. Your worksheet looks okay so you can go ahead and print it from the Print Preview window.

4 Click the Print button while in Print Preview.

The Print Dialog box appears, as shown in Figure 1-29. The Print Dialog box allows you to specify printing options such as which pages to print and the number of copies you want printed. You don't need to worry about any printing options for now.

5 Click OK.

Excel prints the worksheet to the default printer connected to your computer.

NOTE *If you weren't in Print Preview mode, you could also print by clicking the Print button on the Standard toolbar, by selecting File → Print from the menu, or by pressing Ctrl + P. (Actually, this is the method you'll usually use to print something.)*

QUICK REFERENCE

TO PREVIEW A WORKSHEET ON SCREEN:

• CLICK THE PRINT PREVIEW BUTTON ON THE STANDARD TOOLBAR.

OR...

• SELECT FILE → PRINT PREVIEW FROM THE MENU.

TO PRINT A WORKSHEET:

• CLICK THE PRINT BUTTON ON THE STANDARD TOOLBAR.

OR...

• SELECT FILE → PRINT FROM THE MENU.

OR...

• PRESS CTRL + P.

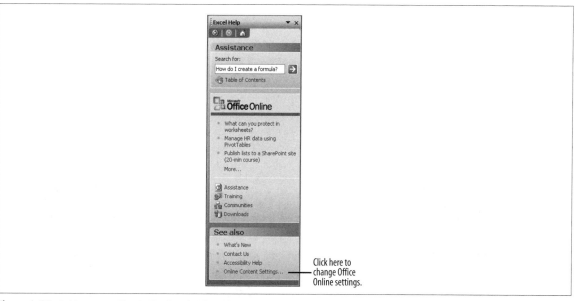

Click here to change Office Online settings.

Figure 1-30. Asking a question in the Excel Help task pane.

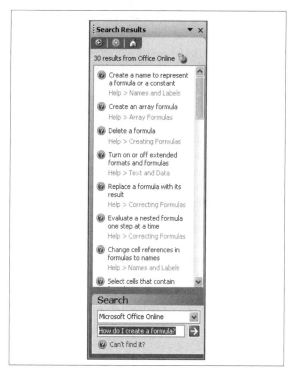

Figure 1-31. Office Online search results.

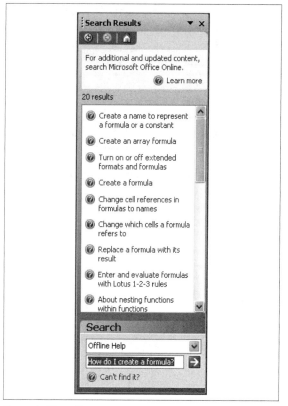

Figure 1-32. Offline Help search results.

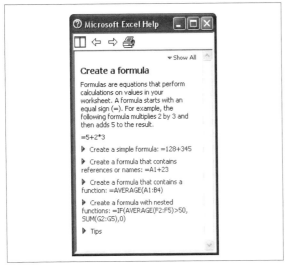

Figure 1-33. Possible topic answers for your question.

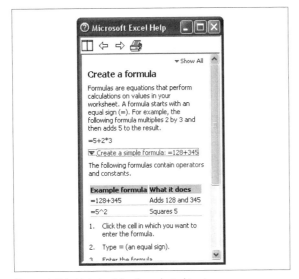

Figure 1-34. Help text for the selected topic.

TIP *The F1 key is the help key for all Windows-based programs.*

When you don't know how to do something in Windows or a Windows based program, don't panic, just look up your question in the Excel Help files. The Excel Help files can answer your questions, offer tips, and provide help for all of Excel's features. Many Excel users forget to use Help, but this is unfortunate, because the Help files know more about Excel than most Excel reference books do!

You can make the Excel Help files appear by pressing the F1 key. Then all you have to do is ask your question in normal English. This lesson will show you how you can get help by asking the Help files a question in normal English.

1 Press the F1 key.

The Excel Help task pane appears, as shown in Figure 1-30.

2 Type How do I create a formula? in the "Search for:" text box, as shown in Figure 1-30.

You can ask Excel Help questions in normal English, just as if you were asking a person instead of a computer. The program identifies keywords and phrases in your questions like "create," and "formula."

NOTE *Microsoft has totally changed the way Help works in Office 2003 with Office Online. Instead of searching for help in the files already stored on your computer, Office Online searches the topic in their online database. The purpose of this feature is to provide current, up-to-date information on search topics, but in their efforts to provide information on more advanced topics, they forget the most basic and important ones, like entering a formula.*

3 Click the Start searching button (→).

Office Online finds results like "Evaluate a nested formula one step at a time," but nothing that will simply help you create a formula to add into your budget worksheet. We have to look in the trusty old Offline Help files for that.

NOTE *Fortunately, you can change your settings to perform Help searches without Office Online. Go to the "See also" section at the bottom of the Excel Help task pane. Click the Online Content Settings option. Uncheck the "Search online content when connected" option and click OK.*

Office Online will refer to Offline Help files if a connection to the Internet is not detected.

4 Click the Search list arrow in the Search area at the bottom of the task pane. Select Offline Help from the list and click the Start searching button (→).

The Offline Help search results appear, including a topic that actually helps us out.

5 Click the Create an array formula **help topic (see Figure 1-31).**

Another window appears with more subtopics, as shown in Figure 1-33.

6 Click the Create a simple formula: =128+345 **help topic.**

Excel displays information on how to create a simple formula, as shown in Figure 1-34.

Notice that the Microsoft Excel Help window has a toolbar that looks like some of the buttons you might have seen on a Web browser. This lets you navigate through help topics just like you would browse the Web.

7 Click the Microsoft Excel Help window's close button **to close the window.**

The Help window closes.

See Table 1-9 for examples of the different Help buttons.

Table 1-9. Help Buttons

Button	Description
	Tiles the Excel program window and the Help window so you can see both at the same time
	Moves back to the previous help topic.
	Moves forward to the next help topic.
	Prints the current help topic.

QUICK REFERENCE

TO GET HELP:

1. PRESS THE F1 KEY.

2. TYPE YOUR QUESTION IN THE SEARCH FOR; TEXT BOX AND EITHER CLICK THE START SEARCHING BUTTON OR PRESS ENTER.

3. CLICK THE HELP TOPIC THAT BEST MATCHES WHAT YOU'RE LOOKING FOR (REPEAT THIS STEP AS NECESSARY.)

TO TURN OFF OFFICE ONLINE:

1. CLICK THE ONLINE CONTENT SETTINGS OPTION IN THE EXCEL HELP TASK PANE.

2. UNCHECK THE SEARCH ONLINE CONTENT WHEN CONNECTED OPTION AND CLICK OK.

Changing the Office Assistant and Using the "What's This" Button

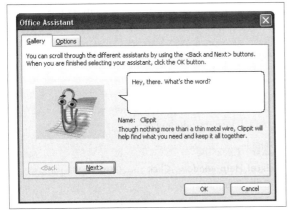

Figure 1-35. You can choose a new Office Assistant.

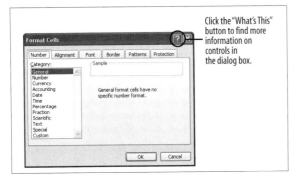

Figure 1-36. Click the "What's This" button (?) to view a brief description of all the controls in a dialog box.

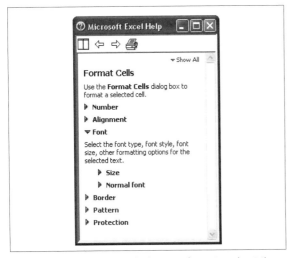

Figure 1-37. Click a link to find more information about the controls in the tab.

The Office Assistant is a cute animated character (a paper clip by default) that can answer your questions, offer tips, and provide help for all of Excel's features. Many Excel users don't use the Office Assistant, but it can be a very helpful tool. If you like using the Office Assistant but want a change of pace from Clippit's antics, you can choose one of eight different Office Assistants to guide you through Excel. Of course, if you really hate the Office Assistant, you can always shut it off.

The other topic covered in this lesson is how to use the "What's This" button. During your journey with Excel, you will undoubtedly come across a dialog box or two with a number of confusing controls and options. To help you find out what the various controls and options in a dialog box are for, many dialog boxes contain a "What's This" (?) button that explains the purpose of each of the dialog box's controls. This lesson will show you how to use the this button, but first, let's start taming the Office Assistant.

1 Select Help → Show the Office Assistant from the menu.

The Office Assistant appears.

2 Right-click the Office Assistant and select Choose Assistant from the shortcut menu.

The Office Assistant dialog box appears (see Figure 1-35).

3 Click the Back or Next button to see the available Office Assistants.

The Office Assistant you select is completely up to you. They all work the same—they just look and act different.

4 Click OK when you find an Office Assistant you like.

If you find the Office Assistant annoying (as many people do) and want to get rid of it altogether, here's how:

5 Right-click the Office Assistant.

A shortcut menu appears.

6 Select Hide from the shortcut menu.

You can always bring the Office Assistant back whenever you need its help.

Now, let's move on to how to use the "What's This" button to discover the purpose of confusing dialog box controls.

7 Select Format → Cells from the menu.

The Format Cells dialog box appears, as shown in Figure 1-36. Notice the "What's This" button located in the dialog box's title bar, just to the left of the dialog box's close button.

8 Click the "What's This" button (?).

A Microsoft Excel Help window appears, as shown in Figure 1-37.

9 Click the Font link.

A brief description of the Font tab of the dialog box appears.

10 Click the close button to close the Microsoft Excel Help window. Click Cancel to close the Format Cells dialog box.

QUICK REFERENCE

TO CHANGE OFFICE ASSISTANTS:

• IF NECESSARY, SELECT HELP → SHOW THE OFFICE ASSISTANT FROM THE MENU.

• RIGHT-CLICK THE OFFICE ASSISTANT AND SELECT CHOOSE ASSISTANT FROM THE SHORTCUT MENU.

• CLICK THE NEXT OR BACK BUTTONS UNTIL YOU FIND AN OFFICE ASSISTANT YOU LIKE, THEN CLICK OK.

TO HIDE THE OFFICE ASSISTANT:

• RIGHT-CLICK THE OFFICE ASSISTANT AND SELECT HIDE FROM THE SHORTCUT MENU.

TO SEE WHAT A CONTROL IN A DIALOG BOX DOES:

• CLICK THE DIALOG BOX "WHAT'S THIS" BUTTON (?) (LOCATED RIGHT NEXT TO THE CLOSE BUTTON).

• FIND THE CONTROL DESCRIPTION IN THE MICROSOFT EXCEL HELP WINDOW.

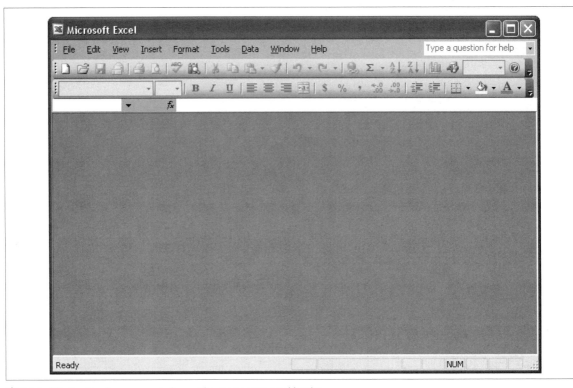

Figure 1-38. The Excel program window without any open workbooks.

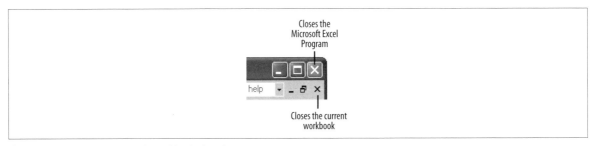

Figure 1-39. The Program and Workbook close buttons.

Because the tasks covered in this lesson are so simple — closing a workbook and exiting the Excel program—this is one of the briefest lessons in the book. Before you close a workbook or exit Excel, you should always make sure you save any changes you've made to the active workbook.

Save button
Other Ways to Save:
• Select **File**→**Save** from the menu.
• Press <**CTRL**> + <**S**>

1 Save the Income and Expenses worksheet by clicking the Save button on the Standard toolbar.

Your disk drive whirs as it saves the changes you've made to the worksheet. Once the worksheet is saved you can close it.

Close button
Other Ways to Close a Workook:
• Select **File**→**Close** from the menu

2 Click the workbook close button. (Make sure you click the worksheet close button, not the Excel Program close button.)

You will probably see two close buttons on your screen—make sure you click the lower close button. The current worksheet closes, but the Excel program does not. The close button located in the far upper-righthand corner of the screen closes the Excel program. You can close a worksheet when you're finished working on it but still want to remain in the Excel program—perhaps to open and work on another worksheet. You've finished both this lesson and this chapter, so now you want to exit or close the Excel program.

Close button
Other Ways to Exit Excel:
• Select **File**→**Exit** from the menu

3 Click the close button on the Microsoft Excel Title Bar.

This time, click the close button in the very far upper-righthand corner of the screen to close Excel. The Excel Program window closes and you return to the Windows desktop.

That's it! You've just completed your first chapter and are well on your way towards mastering Microsoft Excel. You've already learned some very important things; how to start Excel; enter values, labels, and formulas; create, preview, print, and save a worksheet; select and work with cell ranges; and use the AutoFill feature. You will use these skills all the time in your extensive use of Microsoft Excel.

QUICK REFERENCE

TO CLOSE A WORKBOOK:

- CLICK THE WORKBOOK WINDOW CLOSE BUTTON. OR...

- SELECT FILE → CLOSE FROM THE MENU.

TO EXIT MICROSOFT EXCEL:

- CLICK THE EXCEL PROGRAM CLOSE BUTTON. OR...

- SELECT FILE → EXIT FROM THE MENU.

Chapter One Review

Lesson Summary

Starting Excel

Click the Windows Start button and select All Programs → Microsoft Office → Microsoft Office Excel 2003.

Understanding the Excel Screen

Be able to identify the main components of the Excel program screen.

Using Menus

To Open a Menu: Click the menu name with the mouse pointer, or press the Alt key and the letter that is underlined in the menu name.

Excel 2003's new personalized menus hide more advanced commands from view. To display a menu's hidden commands, click the downward-pointing arrow (☒) at the bottom of the menu, or open the menu and wait a few seconds.

To Change How Menus Work: Select View → Toolbars → Customize from the menu, check or clear either the Menus Show Recently Used Commands First and/or Show Full Menus After a Short Delay options, then click Close.

Using Toolbars and Creating a New Workbook

To Use Excel's Toolbars: Simply click the toolbar button you want to use. Leave the pointer over the button to display a screen tip of what the button does.

To Stack the Standard and Formatting Toolbars in Two Separate Rows: Click the ☒ button on either toolbar and select Show Buttons on Two Rows from the drop-down list.

To Create a New Workbook: Click the New button on the Standard toolbar or select File → New from the menu.

Filling Out Dialog Boxes

Be able to identify and use text boxes, list boxes, combo boxes, check boxes, and sheet tabs.

Keystroke and Right-Mouse Button Shortcuts

Keystroke shortcuts: Press Ctrl and the letter that corresponds to the shortcut command at the same time.

Right-Mouse Button Shortcut Menus: Whenever you're unsure or curious about what you can do with an object, click it with the right mouse button to display a list of commands related to the object.

Opening a Workbook

To Open a Workbook: Click the Open button on the Standard toolbar, or select File → Open from the menu, or press Ctrl + O.

Saving a Workbook

To Save a Workbook: Click the Save button on the Standard toolbar, or select File → Save from the menu, or press Ctrl + S.

To Save a Workbook with a Different Name: Select File → Save As from the menu and enter a different name for the workbook.

Moving the Cell Pointer

Using the Mouse: Select the cell you want to edit by clicking it with the mouse pointer or by using the keyboard arrow keys.

Using the Keyboard: Move the cell pointer by pressing the keyboard arrow key that corresponds to the direction you want to move.

Pressing Enter moves the cell pointer down, Tab moves the cell pointer to the right, and Shift + Tab moves the cell pointer to the left.

Use the horizontal and vertical scroll bars and buttons to view portions of the worksheet that are located off-screen.

Navigating a Worksheet

Page Up moves up one screen, Page Down moves down one screen.

Ctrl + Home moves to the first cell (A1) in a worksheet.

Ctrl + End moves to the last cell with data in a worksheet.

F5 opens the Go To dialog box, where you can specify a cell address to jump to.

Entering Labels in a Worksheet

Labels are used for worksheet headings and (usually) text. Excel treats information beginning with a letter as a label, and left-aligns it in the cell.

To Enter a Label: Select the cell you want to contain the label. Type the label—Excel will recognize it as a label if it begins with a letter. Type an ' (apostrophe) if your label begins with a number. Then, confirm the entry.

Entering Values in a Worksheet and Selecting a Cell Range

Values are the numerical information in a worksheet that are usually used in calculations. Excel treats numbers, dates, and times as values and automatically right-aligns it in the cell.

To Select a Cell Range: (Using the mouse) Click the first cell or the range and drag the mouse pointer to the last cell of the range. (Using the keyboard) Make sure the active cell is the first cell of the cell range, then press and hold down the Shift key while using the arrow keys to move the mouse pointer to the last cell of the range.

To Deselect a Cell Range: Click any cell outside the selected cell range.

Calculating Value Totals with AutoSum

Click the cell where you want to insert the total, click the AutoSum button on the Standard toolbar, verify that the cell range selected is correct—if it isn't select the cell range you want to total, and then press Enter.

Entering Formulas

Every formula must start with the equal symbol (=).

To Enter a Formula: Select the cell where you want to insert the formula, press = (the equals sign), enter the formula, using values, cell references, operators, and functions, and then press Enter.

To Reference a Cell in a Formula: Type the cell reference (for example, B5) or simply click the cell you want to reference.

Using AutoFill

Enter at least two values into adjacent cells, select those cells, and click and drag the cell pointer's fill handle to complete the series in the cells you select.

Previewing and Printing a Worksheet

To Print a Worksheet: Click the Print button on the Standard toolbar, or select File → Print from the menu, or press Ctrl + P.

To Preview a Worksheet: Click the Print Preview button on the Standard toolbar or select File → Print Preview from the menu.

Getting Help from the Office Assistant

To Get Help: Press the F1 key. Type your question in the "Search for:" text box and click the Start searching button or press Enter. Click the help topic that best matches what you're looking for. (Repeat as this step as necessary.)

To Turn Off Office Online: Click the Online Content Settings option in the Excel Help task pane. Uncheck the Search online content when connected option and click OK.

Changing the Office Assistant and Using the "What's This" Button

To Change Office Assistants: If necessary, select Help → Show the Office Assistant from the menu. Right-click the Office Assistant and select Choose Assistant from the shortcut menu. Click the Next or Back buttons until you find an Office Assistant you like, then click OK.

To Hide the Office Assistant: Right-click the Office Assistant and select Hide from the shortcut menu.

To See what a Control in a Dialog Box Does: Click the Dialog box "What's This" button (?) (located right next to the close button). Find the control description in the Microsoft Excel Help window.

Closing a Workbook and Exiting Excel

To Close a Workbook: Click the workbook window's close button or select File → Close from the menu.

To Exit Microsoft Excel: Click the Excel program close button or select File → Exit from the menu.

Quiz

1. Right-clicking something in Excel:

   A. Deletes the object.

   B. Opens a shortcut menu that lists several popular commands for a selected item.

   C. Selects the object.

   D. Nothing—the right mouse button is there for left-handed people.

2. Which of the following is NOT a way to complete a cell entry?

   A. Click the Enter button on the Formula bar.

   B. Press any arrow key on the keyboard.

   C. Press Enter.

   D. Press Spacebar.

3. Which of the following formulas is NOT entered correctly?

   A. =B7+14

   B. =B7*B1

   C. 10+50

   D. =10+50

4. Which of the following is NOT an example of a value?

   A. May 10, 2001

   B. Serial Number 50671

   C. 57%

   D. 350

5. Which symbol do formulas begin with?

   A. =

   B. @

   C. +

   D. (

6. You can reference cells in a formula by (select all that apply):

   A. Typing the cell reference; for example, B10.

   B. Clicking the cell(s) you want to reference with the mouse.

   C. Selecting Edit → Reference from the menu and typing the cell reference.

   D. Clicking the Enter button on the Formula bar and clicking the cell with the mouse.

7. Cell ranges consist of two or more cells and are identified by the first and last cell in the range, such as F7:G10. (True or False?)

8. To save a workbook you (select all that apply):

   A. Press Ctrl +F5

   B. Select File → Save from the menu.

   C. Click the Save button on the Standard toolbar.

   D. Click Save on the Windows Start button.

9. You enter "300 Orders" in cell A1 and "250 Orders" in cell A2. You then select both cells and drag the fill handle down to cell A3. When you release the mouse button, which value will appear in cell A3?

   A. 150 Orders

   B. 150

   C. 200 Orders

   D. 200

10. What symbol is used before a number to make it a label?

    A. =

    B. ' (apostrophe)

    C. " (quote)

    D. _ (underscore)

11. Without using the mouse or the arrow keys, what is the fastest way of getting to cell A1 in a spreadsheet?

    A. Press Home

    B. Press Shift + Home

    C. Press Ctrl + Home

    D. Press Alt + Home

12. Which button do you click to add up a series of numbers?

    A. AutoSum button

    B. Formula button

C. Total button

D. QuickTotal button

13. How do you select an entire column?

    A. Select Edit → Select → Column from the menu.

    B. Click the column heading letter.

    C. Hold down the Ctrl key as you click anywhere in the column.

    D. Hold down the Shift key as you click anywhere in the column.

14. You want to spell check a workbook. You open the Tools menu but can't find the Spelling command. What's wrong?

A. The Spelling command is in the Edit menu, silly!

B. You need to display all the options in the Tools menu by clicking the downward-pointing arrow at the bottom of the menu.

C. There isn't a Spelling command.

D. You need to display all the options in the Tools menu by pressing F2.

15. What key can you press to get help in any Windows-based program?

    A. F12

    B. Esc

    C. Scroll Lock

    D. F1

Homework

1. Find cell AA75 in any worksheet.

2. Using the skills you've learned in this chapter, create a worksheet similar to the one shown here (you can fill it in using your own numbers if you want.)

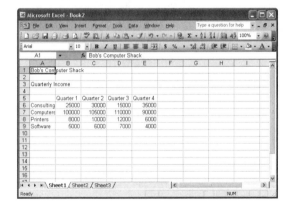

3. Create a Total row in row 10. Use the AutoSum function to find the totals for each quarter.

4. Preview and print your worksheet, and then save it as "Homework 1" in your practice folder or disk.

5. Make a silent vow that from this moment forward you will use Excel anytime you need to add together more than 8 numbers instead of a calculator.

Quiz Answers

1. B. Right-clicking an object displays a shortcut menu for the object.

2. D. There are a lot of ways to complete a cell entry, but pressing the Spacebar isn't one of them.

3. C. 10+50 is missing the equal sign. It should be "=10+50".

4. B. "Serial No. 50671" contains a number, but since it starts with letters Excel treats it as a label.

5. A. All formulas in Excel must begin with an equal sign (=). There's no exception to this rule.

6. A and B. You can reference cells by typing their cell reference or clicking the cell or cell range you want to reference.

7. True. Cells ranges are identified by the first and last cell in the range, such as A1:B10.

8. B and C.

9. 150 Orders.

10. B. Type an ' (apostrophe) before a number to make it a label.

11. C. Press Ctrl + Home to move the cell pointer to cell A1.

12. A. Click the AutoSum button.

13. B. Click the column heading letter of the column you want to select.

14. B. You need to display all the options in the Tools menu by clicking the downward-pointing arrow at the bottom of the menu.

15. D. The F1 key brings up help in every Windows program.

CHAPTER 2
EDITING A WORKSHEET

CHAPTER OBJECTIVES:

Enter and work with date values

Edit, clear, and replace cell contents

Cut, copy, paste, and move cells

Work with and understand absolute and relative cell references

Insert and delete cells, rows, and columns

Use Undo and Redo

Check the spelling of your worksheets

Use advanced print options

Basic file management

Insert cell comments

CHAPTER TASK: EDIT A MILEAGE REIMBURSEMENT REPORT

Prerequisites

- **Know how to start Excel**
- **Know how to use menus, toolbars, dialog boxes, and shortcut keystrokes**
- **Know how to move the cell pointer**

Now that you have the Microsoft Excel basics down, this chapter will show you how to become a sophisticated Excel user. This chapter explains how to enter date values; cut, copy and paste information in your workbook; insert and delete columns and rows; undo any mistakes you might make; and even correct your spelling errors.

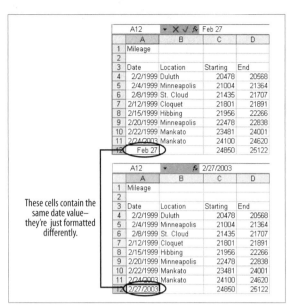

These cells contain the same date value—they're just formatted differently.

Figure 2-1. Enter dates into a worksheet using a variety of formats.

Normally Excel treats dates in your worksheets as values rather than labels. The reason for this is simple—it allows you to perform calculations and formulas on them. For example, you can subtract one date from another to find how many days are between them. You can enter dates using many different types of date formats, as shown in Table 2-1.

1 Start the Microsoft Excel Program.

Open button
Other Ways to Open a Workbook:
• Select **File → Open** from the menu
• Press <**CTRL**> + <**O**>

2 Click the Open button on the Standard toolbar.

The Open dialog box appears.

3 Navigate to your Practice folder or disk.

The Open dialog box displays the Excel files in your Practice folder or disk.

4 Click the workbook named Lesson 2A in the file list box to select it and click Open.

The workbook Lesson 2A opens and appears in the worksheet window. You don't want to modify the

original Lesson 2A workbook, so save it as a new workbook file with a different name—"Mileage Reimbursement."

5 Select File → Save As from the menu. Type Mileage Reimbursement in the File name box and click Save.

Excel saves the workbook with the new name, Mileage Reimbursement, and closes the original document, Lesson 2A. Now you can work on the new workbook without modifying the original workbook.

6 Click cell A11 to make it active.

7 Type 2/24 and press Enter.

Notice that Excel completes the date entry by automatically inserting the current year for you. Excel will always assume that dates are from the current year, unless you specify otherwise.

NOTE *Excel 2003 is Year 2000 compliant, which means you shouldn't have to worry much about the dreaded year 2000 bug that plagues so many computers and applications. You should be aware, however, of how Excel evaluates two-digit years, such as when you type 01/01/99 instead of 01/01/1999.*

Excel assumes any two-digit years entered between 01/01/30 and 12/31/99 are in the 20th century, so when you enter 10/3/54 Excel assumes you mean October 10, 1954. Excel assumes any two-digit years entered between 01/01/00 and 12/31/29 are in the 21st century, so when you enter 10/3/15 Excel assumes you mean October 10, 2015.

You don't have to enter your dates using a 10/5/98 format. Excel understands a variety of date formats. Try entering a date using a different format.

8 Type Feb 27 and press Enter.

Excel converts Feb 27 to You can change how dates are formatted, so that 10/10/98 is displayed as October 10, 1998, but that's in an upcoming lesson.

Excel's *AutoComplete* feature helps speed up data entry, especially if you're using repetitive information.

When you type the first few characters of a label, Excel displays the label if it already appears in the column. Press <Enter> to accept the entry or resume typing to ignore the suggestion.

9 Click cell B11 type Ma.

As soon as you type the "Ma" in "**Ma**nkato," Excel cleverly recognizes what you're typing from the cells in the B column and displays the label "Mankato". If you want to accept "Mankato" simply press Enter to confirm the cell entry. If you're entering a different word, such as "**Ma**nitoba", simply ignore Excel's suggestion and finish typing "Manitoba".

Pick from List

10 Press Enter.

You can also use Excel's *PickList* to help you enter labels in your worksheet. The PickList is a list of labels you've used and helps keep your information consistent. Here's how to use the PickList:

11 Right-click cell B12 and select Pick from Drop-down List from the shortcut menu.

A list containing all the labels in the column appears—simply click the entry you want to use.

12 Select St. Cloud from the PickList.

Table 2-1. Examples of Valid Date and Time Entries

Date Entries	Time Entries
October 17, 1995	5:45 PM
10/17/95	5:45 AM
10-17-95	5:45 (Excel assumes that it's 5:45 AM)
17-Oct-95	17:45 (5:45 PM on a 24-hour clock)
Oct-17(Excel assumes that it's the current year.)	17:45:20 (5:45 PM and 20 seconds)

QUICK REFERENCE

TO ENTER DATE VALUES IN EXCEL:

- EXCEL TREATS DATES AND TIMES AS VALUES, SO ONCE YOU ENTER A DATE IN ONE FORMAT, SUCH AS 4/4/99, YOU CAN REFORMAT THE DATE FORMAT; FOR EXAMPLE, TO APRIL 4, 1999.

TO USE AUTOCOMPLETE:

- TYPE THE FIRST FEW CHARACTERS OF A LABEL; EXCEL DISPLAYS THE LABEL, IF IT APPEARS PREVIOUSLY IN THE COLUMN. PRESS ENTER TO ACCEPT THE ENTRY, OR RESUME TYPING TO IGNORE THE SUGGESTION.

TO USE THE PICKLIST:

- RIGHT-CLICK THE CELL WHERE YOU WANT TO ENTER A LABEL, SELECT PICK FROM DROP-DOWN LIST FROM THE SHORTCUT MENU, AND SELECT THE ENTRY FROM THE LIST.

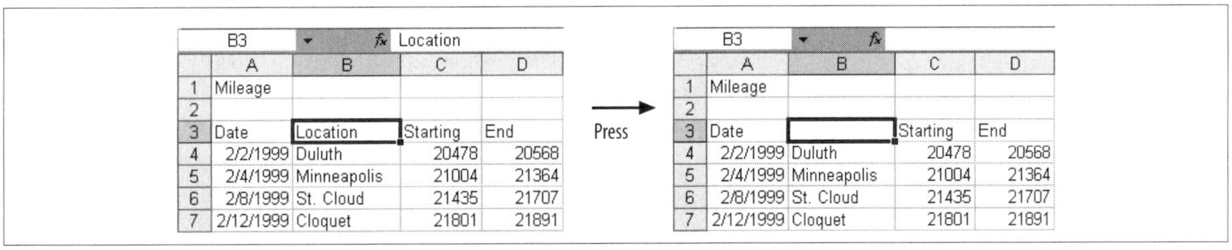

Editing, Clearing, and Replacing Cell Contents

Figure 2-2. Pressing the Delete key clears the contents of the selected cell or cell range.

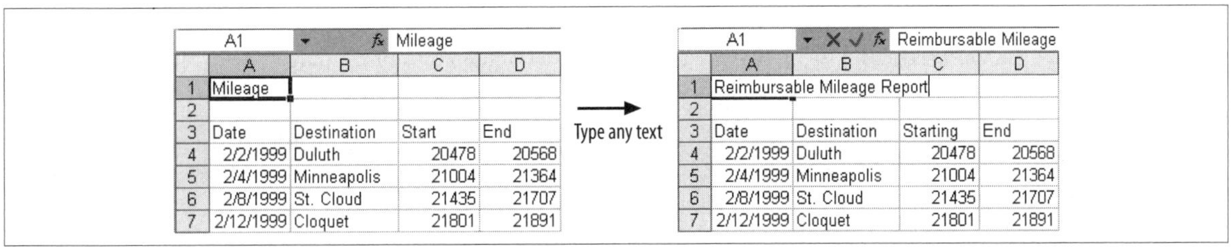

Figure 2-3. Typing replaces the contents of a cell.

You can change or clear the contents of your cells any time. To clear a cell entry simply select the cell or cell range you want to delete and press the Delete key. You don't have to clear a cell entry if you want to replace it altogether—just select the cell and enter the new entry on top of the old entry.

There are a couple methods you can use to edit the contents of a cell. One method is to select the cell you want to edit, click the Formula bar, and then edit the cell contents in the Formula bar. Another method is to double-click the cell you want to edit, then edit the cell contents directly in the cell. Either method causes Excel to go to *Edit mode*, and the Cancel and Enter buttons appear on the Formula bar. In Edit mode the arrow keys move from character to character in the cell instead of from cell to cell. While Excel is in Edit mode you can also can move the insertion point by clicking the I-beam pointer (⌶) where you want to insert text.

1 Click cell B3 to make it active.

2 Press Delete to clear the contents of the active cell.

The contents of cell B3 (see Figure 2-2—the label "location"—is deleted, or cleared, from the cell. Move on to the next step to add a better description for this label.

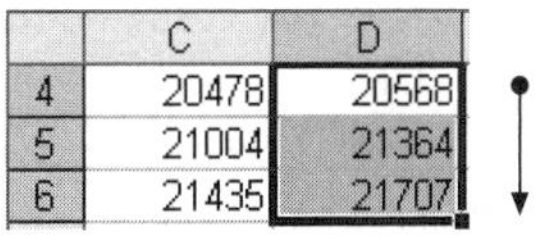

**Selecting a Cell
Range**

3 Type Destination and press Enter.

You can clear the contents of several cells at once by first selecting the cells and then pressing the Delete key.

4 Select the cell range G3:G10 by clicking cell G3, holding down the mouse button, and dragging it to cell G10.

Now clear the selected cell range (G3:G10).

5 Press the Delete key.

The contents of the cells in the selected range are deleted.

You don't have to clear a cell's contents before replacing them—just type in the new entry for the cell.

6 Click cell A1 to make it active, then type Reimbursable Mileage Report and press Enter.

The original content of the cell, the label "Mileage" is replaced with the new label "Reimbursable Mileage Report" as shown in Figure 2-3.

7 Click cell C3.

This cell label needs to be changed from "Starting" to "Beginning." There are several different methods you can use to edit the contents of a cell. The first is to select the cell you want to edit and then click the Formula bar.

Editing a CellEntry with the Formula Bar

8 Click anywhere in the Formula bar.

Notice that the status bar at the bottom of the Excel screen changes from "Ready" to "Edit" indicating Excel is in Edit mode. The blinking vertical line (I) that appears in the Formula bar is called the insertion point. Once Excel is in Edit mode you can move the insertion point in the Formula bar to edit any area by either pressing the arrow keys or by moving the I-beam pointer (I) where you want to place the insertion point and clicking.

9 Press the Backspace key.

Excel deletes one letter to the left of the insertion point.

10 Press and hold the Backspace key to delete the word "Starting", then type Beginning and press Enter.

Another method you can use to edit a cell entry is to edit inside of the cell instead of in the Formula bar, by double-clicking the cell.

Editing a Cell Entry in Place

11 Double-click cell D3.

The insertion point appears directly in the cell so that you can edit the cell's entry.

12 Type ing, so the cell reads "Ending" and press Enter.

You can edit cells that contain values and formulas just like cell entries with labels.

13 Click cell E2, type Cost Per Mile, press Tab or → to move to cell F2, type .32, and then press Enter.

14 Click cell F4 and click anywhere in the Formula bar to enter Edit mode. Or double-click cell F4 to enter Edit mode.

As you can see, a formula is entered in this cell. You want to edit the formula in this cell so that it references whatever value is in cell F2 rather than the fixed value of .30, currently used in the formula.

15 Delete the 0.3 text in the formula of cell F4.

Now that you've deleted the fixed value used in the formula, create a reference to cell F2 to use the value in that cell.

16 Click cell F2.

Excel automatically enters the cell reference, F2, to the formula in cell F4. The formula should now read =E4*F2.

17 Press Enter to confirm the cell entry.

The cell should now read 28.8.

Save button

18 Click the Save button on the Standard toolbar.

QUICK REFERENCE

TO CLEAR A CELL'S CONTENTS:

1. SELECT THE CELL.

2. PRESS THE DELETE KEY.

TO EDIT A CELL'S CONTENTS:

1. SELECT THE CELL.

2. CLICK ANYWHERE IN THE FORMULA BAR.

3. EDIT THE CELL'S CONTENTS (USE THE ARROW, DELETE, AND BACKSPACE KEYS).

4. PRESS ENTER WHEN YOU'RE FINISHED EDITING THE CELL.

TO EDIT A CELL'S CONTENTS IN-PLACE:

1. DOUBLE-CLICK THE CELL YOU WANT TO EDIT.

2. EDIT THE CONTENTS OF THE CELL IN-PLACE.

3. PRESS ENTER WHEN YOU'RE FINISHED EDITING THE CELL.

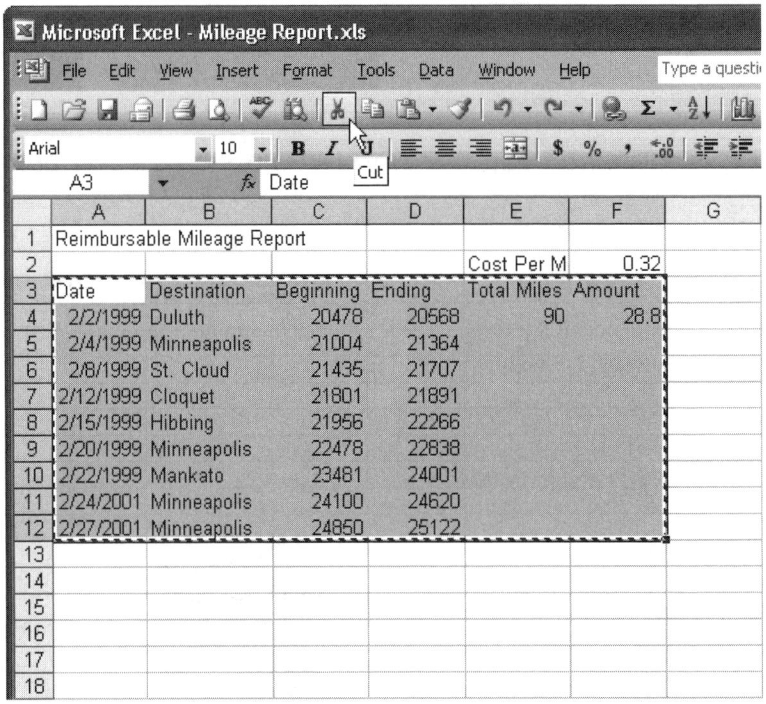

Figure 2-4. Selecting and cutting a range of cells.

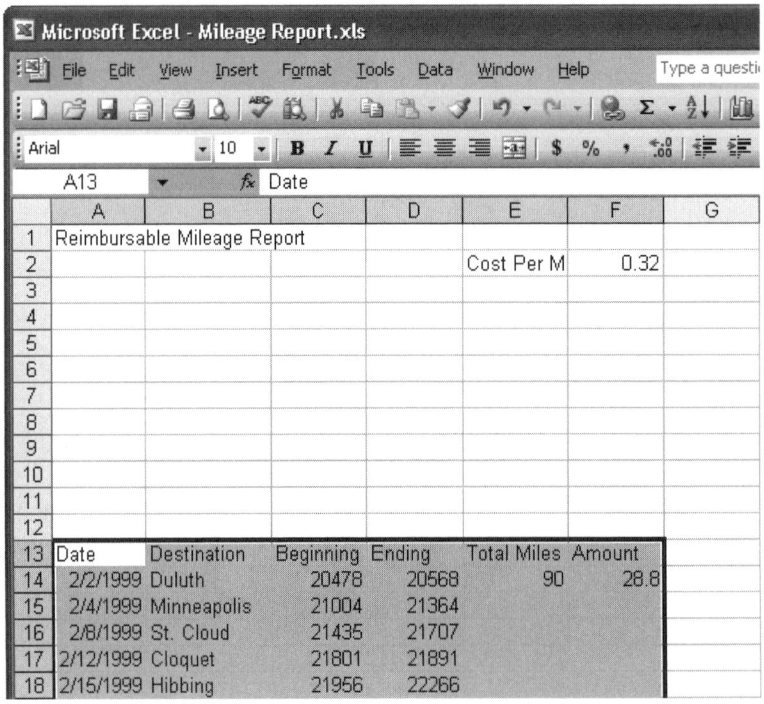

Figure 2-5. Pasting the selected cells in a new location in the workbook.

You already know how to select a cell and ranges of cells using the mouse or keyboard. Once you have selected a cell or cell range, you can cut it, removing it from its original location, and then paste it in another location in the worksheet. Copying is similar to cutting, except the cells are copied instead of removed. Whenever you cut or copy something, it is placed in a temporary storage area called the *Clipboard*. The Clipboard is available to any Windows program, so you can cut and paste between different programs.

Cutting and copying cell entries is one of the more common tasks you're likely to use in Excel (and in many other programs too!). This lesson will give you some practice cutting, copying, and pasting in Excel.

If you are continuing from the previous lesson, you can skip the first step of this exercise; otherwise, you will need to open the Lesson 2B file.

1 If necessary, open the workbook named Lesson 2B on your Practice disk or in your Practice folder then save it as Mileage Report.

First you need to select the cell or cell range you want to copy.

2 Click cell B5 to make it active.

You want to copy this cell to the clipboard so you can paste it in a different location in the worksheet. There are several different methods of copying something—we'll look at all of them. Try out each method and then use the method you prefer.

Copy button
Other Ways to Paste:
• Select **Edit→Copy** from the menu
• Press **<CTRL> + <C>**

3 Click the Copy button on the Standard toolbar.

A line of marching ants appears around the selected cell and the message "Select destination and press ENTER or choose Paste" appears on the status bar. Now you must move the cell pointer to the location where you want to paste the copied cell.

4 Select cell B11.

This is where you want to paste the cell you copied. There are several methods you can use to paste what you copied or cut onto the Windows clipboard.

5 Click the Paste button on the Standard toolbar.

The contents you copied from cell B5 are pasted into the active cell, B11, replacing its original contents. When you use the Paste command, Excel keeps the copied cell(s) in the Clipboard so that you can paste them again in other locations. Try pasting the copied cell in another location.

6 Select cell B12 and repeat Step 5 to paste the copied cell.

The copied cell is inserted in the active cell.

Now that you're familiar with copying, let's try *cutting* several cells. You can cut (or copy) several cells at once by selecting the cells you want to cut (or copy.)

NOTE *To stop the "marching ants" line around cell B5, press the Enter key.*

7 Select the cell range A3:F12.

By now, you should know how to select a cell range.

Cut button
Other Ways to Paste:
• Select **Edit→Cut** from the menu
• Press **<CTRL> + <X>**

8 Click the Cut button on the Standard toolbar.

A line of marching ants appears around the selected cells and the message "Select destination and press ENTER or choose Paste" appears on the status bar. When you select a destination to paste a range of cells you only have to designate the first cell where you want to paste the cell range.

Paste button
Other Ways to Paste:
• Select **Edit→Paste** from the menu
• Press **<CTRL> + <V>**

9 Select cell A13.

This is where you want to paste the selected cell range.

10 Click the Paste button on the Standard toolbar to paste the cut cell range.

Excel removes or "cuts" the selected cells from their original location and inserts them at the new location that begins with the active cell.

11 Save the document by clicking the Save button on the Standard toolbar.

You can also copy, cut, and paste text between two different Windows programs. For example, you could copy information from an Excel worksheet and paste it in a Word document. The cut, copy, and paste commands (the toolbar buttons, menus, and/or keyboard shortcuts) you learned in Excel will work with most Windows applications.

QUICK REFERENCE

TO CUT AND PASTE:

1. SELECT THE CELL OR CELL RANGE YOU WANT TO CUT.

2. CLICK THE CUT BUTTON ON THE STANDARD TOOLBAR.

   OR...

   SELECT EDIT → CUT FROM THE MENU.

   OR...

   PRESS CTRL + X.

3. SELECT THE CELL WHERE YOU WANT TO PASTE THE CUT CELL(S).

4. PRESS ENTER.

TO COPY AND PASTE:

1. SELECT THE CELL OR CELL RANGE YOU WANT TO COPY.

2. CLICK THE COPY BUTTON ON THE STANDARD TOOLBAR.

OR...

SELECT EDIT → COPY FROM THE MENU.

OR...

PRESS CTRL + C.

3. SELECT THE CELL WHERE YOU WANT TO PASTE THE COPIED CELL(S).

4. CLICK THE PASTE BUTTON ON THE STANDARD TOOLBAR.

OR...

SELECT EDIT → PASTE FROM THE MENU.

OR...

PRESS CTRL + V.

LESSON
2.4

Moving and Copying Cells with Drag and Drop

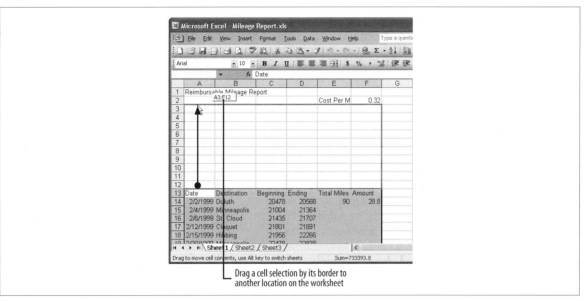

Drag a cell selection by its border to
another location on the worksheet

Figure 2-6. Use drag-and-drop to move a range of cells to a new destination in a worksheet.

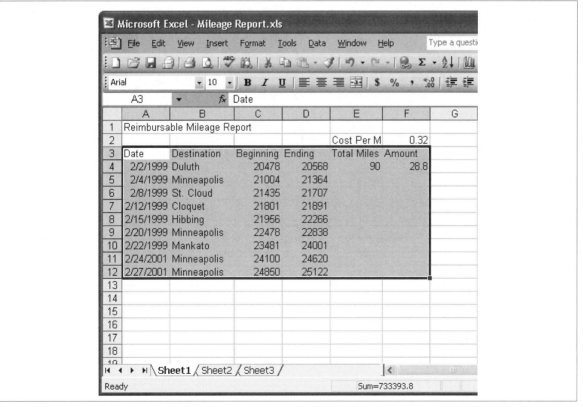

Figure 2-7. The worksheet after moving the cell range.

Figure 2-8. Confirmation to replace occupied cell contents.

In the previous lesson, you learned how to cut, copy, and paste cells. This lesson will show you another way to move or copy cells to different parts of a worksheet: using the drag-and-drop method. Drag-and-drop allows you to pick up a cell or cell range and place it in a new location on the worksheet; all without using any menus, toolbar buttons, or keystrokes!

In this lesson, you use drag-and-drop to move the block of text you cut and pasted in the previous lesson back to its original location.

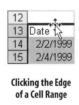

**Clicking the Edge
of a Cell Range**

1 Select the cell range A13:F22.

You may have to scroll down the worksheet in order to see the cell range A13:F22. Once you have selected the cell range, you can move it using drag-and-drop.

2 Position the pointer over any of the edges of the selected range, until it changes to a ⤢, then click and hold the mouse button, drag the selected range to cell A3. and release the mouse button.

As you drag the mouse, an outline of the cell range moves with the pointer, as shown in Figure 2-6. A tip box also appears while you drag the cell range, which displays the current position of the selected cell range as you move it. The selected cell range is dropped in the location, beginning with cell A3 (see Figure 2-7).

NOTE *Dragging-and-dropping can be a bit tricky for some people, especially if they're still new to using a mouse. It may take you several tries before you can drag and drop accurately. If you make a mistake and accidentally drop the cell range in the wrong place, click the Undo button (⮌) on the Standard toolbar and try it again.*

You can also copy cells and cell ranges using the drag-and-drop method. The procedure is almost exactly the same, except you hold down the Ctrl key as you drag the cell or cell range.

3 Select the cell range E2:F2.

Now that you have selected the cells you want to copy, copy them to a new destination in the worksheet using drop-and-drag.

4 Hold down the Ctrl key to copy the selected cell range and repeat Step 2 to copy the cell range to cell E1. Release the Ctrl key when you're finished.

Excel copies the selected cells to the new location.

5 Select the cell range E1:F1.

If you drag-and-drop into occupied cells, Excel will ask you if you want to replace the existing cells, as shown in Figure 2-8.

6 Drag-and-drop the selected cell range to cell A1 (without copying it).

Since this cell is already occupied, Excel asks whether you want to replace the contents of the destination cells.

7 Click Cancel.

Excel cancels the drag-and-drop procedure. You might have noticed that the label "Cost Per Mile" and the value ". 32" appear twice in the worksheet. You don't need this information to appear twice, so delete one of the entries.

8 Select the cell range E1:F1 and press Delete to clear the cell contents.

Now you can save the changes you've made to the workbook.

9 Save your work by clicking the Save button on the Standard toolbar.

If you've made it through the last two lessons, consider yourself an expert on moving and copying cells in Microsoft Excel. Actually, you can consider yourself an expert on copying and moving things in general, because the techniques you've learned in the last two lessons—cutting, copying, pasting, and dragging-and-dropping—will work with almost any Windows program!

QUICK REFERENCE

TO MOVE CELLS WITH DRAG AND DROP:

1. SELECT THE CELL OR THE CELL RANGE YOU WANT TO MOVE.
2. MOVE THE POINTER TO THE BORDER OF THE CELL OR CELL RANGE, CLICK AND HOLD DOWN THE MOUSE BUTTON, AND DRAG THE CELL OR CELL RANGE TO THE UPPER-LEFT CELL OF THE AREA WHERE YOU WANT TO MOVE THE DATA.
3. RELEASE THE MOUSE BUTTON.

TO COPY CELLS WITH DRAG AND DROP:

- FOLLOW THE SAME PROCEDURE, ONLY HOLD DOWN THE CTRL KEY WHILE YOU DRAG AND DROP THE CELL(S).

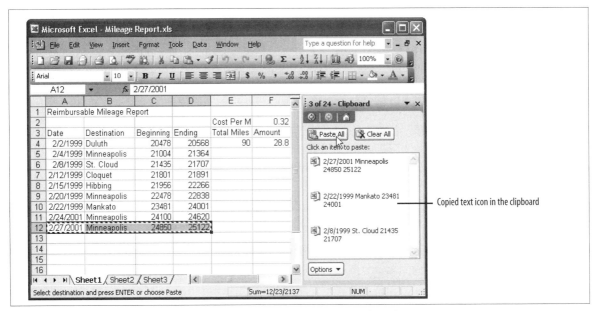

Figure 2-9. The Clipboard task pane displays the cut or copied objects you've collected.

If you do a lot of cutting, copying, and pasting you will probably appreciate Excel's new and improved Office clipboard, which holds not 1, but 24 cut or copied objects.

You can use the Office Clipboard to collect and paste multiple items. For example, you can copy information in a Microsoft Excel workbook, switch to Microsoft Word and copy some text, switch to PowerPoint and copy a bulleted list, switch to Access and copy a datasheet, and then switch back to Excel and paste the collection of copied items.

1 Select Edit → Office Clipboard **from the menu.**

The task pane appears in the right side of the Excel window. Next you need to display the Clipboard task pane.

Anything you cut or copy (up to 24 items) will appear in the Clipboard.

Copy button
Other Ways to Paste:
• Select **Edit→Copy** from the menu.
• Press <**CTRL**> + <**C**>

2 **Select the cell range** A6:D6 **and click the** Copy **button on the Standard toolbar.**

You've just added the contents of the cell range A6:D6 to the Office clipboard.

3 **Select the cell range** A10:D10 **and click the** Copy **button on the Standard toolbar.**

Excel adds the copied cell range to the Office clipboard as shown in Figure 2-9. Several Excel icons appear on the Clipboard toolbar—these represent everything you have cut or copied recently in any Office program. If any additional icons appear in the clipboard it's because you have already cut or copied some information.

Let's add one more item to the clipboard.

4 **Select the cell range** A12:D12 **and click the** Copy **button on the Standard toolbar.**

Another Excel icon appears on the clipboard task pane. The type of clipboard icon indicates which program the object was collected from, as described in Table 2-2.

To paste an object from the Office clipboard, simply click the object you want to paste. Or, you can paste all the objects in the clipboard by clicking the Paste All button in the clipboard task pane.

Paste All button

5 Click cell A13 and click the Paste All button in the task pane.

Excel pastes all the contents of the Office clipboard. Let's see if you remember how to clear cell contents...

6 Select the range of pasted cells (it should be A13:D15) and press the Delete key.

Table 2-2. Icons in the Clipboard Toolbar

Clipboard Icon	Description Contents
	Content cut or copied from a Microsoft Access database
	Content cut or copied from a Microsoft Excel workbook
	Content cut or copied from a Microsoft PowerPoint presentation
	Content cut or copied from a Microsoft Word document
	Web page contents cut or copied from Microsoft Internet Explorer
	Cut or copied graphic object
	Content cut or copied from a program other than Microsoft Office 2003

QUICK REFERENCE

TO DISPLAY THE OFFICE CLIPBOARD:

• SELECT EDIT → OFFICE CLIPBOARD FROM THE MENU.

TO ADD ITEMS TO THE OFFICE CLIPBOARD:

• COPY AND/OR CUT THE ITEMS AS YOU NORMALLY WOULD.

TO VIEW THE CONTENTS OF A CLIPBOARD ITEM:

• POINT TO THE ITEM ON THE CLIPBOARD TOOLBAR.

TO PASTE FROM THE OFFICE CLIPBOARD:

• DISPLAY THE CLIPBOARD TOOLBAR AND THEN CLICK THE ITEM YOU WANT TO PASTE. CLICK THE PASTE ALL BUTTON TO PASTE EVERYTHING.

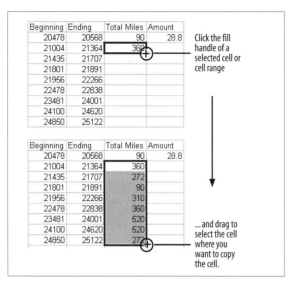

Click the fill handle of a selected cell or cell range

...and drag to select the cell where you want to copy the cell.

Figure 2-10. Use AutoFill to copy a formula to other cells.

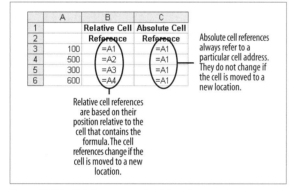

Absolute cell references always refer to a particular cell address. They do not change if the cell is moved to a new location.

Relative cell references are based on their position relative to the cell that contains the formula. The cell references change if the cell is moved to a new location.

Figure 2-11. Relative versus absolute references.

One of the more difficult Excel concepts you need to understand is the difference between *relative* and *absolute* cell references. You should already know that a cell reference identifies a cell or a range of cells on a worksheet and tells Microsoft Excel where to look for values you want to use in a formula. Here is the description and differences between absolute and relative cell references:

- **Relative:** Relative references tell Excel how to find another cell starting from the cell that contains the formula. Using a relative reference is like giving someone directions that explain where to go from where the person is currently standing. When a formula containing relative references is moved, it will reference new cells based on their location to the formula. Relative references are the default type of references used in Excel.

- **Absolute:** Absolute references always refer to the same cell address, even if the formula is moved.

If you're continuing from Lessons 2.3, 2.4, and 2.5, you can skip the first step of this exercise. Otherwise, you will need to open the Lesson 2B file...

1 If necessary, open the workbook named Lesson 2B on your Practice disk or folder then save it as Mileage Report.

First we need to create a simple formula.

2 Click cell E5, type the formula =D5-C5 and press Enter.

You've just created a simple formula that finds out the number of miles driven to a location by subtracting the beginning mileage from the ending mileage. Instead of retyping the total miles formula for every one of the destinations, you can copy the formula using any of the copy and paste methods you've already learned. The easiest and fastest way of copying the formula to the other cells is using the AutoFill function.

3 Click cell E5 and position the pointer over the fill handle of cell E5, until it changes to a +. Click and hold the mouse and drag the fill handle down to cell E12 and release the mouse button, as shown in Figure 2-10.

Poof! AutoFill copies the formula you entered in cell E5 to the cells you selected, saving you a lot of time you would have spent if you manually entered the formulas yourself. Now let's take a look at what is meant by a *relative cell reference*.

Fill Handle

4 Click cell E6 to make it active.

Look at the Formula bar. The formula that Excel copied to this cell isn't exactly the one you entered in cell E5. Instead of the original formula you entered, =D5-C5, this cell contains the formula =D6-C6. Excel copied the formula, but substituted new cell references so that even though the location of the cell has changed, its relationship with the cells in the formula hasn't. This is an example of *relative cell addresses*—they are based on their position relative to the cell that contains the formula.

TIP *Press the F4 key when clicking a cell to create an absolute cell reference to it.*

A1
Relative Reference
$A$1
Absolute Reference
Press the **F4** key when clicking a cell to create
and absolute cell reference to it.

Relative cell addresses are almost always the best way to reference other cells in formulas, which is why they are the default way Excel uses to reference cells. Sometimes, however, you might want a cell reference to always refer to a particular cell address. In this case, you would use an *absolute cell reference*, which always refers to a specific cell address, even if you move the formula to a new location. (See Figure 2-11.) Create another formula to see how to use an absolute cell reference.

5 Select cell F5, type =, click cell E5 (the total miles), type * (the multiplication operator), click cell F2 (the cost per mile), and complete the formula by pressing Enter.

Great! You've just created a formula that multiplies the totals miles driven by the cost per mile, currently .32. Now use AutoFill to copy the formula to the other cells.

6 Position the pointer over the fill handle of cell F5 until it changes to a +, click and hold the mouse, drag the fill handle down to cell F12, and release the mouse button.

Excel copies the formula, but what went wrong? Let's take a look.

7 Click cell F6 to make it active.

Look at the Formula bar. The formula (=E6*F3) that Excel copied to this cell is not correct. Look at cell F3—there's nothing there to multiply (unless you consider the text label), hence the #VALUE! error message. You need to use an *absolute reference* so the formula always refers to cell F2, even if a formula is moved or copied.

8 Click cell F5 to make it active and click anywhere in the Formula bar to change to Edit mode.

9 Verify that the insertion point is touching the F2 in the formula and press the F4 key.

Dollar signs appear, changing the F2 reference to $F$2—indicating it is an absolute reference. You can create an absolute reference to a cell by placing a dollar sign ($) before the parts of the reference that do not change. To create an absolute reference to cell A1, for example, add dollar signs to the formula: $A$1. Pressing F4 changes a relative cell reference to an absolute cell reference.

10 Press Enter and repeat Step 6 to copy the formula to the other cells.

This time the formula is copied correctly. The first cell reference in the formula is relative and changes based on the formula's location. The second cell reference in the formula, ($F$2), on the other hand, is an absolute cell reference and always points to cell F2, regardless of the formula's location.

QUICK REFERENCE

TO CREATE AN RELATIVE REFERENCE IN A FORMULA:

1. CLICK THE CELL YOU WANT TO REFERENCE; FOR EXAMPLE, CLICK CELL B4.

   OR...

2. TYPE THE ADDRESS OF THE CELL; FOR EXAMPLE, TYPE B4.

TO CREATE AN ABSOLUTE REFERENCE IN A FORMULA:

1. PRESS AND HOLD THE F4 KEY AS YOU CLICK THE CELL YOU WANT TO REFERENCE.

   OR...

2. TYPE THE ADDRESS OF THE CELL USING A $ (DOLLAR SIGN) BEFORE EVERY REFERENCE HEADING. (FOR EXAMPLE, TYPE $B$4.)

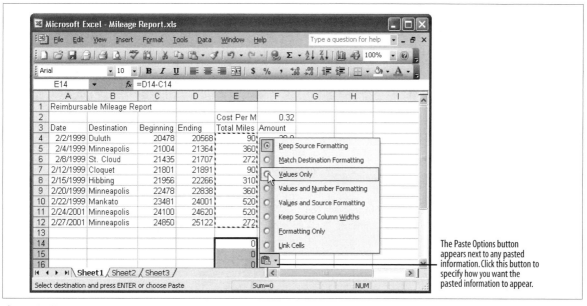

The Paste Options button appears next to any pasted information. Click this button to specify how you want the pasted information to appear.

Figure 2-12. The Paste Options button menu.

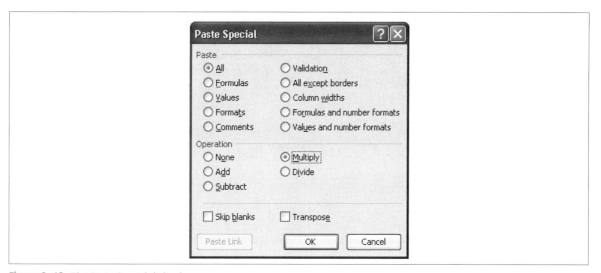

Figure 2-13. The Paste Special dialog box.

Excel's *Paste Special* command lets you specify exactly what you want to copy. For example, you can use the Paste Special command to copy the resulting value of a formula without copying the formula itself, or to copy the values of a range of cells without any of the cell's formatting options.

If you're continuing from the previous lesson, you can skip the first step of this exercise; otherwise, you will need to open the Lesson 2C file…

1 **If necessary, open the workbook named** Lesson 2C **on your Practice disk or in your Practice folder, then save it as** Mileage Report.

First we need to copy something.

Copy button
Other Ways to Copy:
Select **Edit**→**Copy** from the menu.
Press <**Ctrl**> + <**C**>.

2 Select the cell range E4:E12 and click the Copy button on the Standard toolbar (or use the keyboard shortcut Ctrl + C).

The cell range is copied to the clipboard.

3 Select cell E14 and click the Paste button on the Standard toolbar (or use the keyboard shortcut: Ctrl + V).

Excel pastes the contents of the copied cells. Notice, however, that the resulting values from the copied formulas are all 0. Instead of copying the cell formulas, you meant to copy the cell values. You can do this with the Paste Special command. Notice the Paste Options button (🛅) that appears next to the pasted information. You can use this button to specify how you want information pasted.

4 Position the pointer over the Paste Options button (🛅).

A drop-down arrow appears on the Paste Options button. Click this arrow to display a list of various options for how information is pasted into your document.

5 Click the Paste Options button list arrow (🛅 ▾) and select Values Only from the list, as shown in Figure 2-12.

Excel pastes the resulting values from the copied cell range formulas instead of pasting the formulas themselves. The Paste Options button contains the most common paste commands, but not all of them. To see every available paste command (most of which you will never use) you need to use the Edit → Paste Special command.

6 Select cell G4, type 1.25, and press Enter.

7 Select cell G4, copy the cell's contents by clicking the Copy button on the Standard toolbar, select the cell range E4:E12, and then select Edit → Paste Special from the menu.

The Paste Special dialog box reappears (see Figure 2-13. This time you will use an operation to multiply the value of the copied cell with the values in the selected cell range.

8 Select the Multiply option under the Operations section and click OK.

The dialog box closes and the selected cell range is multiplied by the value of cell G4.

Table 2-3 describes the options in the Paste Special dialog box.

Table 2-3. Paste Special Options

Paste Option	Description
All	Pastes all cell contents and formatting. Same as the Paste command.
Formulas	Pastes only the formulas as entered in the Formula bar.
Values	Pastes only the values as displayed in the cells (very useful!).
Formats	Pastes only cell formatting. Same as using the Format Painter button.
Comments	Pastes only comments attached to the cell.
Validation	Pastes data validation rules for the copied cells to the paste area.
All except borders	Pastes all cell contents and formatting applied to the copied cell except borders.
Operations	Specifies which mathematical operation, if any, you want to apply to the copied data. For example, you could multiply the pasted data by 5.
Skip Blanks	Avoids replacing values in your paste area when blank cells occur in the copy area.
Transpose	Changes columns of copied data to rows, and vice versa.
Link	Links the pasted data to the source data.

QUICK REFERENCE

TO USE THE PASTE SPECIAL COMMAND:

1. CUT OR COPY A CELL OR CELL RANGE USING STANDARD CUT AND COPY PROCEDURES.

2. CLICK THE PASTE BUTTON ON THE STANDARD TOOLBAR TO PASTE THE INFORMATION.

3. POSITION THE POINTER OVER THE  PASTE OPTIONS BUTTON THAT APPEARS, CLICK THE PASTE OPTIONS BUTTON LIST ARROW, AND SELECT THE DESIRED PASTE OPTION.

OR...

SELECT EDIT → PASTE SPECIAL FROM THE MENU.

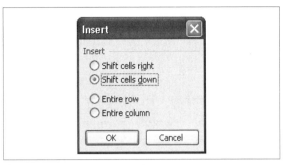

Figure 2-14. The Insert dialog box.

Figure 2-15. The Delete dialog box.

	A	B	C	D	E	F	G
1	Reimbursable Mileage Report						
2					Cost Per M	0.32	
3	Date	Destination	Beginning	Ending	Total Miles	Amount	
4	2/2/1999	Duluth	20478	20568	112.5	36	1.25
5	2/4/1999	Minneapolis	21004	21364	450	144	
6	2/8/1999	St. Cloud	21435	21707	340	108.8	

Figure 2-16. Selecting a cell range to insert.

	A	B	C	D	E	F	G
1	Reimbursable Mileage Report						
2							
3					Cost Per M	0.32	
4	Date	Destination	Beginning	Ending	Total Miles	Amount	1.25
5	2/2/1999	Duluth	20478	20568	112.5	36	
6	2/4/1999	Minneapolis	21004	21364	450	144	

↓ Existing cells move to make room for the inserted cells

Figure 2-17. Two inserted cell ranges.

While working on a worksheet, you may need to insert new cells, columns, or rows. Other times you may need to delete existing cells, columns, or rows. When you insert cells, you must shift any existing cells down or to the right to make room for the new cells. Likewise, when you delete cells (which is not the same as clearing the cell contents) you must shift any existing cells to fill the space left by the deletion.

In this lesson, you will get some practice inserting and deleting cells, rows, and columns. If you're continuing from the previous Absolute and Relative Address lesson, you can skip the first step of this exercise. If not, you will need to open the Lesson 2C file...

1 **If necessary, open the workbook named** Lesson 2C **on your Practice disk or in your Practice folder then save it as** Mileage Report.

First you need to specify where you want to insert the new cells.

Click the heading for the first row or column you want to select, then drag the mouse pointer to the last row or column heading

2 **Select the cell range** A2:F2.

This is where you want to insert the new cells.

3 **Select** Insert → Cells **from the menu.**

The Insert dialog box appears, as shown in Figure 2-14. You can choose to shift the existing cells to the right or down, or you can insert an entire row or entire column. The "Shift cells down" option is selected by default. This is the option you want to use. You're going to be inserting a new row of cells.

4 Click OK.

Excel inserts six new cells and shifts the cells that are below down one row.

You can also insert entire columns and rows using a couple different methods:

- **Menu:** Select the column or row heading where you want to insert the new column or row, and then select Insert → Rows, or Insert → Columns from the menu.

- **Shortcut Menu:** Right-click the selected row or column heading(s) and select Insert from the shortcut menu.

5 Select the second and third rows by clicking the 2 row heading and dragging the pointer to the 3 row heading and then releasing the mouse button.

Both the second and third rows are selected.

6 Right-click either of the selected row headings and select Insert from the shortcut menu.

Excel inserts two new rows. Inserting a column is almost the same as inserting a row.

7 Select the cell range F3:F15 and select Insert → Cells from the menu.

The Insert dialog box reappears. This time you want to shift the existing cells to the right. Based on the selected cell range, Excel recognizes this is the most likely option, so the Shift cells right option is selected by default.

8 Click OK.

Excel inserts the new cells and shifts the selected cell range to the right.

Deleting cells, cell ranges, columns, and rows is just as easy and straightforward as inserting them.

9 Repeat the procedure you learned in Step 5 to select the second, third, and fourth rows.

10 Select Edit → Delete from the menu.

The selected rows are deleted. You can also delete cells using the shortcut menu method:

11 Right-click the F column heading and select Delete from the shortcut menu.

Excel deletes the entire F column.

That's it! You've learned how to insert and delete cells, columns, and rows to and from your worksheets.

QUICK REFERENCE

TO INSERT A ROW OR COLUMN:

1. SELECT THE ROW OR COLUMN HEADINGS WHERE YOU WANT TO INSERT THE COLUMN OR ROW.

2. RIGHT-CLICK THE SELECTED ROW OR COLUMN HEADING(S) AND SELECT INSERT FROM THE SHORTCUT MENU.

   OR...

   SELECT INSERT → COLUMNS OR INSERT → ROWS FROM THE MENU.

TO DELETE A ROW OR COLUMN:

1. SELECT THE ROW OR COLUMN HEADING(S) YOU WANT TO DELETE.

2. RIGHT-CLICK THE SELECTED ROW OR COLUMN HEADING(S) AND SELECT DELETE FROM THE SHORTCUT MENU.

   OR...

   SELECT EDIT → DELETE FROM THE MENU.

TO DELETE A CELL RANGE:

1. SELECT THE CELL RANGE YOU WANT TO DELETE.

2. RIGHT-CLICK THE SELECTION AND SELECT DELETE FROM THE SHORTCUT MENU.

   OR...

1. SELECT EDIT → DELETE FROM THE MENU.

2. SPECIFY HOW YOU WANT THE ADJACENT CELLS SHIFTED.

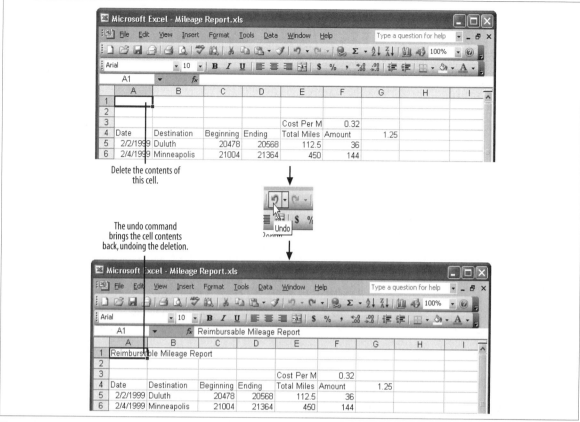

Figure 2-18. Undoing a command.

You may not want to admit this, but you're going to make mistakes when you use Excel. You might accidentally delete a column or row you didn't mean to delete, or paste something you didn't mean to paste. Fortunately, Excel has a wonderful feature called *undo* that does just that—undoes your mistakes and actions, making them as though they never happened. Excel can undo up to 16 of your last actions or mistakes. This lesson explains how you can undo both single and multiple mistakes, and how to redo your actions in case you change your mind.

1 Select cell A1 to make it active and press the Delete key to delete the worksheet's title.

The worksheet's title, "Reimbursable Mileage Report," disappears (see Figure 2-18). Oops! You didn't really want to delete that! Watch how you can undo your "mistake."

Undo button
Other Ways to Undo:
• Select **Edit→Undo** from the menu.
• Press <**CTRL**> + <**Z**>

2 Click the Undo button.

Poof! The deleted title "Reimbursable Mileage Report" is back again. Hmmm… maybe you did want to erase the worksheet title after all. Anything that can be undone can be redone if you change you change your mind or want to "undo an undo." Here's how you can redo the previous clear command.

Redo button
Other Ways to Redo:
• Select **Edit→Redo** from the menu

3 Click the Redo button.

The contents of cell A1, the worksheet title, disappear again.

Often you will probably make not one, but several mistakes, and it may be a minute or two before you've even realized you've made them. Fortunately, the programmers at Microsoft thought of this when they developed Excel, because the undo feature is multileveled—meaning you can undo up to 16 of the last things you did. The next few stops will show you how you can undo multiple errors.

Multilevel Undo

4 Select cell F2 to make it active, type .35, and press Enter.

There's your second mistake (the first was deleting the worksheet title in cell A1.)

5 Select the fourth and fifth rows in the worksheet by clicking the 4 row heading, holding down the mouse button, dragging the pointer over the 5 row heading, and releasing the mouse button.

Now that you have selected the fourth and fifth rows, you can delete them.

6 Right-click the selected 4 or 5 row heading and select Delete from the shortcut menu.

The fourth and fifth rows are deleted from the worksheet. Mistake number three. You've made enough mistakes now to see how multilevel undo works. Here's how to undo all of your mistakes.

7 Click the downward pointing arrow to the right of the Undo button.

A list of your recent actions appear beneath the Undo button. Notice that there are more actions listed than just your three recent "mistakes." If you wanted you could undo the last sixteen actions. You don't want to undo the sixteen actions—just the last three mistakes.

8 Select the word Clear from the undo list, as shown in Figure 2-19.

The last three changes you made to the workbook— deleting two rows, typing .35 in cell F2, and clearing the worksheet's title—are all undone.

The opposite of the Undo command is the Repeat command, which repeats your last command or action, if possible. Here's how to use it.

9 Select the cell range A3:A12, right-click the selection, select Delete from the shortcut menu, make sure the Shift cells left option is selected, and click OK.

You've just deleted the Date column. Now you can repeat your last command…

10 Select the cell range D3:D12 and press Ctrl + Y.

Excel repeats your last command and deletes the Total Miles range.

11 Click the Undo button on the Standard toolbar twice to undo your deletions, and then save your work.

QUICK REFERENCE

TO UNDO:

- CLICK THE UNDO BUTTON ON THE STANDARD TOOLBAR.

OR...

- SELECT EDIT → UNDO FROM THE MENU.

OR...

- PRESS CTRL + Z.

TO REDO:

- CLICK THE REDO BUTTON ON THE STANDARD TOOLBAR.

OR...

- SELECT EDIT → REDO FROM THE MENU.

OR...

- PRESS CTRL + Y.

TO REPEAT YOUR LAST COMMAND:

- PRESS CTRL + Y.

OR...

- SELECT EDIT → REPEAT FROM THE MENU.

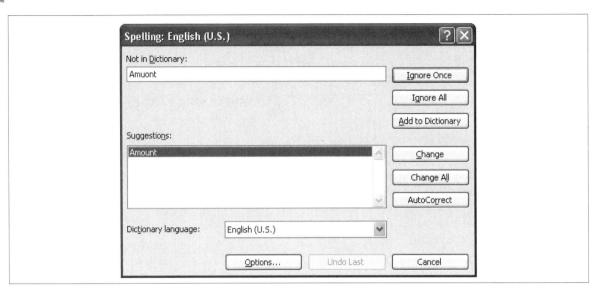

Figure 2-19. The Spelling dialog box.

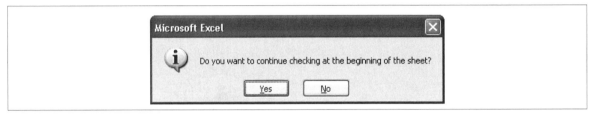

Figure 2-20. When Excel reaches the end of the worksheet, it asks if you want to continue checking from the beginning.

Figure 2-21. The spell check complete dialog box.

In the past, the spell check feature was only available in word-processing programs—but no more! You can use Excel's spell checker to find and correct any spelling errors you might have made in your workbooks. Excel's spell checker is shared and used by the other programs in the Microsoft Office suite. Any words you add to the custom spelling dictionary in one Microsoft Office program will be available in all the other programs. Worksheets are not the same as documents created by word processors and may contain abbreviations that the spell checker may not recognize. When this happens, click either Ignore to ignore the abbreviation, or Add to add the abbreviation to the custom spelling dictionary.

1 Press Ctrl + Home **to move to the first cell in the worksheet, A1.**

Excel starts checking the spelling of the words in a worksheet at the active cell and stops whenever it encounters a word that is not found in its dictionary.

Spelling button
Other Ways to Spell Check:
• Select **Tools**→**Spelling** from the menu.
• Press <**F7**>

2 Click the Spelling button on the Standard toolbar.

The Spelling dialog box appears as shown in Figure 2-19, with the misspelled word "Amuont" listed as the first misspelled word in the worksheet. Excel lists several possible suggestions for the correct spelling of the word.

3 Click Amount in the Suggestions list and click Change.

Excel makes the spelling correction for you. The spell checker moves on and selects the word "Cloquet" as the next misspelled word in the worksheet. Excel couldn't find the word "Cloquet" in its dictionary, but since it is the name of a city and is spelled correctly, you can ignore it.

Spell check begins at the active cell. When it reaches the end of the worksheet, it asks if you want to continue checking at the beginning of the document, as shown in Figure 2-20.

4 Click Ignore All to ignore all occurrences of the word "Cloquet" in the worksheet.

When the spell checker can't find any more incorrectly spelled words, Excel will indicate the spelling check is complete by displaying the dialog box shown in Figure 2-21.

Save button

5 Click the Save button on the Standard toolbar to save the changes you've made to the worksheet.

No doubt about it, the spell checker is a great tool to assist you in creating accurate worksheets. It's important to note, however, that Excel won't catch all of your spelling errors. For example, if you mistakenly type the word "Repeat" when you meant to type "Report" Excel won't catch the mistake because "Repeat" is a correctly spelled word.

QUICK REFERENCE

TO CHECK THE SPELLING IN A WORKSHEET:

- CLICK THE SPELLING BUTTON ON THE STANDARD TOOLBAR.

  OR...

- SELECT TOOLS → SPELLING FROM THE MENU.

  OR...

- PRESS F7.

Finding and Replacing Information

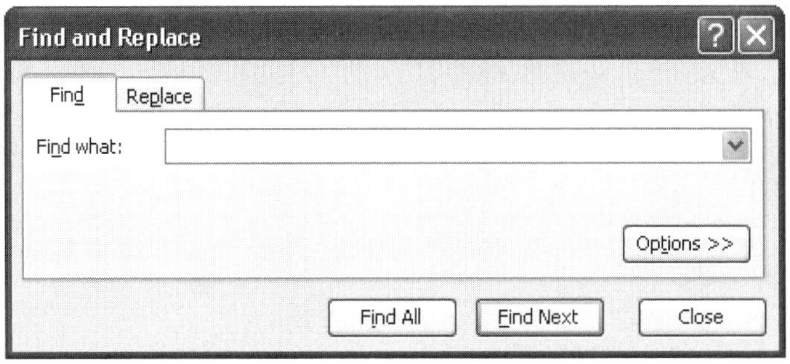

Figure 2-22. The Find dialog box.

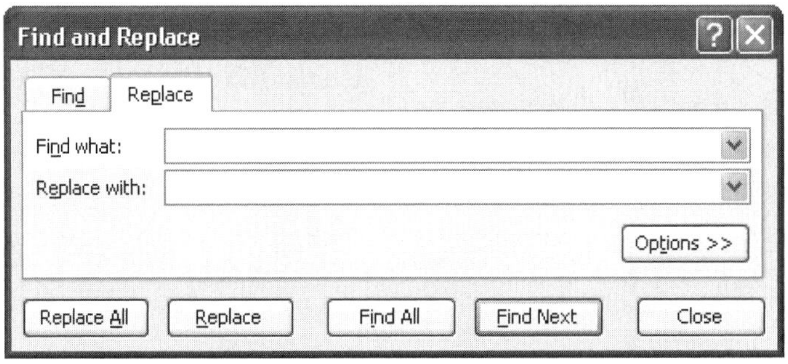

Figure 2-23. The Replace dialog box.

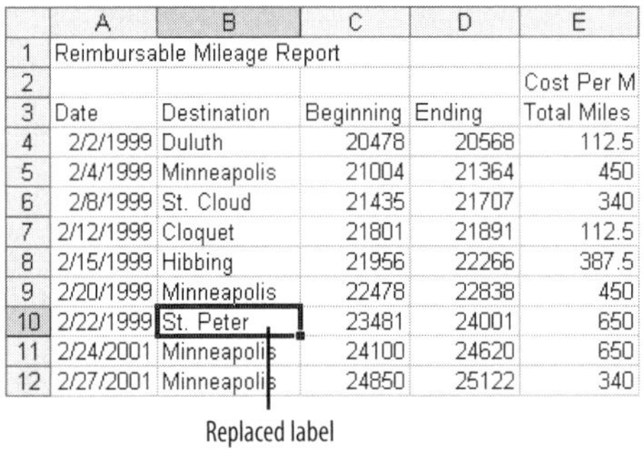

Replaced label

Figure 2-24. Replaced labels.

Imagine you are working on a huge worksheet that tracks the feeding patterns of various squirrels. You're almost finished with the worksheet when you realize that you've mistakenly referred to one of the species of squirrels you're tracking—flying squirrels—not by their proper scientific name "Sciuridae Glaucomys," but by the scientific name for the common gray squirrel "Sciuridae Sciurus." Yikes! It will take hours to go back and find every instance of "Sciuridae Sciurus" and replace it with "Sciuridae Glaucomys." Or it could take you less than a minute if you use Excel's find and replace function.

This lesson explains how to find specific words, phrases, and values in your workbooks, and how you can automatically replace those words, phrases, and values.

1 **If necessary, open the workbook named** Lesson 2D **and save it as** Mileage Report**.**

2 **Press** Ctrl + Home **to move to the beginning of the worksheet, cell A1.**

3 Select Edit → Find **from the menu.**

The Find dialog box appears, as shown in Figure 2-22.

4 **In the** Find what **box type** Minneapolis.

You want to find every occurrence of the phrase "Minneapolis" in the worksheet.

5 **Click the** Find Next button.

Excel jumps to the first occurrence of the word "Minneapolis" it finds in the worksheet.

6 **Click the** Find Next button.

Excel jumps to the next occurrence of the word "Minneapolis" in the worksheet.

7 **Click** Close **to close the Find dialog box.**

The Find dialog box closes. You can also replace information in a worksheet.

8 Select Edit → Replace **from the menu.**

The Replace dialog box appears, as shown in Figure 2-23.

9 **In the** Find what **box, type** Mankato.

You want to replace every occurrence of the word "Mankato" with the word "St. Peter."

10 **Select the** Replace with **box by clicking it or by pressing the** Tab **key, and then type** St. Peter.

11 **Click** Replace All.

Excel finds all the occurrences of the word "Mankato" in the worksheet and replaces them with the word "St Peter."

NOTE *Think before you use the Replace All button—you might not want it to replace every instance of a label or value! You can find and replace each individual occurrence of a label or value by clicking Find Next and then Replace.*

12 **Click** OK **to confirm the changes. Click** Close **to close the Replace dialog box.**

The Replace dialog box disappears and you're back to your worksheet. Notice how all the occurrences of the

word "Mankato" have been replaced by "St. Peter" (see Figure 2-24).

QUICK REFERENCE

TO FIND INFORMATION IN A WORKBOOK:

1. SELECT EDIT → FIND FROM THE MENU.

   OR...

   PRESS CTRL + F.

2. ENTER THE TEXT YOU WANT TO SEARCH FOR IN THE FIND WHAT BOX.

3. CLICK THE FIND NEXT BUTTON.

4. REPEAT STEP 3 UNTIL YOU FIND THE TEXT YOU'RE LOOKING FOR.

TO FIND AND REPLACE INFORMATION:

1. SELECT EDIT → REPLACE FROM THE MENU.

   OR...

2. PRESS CTRL + H.

3. ENTER THE TEXT YOU WANT TO SEARCH FOR IN THE FIND WHAT BOX.

4. ENTER THE TEXT YOU WANT TO REPLACE THAT TEXT WITH IN THE REPLACE WITH BOX.

5. CLICK THE FIND NEXT BUTTON.

6. CLICK THE REPLACE BUTTON TO REPLACE THE TEXT.

7. REPEAT STEPS 4 AND 5 IF THERE IS MORE THAN ONE OCCURRENCE THAT YOU WANT TO REPLACE.

   OR...

   CLICK REPLACE ALL TO SEARCH AND REPLACE EVERY OCCURRENCE OF TEXT IN THE WORKBOOK.

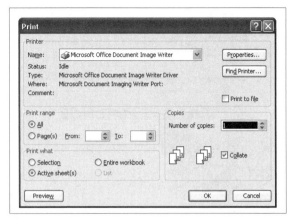

Figure 2-25. The Print dialog box.

You already know how to print, but in this lesson you will become an expert at printing. This lesson explains how to print more than one copy of a document, send a document to a different printer, and print specific pages of a document.

1 Click File → Print from the menu.

The Print dialog box opens, as shown in Figure 2-25. The Print dialog box is where you can specify printing options when you print your workbook. Several commonly used print options you might specify would be: how many pages to print, specific pages to print, or to which printer to print (if your computer is attached to more than one printer). See Table 2-4 for a description of what print options are available.

2 In the Number of copies box, type 2.

3 Click OK.

The Print dialog box closes, and Excel prints two copies of your worksheet (if your computer is attached to a printer).

Table 2-4 explains some of the other print options you can use when printing a worksheet; for example, how to print a specific page or a range of pages.

Table 2-4. Print Dialog Box Options

Print option	Description
Name	Select which printer to send your workbook to when it prints (if you are connected to more than one printer). The currently selected printer is displayed.
Properties	Displays a dialog box with options available for your specific printer such as what paper size you're using, if your document should be printed in color or black and white, etc.
Print to file	Prints the workbook to a file instead of sending to the printer.
Page range	Allows you to specify what pages you want printed. There are several options here: **All:** Prints the entire document **Current page:** Prints only the page of the workbook on which you're currently working. **Selection:** Prints only selected cells. **Pages:** Prints only the pages of the workbook you specify. Select a range of pages with a hyphen (like 5-8) and separate single pages with a comma (like 3,7).
Number of copies	Specifies the number of copies you want to print.
Print what	Allows you to select what is printed: the currently selected cells, the active sheet(s), or the entire workbook.
Options	Lets you specify other printing options, such as printing a document in reverse order (from the last page to the first).

QUICK REFERENCE

FOR ADVANCED PRINTING OPTIONS:

1. SELECT FILE → PRINT FROM THE MENU.

2. REFER TO TABLE 2-4 FOR INFORMATION ON VARIOUS PRINTING OPTIONS.

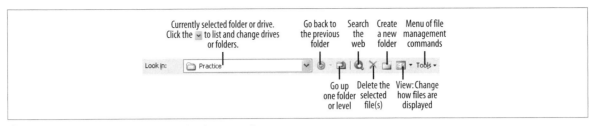

Figure 2-26. The Open and Save As dialog boxes' toolbar.

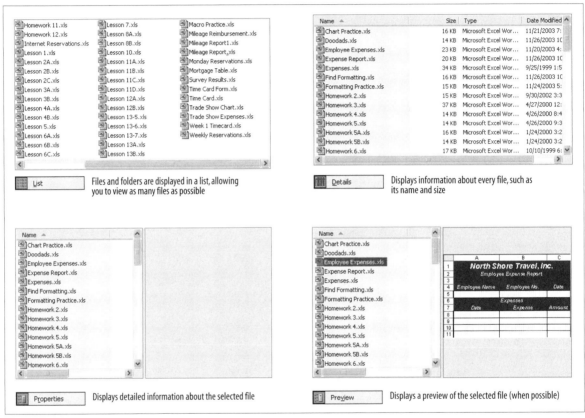

Figure 2-27. The View list button lets you change how files are displayed in the Open or Save As dialog boxes.

Tools menu

File management includes moving, copying, deleting, and renaming the files you've created. Although it's a little easier to work with and organize your files using Windows Explorer or My Computer, you can also perform a surprising number of file management chores right from inside Microsoft Excel XP—especially with its new and improved Open and Save dialog boxes. See Figure 2-26 for an example of the Open and Save As dialog boxes toolbar.

Open button

1 Click the Open button **on the Standard toolbar.**

The Open dialog appears. The Open dialog box is normally used to open files, but you can also use it to perform several file management functions. There are two different ways to access file management commands from inside the Open or Save As dialog boxes:

File Shortcut Menu

- Select a file and then select the command you want from the dialog box's Tools menu.
- Right-click a file and select the command you want from a shortcut menu.

2 **Right-click the** Rename Me **file.**

A shortcut menu appears with a list of available file management commands for the selected file. See Table 2-5 for a description of the File Shortcut menu commands.

3 **Select** Rename **from the shortcut menu, type** Home Budget, **and press** Enter.

You have just changed the name of the selected file from "Rename Me" to "Home Budget". Instead of right-clicking the file, you could have selected it and then selected Rename from the Tools menu. Move on to the next step to learn how to delete a file.

4 **Click the** Home Budget **file to select it and press the** Delete **key.**

A dialog box appears, asking you to confirm the deletion of the Home Budget file.

5 **Click** Yes.

The Home Budget file is deleted. If you work with and create numerous files, you may find it difficult to remember what you named a file. To find the file(s) you're looking for, it can help to preview your files without opening them.

Views Button List Arrow

6 **Click the** Views button **list arrow and select** Preview.

The Open dialog changes the display of Excel files on your Practice folder or disk from List View to Preview View. To see the contents of a file, select it in the file list on the left side of the dialog box. It appears in the Preview area to the right side of the dialog box. Try previewing the contents of a file without opening it now.

NOTE *You must save Excel workbooks with a Picture Preview in order to display a preview in the Open dialog box. To do this, before saving any file select File → Properties, click the Summary tab, and verify that the Save picture preview check box is checked.*

7 **Click the** Lesson 1A **file.**

The Lesson 1A file is selected and a preview of its contents appear in the Preview section. Change back to List mode to display as many files in the window as possible.

8 **Click the** Views button **list arrow, select** List **to display the files in list view (see Figure 2-27), then close the dialog box by clicking** Cancel.

Table 2-5. File Shortcut Menu Commands

Command	Description
Open	Opens the selected file.
Open Read-Only	Opens the selected file so that it can be read but not changed.
Open as Copy	Creates a copy of the selected file with the name "Copy of" and the name of the original file, and then opens the new, copied file.
Print	Sends the selected file to the default printer.
Quick View	Displays the contents of the selected file without opening the file.
Send To	Depending on how your computer is set up, it lets you send the selected file to a printer, to an e-mail recipient, to a fax, or to a floppy drive.
Cut	Used in conjunction with the Paste command to move files. Cuts, or removes the selected file from its current folder or location.
Copy	Used in conjunction with the Paste command to copy files. Copies the selected file.
Paste	Pastes a cut or copied file or files.
Create Shortcut	Creates a shortcut—a quick way to a file or folder without having to go to its permanent location—to the file.
Delete	Deletes the selected file or files.
Rename	Renames the selected files.
Properties	Displays the properties of the selected file, such as when the file was created or last modified, or how large the file is.

QUICK REFERENCE

BASIC FILE MANAGEMENT IN THE OPEN DIALOG BOX:

1. OPEN THE OPEN OR SAVE AS DIALOG BOXES BY SELECTING OPEN OR SAVE AS FROM THE FILE MENU.

2. RIGHT-CLICK THE FILE AND REFER TO TABLE 2-5 FOR A LIST OF THINGS YOU CAN DO TO THE SELECTED FILE.

OR...

SELECT THE FILE AND SELECT A COMMAND FROM THE TOOLS MENU.

TO CHANGE HOW FILES ARE DISPLAYED:

- CLICK THE VIEW BUTTON LIST ARROW AND SELECT A VIEW.

Inserting Cell Comments

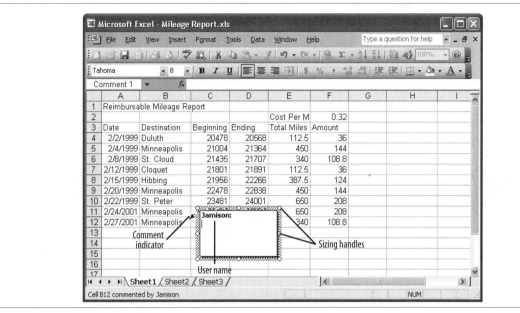

Figure 2-28. Inserting a cell comment.

Sometimes you may need to add notes to your workbook to document complicated formulas or questionable values, or to leave a comment to another user. Excel's cell comments command helps you document your worksheets and make them easier to understand. Think of cell comments as Post-It Notes that you can attach to any cell. Cell comments appear whenever you point at the cell to which they're attached.

1 If necessary, open the workbook named Lesson 2E and save it as Mileage Report.

2 Right-click cell B12.

A shortcut menu appears.

3 Select Insert Comment from the shortcut menu.

A comment box appears by the cell, as shown in Figure 2-28. Notice a name appears at the beginning of the comment—this is the user name, which can be found by selecting Tools → Options from the menu and clicking the General tab. The user name appears on the comment so that other users will know who added the comment. You can add a note to the comment box by just typing.

4 Type This date may be incorrect.

Now that you've finished writing the note, you can close the comment box.

Comment Indicator

5 Click anywhere outside the comment box to close it.

The comment box closes. Notice a small red triangle now appears in the upper-right corner of cell B12. This triangle indicates that there is a comment attached to the cell. Displaying a comment is very, very easy.

6 Position the pointer over cell B12.

The comment appears next to the cell whenever the pointer is positioned over it. Here's how to edit a comment:

7 Right-click cell B12.

A shortcut menu appears.

8 Select Edit Comment from the shortcut menu.

An insertion point (|) appears at the end of the text in the comment box, indicating that you can edit the text in the comment box. Add some more text to the comment box.

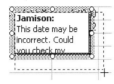

Resize a comment box by clicking and dragging any of its sizing handles until the comment box is the size you want.

9 Press the Spacebar, then type Could you check my receipts to verify this?

You can also change the size and position of a comment box while in edit mode. Notice the white boxes that appear at the corners and sides of the comment box, as shown in Figure 2-28. These are sizing handles, which you can use to change the size of the box.

10 Position the pointer over the lower-right sizing handle, until the pointer changes to a ↖, click and hold the left mouse button and drag the mouse diagonally up and to the left about a half-inch, then release the mouse button.

The comment is resized, and the text is wrapped accordingly. You can also move a comment to a different location on the screen.

11 Position the pointer over the border of the comment box until it changes to a ✛, click and drag the comment down an inch, then release the mouse button to drop the comment.

You've just moved the comment to a new position on the worksheet. Now delete the comment.

12 Right-click cell B12 and select Delete Comment from the shortcut menu.

QUICK REFERENCE

TO INSERT A COMMENT:

1. RIGHT-CLICK THE CELL YOU WANT TO ATTACH A COMMENT TO.

2. SELECT INSERT COMMENT FROM THE SHORTCUT MENU.

3. TYPE THE COMMENT.

4. CLICK ANYWHERE OUTSIDE THE COMMENT AREA WHEN YOU'RE FINISHED.

TO EDIT A COMMENT:

1. RIGHT-CLICK THE CELL THAT CONTAINS THE COMMENT YOU WANT TO EDIT.

2. SELECT EDIT COMMENT FROM THE SHORTCUT MENU.

3. EDIT THE COMMENT.

4. CLICK ANYWHERE OUTSIDE THE COMMENT AREA WHEN YOU'RE FINISHED.

TO DELETE A COMMENT:

1. RIGHT-CLICK THE CELL THAT CONTAINS THE COMMENT YOU WANT TO EDIT.

2. SELECT DELETE COMMENT FROM THE SHORTCUT MENU.

Understanding Smart Tags

LESSON
2.15

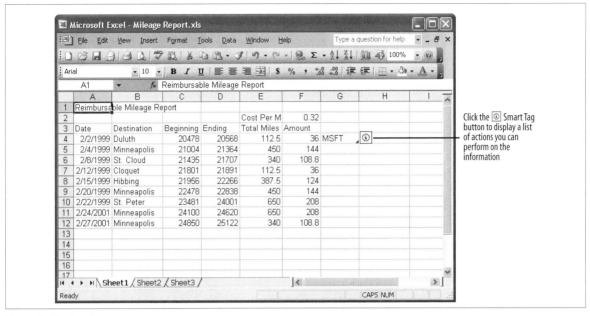

Figure 2-29. Smart Tags.

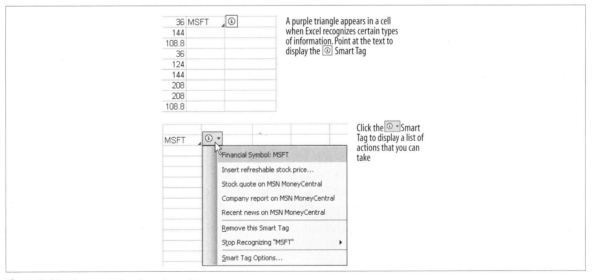

Figure 2-30. The Smart Tag drop-down list.

TIP *You can change the Smart Tag options by selecting Tools → AutoCorrect Options from the menu and clicking the Smart Tag tab.*

Smart tags were new in Microsoft Office XP, and they still make working with Excel 2003 a lot easier. Smart tags are similar to right-mouse button shortcuts—you click Smart Tags to perform actions on various items. Smart tags appear when Excel recognizes certain types of infor-

mation, such as the name of a person in your Address Book. Excel marks these items with a ◢ purple triangle and a Smart Tag indicator (⊚). Clicking a Smart Tag indicator (⊚) displays a list of things that you can do to the Smart Tag, such as finding the current stock price for a financial symbol. Other Smart Tag–like buttons appear when you paste information or make a mistake in a formula. Clicking these buttons specifies how Excel pastes or corrects information.

In this lesson you will learn what Smart Tags look like and how to use them. First, we need to ensure that the all the Smart Tag options are active. The following describes how to view Excel's Smart Tag options.

1 **Select** Tools → AutoCorrect Options **from the menu and click the** Smart Tags **tab.**

The Smart Tags tab of the AutoCorrect Options dialog box appears.

2 **Ensure that the** Label data with Smart Tags **box is checked.**

Selecting this option will tell Microsoft Excel to mark certain types of information with Smart Tags.

3 **Click** OK.

The AutoCorrect Options dialog box closes. Let's see how these Smart Tags work.

4 **Click any blank cell, type** MSFT, **and press** Enter.

In case you're not a stockbroker, MSFT is the stock ticker symbol for Microsoft. Shortly after you press Enter, Microsoft Excel recognizes the MSFT stock ticker symbol and marks it with a Smart Tag—a ◢ purple triangle in the bottom of the cell.

5 **Position the pointer over the** MSFT **cell.**

A Smart Tag button (⊙) appears next to the MSFT. Click this button to specify what actions you can perform on the MSFT information.

6 **Click the** Smart Tag button **list arrow (**⊙ ▾**) and select** Stock quote on MSN MoneyCentral **from the list (see Figure 2-30).**

If you are connected to the Internet, your computer's Web browser will open and display the current stock price for Microsoft (how are they doing today?).

7 **Close your Web browser.**

Table 2-6. Smart Tags and Buttons

Smart Tag Button	Smart Tag Name	Description
⊛	Smart Tag	When Excel recognizes certain types of data, such as a stock ticker symbol, the data is marked with a Smart Tag indicator (⊙), or a purple dotted underline. To find out what actions you can take with a Smart Tag, move the insertion point over the text with a Smart Tag indicator until the Smart Tag button (⊛) appears. Click the Smart Tag button (⊛) to see a menu of actions.
🖹	Paste Options	The Paste Options button appears after you paste something. Click the Paste Options button to specify how information is pasted into your workbook. The available options depend on the type of content you are pasting and the program you are pasting from.
◈	Formula Error	The Formula Error button appears when Excel formula checker detects an error in a formula, such as a division by zero.

QUICK REFERENCE

UNDERSTANDING SMART TAGS:

- AS YOU ENTER INFORMATION IN A DOCUMENT, SMART TAG BUTTONS () WILL APPEAR. CLICK THESE BUTTONS TO DO SOMETHING TO THE SPECIFIED INFORMATION.

TO USE A SMART TAG:

- CLICK THE SMART TAG LIST ARROW AND SELECT THE DESIRED ACTION OR OPTION.

TO VIEW/CHANGE SMART TAG OPTIONS:

SELECT TOOLS → AUTOCORRECT OPTIONS FROM THE MENU AND CLICKING THE SMART TAG TAB.

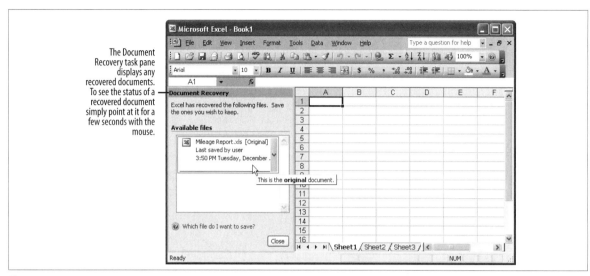

The Document Recovery task pane displays any recovered documents. To see the status of a recovered document simply point at it for a few seconds with the mouse.

Figure 2-31. The Document Recovery task pane.

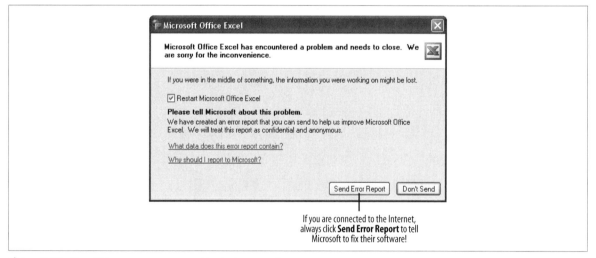

If you are connected to the Internet, always click **Send Error Report** to tell Microsoft to fix their software!

Figure 2-32. Oops! There goes your annual budget proposal!

If you haven't found this out already, sooner or later you're going to discover that computers don't always work the way they're supposed to. Nothing is more frustrating than when a program, decides to take a quick nap for no apparent reason, locks up, and stops responding to your commands—especially if you lose the precious workbook that you're working on!

Fortunately, after more than 10 years and roughly 9 software versions, Microsoft has finally realized that people might want to recover their workbooks if Microsoft Excel locks up or stops responding. If Excel 2003 encounters a problem and stops responding, after you finish hitting your computer's monitor, you can restart Microsoft Excel or your computer and try to recover your lost workbooks. Sometimes Excel will display a dialog box similar to the one shown in Figure 2-32 and automatically restart itself.

In this lesson, you will learn how to use Microsoft Excel's new document recovery features, should disaster strike (heaven forbid).

1 If necessary, restart your computer and/or Microsoft Excel.

You may not need to restart your computer or Excel at all—often Excel will display the dialog box shown in Figure 2-32 and automatically restart itself when it encounters a problem.

When you restart Microsoft Excel, hopefully the Document Recovery pane will appear, as shown in Figure 2-31. If the Document Recovery pane doesn't appear you're out of luck—Excel didn't recover any of your workbooks. Hope you made a backup!

Sometimes Excel will display several recovered workbooks in the Document Recovery task pane, such as the original workbook that was based on the last manual save and a recovered workbook that was automatically saved during an AutoRecovery save process. You can see the status of any recovered workbook by simply pointing at the recovered workbook for a second or two. See Table 2-7 for a description of the different status indicators.

2 To view details about any recovered workbook simply point at the workbook in the Document Recovery task pane for a few seconds.

Hopefully you will find a version of your workbook—either original or recovered—that isn't missing too much of your work.

Here's how to select and then save a recovered workbook…

3 Click the desired recovered workbook from the task pane.

The workbook appears in Excel's worksheet window.

4 Select File → Save As from the menu and save the workbook.

You can further protect your work by using the AutoRecovery feature to periodically save a temporary copy of the workbook on which you're working. To recover work after a power failure or similar problem, you must have turned on the AutoRecovery feature before the problem occurred. You can set the AutoRecovery save interval to occur more often than every 10 minutes (its default setting). For example, if you set it to save every 5 minutes, you'll recover more information than if you set it to save every 10 minutes. Here's how to change the AutoRecovery save interval…

5 Select Tools → Options from the menu and click the Save tab.

The Save tab of the Options dialog box appears.

6 Ensure that the Save AutoRecovery info every: box is checked, and specify the desired interval, in minutes, in the minutes box. Click OK when you're finished.

Even with document recovery features, the best way to ensure that you don't lose much information if your computer freezes up is to save your work regularly.

Table 2-7. Status Indicators in the Document Recovery Task Pane

Status Indicator	Description
Original	Original file based on last manual save.
Recovered	File recovered during recovery process or file saved during an AutoRecovery save process
Repaired	Excel encountered problems while recovering the workbook and has attempted to repair them. Make sure that you double-check your workbook to make sure that there isn't any corruption.

QUICK REFERENCE

TO RECOVER A DOCUMENT:

1. RESTART MICROSOFT EXCEL (IF IT DOESN'T RESTART BY ITSELF).

2. FIND AND THEN CLICK THE BEST RECOVERED DOCUMENT IN THE DOCUMENT RECOVERY TASK PANE.

3. SAVE THE DOCUMENT BY SELECTING FILE → SAVE AS FROM THE MENU.

TO CHANGE THE AUTORECOVERY SETTINGS:

1. SELECT TOOLS → OPTIONS FROM THE MENU AND CLICK THE SAVE TAB.

2. ENSURE THAT THE SAVE AUTORECOVERY INFO EVERY BOX IS CHECKED AND SPECIFY THE DESIRED INTERVAL, IN MINUTES, IN THE MINUTES BOX. CLICK OK WHEN YOU'RE FINISHED.

Chapter Two Review

Lesson Summary

Entering Data Values and Using AutoComplete

Excel treats dates and times as values.

You can enter dates in cells using almost any type of date format: 1/1/99, 1-1-99, January 1, 1999, etc.

To Use AutoComplete: Type the first few characters of a label; Excel displays the label, if it appears previously in the column. Press Enter to accept the entry or resume typing to ignore the suggestion.

To Use the PickList: Right-click the cell where you want to enter a label, select Pick from List from the shortcut menu, and select the entry from the list.

Editing, Clearing, and Replacing Cell Contents

To Clear Cell Contents: Select the cell or cell range and press the Delete key.

Entering information into a cell replaces its previous contents.

To Edit a Cell's Contents: Select the cell, click the Formula bar, edit the cell contents, and press Enter when you're finished.

To Edit a Cell In-Place: Double-click the cell you want to edit, edit the cell's contents in-place, and press Enter when you're finished.

Cutting, Copying, and Pasting Cells

How to Cut: Cut cells or cell ranges by selecting the cell or cell range and using one of four methods to cut:

- Click the Cut button on the Standard toolbar.
- Select Edit → Cut from the menu.
- Press Ctrl + X.
- Right-click and select Cut from the shortcut menu.

How to Copy: Copy cell or cell ranges by selecting the cell or cell range and using one of four methods to copy:

- Click the Copy button on the Standard toolbar.
- Select Edit → Copy from the menu.
- Press Ctrl + C.
- Right-click and select Copy from the shortcut menu.

How to Paste a Copied Object: Paste copied cells by selecting the cell where you want to paste the copied cell(s) and using one of four methods:

- Click the Paste button on the Standard toolbar.
- Select Edit → Paste from the menu.
- Press Ctrl + V.
- Right-click select Paste from the shortcut menu.

How to Paste a Cut Object: Select the cell where you want to paste the cut cell(s) and press Enter.

Moving and Copying Cells with Drag and Drop

To Move Cells with Drag and Drop: Select the cell or cell range you want to move, drag the selection by its outside border to the upper-left cell of the area where you want to move the cells, and release the mouse button.

To Copy Cells with Drag and Drop: Follow the above procedure, but hold down the Ctrl key while you drag and drop the cell(s).

Collecting and Pasting Multiple Items

To Display the Clipboard Task Pane: Select Edit → Office Clipboard from the menu.

To Add Items to the Office Clipboard: Copy and/or cut the items as you normally would.

To View the Contents of a Clipboard Item: Point to the item on the Clipboard toolbar.

To Paste from the Office Clipboard: If necessary, display the Clipboard task pane, then click the item you want to paste. Click the Paste All button to paste all collected items.

Working with Absolute and Relative Cell References

Relative cell references are based on their position relative to the cell that contains the formula. The cell references change if the cell is moved to a new location.

Absolute cell references are preceded by $ signs and always refer to a particular cell address. They do not change if the cell is moved to a new location.

Press F4 after selecting a cell range to make it an absolute reference.

Using the Paste Special Command

To Use the Paste Special Command: Cut or copy a cell or cell range using standard cut and copy procedures. Click the Paste button on the Standard toolbar to paste the information. Position the pointer over the Paste Options button, click the Paste Options button list arrow, and select the desired paste option.

Inserting and Deleting Cells, Rows, and Columns

To Insert a Row or Column: Select the row or column headings to insert the column or row, right-click the selected row or column heading(s), and select Insert from the shortcut menu. Or select the row or column headings where you want the row or column to be inserted, and select Insert → Columns or Insert → Rows from the menu.

To Delete a Row or Column: Select the row or column heading(s) you want to delete and either right-click the selected row or column heading(s) and select Delete from the shortcut menu or select Edit → Delete from the menu.

To Delete a Cell Range: Select the cell range you want to delete, either right-click the selection and select Delete from the shortcut menu or select Edit → Delete from the menu, and then specify how you want adjacent cells shifted.

Using Undo and Redo

Undo: Undo your mistake or last action by clicking the Undo button on the Standard toolbar, by selecting Edit → Undo from the menu, or by pressing Ctrl + Z.

Redo: Redo an undone action by clicking the Redo button on the Standard toolbar, by selecting Edit → Redo from the menu, or by pressing Ctrl + Y.

Multilevel Undo/Redo: Click the arrows on the Undo or Redo buttons on the Standard toolbar to undo or redo several actions at once.

Repeat: Repeat your last command by pressing Ctrl + Y or by selecting Edit → Repeat from the menu.

Checking Your Spelling

To Check for Spelling Errors: Click the Spelling button on the Standard toolbar or select Tools → Spelling from the menu.

Finding and Replacing Information

To Find Information: Select Edit → Find from the menu, or press Ctrl + F. Enter the text you want to search for in the Find what box and click the Find next button. You can click the Find next button multiple times until you find the text you're looking for.

To Replace Information: Select Edit → Replace from the menu or press Ctrl + H. Enter the text you want to search for in the Find what box and enter the text you want to replace it with in the Replace with box. Click the Find next button to find the text and the Replace button to replace the text. Click Replace All to replace every occurrence of the text in the workbook.

Advanced Printing Options

Open the Print Dialog box by selecting File → Print from the menu. You can specify the number of copies and which pages to print.

File Management

You can perform most file management functions, such as delete, rename, and copy, from the Open File or Save As dialog boxes. Right-click a file and select a file command from the shortcut menu or select the file and select a command from the Tools menu.

To Change How Files are Displayed: Click the Views button list arrow and select a view.

Inserting Cell Comments

To Insert a Comment: Right-click the cell you want to attach a comment to and select Insert Comment from the shortcut menu. Enter the comment and click anywhere outside the comment area when you're finished.

To Edit a Comment: Right-click the cell that contains the comment you want to edit and select Edit Comment from the shortcut menu. Edit the comment and click anywhere outside the comment area when you're finished adding to the comment.

To Delete a Comment: Right-click the cell that contains the comment you want to edit and select Delete Comment from the shortcut menu.

Understanding Smart Tags

As you enter information in a document, Smart Tag buttons (⊚) will appear. Click these buttons to do something to the specified information.

To Use a Smart Tag: Click the Smart Tag list arrow to select the desired action or option.

To View/Change Smart Tag Options: Select Tools → AutoCorrect Options from the menu and click the Smart Tag tab.

Recovering Your Workbooks

To Recover a Document: Restart Microsoft Excel (if it doesn't restart by itself). Find and then click the best recovered workbook in the Document Recovery task pane. Save the workbook by choosing File → Save As from the menu.

To Change the AutoRecovery Settings: Select Tools → Options from the menu and click the Save tab. Ensure that the Save AutoRecovery info every: box is checked and specify the desired interval, in minutes, in the minutes box. Click OK when you're finished.

Quiz

1. You're going to the bank on Monday and somehow lose the daily receipts that you're supposed to deposit at the end of every day. When you complete the daily receipts summary worksheet on Friday how can you add a note to the Monday cell to explain what happened to your boss?

   A. Who cares about adding a note? You better start brushing up your résumé.

   B. Print out the worksheet and add a Post-It note by the Monday receipt cell.

   C. Select the Monday receipt cell and select Insert → Comment from the menu to add a comment.

   D. Don't add a note—just guess what the amount of the deposit would be and enter that. Let your boss figure it out when she gets the bank statement.

2. Which is the fastest method of replacing the contents of a cell?

   A. Press Delete to clear the cell's contents and enter the new contents.

   B. Enter the new contents—they will replace the old contents.

   C. Click the Formula bar to edit the cell contents, press Backspace to erase the old contents, and enter the new contents.

   D. Double-click the cell to edit it in-place, press Backspace to erase the old contents, and enter the new contents.

3. Which of the following will NOT cut information?

   A. Clicking the Cut button on the Standard toolbar.

   B. Pressing Ctrl + C.

   C. Pressing Ctrl + X.

   D. Selecting Edit → Cut from the menu.

4. Relative references always refer to a particular cell address. They don't change if they are moved to a new location (True or False?)

5. The Paste Special command lets you copy and paste (select all that apply):

   A. The resulting values of a formula instead of the actual formula.

   B. Formatting options.

   C. Cell comments.

   D. Multiply the selection by a copied value.

6. Which of the following statements is NOT true?

   A. You can spell check your worksheets by clicking the Spelling button on the Standard toolbar.

   B. To find information in a worksheet select Edit → Find from the menu.

   C. The Undo function can only undo the most recent action you performed.

   D. When you delete a cell range, row, or column, you must shift any existing cell to take the place of the deleted cells.

7. You can edit a cell by (select all that apply):

    A. Double-clicking the cell to edit it in place.

    B. Selecting Edit → Edit Workbook → Edit Worksheet → Edit Cell from the menu.

    C. You can't—you're just going to have to retype all that information over again.

    D. Clicking the Formula bar.

8. The spell checker always marks your name as a spelling error. How can you get Excel to stop saying your name is spelled incorrectly?

    A. Select Tools → Spelling from the menu and click Add when your name appears.

    B. Right-click your name and select Add from the shortcut menu.

    C. Select Tools → Spelling and Grammar from the menu and click Add to Dictionary.

    D. You can't do anything about it.

9. How can you print three copies of a workbook?

    A. Select File → Print from the menu and type 3 in the "Number of copies" text box.

    B. Press Ctrl + P + 3.

    C. Select File → Properties from the menu and type 3 in the "Copies to print" text box.

    D. Click the Print button on the Standard toolbar to print the document, then take it to Kinko's and have two more copies made.

10. You discover you've made minor calculation error in a worksheet. How can you replace every instance of the word "profit" in your worksheet with the word "loss"?

    A. Select Edit → Replace from the menu, type "profit" in the Find what box, type "loss" in the Replace with box and click Replace All.

    B. There isn't any easy way. You'll have to go through your novel and replace the words yourself.

    C. Click the Find and Replace button on the Standard toolbar, then follow the Find and Replace Wizard's on-screen instructions to replace the word.

    D. Select Tools → Replace from the menu, type "profit" in the Find what box, type "loss" in the Replace with box and click Replace All.

11. Which of following is an absolute cell reference?

    A. A1

    B. #A#1

    C. !A!1

    D. $A$1

12. You can use the Copy button on the Standard toolbar to copy a worksheet's values but not its formulas. (True or False?)

13. How do you insert a row? (Select all that apply.)

    A. Right-click the row heading where you want to insert the new row and select Insert from the shortcut menu.

    B. Select the row heading where you want to insert the new row and select Edit → Insert Row from the menu.

    C. Select the row heading where you want to insert the new row and click the Insert Row button on the Standard toolbar.

    D. Select the row heading where you want to insert the new row and select Insert → Row from the menu.

14. How do you delete a column? (Select all that apply.)

    A. Right-click the column heading you want to delete and select Delete from the shortcut menu.

    B. Select the column heading you want to delete and select Edit → Delete from the menu.

    C. Select the column heading you want to delete and select the Delete Row button on the Standard toolbar.

    D. Select the column heading you want to delete and select Insert → Delete from the menu.

Homework

1. Open the Homework 2 workbook and save it as "Doodads."

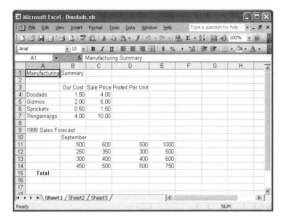

2. Change the worksheet title in cell A1 to "2000 Manufacturing Summary".

3. Create a formula that finds the profit per unit in cell D4 (hint: you'll have to subtract cell C4 from cell B4.)

4. Copy the formula you created in cell D4 to the remaining cells under the Profit Per Unit heading (the cell range D5:D7).

5. Copy the labels in cell range A4:A7 to the cell range A11:A14.

6. Use AutoFill to add the remaining months in row 10.

7. Check the worksheet for spelling errors.

Extra Credit: Create a formula in cell B15 that totals the September column, then multiplies by the value in cell D4. Only make the reference to the D column an *absolute reference*. Copy the formula to the remaining cells in the Sales Forecast table.

Can't figure out the formula? Okay, it's =SUM(B11:B14)*$D4.

Quiz Answers

1. C. Selecting Insert → Comment attaches a note to the current cell.

2. B. Typing replaces the previous contents of a cell. The other methods also work—they're just not nearly as fast.

3. B. Ctrl + C copies information instead of cutting it.

4. False. Relative references reference cells based on their position from the cell that contains the formula, and change if the cell that contains the formula is moved.

5. A, B, C, and D. You can use the Paste Special command to copy and paste all of these items.

6. C. The Undo function can undo up to 16 of your last actions.

7. A and D. You can edit the contents of a cell by clicking the Formula bar or by double-clicking the cell.

8. A. Add your name to the dictionary by selecting Tools → Spelling from the menu and clicking Add when your name appears.

9. A. You need to open the Print dialog box and specify the number of copies you want to print.

10. A. Select Edit → Replace from the menu, type "profit" in the "Find what" box, type "loss" in the "Replace with" box and click Replace All.

11. D. Absolute cell references have $ (dollar signs) before the column and/or number cell indicator.

12. False. The Copy button on the Standard toolbar can copy both values and formulas.

13. A and D. Either of these procedures will insert a new row.

14. A and B. Either of these procedures will delete a column.

CHAPTER 3
FORMATTING A WORKSHEET

CHAPTER OBJECTIVES:

Format fonts with the Formatting toolbar and menus

Format values

Adjust row height and column width

Align a cell's contents

Add borders, colors, and patterns to cells

Use the format painter to copy formatting

Create a custom number format

Create, apply, and modify a style

Use conditional formatting

Merge cells

CHAPTER TASK: FORMAT AN EXPENSE REPORT

Prerequisites

- **Understand how to use menus, toolbars, dialog boxes, and shortcut keystrokes**
- **Understand how to select cell ranges**

You probably have several colleagues at work that dazzle everyone at meetings with their sharp-looking spreadsheets that use colorful fonts and neat-looking borders. This chapter explains how to format your worksheet to make it more visually attractive and easier to read. You will learn how to change the appearance, size, and color of fonts and how to align text inside a cell as well as learn how to increase the height of a row and the width of a column. This chapter also describes how you can make your worksheets more organized and professional looking by adding borders and shading.

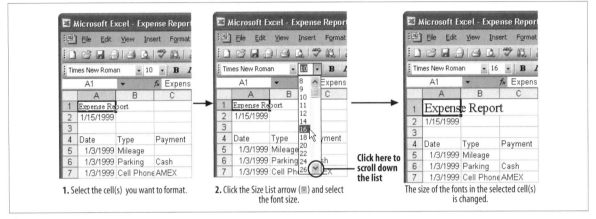

Figure 3-1. The Formatting toolbar.

Figure 3-2. Changing font size.

You can emphasize text in a worksheet by making the text darker and heavier (**bold**), slanted (*italics*), or in a different typeface (or font). The Formatting toolbar (see Figure 3-1) makes it easy to apply character formatting. The Formatting toolbar includes buttons for applying the most common character and paragraph formatting options.

1 **Start Microsoft Excel, open the workbook named** Lesson 3A **and save it as** Expense Report.

Excel saves the worksheet in a new file with the name "Expense Report." The first thing you need to do is make the title "Expense Report" stand out from the rest of the worksheet.

2 **Click cell** A1 **to make it active.**

Once you have selected a cell or cell range you can format it.

Font List

3 **Click the** Font list arrow **(▼) on the Formatting toolbar, then scroll down and select** Times New Roman **from the list of fonts.**

The contents of the active cell, the title "Expense Report," appear in Times New Roman font. Arial and Times New Roman are two of the most commonly used fonts in Windows. (Table 3-1 lists these and other common font types and sizes.)

Font Size List

4 **With cell A1 still selected, click the** Font Size list arrow **(▼) on the Formatting toolbar and select** 16, **as shown in Figure 3-2.**

The label "Expense Report" appears in a larger font size (16 point type instead of the previous 12 point type). Wow! That font formatting really makes the title stand out from the rest of the worksheet, doesn't it? Font sizes are measured in points (pt.), which are 1/72 of an inch. The larger the number of points, the larger the font.

5 Select the cell range A4:G4 and click the Bold button on the Formatting toolbar.

The cells in the selected range—the column headings for the worksheet—appear in bold.

Bold button
Other Ways to Bold:
• Select **Formats**→**Font** from the menu select **Bold**, and click **OK**.
• Press <**Ctrl**>+<**B**>

6 Click the Italics button on the Formatting toolbar.

The text in the selected cells is formatted with italics. Notice that both the Bold and Italics buttons are shaded on the Formatting toolbar, indicating that the selected cells are formatted with Bold and Italics formatting.

Another way you can format fonts is by changing their color:

7 Click cell A1 to make it active.

8 Click the Font Color arrow (▼) on the formatting toolbar and select the dark red color from the color palette.

The text in the selected cell changes from black to dark red.

So far, you have been formatting all the fonts in a cell at once. What if you want to use different font for-

matting in the same cell—is that possible? Yes it is. Go to the next step to find out how.

9 Click cell G2 to make it active.

Here you want only the words "Submitted By:" in bold. Leave the rest of the text, "Bill Smith," formatted the way it is.

10 Position the ⌶ pointer at the very beginning of the Formula bar, immediately before the word Submitted.

The insertion point—the blinking vertical bar (⌶)—appears at the beginning of the Formula bar.

11 Click and hold down the mouse button and drag the ⌶ across the words Submitted By:. Release the left mouse button when the text is selected.

Another way to select text is to hold down the Shift key, move the insertion point with the arrow keys, and release the Shift key when you're finished. Now you can format the selected text.

12 Click the Bold button on the Formatting toolbar.

Only the selected text "Submitted By:" is formatted with Bold. The remaining text in the cell is left unchanged.

13 Click the Save button on the Standard toolbar to save your work.

Table 3-1. Examples of Common Font Types and Sizes

Common Font Types	Common Font Sizes
Arial	Arial 8 point
Comic Sans MS	Arial 10 point
Courier New	Arial 12 point
Times New Roman	Arial 14 point

QUICK REFERENCE

TO BOLD TEXT:

- CLICK THE BOLD BUTTON ON THE FORMATTING TOOLBAR OR PRESS CTRL + B.

TO ITALICIZE TEXT:

- CLICK THE ITALICS BUTTON ON THE FORMATTING TOOLBAR OR PRESS CTRL + I.

TO UNDERLINE TEXT:

- CLICK THE UNDERLINE BUTTON ON THE FORMATTING TOOLBAR OR PRESS CTRL + U.

TO CHANGE FONT SIZE:

- SELECT THE PT. SIZE FROM THE [10 ▾] FONT SIZE LIST ON THE FORMATTING TOOLBAR.

TO CHANGE FONT TYPE:

- SELECT THE FONT FROM THE [Times New Roman ▾] FONT LIST ON THE FORMATTING TOOLBAR.

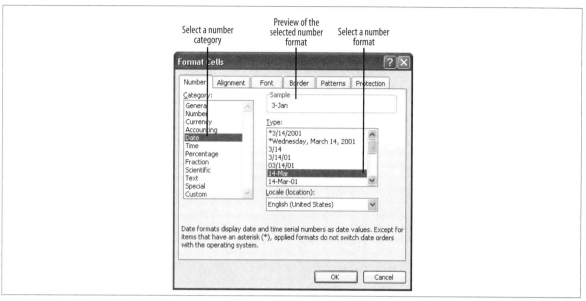

Figure 3-3. The Number tab of the Format Cells dialog box.

	A	B	C	D	E	F	G
1	Expense Report						
2	1/15/1999						Submitted
3							
4	*Date*	*Type*	*Payment*	*Price Per*	*Quantity*	*Tax*	*Total*
5	1/3/1999	Mileage		0.32	46	0	14.72
6	1/3/1999	Parking	Cash	7	1	0	7
7	1/3/1999	Cell Phone	AMEX	0.15	23	0.065	4.95475
8	1/5/1999	Mileage		0.32	35	0	11.2
9	1/5/1999	Airfare	VISA	1299	1	0.01	1312
10	1/7/1999	Lodging	Check	69	1	0.09	75.3
11	1/7/1999	Meals	AMEX	8.5	1	0.07	9.165
12	1/7/1999	Taxi	Cash	22	1	0	22
13	1/8/1999	Incidental	VISA	14.99	1	0.07	16.1093
14	1/8/1999	Postage	Cash	2.75	1	0	2.75
15	1/10/1999	Mileage		0.32	64	0	20.48
16	1/11/1999	Other	VISA	15	1	0.065	16.04
17	1/12/1999	Cell Phone	Call	0.15	10	0	1.5

Figure 3-4. The preformatted Expense Report worksheet values.

	A	B	C	D	E	F	G
1	Expense Report						
2	1/15/1999						Submitted
3							
4	Date	Type	Payment	Price Per U	Quantity	Tax	Total
5	3-Jan	Mileage		$ 0.32	46	0.0%	14.72
6	3-Jan	Parking	Cash	$ 7.00	1	0.0%	7.00
7	3-Jan	Cell Phone	AMEX	$ 0.15	23	6.5%	4.95
8	5-Jan	Mileage		$ 0.32	35	0.0%	11.20
9	5-Jan	Airfare	VISA	$ 1,299.00	1	1.0%	1,312.00
10	7-Jan	Lodging	Check	$ 69.00	1	9.0%	75.30
11	7-Jan	Meals	AMEX	$ 8.50	1	7.0%	9.17
12	7-Jan	Taxi	Cash	$ 22.00	1	0.0%	22.00
13	8-Jan	Incidental I	VISA	$ 14.99	1	7.0%	16.11
14	8-Jan	Postage	Cash	$ 2.75	1	0.0%	2.75
15	10-Jan	Mileage		$ 0.32	64	0.0%	20.48
16	11-Jan	Other	VISA	$ 15.00	1	6.5%	16.04
17	12-Jan	Cell Phone Call		$ 0.15	10	0.0%	1.50

Figure 3-5. The Expense Report worksheet values after being formatted.

In this lesson, you will learn how to apply number formats. Applying *number formatting* changes how values are displayed—it doesn't change the actual information in any way. Excel is often smart enough to apply some number formatting automatically. For example, if you use a dollar sign to indicate currency, such as $548.67, Excel will automatically apply the currency number format for you.

The Formatting toolbar has five buttons—Currency, Percent, Comma, Increase Decimal, and Decrease Decimal—that you can use to quickly apply common number formats. (See Table 3-2 for examples of each of these buttons.) If none of these buttons has what you're looking for, you need to use the Format Cells dialog box by selecting Format → Cells from the menu and clicking the Number tab. Formatting numbers with the Format Cells dialog box isn't as fast as using the toolbar, but it gives you more precision and more formatting options. We'll use both methods in this lesson.

Currency Style button

1 Select the cell range D5:D17 and click the Currency Style button on the Formatting toolbar.

A dollar sign and two decimal places are added to the values in the selected cell range.

Comma Style button

2 Select the cell range G5:G17 and click the Comma Style button on the Formatting toolbar.

Excel adds a comma and two decimal places to the selected cell range.

Percent Style button

3 Select the cell range F5:F17 and click the Percent Style button on the Formatting toolbar.

Excel applies percentage style number formatting to the information in the Tax column. Notice there isn't a decimal place; Excel rounds any decimal places to the nearest whole number, but that isn't suitable here. You want to include a decimal place to accurately show the tax rate.

Increase Decimal button

4 With the Tax cell range still selected, click the Increase Decimal button on the Formatting toolbar.

Excel adds one decimal place to the information in the tax rate column.

Next, you want to change the date format in the date column. There isn't a "Format Date" button on the Formatting toolbar, so you will have to format the date column using the Format Cells dialog box.

The Formatting toolbar is great for quickly applying the most common formatting options to cells, but it doesn't offer every available formatting option. To see and/or use every possible character formatting option, you have to use the Format Cells dialog box. You can open the Format Cells dialog box by either selecting Format → Cells from the menu, or right-clicking and selecting Format Cells from the shortcut menu.

5 Select the cell range A5:A17, select Format → Cells from the menu, and click the Number tab if necessary.

The Format Cells dialog box appears with the Number tab in front and Date format category selected, as shown in Figure 3-3. You can also use the Number tab of the Format Cells dialog box to format cells with any type of number option: percentages, currencies, dates, and—as you can see in the Category list—many more.

6 From the Category list, select Date, select the format 14-Mar from the Type list box, and click OK.

The Format Cells dialog box closes and the selected cell range is formatted with the date format you selected. Try using another date format.

7 With the Date cell range still selected, select Format → Cells from the menu.

The Format Cells dialog box reappears.

8 Select 14-Mar-01 from the Type list box and click OK.

The dates are now formatted to display the year. See Figures 3-4 and 3-5 for examples of a worksheet in both the preformatted and formatted state.

9 Save your work.

Table 3-2. Number Formatting Buttons on the Formatting Toolbar

Button Icon	Button Name	Example	Formatting
$	Currency	$1,000.00	Adds a dollar sign, comma, and two decimal places
%	Percent	100%	Displays the value as a percentage with no decimal places
,	Comma	1,000	Separates thousands with a comma and adds two decimal places
.00	Increase Decimal	1000.00	Increases the number of digits after the decimal point by one
.00	Decrease Decimal	1000.0	Decreases the number of digits after the decimal point by one

QUICK REFERENCE

TO APPLY NUMBER FORMATTING:

• SELECT THE CELL OR CELL RANGE YOU WANT TO FORMAT AND CLICK THE APPROPRIATE NUMBER FORMATTING BUTTON(S) ON THE FORMATTING TOOLBAR.

OR...

• SELECT THE CELL OR CELL RANGE YOU WANT TO FORMAT, SELECT FORMAT → CELLS FROM THE MENU, CLICK THE NUMBER TAB, AND SPECIFY THE NUMBER FORMATTING YOU WANT TO APPLY.

OR...

• SELECT THE CELL OR CELL RANGE YOU WANT TO FORMAT, RIGHT-CLICK THE CELL OR CELL RANGE, SELECT FORMAT CELLS FROM THE SHORTCUT MENU, CLICK THE NUMBER TAB, AND SPECIFY THE NUMBER FORMATTING YOU WANT TO APPLY.

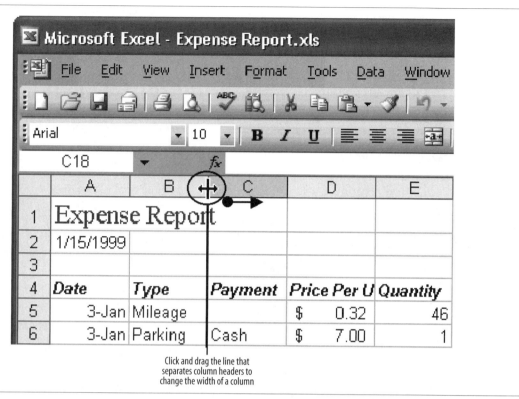

Figure 3-6. Adjusting the width of a column.

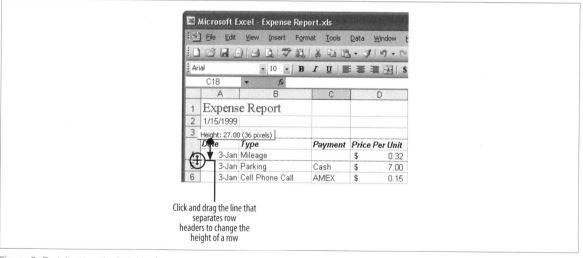

Figure 3-7. Adjusting the height of a row.

Figure 3-8. The Row Height dialog box.

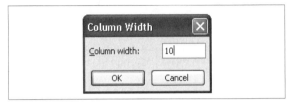

Figure 3-9. The Column Width dialog box.

When you start working on a worksheet, all the rows and columns are the same size. As you enter information into the worksheet, you will quickly discover that some of the columns or rows are not large enough to display the information they contain. This lesson explains how to change the width of a column and the height of a row.

1 Carefully position the pointer over the line between the B and C in the column header area, until it changes to a ✛.

Once the pointer is positioned over the column line and appears as a ✛, you can adjust the column width to make it smaller or wider.

2 Click and hold the mouse button and drag the line to the right until Column B is wide enough to see all of the Type labels, as shown in Figure 3-6.

Notice that while you are dragging the column line, a tip box appears displaying the current width of the column.

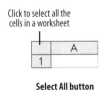

Click to select all the cells in a worksheet

Select All button

3 Position the pointer over the line between the D and E in the column header area until it changes to a ✛, then double-click the left mouse button.

Excel automatically adjusts the width of the selected column so that it can hold the widest cell entry. This

neat feature is called *AutoFit*. You can also use AutoFit by selecting Format → Column (or Row) → AutoFit from the menu.

The procedure for adjusting the height of a row is almost the same as adjusting the width of a column:

4 Carefully position the pointer over the line between the 4 and 5 in the row header area, until it changes to a ✛.

Once the pointer is positioned over the column line and appears as a ✛, you can adjust the row height to make it smaller or wider.

5 Click and hold the mouse button and drag the line down until the height of Row 4 is doubled, as shown in Figure 3-7.

Notice that while you are dragging the column, a tip box appears displaying the current height of the row.

In most instances, using the mouse is the fastest and easiest method to adjust the height of a row or the width of a column. There are times, however, when you may want to adjust the height of a row or the width of a column by using a dialog box. For example, you can select and adjust the width of several columns at the same time with a dialog box.

6 Click the Select All button (the gray rectangle in the upper-left corner of the worksheet where the row and column headings meet) to select the entire worksheet.

Excel selects all the cells in the worksheet.

7 Select Format → Row → Height from the menu.

The Row Height dialog box appears, as shown in Figure 3-8. Here you can enter an exact measurement to adjust the row height. The default row height is 12.75.

8 Type 14 in the Row Height text box and click OK.

The height of all the rows in the worksheet changes to 14. Notice, however that the new row height is not sufficient to accommodate the worksheet's title, so you will need to adjust the height of row A. You can use the AutoFit feature to automatically adjust the height of row 1.

9 Deselect the entire worksheet by clicking any cell in the worksheet.

The entire worksheet is no longer selected.

10 Double-click the line between the 1 and 2 in the row header area.

Excel automatically adjusts the height of the first row so the title Expense Report fits in the row. A faster way to open either the Row Height or the Column Width dialog box is to use the right mouse button shortcut menu.

11 Right-click the A column header.

A shortcut menu containing the most commonly used commands used with columns appears. Had you right-clicked a row heading, a shortcut menu with the most commonly used row commands would have appeared.

12 Select Column Width from the shortcut menu.

The Column Width dialog box appears, as shown in Figure 3-9. Here you can enter an exact measurement to adjust the column width. The default column width is 8.43.

13 Type 10 in the Column Width box and click OK.

The width of the selected column, Column A, changes to 10.

14 Save your work.

Splendid! In just one lesson you've learned how to adjust the width of columns and height of rows using several different methods.

QUICK REFERENCE

TO ADJUST THE WIDTH OF A COLUMN:

- DRAG THE COLUMN HEADER'S RIGHT BORDER TO THE LEFT OR RIGHT.

  OR...

- RIGHT-CLICK THE COLUMN HEADER(S), SELECT COLUMN WIDTH FROM THE SHORTCUT MENU, AND ENTER THE COLUMN WIDTH.

  OR...

- SELECT THE COLUMN HEADER(S), SELECT FORMAT → COLUMN → WIDTH FROM THE MENU, AND ENTER THE COLUMN WIDTH.

TO ADJUST THE HEIGHT OF A ROW:

- DRAG THE ROW HEADER'S BOTTOM BORDER UP OR DOWN.

  OR...

- RIGHT-CLICK THE ROW HEADER(S), SELECT ROW HEIGHT FROM THE SHORTCUT MENU, AND ENTER THE ROW HEIGHT.

  OR...

- SELECT THE ROW HEADER(S), SELECT FORMAT → ROW → HEIGHT FROM THE MENU, AND ENTER THE ROW HEIGHT.

TO AUTOMATICALLY ADJUST THE WIDTH OF A COLUMN OR ROW (AUTOFIT):

- DOUBLE-CLICK THE RIGHT BORDER OF THE COLUMN OR BOTTOM BORDER OF A ROW.

  OR...

- CLICK THE COLUMN HEADING TO SELECT THE COLUMN AND SELECT FORMAT → ROW (OR COLUMN) → AUTOFIT FROM THE MENU.

Changing Cell Alignment

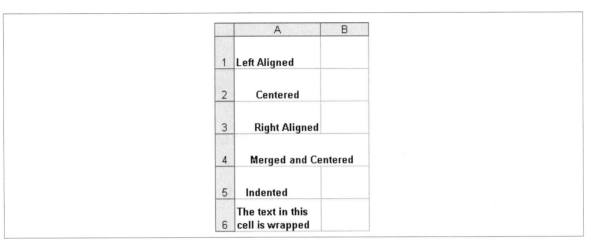

Figure 3-10. Examples of different cell alignment options.

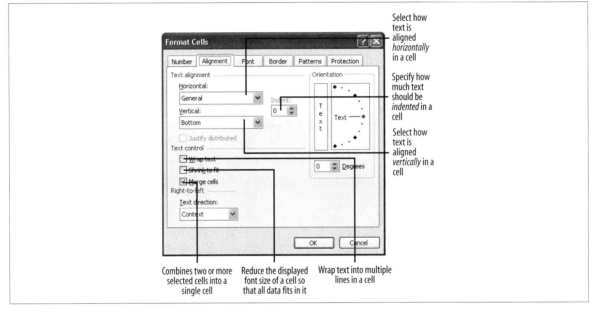

Figure 3-11. The Alignment tab of the Format Cells dialog box.

	A	B	C	D	E	F	G	
1				Expense Report				← Merged and centered cell
2	1/15/1999					**Submitted By:** Bill Smith		
3								
4	*Date*	*Type*	*Payment*	*Price Per Unit*	*Quantity*	*Tax*	*Total*	
5	3-Jan	Mileage		$ 0.32	46	0.0%	14.72	
6	3-Jan	Parking	Cash	$ 7.00	1	0.0%	7.00	
7	3-Jan	Cell Phone Call	AMEX	$ 0.15	23	6.5%	4.95	
8	5-Jan	Mileage		$ 0.32	35	0.0%	11.20	
9	5-Jan	Airfare	VISA	$ 1,299.00	1	1.0%	1,312.00	
10	7-Jan	Lodging	Check	$ 69.00	1	9.0%	75.30	
11	7-Jan	Meals	AMEX	$ 8.50	1	7.0%	9.17	
12	7-Jan	Taxi	Cash	$ 22.00	1	0.0%	22.00	
13	8-Jan	Incidental Expenses	VISA	$ 14.99	1	7.0%	16.11	
14	8-Jan	Postage	Cash	$ 2.75	1	0.0%	2.75	
15	10-Jan	Mileage		$ 0.32	64	0.0%	20.48	
16	11-Jan	Other	VISA	$ 15.00	1	6.5%	16.04	
17	12-Jan	Cell Phone Call		$ 0.15	10	0.0%	1.50	
18								
19				Notes:	I misplaced several of the			← Merged cell
20					receipts for my trip to Boston.			
21					Are they absolutely necessary?			

Figure 3-12. The worksheet with new alignment formatting.

By default, the contents of a cell appear at the bottom of the cell, with values (numbers) aligned to the right and labels (text) aligned to the left. This lesson explains how to control how data is aligned in a cell using the Formatting toolbar and the Format Cells dialog box. Figures 3-10 and 3-11 show examples of alignment formatting.

1 If necessary, open the workbook named Lesson 3B and save it as Expense Report.

Center button

2 Select the cell range A4:G4 and click the Center button on the Formatting toolbar.

Excel centers the selected headings inside the cells. Notice the Center button on the Formatting toolbar is shaded, indicating the cells are center aligned.

3 Select the cell range A5:A17 and click the Center button on the Formatting toolbar.

The dates in the A column are centered.

Align Right button

4 Select cell G2, then click the Align Right button on the Formatting toolbar.

Excel aligns the label to the right side of the cell. Notice the text spills over into the cells to the left of the cells, since they are currently unoccupied.

Merge and Center button

5 Select the cell range A1:G1 and click the Merge and Center button on the Formatting toolbar.

Excel merges, or combines, the seven selected cells into a single larger cell that spans across seven columns, and centers the text inside the single merged cell. A merged cell is a single cell created by combining two or more selected cells. The cell reference for a merged cell is the upper-left cell in the original selected range.

6 Select the cell range E19:G21.

You want to combine all the cells in the selected range into a single merged cell.

7 Select Format → Cells from the menu and click the Alignment tab.

See Figure 3-11. Here you can specify more advanced cell alignment options.

8 Check the Merge cells check box and click OK.

The Format Cells dialog box closes and the selected cell range is merged into a single cell. Hey! The new merged cell is large enough to hold all of the notes text, so why is only a single line of text displayed? To display multiple lines of text in a cell you must select the Wrap Text option on the Alignment tab of the Format Cells dialog box.

9 With the merged cell still selected, select Format → Cells from the menu.

The Format Cells dialog box reappears with the Alignment tab in front.

10 Check the Wrap text check box and click OK.

The notes wrap on multiple lines so that all the text fits inside the merged cell. Sometimes you might want to indent the contents of several cells to make a worksheet appear more organized and easy to read.

Increase Indent button

11 Select the cell range B5:B17 and click the Increase Indent button on the Formatting toolbar.

The labels in the selected cells are indented one space to the right.

Decrease Indent button

12 With the same cell range selected, click the Decrease Indent button on the Formatting toolbar, then save your work.

Table 3-3 lists the Formatting toolbar's alignment formatting buttons.

Table 3-3. Alignment Formatting Buttons on the Formatting Toolbar

Button Icon	Button Name	Example	Formatting
	Align Left	Left	Aligns the cell contents to the left side of the cell
	Center	Center	Centers the cell contents in the cell
	Merge and Center	Center	Merges the selected cells and centers the cell contents
	Align Right	Right	Aligns the cell contents to the right side of the cell
	Increase Indent	Indent	Indents the cell contents by one character
	Decrease Indent	Indent	Decreases indented cell contents by one character

QUICK REFERENCE

TO CHANGE CELL ALIGNMENT:

1. SELECT THE CELL OR CELL RANGE YOU WANT TO ALIGN.

2. CLICK THE APPROPRIATE ALIGNMENT BUTTON(S) ON THE FORMATTING TOOLBAR.

OR...

1. SELECT THE CELL OR CELL RANGE YOU WANT TO ALIGN.

2. EITHER RIGHT-CLICK THE SELECTION AND SELECT FORMAT CELLS FROM THE SHORTCUT MENU OR SELECT FORMAT → CELLS FROM THE MENU.

3. CLICK THE ALIGNMENT TAB AND SELECT THE DESIRED ALIGNMENT OPTION.

Display/Hide gridlines

Figure 3-13. The View tab of the Options dialog box.

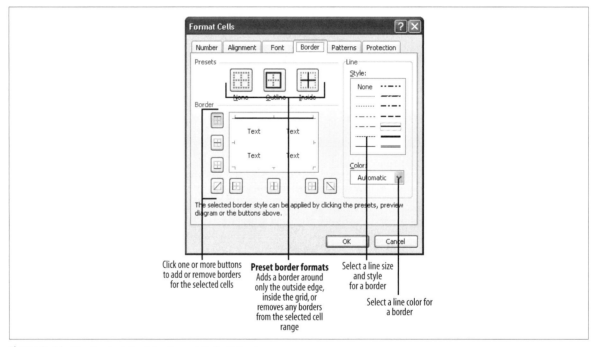

Click one or more buttons to add or remove borders for the selected cells

Preset border formats Adds a border around only the outside edge, inside the grid, or removes any borders from the selected cell range

Select a line size and style for a border

Select a line color for a border

Figure 3-14. The Border tab of the Format Cells dialog box.

	A	B	C	D	E	F	G
1				Expense Report			
2	1/15/1999					**Submitted By:** Bill Smith	
3							
4	*Date*	*Type*	*Payment*	*Price Per Unit*	*Quantity*	*Tax*	*Total*
5	3-Jan	Mileage		$ 0.32	46	0.0%	14.72
6	3-Jan	Parking	Cash	$ 7.00	1	0.0%	7.00
7	3-Jan	Cell Phone Call	AMEX	$ 0.15	23	6.5%	4.95
8	5-Jan	Mileage		$ 0.32	35	0.0%	11.20
9	5-Jan	Airfare	VISA	$ 1,299.00	1	1.0%	1,312.00
10	7-Jan	Lodging	Check	$ 69.00	1	9.0%	75.30
11	7-Jan	Meals	AMEX	$ 8.50	1	7.0%	9.17
12	7-Jan	Taxi	Cash	$ 22.00	1	0.0%	22.00
13	8-Jan	Incidental Expenses	VISA	$ 14.99	1	7.0%	16.11
14	8-Jan	Postage	Cash	$ 2.75	1	0.0%	2.75
15	10-Jan	Mileage		$ 0.32	64	0.0%	20.48
16	11-Jan	Other	VISA	$ 15.00	1	6.5%	16.04
17	12-Jan	Cell Phone Call		$ 0.15	10	0.0%	1.50
18							
19				Notes:		I misplaced several of the	
20						receipts for my trip to Boston.	
21						Are they absolutely necessary?	

Figure 3-15. The Expense Report worksheet with borders added.

Borders make worksheets more visually attractive. Adding borders to ranges of similar cells also makes them more organized and easier to read. Just like any other formatting attributes, you can add a variety of borders to the cells in your worksheet using the Formatting toolbar (specifically, the Border button) or the Format cells dialog box. Just like the previous formatting lessons, we'll cover both methods of adding borders in this lesson.

Although it isn't absolutely necessary, removing the gridlines in the worksheet makes it easier to see borders.

Border button arrow list

1 Select Tools → Options **from the menu and click the** View tab.

The Options dialog box appears with the View tab selected, as shown in Figure 3-13. Here you can change how the worksheet is displayed. You're only interested in one view option here: you want to remove the cell gridlines in this worksheet so you can more easily see the borders you will be adding in this lesson.

2 Uncheck the Gridlines check box **and click** OK.

The dialog box closes and the cell gridlines no longer appear on the worksheet. Don't worry—the worksheet works exactly the same with or without the gridlines. Gridlines are only a visual aid to help to you determine which column and row a cell is in.

Selecting a Thick Border Line

3 Select the cell range A4:G4, click the Border button list arrow (⬛) on the Formatting toolbar, and select Bottom Border (located in the second column, first row).

A single, thin border appears at the bottom of the selected cells. You can choose from several different border styles. Try using a different border style in the next step.

4 Select the cell G17, click the Border button list arrow on the Formatting toolbar and select the double bottom border (located in the first column, second row).

Excel adds a double-lined border to the bottom of the selected cell. The Border button is usually the fastest and easiest way to add borders to your worksheets, but you can also add borders using the Borders tab of the Format Cells dialog box.

5 Select the cell range A5:G17, select Format → Cells from the menu and click the Border tab.

The Format Cells dialog box appears with the Border tab selected, as shown in Figure 3-14. The Border tab of the Format Cells dialog box gives you more options for adding borders than the Borders button on the Formatting toolbar does.

6 Select the thickest line style in the Style list (the second to the last option in the second column). Click the Color list arrow and select a dark blue color, then click the Outline button to apply the specified border style to the outside of the selected cell range.

This will add a thick, dark blue border around the outside of the selected cell range.

7 Click OK.

The Format Cells dialog box closes and the borders you specified are added to the selected cell range. Let's add a different border style inside the cell range.

8 With the cell range A5:G17 still selected, select Format → Cells from the menu.

The Format Cells dialog box appears.

9 Select the thinnest solid line style (the last option in the first column). Click the Color list arrow and select Automatic, then click the Inside button to apply the specified border style to the inside of the selected cell range.

Notice a preview of how your borders will look appears in the Border section of the dialog box.

10 Click OK.

The Format Cells dialog box closes and the borders you specified are added to the selected cell range, as shown in Figure 3-15.

11 Select the cell range E19:G21 (the merged notes cell), click the Border button arrow, and then select the thick box border option (located in the last column and last row) and click OK.

Excel adds a thick border around the outside of the selected cells. You decide you want to remove the border. It is just as easy to remove a border as it is to add it.

12 With the cell range E19:G21 selected, click the Border button arrow and select the No Border option (located in the first column, first row).

The border is removed from the selected cell range. Before we finish this lesson we must once again display the worksheet gridlines.

13 Select Tools → Options from the menu, click the View tab, check the Gridlines check box, and click OK.

QUICK REFERENCE

TO ADD A BORDER:

1. SELECT THE CELL OR CELL RANGE TO WHICH YOU WANT TO ADD THE BORDER(S).

2. CLICK THE BORDER BUTTON LIST ARROW ON THE FORMATTING TOOLBAR AND SELECT THE BORDER YOU WANT.

OR...

• EITHER RIGHT-CLICK THE SELECTION AND SELECT FORMAT CELLS FROM THE SHORTCUT MENU OR SELECT FORMAT → CELLS FROM THE MENU. CLICK THE BORDER TAB AND SELECT THE BORDER(S) YOU WANT TO ADD.

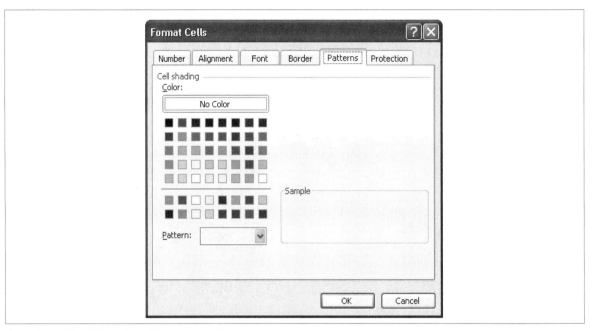

Figure 3-16. The Patterns tab of the Format Cells dialog box.

	A	B	C	D	E	F	G
1				Expense Report			
2	1/15/1999					**Submitted By:**	Bill Smith
3							
4	*Date*	*Type*	*Payment*	*Price Per Unit*	*Quantity*	*Tax*	*Total*
5	3-Jan	Mileage		$ 0.32	46	0.0%	14.72
6	3-Jan	Parking	Cash	$ 7.00	1	0.0%	7.00
7	3-Jan	Cell Phone Call	AMEX	$ 0.15	23	6.5%	4.95
8	5-Jan	Mileage		$ 0.32	35	0.0%	11.20
9	5-Jan	Airfare	VISA	$ 1,299.00	1	1.0%	1,312.00
10	7-Jan	Lodging	Check	$ 69.00	1	9.0%	75.30
11	7-Jan	Meals	AMEX	$ 8.50	1	7.0%	9.17
12	7-Jan	Taxi	Cash	$ 22.00	1	0.0%	22.00
13	8-Jan	Incidental Expenses	VISA	$ 14.99	1	7.0%	16.11
14	8-Jan	Postage	Cash	$ 2.75	1	0.0%	2.75
15	10-Jan	Mileage		$ 0.32	64	0.0%	20.48
16	11-Jan	Other	VISA	$ 15.00	1	6.5%	16.04
17	12-Jan	Cell Phone Call		$ 0.15	10	0.0%	1.50
18							
19				Notes:	I misplaced several of the		
20					receipts for my trip to Boston.		
21					Are they absolutely necessary?		
22							

Figure 3-17. The Expense Report with Pattern formatting.

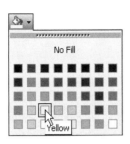

Selecting a Fill color

In the last lesson, you learned how to add borders to the cells in your worksheet. In this lesson, you will see how you can change the background colors and patterns of cells. Applying colors and patterns to cells is actually a very, very, easy procedure, so let's get started!

1 Click cell E19 (the merged cell that contains the notes) to make it active, click the Fill Color button arrow on the Formatting toolbar and select the Yellow color from the color palette.

The background of the selected cell changes to the yellow. Like all other formatting options in Excel, you can also change the background color of cells with the Format Cells dialog box.

2 Select the cell range A5:G17, select Format → Cells from the menu, and click the Patterns tab.

The Format Cells dialog appears with the Patterns tab selected, as shown in Figure 3-16. Here you can add both colors and patterns to the background of cells.

3 Select the light blue color and click OK.

The dialog box closes and the selected light blue color is added to the selected cell range. The procedure for adding a pattern to the background of a cell range is the same as adding colors.

4 Click cell A1 to make it active and select Format → Cells from the menu.

The Format Cells dialog appears with the Patterns tab selected.

5 Click the Pattern List Arrow, select the thin vertical stripe option and click OK.

The Format Cells dialog box closes and the selected pattern, the thin vertical stripe, is applied to the background of the cell (see Figure 3-17).

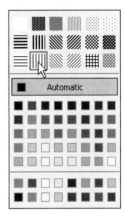

Selecting a Pattern

NOTE *If you intend to print a worksheet, be careful of which colors and patterns you use, especially if you don't have a color printer. Some colors may look great on the computer screen, but not when printed. Some background colors and patterns can even cause the cell information to be illegible when printed. You are usually better off if you use lighter background colors and patterns, such as yellow, light gray, or light blue.*

6 Save your work.

QUICK REFERENCE

TO APPLY BACKGROUND COLORS AND PATTERNS:

1. SELECT THE CELL OR CELL RANGE YOU WANT TO FORMAT.

2. CLICK THE FILL COLOR LIST ARROW ON THE FORMATTING TOOLBAR AND SELECT THE COLOR YOU WANT.

OR...

1. EITHER RIGHT-CLICK THE SELECTION AND SELECT FORMAT CELLS FROM THE SHORTCUT MENU, OR SELECT FORMAT → CELLS FROM THE MENU.

2. CLICK THE PATTERNS TAB AND SELECT THE COLOR OR PATTERN YOU WANT TO USE.

Using the Format Painter

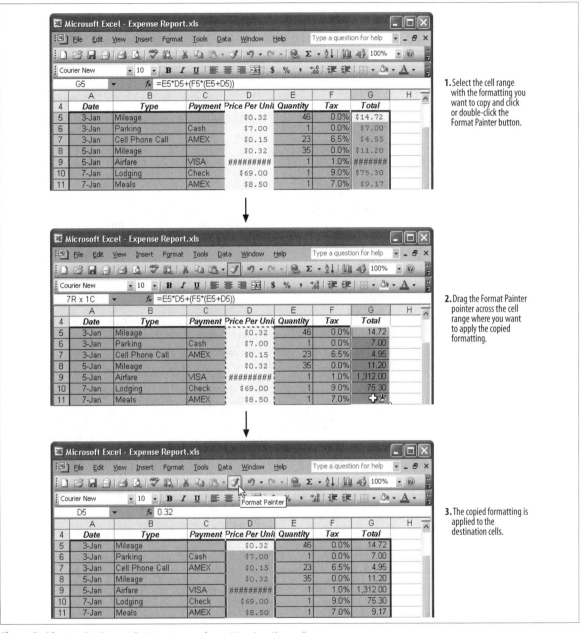

1. Select the cell range with the formatting you want to copy and click or double-click the Format Painter button.

2. Drag the Format Painter pointer across the cell range where you want to apply the copied formatting.

3. The copied formatting is applied to the destination cells.

Figure 3-18. Use the Format Painter to copy formatting to other cells.

If you find yourself applying exactly the same formatting to cells repeatedly, the Format Painter is the tool for you. The Format Painter allows you to copy formatting attributes from a cell or cell range and apply them elsewhere. Sound confusing? It won't be once you have finished this lesson.

1 **If necessary, open the workbook named** Lesson 3C **and save it as** Expense Report.

2 **Select the cell range** D5:D17 **and select** Format → Cells **from the menu.**

The Format Cell dialog box appears. You want to change several of the formatting options for the selected cell range. Start by changing the number format.

3 Select the Number tab, select Currency under the Category list, and select the fourth option in the Negative numbers list (the ($1,234.10) option).

The next formatting option you need to change for the selected cell range is the font formatting.

4 Select the Font tab, select Courier New from the Font list, and then select a dark red color from the color list.

The last two formatting options you want to modify are the borders and shading options.

5 Select the Border tab and click the None button, then select the Patterns tab, select the yellow color, and click OK.

The Format Cells dialog box closes and the selected cell range is formatted with all the formatting options you specified. It took a lot of clicking to do all of that formatting, didn't it? Now imagine you want to format the cell range G5:G17 (the Totals column) with exactly the same formatting options. Instead of doing all those steps again, you can use the Format Painter tool to copy the formatting from the Price Per Unit cells and then paste, or apply, the copied formatting to the Totals column. First, you need to select the cell or cell range that contains the formatting you want to copy.

Format Painter button

6 With the cell range (D5:D17) still selected, click the Format Painter button on the Standard toolbar.

Notice the pointer changes to a ⊹🖌. Next, you need to paste, or apply, the copied formatting.

7 Select the cell range G5:G17 with the Format Painter (⊹🖌).

Like other mouse-intense operations, this can be a little tricky for some people the first time they try it. Once you have selected the cell range, the cell formatting from the Price Per Unit cell range is applied to the Total cell range, saving you a lot of time and work had you manually formatted the cells (see Figure 3-18). Notice cell G8 displays a series of ####. That's because the G column is no longer wide enough to display the contents of cell G8. To fix this problem, you merely have to adjust the column width.

8 Adjust the width of the G column so that you can see the contents of cell G9.

Remember how to adjust the width of a column? Move the pointer to the column header area and drag the column's right edge with the mouse to adjust its width. The G column will correctly display the contents of all its cells when it's wide enough.

9 Save your work.

QUICK REFERENCE

TO COPY FORMATTING WITH THE FORMAT PAINTER:

1. SELECT THE CELL RANGE WITH THE FORMATTING OPTIONS YOU WANT TO COPY.

2. CLICK THE FORMAT PAINTER BUTTON ON THE STANDARD TOOLBAR.

3. SELECT THE CELL RANGE WHERE YOU WANT TO APPLY THE COPIED FORMATTING.

TO COPY SELECTED FORMATTING TO SEVERAL LOCATIONS:

1. SELECT THE CELL RANGE WITH THE FORMATTING OPTIONS YOU WANT TO COPY.

2. DOUBLE-CLICK THE FORMAT PAINTER BUTTON.

3. SELECT THE CELL RANGE WHERE YOU WANT TO APPLY THE COPIED FORMATTING.

4. CLICK THE FORMAT PAINTER BUTTON WHEN YOU'RE FINISHED.

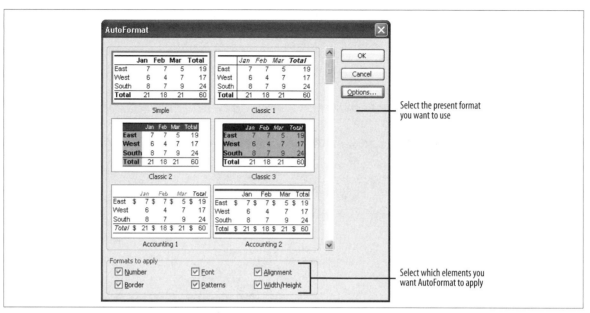

Figure 3-19. The AutoFormat dialog box.

	A	B	C	D	E	F	G
4	Date	Type	Payment	Price Per Unit	Quantity	Tax	Total
5	3-Jan	Mileage		$0.32	46	0.0%	$14.72
6	3-Jan	Parking	Cash	$7.00	1	0.0%	$7.00
7	3-Jan	Cell Phone Call	AMEX	$0.15	23	6.5%	$4.95
8	5-Jan	Mileage		$0.32	35	0.0%	$11.20
9	5-Jan	Airfare	VISA	$1,299.00	1	1.0%	$1,312.00
10	7-Jan	Lodging	Check	$69.00	1	9.0%	$75.30
11	7-Jan	Meals	AMEX	$8.50	1	7.0%	$9.17
12	7-Jan	Taxi	Cash	$22.00	1	0.0%	$22.00
13	8-Jan	Incidental Expense:	VISA	$14.99	1	7.0%	$16.11
14	8-Jan	Postage	Cash	$2.75	1	0.0%	$2.75
15	10-Jan	Mileage		$0.32	64	0.0%	$20.48
16	11-Jan	Other	VISA	$15.00	1	6.5%	$16.04
17	12-Jan	Cell Phone Call		$0.15	10	0.0%	$1.50

Figure 3-20. A worksheet AutoFormatted with the Colorful 2 option.

This lesson explains how Excel can automatically format your worksheets with the AutoFormat command. Auto-Format is a built-in collection of formats such as font sizes, patterns, and alignments that you can quickly apply to a cell range or entire worksheet. AutoFormat lets you choose from 16 different preset formats. It is a great feature if you want your worksheet to look sharp and professional, but don't have the time to format it yourself.

1 Place the cell pointer anywhere in the table (the cell range A4:G17).

Excel will automatically determine the table's boundaries. You can also manually select the cell range.

2 Select Format → AutoFormat from the menu.

The AutoFormat dialog box appears, as shown in Figure 3-19. The 16 present formats are listed in the Table format list. You can see what a present format looks like by selecting it and looking at the sample area of the dialog box.

3 Click the Options button.

The AutoFormat dialog box expands to show six check boxes. You can control the type of formatting that is applied by checking or unchecking any of the boxes. If you want AutoFormat to skip one of the formatting categories, simply uncheck the appropriate box.

4 Select the Colorful 2 option from the Table format list and click OK.

The dialog box closes and the selected cell range is formatted with the Colorful 2 formatting options, as shown in Figure 3-20.

5 Save your work.

QUICK REFERENCE

TO FORMAT A TABLE USING AUTOFORMAT:

1. PLACE THE CELL POINTER ANYWHERE WITHIN A TABLE YOU WANT TO FORMAT, OR ELSE SELECT THE CELL RANGE YOU WANT TO FORMAT.

2. SELECT FORMAT → AUTOFORMAT FROM THE MENU.

3. SELECT ONE OF THE AUTOFORMATS FROM THE LIST AND CLICK OK.

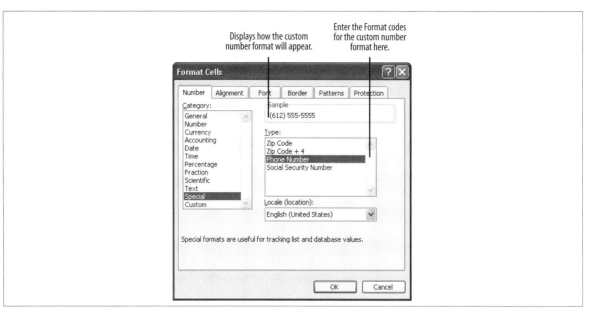

Displays how the custom number format will appear.

Enter the Format codes for the custom number format here.

Figure 3-21. Entering a custom number format in the Format Cells dialog box.

	A	B
16	*11-Jan*	*Other*
17	*12-Jan*	*Cell Phone Call*
18		
19	(612) 555-5555	
20	52-1876	

Figure 3-22. Cells formatted using custom number formats.

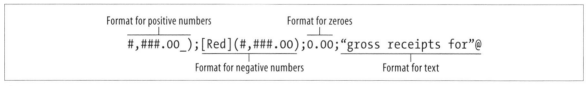

Format for positive numbers

Format for zeroes

#,###.00_);[Red](#,###.00);0.00;"gross receipts for"@

Format for negative numbers

Format for text

Figure 3-23. Example of how to use Format codes to create a custom number format.

You learned how to format values (numbers) in a previous lesson in this chapter. Excel comes with a huge number of predefined number formats you can use. With so many available number formats, it is unlikely that you will ever need to create your own custom number, but if you do, this lesson explains how to do it.

1 Select cell A19 to make it active, type 6125555555, and press Enter.

This cell contains the employee's telephone number. To make the phone number easier to read, you can apply special number formatting to the cell.

2 Select cell A19 again, select Format → Cells from the menu, then click the Number tab (see Figure 3-21).

The Format Cells dialog box appears with the Numbers tab selected.

3 Select Special under the Category list and select Phone Number under the Type list.

This will add area code parenthesis and a prefix separator (hyphen) format to the number, making it easy to recognize as a telephone number. A preview of how the number will look with the selected formatting appears in the Sample area of the dialog box.

4 Click OK.

The Format Cells dialog box closes and the Phone Number format is applied to the active cell. Whoops! You're going to have to widen the A column in order to see the newly formatted number.

5 Double-click the right border of the A column heading.

Excel automatically adjusts the width of the A column. There's the phone number!

If you find that none of the formatting options is satisfactory, here's how to create your own:

6 Enter 521876 into cell A20, and press Enter.

The number you just entered is the employee ID, and should be displayed like 52-1876, as shown in Figure 3-22. Excel already tried to AutoCorrect it, however, so the formatting for this cell must be changed.

7 Make sure cell A20 is the active cell, select Format → Cells from the menu, and click the Number tab.

The Format Cells dialog box appears.

8 Select Custom under the Category list.

This is where you can create your own number formats. You create a custom number format by specifying format codes that describe how you want to display a number, date, time, or text (see Figure 3-23). Table 3-4 gives some examples of how to use these codes when creating custom number formats.

9 In the Type box, replace the text with ##-#### and click OK.

The dialog box closes and Excel formats cell A20 with the custom number format you created.

NOTE *The sample area of the number dialog box becomes very important when you're creating custom number formats. Watch the sample area carefully to see how the custom number format you create will be displayed.*

You can create custom number formats by entering format codes that describe how you want to display a number, date, time, or text. Table 3-4 shows several examples that demonstrate how you can use number codes to create your own custom number formats.

Table 3-4. Format Codes for Numbers and Dates

Numbers		Dates and Times	
To Display	**Use this Code**	**To Display**	**Use this Code**
1234.59 as 1234.6	####.#	1/1/99 as 1-1-99	m-d-yy
12499 as 12,499	#,###	1/1/99 as Jan 1, 99	mmm d, yy
12499 as 12,499.00	#,###.##	1/1/99 as January 1, 1999	mmmm, d, yyyy
1489 as $1,489.00	$#,###.##	1/1/99 as Fri 1/1/99	ddd m/d/yy
.5 as 50%	0%	1/1/99 as Friday, January 1	dddd, mmmm, d
.055 as 5.5%	0.0%	4:30 PM as 4:30 PM	h:mm AM/PM
Hide value	;;	4:30 PM as 16:30	h:mm

QUICK REFERENCE

TO CREATE A CUSTOM NUMBER FORMAT:

1. SELECT THE CELL OR CELL RANGE YOU WANT TO FORMAT.

2. SELECT FORMAT → CELLS FROM THE MENU AND CLICK THE NUMBER TAB.

3. SELECT THE CUSTOM CATEGORY AND TYPE A NUMBER FORMAT IN THE TYPE BOX USING THE FORMAT CODES SHOWN IN TABLE 3-4.

	A	B	C	D	E	F	G
4	Date	Type	Payment	Price Per Unit	Quantity	Tax	Total
5	3-Jan	Mileage		$0.32	46	0.0%	$14.72
6	3-Jan	Parking	Cash	$7.00	1	0.0%	$7.00
7	3-Jan	Cell Phone Call	AMEX	$0.15	23	6.5%	$4.95
8	5-Jan	Mileage		$0.32	35	0.0%	$11.20
9	5-Jan	Airfare	VISA	$1,299.00	1	1.0%	$1,312.00
10	7-Jan	Lodging	Check	$69.00	1	9.0%	$75.30
11	7-Jan	Meals	AMEX	$8.50	1	7.0%	$9.17
12	7-Jan	Taxi	Cash	$22.00	1	0.0%	$22.00
13	8-Jan	Incidental Expense:	VISA	$14.99	1	7.0%	$16.11
14	8-Jan	Postage	Cash	$2.75	1	0.0%	$2.75
15	10-Jan	Mileage		$0.32	64	0.0%	$20.48
16	11-Jan	Other	VISA	$15.00	1	6.5%	$16.04
17	12-Jan	Cell Phone Call		$0.15	10	0.0%	$1.50

Figure 3-24. The Expense Report worksheet with the Money Style applied.

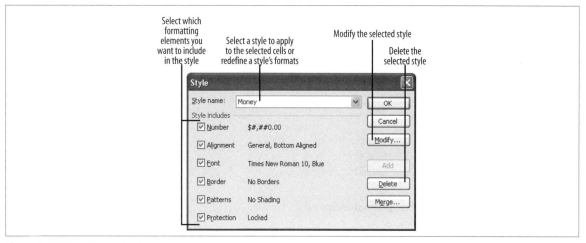

Select which formatting elements you want to include in the style

Select a style to apply to the selected cells or redefine a style's formats

Modify the selected style

Delete the selected style

Figure 3-25. The Style dialog box.

If you find yourself applying the same formatting options repeatedly, you could probably save a lot of time by using a *style*. A style is a collection of formats—such as font size, color, patterns, and alignment—that you can define and save as a group. Once you have defined and saved a style, you can apply all of the formatting elements at once.

A style can contain any (or all) of the following formatting attributes:

- Number
- Font (type, size, and color)
- Borders
- Alignment
- Pattern
- Protection (locked and hidden)

In this lesson, you will learn how to create, apply, and modify a style. The easiest way to create a style is by example. This means you have to format a cell or cell range and then create a style based on that cell or cell range.

1 If necessary, open the workbook named Lesson 3D and save it as Expense Report.

2 Select the cell range D5:D17 and select Format →
Cells from the menu.

The Format Cells dialog box appears. Specify how you
want to format the selected cell range.

3 Click the Number tab, select Currency from the
Category list, and select the first option, -$1,234.00,
from the Negative numbers list.

The next formatting option you want to change is the
font formatting.

4 Click the Font tab, select Times New Roman from
the Font list, select Regular from the Font style list,
click the Font color list arrow and select the blue color.

The last formatting option you want to change is the
pattern.

5 Click the Patterns tab, select No Color, and then
click OK.

The Format Cells dialog box closes and the formatting
options you specified are applied to the selected cell
range.

Instead of applying the same formatting options to
other cells by repeating Steps 2–4, you can create a
Style based on the cells you just formatted.

6 Verify the cell range D5:D17 is selected and select
Format → Style from the menu.

The Style dialog box appears, as shown in Figure 3-25.
Here you can create, define, or apply a style. You want
to create a new style named Money based on the
selected cell range.

7 Type Money in the Style name text box and click
OK.

You've just created a new Style named money. Try
applying the Money style to a new cell range in the
worksheet.

8 Select the cell range G5:G17, select Format →
Style from the menu, select Money from the Style
name list, and click OK.

The dialog box closes and the selected cell range is
formatted with the Money style, as shown in
Figure 3-24. See how quickly and easily you can apply
cell formatting to using styles?

Now that you know how to create and apply styles, we
can move on to what's really neat about styles: modifying them. You can modify the formatting options
for a style just like you would modify the formatting
for a cell or cell range. However, when you modify a
style, *every cell formatted with that style is updated to
reflect the formatting changes.* Here is how to modify a
style:

9 Select Format → Style from the menu, select
Money from the Style list, and click Modify.

The Format Cells dialog box appears.

10 Click the Font tab and select Arial from the Font
list. Click OK to close the Format cells dialog box, then
click OK again to close the Style dialog box.

The dialog box closes and every cell formatted with
the Money style is updated to reflect the change in
fonts.

You can delete the Money style, since you will no
longer be using it.

11 Select Format → Style from the menu, select
Money from the Style list, and click Delete.

Excel deletes the Money style.

Look how much time you just saved by modifying the
Money style. If you hadn't used a style, you would have
had to go and change the font formatting manually. Plus,
there is always the chance that you might miss reformat-
ting something.

QUICK REFERENCE

TO CREATE A STYLE BY EXAMPLE:

1. SELECT A CELL OR CELL RANGE AND APPLY THE FORMATTING YOU WANT TO USE IN THE STYLE.

2. MAKE SURE THE CELL OR CELL RANGE YOU FORMATTED IN STEP 1 IS SELECTED, THEN SELECT FORMAT → STYLE FROM THE MENU.

3. ENTER A NAME FOR THE STYLE IN THE STYLE NAME BOX.

4. (OPTIONAL) REMOVE THE CHECKMARKS FOR ANY FORMATTING ATTRIBUTES THAT YOU DON'T WANT TO BE PART OF THE STYLE.

5. CLICK OK.

TO APPLY A STYLE:

1. SELECT A CELL OR CELL RANGE YOU WANT TO FORMAT.

2. SELECT FORMAT → STYLE FROM THE MENU, SELECT THE STYLE FROM THE STYLE LIST, AND CLICK OK.

TO MODIFY A STYLE:

1. SELECT FORMAT → STYLE FROM THE MENU, SELECT THE STYLE YOU WANT TO MODIFY FROM THE STYLE LIST, AND CLICK MODIFY.

2. MODIFY ANY OF THE STYLES FORMATTING ATTRIBUTES AND CLICK OK WHEN YOU'RE FINISHED.

Formatting Cells with Conditional Formatting

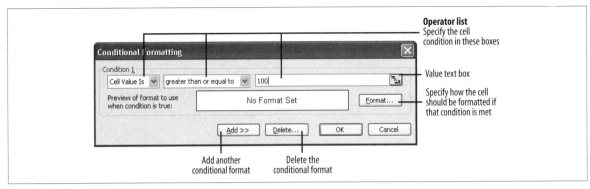

Figure 3-26. The Conditional Formatting dialog box.

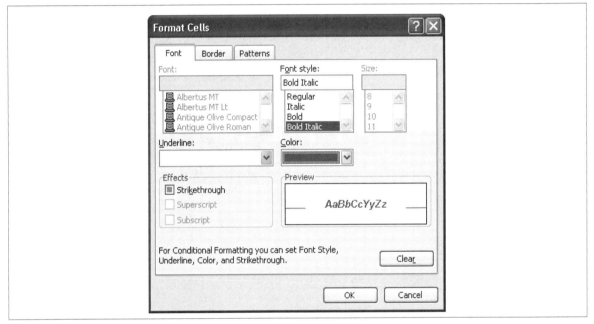

Figure 3-27. The Format Cells dialog box.

Figure 3-28. The Total cells with conditional formatting applied (note the numbers displayed in blue and in green).

Figure 3-29. The Delete Conditional Format dialog box.

You already know how to format most attributes of a cell: color, font and font size, and borders, to name only a few. In this lesson, you will learn how to use *conditional formatting*. Conditional formatting formats cells only if a specified condition is true. For example, you could use conditional formatting to display weekly sales totals that exceeded $50,000 in bright red boldface formatting, and in bright blue italics formatting if the sales totals were under $20,000. If the value of the cell changes and no longer meets the specified condition, the cell returns to its original formatting.

1 Select the cell range G5:G17.

You want to apply conditional formatting to the Totals column to highlight any values that meet a certain condition.

2 Select Format → Conditional Formatting from the menu.

The Conditional Formatting dialog box appears, as shown in Figure 3-26. This is where you can add conditional formatting options to the selected cell range.

You want to conditionally format the selected cell range (the Totals column) so that any values over 100 are formatted in a green, bold, italics font.

3 Click the Operator list arrow (the second field) and select greater than or equal to.

Next, you need to specify what value the cell must be equal or greater in order to apply the conditional formatting.

4 Click the Value text box (the third field) and type 100.

Next, you must specify how you want the cells to be formatted if the condition is met (if the cell value is equal to or greater than 100).

5 Click the Format button.

The Format Cells dialog box appears, as shown in Figure 3-27.

6 Select Bold Italic from the Style list, click the Color list arrow, select a Green color, and click OK.

You return to the Conditional Formatting dialog box. You have finished entering a conditional format for the selected cell range. You are not limited to adding a single conditional format—you can specify up to three.

Here's how to add another conditional formatting option:

7 Click the Add button.

The Conditional Formatting dialog box expands to display a second condition.

8 Click the Condition 2 Operator list arrow, select less than, click the Value text box, and type 5.

Now specify how you want the cell to be formatted if its value is less than 5. Make sure you're selecting the Condition 2 options and not the Condition 1 options!

9 Click the Format button, select Bold from the Style list, click the Color list arrow, select the blue color, and click OK.

You return to the Conditional Formatting dialog box. Since you've finished entering your conditional formatting options for the selected cell range, you can close the dialog box.

10 Click OK.

The dialog box closes and the cells are conditionally formatted according to their values, as shown in Figure 3-28.

You can easily delete conditional formatting from a cell if you decide you no longer need it.

11 With the cell range G5:G17 still selected, select Format → Conditional Formatting from the menu, then click the Delete button.

The Delete Conditional Format dialog box appears, as shown in Figure 3-29.

12 Check both the Condition 1 and Condition 2 check boxes, click OK, then click OK again to close the Conditional Formatting dialog box.

The conditional formatting for the selected cells is removed.

QUICK REFERENCE

TO CONDITIONALLY FORMAT A CELL OR CELL RANGE:

1. SELECT THE CELL OR CELL RANGE YOU WANT TO FORMAT CONDITIONALLY.

2. SELECT FORMAT → CONDITIONAL FORMATTING FROM THE MENU.

3. ENTER THE CONDITION (FOR EXAMPLE, CELL VALUE IS GREATER THAN 10).

4. CLICK THE FORMAT BUTTON AND SPECIFY THE FORMATTING YOU WANT TO USE IF THE CONDITION IS TRUE.

5. IF YOU WANT TO SPECIFY ADDITIONAL CONDITIONS FOR THE SELECTED CELLS, CLICK THE ADD BUTTON AND REPEAT STEPS 3 AND 4.

Change the *vertical*
alignment of text in the
selected cell

Text Rotation Tool
Rotate text in the
selected cell

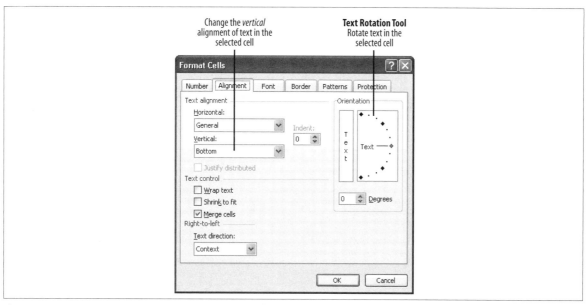

Figure 3-30. The Alignment tab of the Format Cells dialog box.

Merged cell with 90-degree
vertical alignment.

	A	B	C	D	E	F	G	H
4		Date	Type	Payment	Price Per Unit	Quantity	Tax	Total
5		3-Jan	Mileage		0.32	46	0.0%	14.72
6		3-Jan	Parking	Cash	7	1	0.0%	7
7	Boston Trip	3-Jan	Cell Phone	AMEX	0.15	23	6.5%	4.95475
8		5-Jan	Mileage		0.32	35	0.0%	11.2
9		5-Jan	Airfare	VISA	1299	1	1.0%	1312
10		7-Jan	Lodging	Check	69	1	9.0%	75.3
11		7-Jan	Meals	AMEX	8.5	1	7.0%	9.165
12		7-Jan	Taxi	Cash	22	1	0.0%	22
13		8-Jan	Incidental E	VISA	14.99	1	7.0%	16.1093
14		8-Jan	Postage	Cash	2.75	1	0.0%	2.75
15		10-Jan	Mileage		0.32	64	0.0%	20.48
16		11-Jan	Other	VISA	15	1	6.5%	16.04
17		12-Jan	Cell Phone	Call	0.15	10	0.0%	1.5

Figure 3-31. The Expense Report workbook with a merged, 90-degree vertically aligned cell.

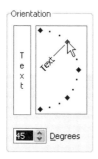

The Text Rotation tool

Fasten your seat belts; we've got a lot of ground to cover in this lesson! You'll learn how to merge several cells together into a single, larger cell, how to rotate text within a cell, and how to automatically adjust the width of a column to fit the column's widest entry.

1 Select the cell range A4:A17, select Insert → Cells from the menu, and click OK.

Excel inserts a cell range, shifting the other cells in the worksheet to the right.

2 Select the cell range A5:A12.

You want to merge the cells in the selected cell range.

3 Select Format → Cells from the menu and click the Alignment tab.

The Format Cells dialog box appears with the Alignment tab in front, as shown in Figure 3-30. The text control section of the Alignment tab has three options:

- **Wrap text:** Wraps text into multiple lines in a cell. The number of wrapped lines depends on how wide the column is and how much text is in the cell.

- **Shrink to fit:** Automatically reduces the displayed font size of a cell so that all data fits within the cell.

- **Merge cells:** Combines two or more selected cells into a single cell. The reference for a merged cell is the upper-left side of the cell.

Try merging the selected cell range into a single cell.

4 Click the Merge cells check box, and then click OK.

The dialog box closes, and the selected cells are merged into a single, larger cell.

5 With cell A5 still selected (the merged cell), type Boston Trip and click the Enter button on the Formula bar.

You already know how to change the horizontal alignment of text in a cell. Now you'll learn how to change a cell's *vertical* alignment.

6 Select Format → Cells from the menu, drag the text rotation tool in the Orientation section to a 45-degree angle, and click OK.

The dialog box closes and the text in cell A5 is aligned at a 45-degree angle.

7 With cell A5 still selected (the merged cell), select Format → Cells from the menu, drag the text rotation tool in the Orientation section to a 90-degree angle, click the Vertical list arrow, and select Center.

This will align the text at a 90-degree angle in the cell and center the text vertically. Add a colored background to the cell to make it stand out.

8 Click the Patterns tab, select the light blue color, and click OK.

The dialog box closes and cell A5 is formatted with the selected background color and vertical alignment formatting options. To finish the lesson, reduce the width of Column A using AutoFit.

9 Position the pointer on the right border of the A column heading until it changes to a ✛. Then resize the column to match the size of the A column shown in Figure 3-31.

10 Save your work and exit Microsoft Excel.

QUICK REFERENCE

TO MERGE CELLS:

1. SELECT THE CELLS THAT YOU WANT TO MERGE.

2. SELECT FORMAT → CELLS FROM THE MENU, CLICK THE ALIGNMENT TAB, SELECT THE MERGE CELLS CHECK BOX AND CLICK OK.

TO ROTATE TEXT IN A CELL:

1. SELECT THE CELL OR CELL RANGE YOU WANT TO MODIFY.

2. SELECT FORMAT → CELLS FROM THE MENU AND CLICK THE ALIGNMENT TAB.

3. SELECT ONE OF THE OPTIONS IN THE ORIENTATION SECTION OR ADJUST THE ANGLE BY DRAGGING THE TEXT ROTATION TOOL.

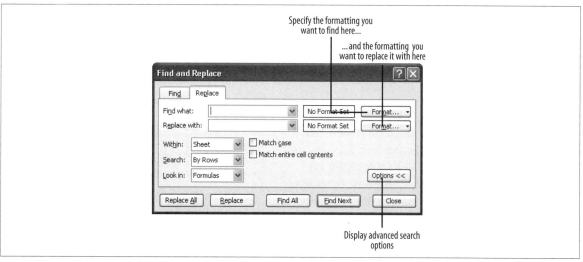

Figure 3-32. The Find and Replace dialog box.

Specify the formatting you
want to find here...

...and the formatting you
want to replace it with here

Display advanced search
options

Here Excel finds all the white-colored text...

...and changes it to black

Figure 3-33. Excel 2003 can find and replace formatting in addition to text.

After seeing a printed copy of your annual snowfall workbook, you realize that your "clever" scheme of formatting the workbook using white fonts on a white background maybe isn't such a great idea. Now you'll have to go back to your snowfall workbook, find every white colored font and replace it with a slightly more visible font. Good luck!

Actually this task will be much easier than it sounds. Find and Replace has been greatly enhanced in Microsoft Excel 2003 (see Table 3-5 for a description of the Find and Replace options). Find and Replace can now find and/or replace formatting in addition to text and information. So you can use it to replace every white-colored font in a workbook with a black-colored font.

In this lesson, you will learn how to use Find and Replace to find specific formatting in a workbook, and how to easily change that formatting.

1 **Open the workbook named** Lesson 3E **and save it as** Find Formatting.

Here's your snowfall workbook. You need to change all the white-colored text to black. Since you don't even know where all the white-colored text is (how did you create this workbook anyway?), you will use Find and Replace to automatically find all the white-colored text and change it to black.

2 Select Edit → Replace from the menu.

The Find and Replace dialog box appears. You need to click the Options button to display more advanced find and replace controls.

3 Click Options.

The Find and Replace dialog box expands and displays more advanced options, as shown in Figure 3-32. Notice that two Format buttons appear after clicking the Options button. You use the top Format button to specify the cell formatting you want to find and the bottom Format button to specify the cell formatting you want to replace it with.

4 Click the top Format button.

The Find Format dialog box appears. This is where you specify the cell formatting you want to look for.

5 Click the Font tab.

You want to search for white-colored fonts.

6 Click the ⌄ Color list arrow and select a white color.

That's the only formatting option you want to look for, so you can close the Find Format dialog box.

7 Click OK.

The Find Format dialog box closes. Next you need to specify the cell formatting you want to replace the white-colored fonts with.

8 Click the bottom Format button.

The Replace Format dialog box appears.

9 If necessary, click the Font tab, then click the ⌄ Color list arrow and select Automatic.

Move on to the next step and close the Replace Format dialog box.

10 Click OK.

The Replace Format dialog box closes.

Now that you've specified the cell formatting you want to look for and the cell formatting you want to replace it with, you can start finding and replacing the formatting. Just like finding and replacing text, you can review and replace each occurrence of formatting, or you can automatically replace all occurrences at once.

11 Click Replace All.

Excel replaces all the white-colored text formatting with black-colored text formatting, as shown in Figure 3-33.

12 Click OK, then Close. Close Microsoft Excel without saving any changes.

Congratulations! You've worked your way through a long and rather difficult chapter! The next time you're called on to create a worksheet, make sure you use some of the formatting techniques you've learned to impress your colleagues.

Table 3-5. Find and Replace Options

Option	Description
Replace All	Replaces all occurrences of the search criteria in your worksheet. If you want to review and selectively replace each occurrence, click Replace instead of Replace All.
Replace	Replaces the selected occurrence of the criteria in the Find what box, finds the next occurrence, and then stops. If you want to automatically replace all occurrences of the search criteria in your document, click Replace All.
Find All	Finds all occurrences of the search criteria in your document. If you want to find and review each occurrence separately, click Find Next instead of Find All.
Find Next	Searches for the next occurrence of the characters specified in the Find what box. To find the previous occurrence, hold down SHIFT and click Find Next.

QUICK REFERENCE

TO FIND AND REPLACE CELL FORMATTING:

1. SELECT EDIT → REPLACE FROM THE MENU.

2. CLICK OPTIONS.

3. CLICK THE TOP FORMAT BUTTON, SPECIFY THE FORMATTING OPTIONS YOU WANT TO SEARCH FOR, AND CLICK OK.

4. CLICK FIND NEXT TO FIND EACH OCCURRENCE OF CELL FORMATTING AND REPLACE TO REPLACE THE CELL FORMATTING.

OR...

CLICK REPLACE ALL TO REPLACE ALL OCCURRENCES OF THE CELL FORMATTING.

Chapter Three Review

Lesson Summary

Formatting Fonts with the Formatting Toolbar

Change the style of text by clicking the Bold button, Italics button, or Underline button on the Formatting toolbar.

Change the font type by selecting a font from the Font list on the Formatting toolbar.

Change the font size by selecting the pt. size from the Font Size list.

Formatting Values

To Apply Number Formatting Using the Formatting Toolbar: Select the cell or cell range you want to format, and click the appropriate number formatting button(s) on the Formatting toolbar.

The Number Formatting Buttons on the Formatting toolbar include Currency, Percent, Comma, Increase Decimal, and Decrease Decimal.

To Apply Number Formatting using the Format Cells Dialog Box: Select the cell or cell range you want to format, right-click the cell or cell range, select Format Cells from the shortcut menu, click the Number tab, and specify the number formatting you want to apply.

Adjusting Row Height and Column Width

To Adjust the Width of a Column: There are three methods:

- Drag the column header's right border to the left or right.
- Right-click the column header, select Column Width from the shortcut menu, and enter the column width.
- Select the column header(s), select Format → Column → Width from menu and enter the column width.

To Adjust the Height of a Row: There are three methods:

- Drag the row header's bottom border up or down.
- Right-click the row header(s), select Row Height from the shortcut menu, and enter the row height.
- Select the row header(s), select Format → Row → Height from menu, and enter the row height.

To Automatically Adjust the Width of a Column or Row (AutoFit): Double-click the right border of the column or click the column heading to select the column and select Format → Column → AutoFit from the menu.

Changing Cell Alignment

Using the Formatting Toolbar: Select the cell or cell range and click the appropriate alignment button (Left, Center, Right, or Merge and Center) on the Formatting toolbar.

Using the Format Cells Dialog Box: Select the cell or cell range and either right-click the selection and select Format Cells from the shortcut menu or select Format → Cells from the menu. Click the Alignment tab and select the desired alignment option.

Adding Borders

Using the Formatting Toolbar: Select the cell or cell range you want to add a border(s) to, click the Border button list arrow on the Formatting toolbar, and select the border you want.

Using the Format Cells Dialog Box: Either right-click the selection and select Format Cells from the shortcut menu or select Format → Cells from the menu. Click the Border tab and select the border(s) you want to add.

Applying Colors and Patterns

Using the Formatting Toolbar: Select the cell or cell range, click the Fill Color list arrow on the Formatting toolbar, and select the color you want.

Using the Format Cells Dialog Box: Either right-click the selection and select Format Cells from the shortcut menu, or select Format → Cells from the menu. Click the Patterns tab and select the color or pattern you want to use.

Using the Format Painter

The Format Painter lets you copy the formatting of a cell or cell range and apply or paste the formatting to other cells.

To Use the Format Painter: Select the cells with the formatting options you want to copy, click the Format Painter button on the Standard toolbar, and select the cell range where you want to apply the copied formatting.

Double-click the Format Painter button to apply formatting to several locations. Click the Format Painter button again when you're finished.

Using AutoFormat

AutoFormat automatically formats your worksheets using one of 16 preset formatting schemes.

Select Format → AutoFormat from the menu and select one of the AutoFormats from the list and click OK.

Creating a Custom Number Format

To Create a Custom Number Format: Select the cell or cell range you want to format, select Format → Cells from the menu, click the Number tab, and select the Custom category. Type a number format in the Type box using the appropriate format codes.

Creating, Applying, and Modifying a Style

A style is a collection of formats (Number, Font, Borders, Alignment, Pattern, and Protection) you can define and save as a group so you can apply all of the formatting elements at once.

To Create a Style by Example: Select a cell or cell range and apply the formatting you want to use in the style. Once the cell or cell range is formatted, select it and select Format → Style from the menu. Enter a name for the style in the Style name box.

To Apply a Style: Select a cell or cell range you want to format, select Format → Style from the menu, select the style from the Style list, and click OK.

To Modify a Style: Select Format → Style from the menu, select the style you want to modify from the Style list, and click Modify. Modify any of the styles formatting

attributes and click OK when you're finished. Every cell formatted using that style will be updated.

Formatting Cells with Conditional Formatting

Conditional formatting is a format, such as cell shading or font color, which Excel automatically applies to cells if a specified condition is true.

To Conditionally Format a Cell or Cell Range: Select the cell or cell range you want to format conditionally and select Format → Conditional Formatting from the menu. Enter the condition (for example, Cell Value is greater than 10), click the Format button, and specify the formatting you want to use if the condition is true. If you want to specify additional conditions for the selected cells, click the Add button; otherwise, click OK.

Merging Cells, Rotating Text, and using AutoFit

To Merge Cells: Select the cells that you want to merge, select Format → Cells from the menu, click the Alignment tab, select the Merge cells check box, and click OK.

To Rotate Text in a Cell: Select the cell or cell range, select Format → Cells from the menu, and click the Alignment tab. Select one of the options in the Orientation section or adjust the angle by dragging the text rotation tool.

Finding and Replacing Formatting

To Find and Replace Cell Formatting: Select Edit → Replace from the menu and click Options. Click the top Format button, specify the formatting options you want to search for, and click OK. Click the bottom Format button, specify the new formatting options, and click OK. Click Find Next to find each occurrence of cell formatting and Replace to replace the cell formatting, or click Replace All to replace all occurrences of the cell formatting.

Quiz

1. Which of the following procedures changes the font size?

    A. Select the text and choose a point size from the Font list on the Formatting toolbar.

    B. Select the cell(s) and right-click the selection, select Format Cells from the shortcut menu, click the Font tab, select the font size, and click OK.

    C. Select the cell(s), select Format → Cells from the menu, click the Font tab, select the font size, and click OK.

    D. All of the above.

2. Which is NOT a method for applying boldface to a selected cell range?

    A. Select Format → Cells from the menu, click the Font tab, and select Bold from the Font style list.

    B. Press Ctrl + B.

    C. Right-click the text and select Boldface from the shortcut menu.

    D. Click the Bold button on the Formatting toolbar.

3. To copy formatting from one cell in a worksheet and apply it to another cell you would use:

    A. The Edit → Copy Format and Edit → Paste Format commands from the menu.

    B. The Format Painter button on the Standard toolbar.

    C. There is no way to copy and apply formatting in Excel—you would have to do it manually.

    D. The Copy and Apply Formatting dialog box, located under the Format → Copy and Apply menu.

4. The numbers in your worksheet look like this: 1000. You want them to look like this: $1,000.00. How can you accomplish this?

    A. Click the Currency Style button on the Formatting toolbar.

    B. Select Format → Money from the menu.

    C. You have to retype everything and manually add the dollar signs, commas, and decimals.

    D. None of the above.

5. A date is considered a value, and therefore you can change how it is displayed. For example, 5/12/99 could be reformatted to May 12, 1999 (True or False?)

6. Which of the following is NOT a method for adjusting the width of a column?

    A. Drag the column header's right border to the left or right.

    B. Double-click the column header's right border.

    C. Select the column header and click the Column Width button on the Standard toolbar.

    D. Right-click the column header, select Column Width from the shortcut menu, and enter the column's width.

7. Which of the following statements is NOT true:

    A. Clicking the Center button centers the text or numbers inside the cell.

    B. The Merge and Center button merges several cells into a single larger cell and centers the contents inside the cell.

    C. You can change cell alignment by clicking Format → Cells from the menu and clicking the Alignment tab.

    D. Cells can only display one line of text—they can't wrap text inside the cell.

8. What is the procedure(s) for adding a border above and below a selected cell range? (Select all that apply)

    A. Select Format → Cells from the menu, click the Borders tab, click the top and bottom lines in the border preview diagram, and click OK.

    B. Type several underscore (_) characters in cells above and below the cell range.

    C. Click the Border button arrow on the Formatting toolbar and select the appropriate border formatting from the list.

    D. Click the Underline button on the Formatting toolbar.

9. AutoFormat automatically formats your worksheet using 1 of 16 present formatting styles (True or False?)

10. How can you make a certain cell yellow?

    A. Click the Highlight button on the Standard toolbar.

    B. Click the Fill button arrow on the Formatting toolbar and click the yellow color.

    C. Select Format → Color → Yellow from the menu.

    D. Click the Borders button arrow on the Formatting toolbar and click the yellow color.

11. You have four cells that you want to combine into one. How can you do this?

    A. Select the cells and click the Merge Cells button on the Formatting toolbar.

    B. Select the cells and select Tools → Merge Wizard from the menu.

    C. Select the cells and click the Merge and Center button on the Formatting toolbar.

    D. Select the cells and select Edit → Merge Cells from the menu.

12. You want to use the Format Painter to apply formatting to several cells in a worksheet that are not next to each other. How can you do this?

    A. Click the Format Painter button on the Standard toolbar.

    B. Double-click the Format Painter button on the Standard toolbar.

    C. This isn't possible.

    D. Open the Copy and Apply Formatting dialog box by selecting Format → Copy Formatting from the menu.

13. How can you rotate text in a cell?

    A. Select Format → Cells from the menu and click the Alignment tab.

    B. Click the Alignment button arrow from the Formatting toolbar and select the desired alignment.

    C. Select Format → Text Direction from the menu.

    D. Right-click the cell and select Text Direction from the shortcut menu.

14. You want to change the dates in a worksheet so that they appear as October 15, 2001 instead of 10/15/01. How can you do this?

    A. Select the cells and click the Long Date button on the Formatting toolbar.

    B. You will have retype all the dates, as there is no way to reformat them.

    C. Select the cells and select Format → Cells from the menu, click the Number tab, select Date from the Number list, and select the date format you want.

    D. You will need to call your system administrator have him or her install the Microsoft Long Date patch for you.

Homework

1. Open the Homework 3 workbook and save it as "Formatting Practice."

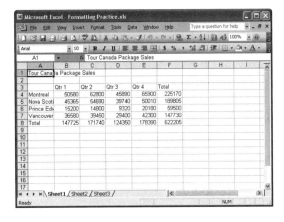

2. Resize the A column so that you can completely see all the tour packages.

3. Change the font of the worksheet title to Times New Roman.

4. Make the worksheet title bold, change its color to dark blue, and its size to 14 pt.

5. Change the tour package sales amounts to currency formatting.

6. Center the column headings (Qtr 1 to Total) and apply bold formatting to them.

7. Add a bottom border to cell range B7:F7.

8. Merge the cell range A1:F1 into a single cell that spans the worksheet.

Quiz Answers

1. D. All of these procedures change the font size.

2. C. There is not a Boldface option in the shortcut menu.

3. B. The Format Painter copies formatting from one area of a worksheet and applies it to another area.

4. A. The currency button on the Formatting toolbar applies the currency number formatting.

5. True. Date value can be displayed in a number of ways, but they're still the same date.

6. C. There isn't a Column Width button on the Standard toolbar.

7. D. Cell can display multiple lines of text. Select Format → Cells, click the Alignment tab, and check the Wrap Text check box.

8. A and C. You can add a border to a select cell range by selecting a border from the Border button on the Formatting toolbar or by selecting Format → Cells from the menu and clicking the Borders tab.

9. True. AutoFormat automatically applies 1 of 16 formatting styles to your worksheet.

10. B. You can make a cell yellow by clicking the Fill button arrow on the Formatting toolbar and selecting a yellow color.

11. C. You can merge several selected cells into a single cell by clicking the Merge and Center button on the Formatting toolbar.

12. B. Double-click the Format Painter button on the Standard toolbar to apply formatting to several non-adjacent cells in a worksheet. Click the Format Painter button when you're finished applying the formatting.

13. A. You can rotate text in a cell by selecting Format → Cells from the menu and clicking the Alignment tab.

14. C. You can format date values by selecting Format → Cells from the menu, clicking the Number tab, selecting Date from the Number list, and selecting the date format.

CHAPTER 4

CREATING AND WORKING WITH CHARTS

CHAPTER OBJECTIVES:

Create a chart

Move and resize a chart

Format objects in a chart

Arrange a chart's source data

Arrange a chart type

Add titles, gridlines, annotations, and a data table to a chart

Work with a 3-D chart

Create and work with a custom chart

Plot data on a map

CHAPTER TASK: CREATE A CHART THAT PLOTS SURVEY DATA

Prerequisites

- **Understand how to use menus, toolbars, dialog boxes, and shortcut keystrokes**
- **Understand how to select cell ranges**

You already know what a chart is—charts illustrate data, relationships, or trends graphically. Like the saying "a picture is worth a thousand words," charts are often better at presenting information than hard-to-read numbers in a table or spreadsheet.

In this chapter, you will learn just about everything there is to know about charts: how to create dynamic looking charts, how to edit and format them, and how to work with different types. Creating and working with charts in Excel is easier than you might think and is actually quite fun. The dazzling charts you will be able to create after you finish this chapter will impress both you and your colleagues.

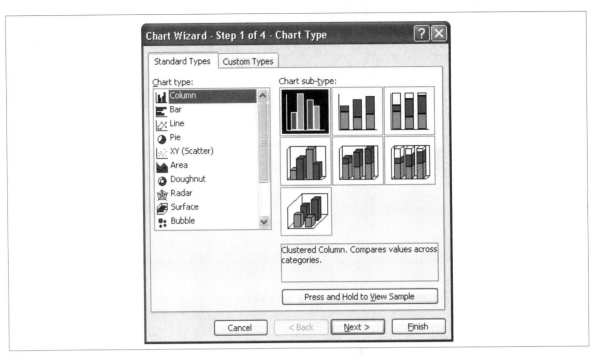

Figure 4-1. Step One of the Chart Wizard: selecting a type of chart.

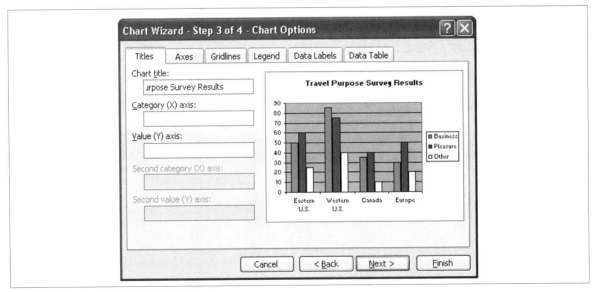

Figure 4-2. Step Three of the Chart Wizard: specifying chart options.

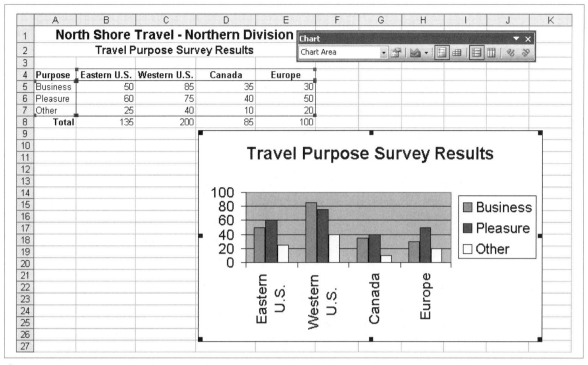

	A	B	C	D	E	F	G	H	I	J	K
1	**North Shore Travel - Northern Division**										
2	Travel Purpose Survey Results										
3											
4	Purpose	Eastern U.S.	Western U.S.	Canada	Europe						
5	Business	50	85	35	30						
6	Pleasure	60	75	40	50						
7	Other	25	40	10	20						
8	Total	135	200	85	100						

Figure 4-3. The new chart.

You can plot most of the information in a worksheet on a chart—and that's what this lesson is about! This lesson will give you practice creating a chart based on data that's already been entered in a worksheet. The most common (and by far the easiest method) of creating a chart is to use the *Chart Wizard*. Get that image of mysterious old bearded men wearing purple robes and pointy hats with stars and moons on them out of your mind—the Chart Wizard is a feature that walks you through the process of creating a chart.

1 Start Excel, open the workbook named Lesson 4A, and save it as Survey Results.

The first step in creating a chart is to select the cells that contain *both the values and labels* you want to chart.

**Chart Wizard
button**
Other Ways to insert a Chart:
• Select **Insert→Chart** from the menu.

2 Select the cell range A4:E7, then click the Chart Wizard button **on the Standard toolbar.**

The Chart Wizard opens, as shown in Figure 4-1.

The first step in creating a chart is selecting the type of chart you want to create from the Chart type list. You can preview how your data will appear in each type of chart by selecting the chart type and clicking the "Press and Hold to View Sample" button. You want to create a Column chart, and since the Column chart type is already selected, you can move on to the next step.

3 Click Next to accept the Column chart type and move to the second step in the Chart Wizard.

The second step in the Chart Wizard lets you select the cell range you want to chart. You also have to specify if the data series (the information you're plotting in your chart) is from the rows or columns of the worksheet. In this case, use the rows option so your chart will be plotted by destination. Since this is currently selected, you don't need to change anything. The cell range A4:E7 appears in the Data range text box because you have already selected the cell range before starting the Chart Wizard. The chart options here are correct, so you can move on to the next step.

4 Click Next **to move to the third step in the Chart Wizard.**

The third step in the Chart Wizard presents you with a sample of your chart, as shown in Figure 4-2. Here you can add titles to the chart, axis, legend, data labels, gridlines, and data table.

5 Click the Chart title box **and type** Travel Purpose Survey Results.

The Chart title appears in the Sample Chart.

6 Click Next **to move to the fourth step in the Chart Wizard.**

The fourth and final step in the Chart Wizard is to determine the chart's location. There are two options:

• **As new sheet:** The chart will be placed on a separate, new sheet in the workbook. You can enter a name for this new sheet or accept Excel's default sheet name.

• **As object in:** The chart will be placed on the same sheet as the data.

You want to place your chart on the current worksheet, which is already selected, so you can finish the Chart Wizard.

7 Click Finish **to complete the Chart Wizard.**

The Chart Wizard dialog box closes, and the column chart appears in the active worksheet, as shown in Figure 4-3. Your chart may be covering a large portion of the worksheet data—don't worry about it. You'll learn how to move and resize a chart in the next lesson.

8 Save your work.

Congratulations! You've just created your first chart. Turn the page to learn how you can move and resize the chart.

QUICK REFERENCE

TO CREATE A CHART WITH THE CHART WIZARD:

1. SELECT THE CELL RANGE THAT CONTAINS THE DATA YOU WANT TO CHART AND CLICK THE CHART WIZARD BUTTON ON THE STANDARD TOOLBAR.

   OR...

   SELECT THE CELL RANGE AND SELECT INSERT → CHART FROM THE MENU.

2. SELECT THE CHART TYPE AND CLICK NEXT.

3. VERIFY (OR CHANGE) THE CELL RANGE USED IN THE CHART AND CLICK NEXT.

4. ADJUST THE CHART OPTIONS BY CLICKING THE CATEGORIZED TABS AND SELECTING ANY OPTIONS AND THEN CLICKING NEXT.

5. SPECIFY WHERE YOU WANT TO PLACE THE CHART (AS AN EMBEDDED OBJECT OR ON A NEW SHEET) AND CLICK FINISH.

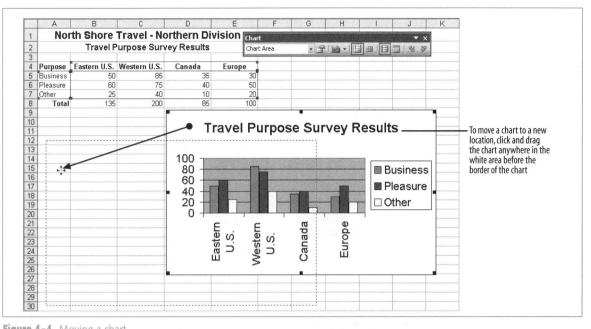

Figure 4-4. Moving a chart.

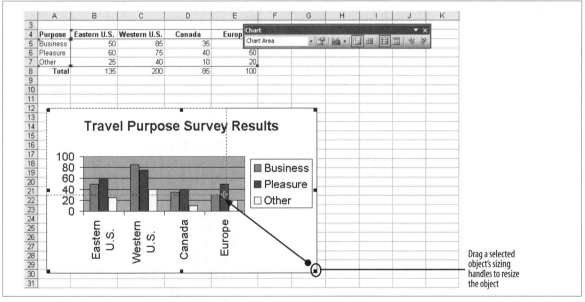

Figure 4-5. Resizing a chart.

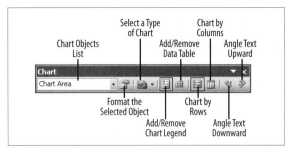

Figure 4-6. The Chart toolbar.

More often than not, charts are not the size you want them to be after they are created. In this lesson, you will learn how to resize a chart to make it larger or smaller. You will also learn how to move a chart to a new location in the worksheet.

1 Make sure the chart is selected.

If the chart isn't selected, all you have to do is click it to select it. Six boxes, called *sizing handles*, appear along the edges of a chart any time it is selected. Sizing handles are used to change the size of charts and other objects.

2 Click and hold the blank area just before the border of the chart. Drag the chart down and to the left, below the Total row and release the mouse button.

The pointer changes to a ✛ (see Figure 4-4), and a dotted outline of the chart appears as you move the chart to a new location.

You can resize a chart by clicking and dragging any of its *sizing handles*, located along the border of any selected chart, as shown in Figure 4-5.

3 Position the pointer over the lower-right sizing handle, until the pointer changes to a ↖, then drag the mouse diagonally up and to the left, until the chart is about 25% smaller.

The chart is resized. You can also make a chart or object larger by dragging the sizing handles down and to the right. You can also move and resize objects in a chart using the same procedures.

4 Click the chart legend to select it.

Selection handles appear around the legend. Once you have selected an object you can move or resize it.

5 Drag the legend to the lower-right corner of the chart, so that it is at the same level as the destination titles.

The chart legend is moved to the new location.

6 Click anywhere outside the chart to deselect the legend and the chart.

7 Save your work.

The skills you've just learned (moving and resizing objects) are important because you can use them to move and resize just about any type of object. You can even use these skills to move and resize objects in other programs, such as Microsoft Word or PowerPoint.

QUICK REFERENCE

TO RESIZE A CHART:

- CLICK THE CHART TO SELECT IT, THEN DRAG ITS SIZING HANDLES UNTIL THE CHART IS THE SIZE YOU WANT.

TO MOVE A CHART:

- CLICK AND HOLD DOWN THE MOUSE BUTTON ON THE BLANK AREA AROUND THE CHART, DRAG IT TO A NEW LOCATION IN THE WORKBOOK, THEN RELEASE THE MOUSE BUTTON.

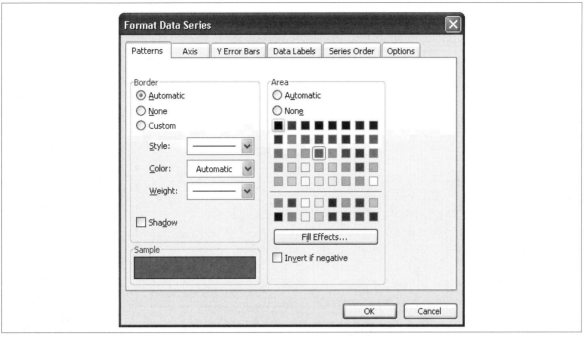

Figure 4-7. The Patterns tab of the Format Data Series dialog box.

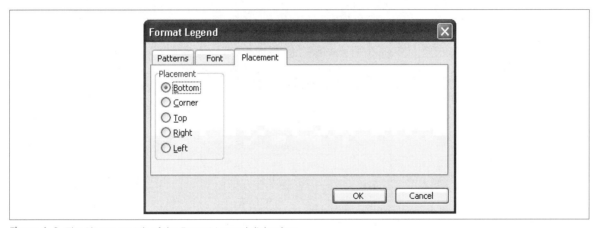

Figure 4-8. The Placement tab of the Format Legend dialog box.

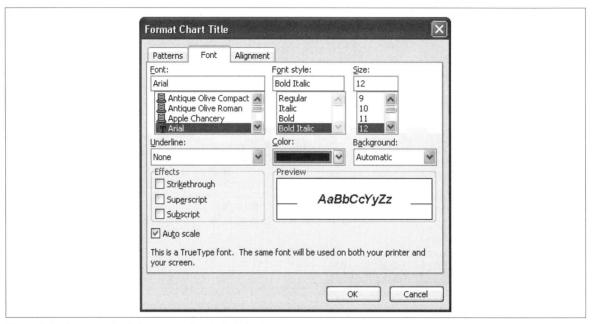

Figure 4-9. The Font tab of the Format Chart Title dialog box.

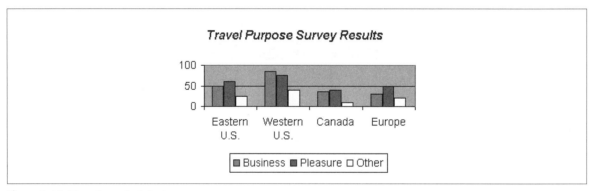

Figure 4-10. The reformatted chart.

Here's an important fact you need to know: you can select, format, and edit every object in a chart. For example, you can change the style, size, and color of any of the fonts used in a chart, or you can change the background color of the chart. After you've completed this lesson you'll be a pro at formatting anything and everything in a chart. Some items that can be formatted and edited in a chart include:

• Chart Title

• Any Data Series

• Chart's Gridlines

• Chart Legend

• Chart Background Area

• Chart Plot Area

• Data tables

• Category Axis

There are two methods you can use to select a chart object. The first method is to simply click an object to select it. Sometimes it can be tricky to know exactly where or what to click when selecting a chart object. For example, what would you click to select the chart's plot area? In these cases it is easier to use the second method, which is to select the object from the Chart Object list on the Chart toolbar.

Format Data Series button
Other Ways to Format a Data Series:
• Double-click the object.
• Right click the object and select **Format Data Series** from the shortcut menu.
• Click the object to select it and select
Format→Selected Data Series from the menu.

1 Click the chart to select it.

The first object you want to format on the chart is the Pleasure Data series. Of course, you must first select the Pleasure Data series before you can format it. You can select the Pleasure Data series from the Chart Object list on the Chart toolbar.

2 Click the Chart Objects list arrow on the Chart toolbar and select Series "Pleasure" from the list.

NOTE *If the Chart toolbar doesn't appear on your screen, you can display it by selecting View → Toolbars → Chart from the menu.*

Selection boxes appear on the three columns of the Pleasure data series in the chart. Now that you've selected the Pleasure series, you can format it.

3 Click the Format Data Series button on the Chart toolbar and click the Patterns tab if necessary.

The Format Data Series dialog box appears, as shown in Figure 4-7. You are presented a variety of different formatting options that you can apply to the selected data series. We'll take a closer look at how to format a data series in an upcoming lesson; for now, just change the color of the data series.

4 Select a green color from the color palette in the Area section and click OK.

The dialog box closes and the color of the Pleasure data series changes to green. Next, try formatting the

chart's legend so you can place it in a better location on the chart.

5 Double-click the chart's legend to format it and select the Placement tab.

The Format Legend dialog box appears, as shown in Figure 4-8.

6 Select the Bottom option and click OK.

The dialog box closes and the legend appears at the bottom of the chart.

The last thing to format in this lesson is the chart's title.

7 Double-click the Chart's title (Travel Purpose Survey Results) to format it, and click the Font tab.

The Format Chart Title dialog box appears, as shown in Figure 4-9. Change the font of the chart's title as follows:

8 Select Bold Italic from the Font Style list, click the Color list arrow and select a Blue color, then click OK.

The dialog box closes and the chart title is formatted with the font options you selected.

9 Compare your chart to the one in Figure 4-10 and save your work.

There are so many different types of chart objects, each with their own individual formatting options, that it would take days to go through all of them. Instead, this lesson has given you a general guideline to follow to select and format any type of chart object you encounter.

QUICK REFERENCE

TO SELECT A CHART OBJECT:

- CLICK THE CHART OBJECTS LIST ARROW ON THE CHART TOOLBAR AND SELECT THE OBJECT.

  OR...

- CLICK THE OBJECT.

TO FORMAT A CHART OBJECT:

1. DOUBLE-CLICK THE OBJECT.

   OR...

   SELECT THE OBJECT AND CLICK THE FORMAT DATA SERIES BUTTON ON THE CHART TOOLBAR.

OR...

RIGHT-CLICK THE OBJECT AND SELECT FORMAT DATA SERIES FROM THE SHORTCUT MENU.

OR...

SELECT THE OBJECT AND SELECT FORMAT → FORMAT DATA SERIES FROM THE MENU.

2. CLICK THE TAB THAT CONTAINS THE ITEMS YOU WANT TO FORMAT AND SPECIFY YOUR FORMATTING OPTIONS.

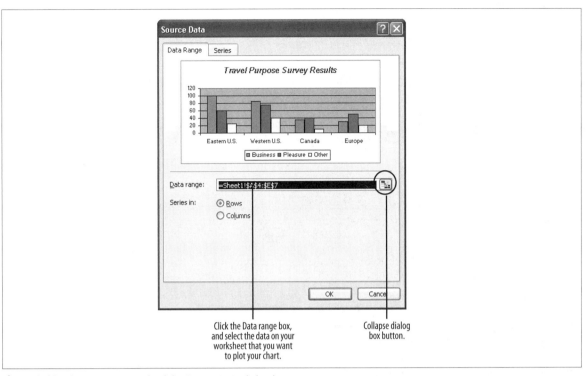

Figure 4-11. The Data Range tab of the Source Data dialog box.

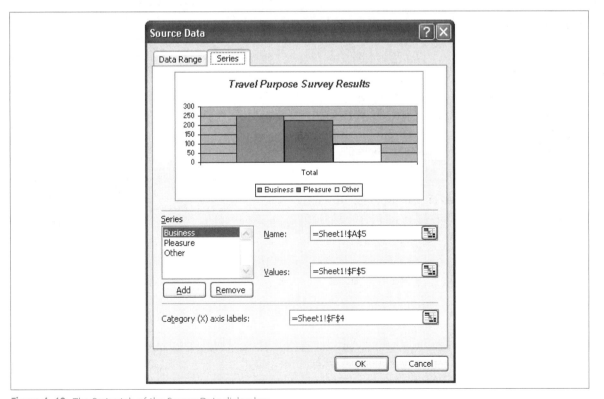

Figure 4-12. The Series tab of the Source Data dialog box.

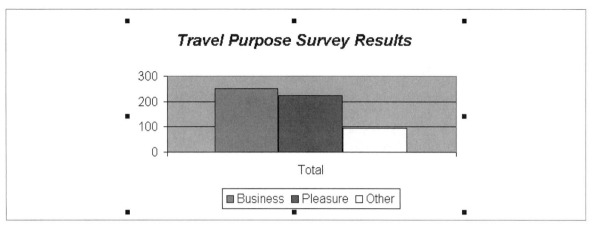

Figure 4-13. The updated chart.

Once you create a chart, you may decide to change which worksheet cells contain the values and labels you want to plot in the chart. For example, you might add a new column or row to a worksheet and then want to include it in an existing chart. Or you might want to remove some cells that you no longer want to be plotted in a chart. This lesson shows you how to change a chart's *source data*; i.e., which worksheet cells that contain the values and labels on which the chart is based.

1 If necessary, open the workbook named Lesson 4B and save it as Survey Results.

2 Click cell B5, type 100, and press Enter.

Notice that the chart is updated, reflecting the change in value. You decide to add another column to display the total purposes for traveling for all the destinations. First, you need to add a column heading.

3 Click cell F4, click the Bold button and the Center button on the Formatting toolbar, type Total, and press Enter.

Next, total the purposes for traveling for all of the destinations.

Σ

AutoSum button

4 Make sure cell F5 is the active cell, click the Auto-Sum button on the Standard toolbar (note that Excel automatically selects the correct cell range, B5:E5) and click the Enter button on the Formula bar.

Excel totals all the values in the Business row. Use AutoFill to copy the formula you just created to the remaining cells.

5 Copy the formula in cell F5 to the cell range F6:F8.

You can copy the formula using AutoFill (the fastest and easiest method) or by copying and pasting. Next, you want to modify the chart so it displays only the data from the Total column you just added.

6 Click the chart to select it.

Selection handles appear at the corners and sides of the chart and the Chart toolbar appears. Now you need to change the source data for the chart.

7 Select Chart → Source Data from the menu and click the Data Range tab.

The Source Data dialog box appears, as shown in Figure 4-11. This is where you can change the chart's source data. Notice the Data range box currently contains =Sheet1!$A$4:$E$7, which is the cell range for the chart's current data source. You want the data source to include the cells from the Purpose column—A4:A7—and the values from the Total column—F4:F7.

TIP *To select nonadjacent cell ranges, press and hold the Ctrl key while you select additional cells.*

8 Select the cell range A4:A7.

If the dialog box is in the way, you can temporarily hide it by clicking the data range box's *Collapse dialog button.*

Okay, you've got the A (Purpose) column selected. So how can you select the F (Total) column since the two columns are not next to each other? Move on to the next step to find out.

9 Press and hold the Ctrl key, select the cell range F4:F7, release the Ctrl key, and press Enter.

Pressing and holding the Ctrl key lets you select cells that are not next to each other. The chart plots the new cells you specified as a data source. We have one more thing to look at while the Source Data dialog box is still open.

10 If necessary, select Chart → Source Data from the menu, then click the Series tab.

The Series tab of the Source Data dialog box appears, as shown in Figure 4-12. You don't have to touch anything here: we just want to take a quick look at this screen. Once you have selected the source data for the chart, you can add, change, and delete the data series and name series used here, on the Series tab.

11 Click OK.

Compare your chart with the one in Figure 4-13.

QUICK REFERENCE

TO CHANGE A CHART'S DATA SOURCE:

1. SELECT THE CHART, SELECT CHART → SOURCE DATA FROM THE MENU, AND CLICK THE DATA RANGE TAB.

2. CLICK IN THE DATA RANGE BOX AND SELECT THE CELL RANGE ON WHICH YOU WANT TO BASE THE CHART. (CLICK THE COLLAPSE DIALOG BOX BUTTON IF NECESSARY.)

3. CLICK OK.

TO USE NONADJACENT CELL RANGES IN A CHART:

• SELECT THE FIRST CELL RANGE, THEN PRESS AND HOLD THE CTRL KEY AS YOU SELECT THE REMAINING NONADJACENT RANGES.

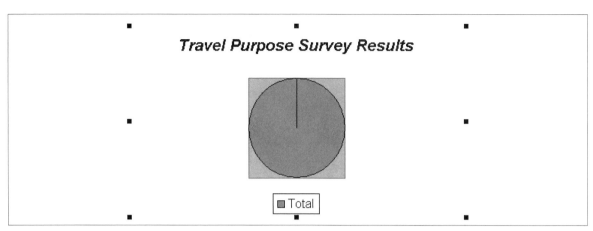

Figure 4-14. A pie chart incorrectly plotted by rows.

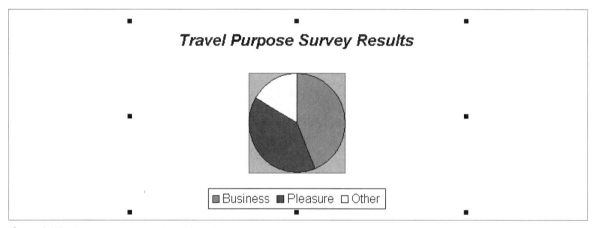

Figure 4-15. The same pie chart plotted by columns.

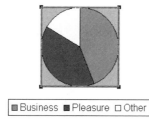

Travel Purpose Survey Results

■ Business ■ Pleasure □ Other

1. Click the chart area to enter Edit Mode

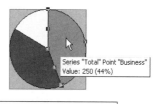

Travel Purpose Survey Results

Series "Total" Point "Business"
Value: 250 (44%)

■ Business ■ Pleasure □ Other

2. Click a slice of the chart to select it

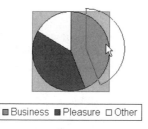

Travel Purpose Survey Results

■ Business ■ Pleasure □ Other

3. Hold down the mouse button and drag the slice away from the chart

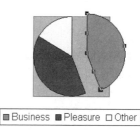

Travel Purpose Survey Results

■ Business ■ Pleasure □ Other

4. Release the mouse button to drop the slice

Figure 4-16. Pulling a slice from a pie chart.

Chart Type button

Just as some lures are better than others for catching certain types of fish, different types of charts are better than others for presenting different types of information. So far, you have been working on a *column chart*, which is great for comparing values for different items, but not so great for illustrating trends or relationships. In this lesson, you will learn how and when to use different types of charts. You will also learn a valuable tip when working with pie charts: how to pull a slice of the pie away from the chart.

Selecting a Pie Chart

1 Click the chart to select it.

2 Click the Chart Type List arrow from the Chart toolbar and select the Pie Chart.

The chart changes to a pie chart, as shown in Figure 4-14. What happened? Why is there only one piece of the pie instead of three? It's because Excel is still plotting the data by rows (destinations) instead of by columns (purpose).

NOTE   *Sometimes when you change chart types, the formatting options for one chart type may not be appropriate for another chart type. An improperly formatted chart appears cluttered and difficult to read. To solve this problem: Select Chart → Chart Type from the menu, next select the chart type and sub-type you want to use, and then select the Default formatting check box and click OK.*

By Column button

3   Click the By Column button **on the Chart toolbar.**

Excel changes the data series for the chart from rows to columns and properly displays the chart (see Figure 4-15). You decide you want to pull the business slice of the pie away from the pie chart to emphasize it.

4   Click the actual Chart Plot Area **to enter edit mode.**

The chart plot area is the actual chart, in this case, the circular pie chart. Sizing handles appear on the business slice.

5   Click the business slice **of the pie to select it (selection handles should appear on the slice) and then click and drag it away from the chart about a half-inch (see Figure 4-16).**

NOTE   *Make sure you click the slice of the pie you want to pull away from a chart before you drag it. You will pull all the pieces of a pie chart away if you simply drag-and-drop a piece without clicking and selecting it first.*

Because Excel offers so many different types of charts and graphs, you should have a general idea which type of chart to use in which circumstances. Table 4-1 shows some of the more commonly used charts and graphs and gives explanations on how and when they are used.

Table 4-1. Types of Charts and Graphs

Chart or Graph	Chart or Graph Type	Description
	Column	Column charts are used when you want to compare different values vertically side by side. Each value is represented in the chart by a vertical bar. If there are several series, each series is represented by a different color.
	Bar	Bar charts are just like column charts, except they display information in horizontal bars rather than in vertical columns.
	Line	Line charts are used to illustrate trends. Each value is plotted as a point on the chart and connected to other values by a line. Multiple items are plotted using different lines.
	Area	Area charts are the same as line charts, except the area beneath the lines is filled with color.
	Pie	Pie charts are useful for showing values as a percentage of a whole. The values for each item are represented by different colors.

Table 4-1. Types of Charts and Graphs (Continued)

Chart or Graph	Chart or Graph Type	Description
	Scatter	Scatter charts are used to plot clusters of values using single points. Multiple items can be plotted by using different colored points or different point symbols.
	Combination	Combination charts combine two different types of charts together. For example, a combination chart might contain both a column chart and a line chart.

QUICK REFERENCE

TO CHANGE THE CHART TYPE:

- SELECT THE CHART AND SELECT CHART → CHART TYPE FROM THE MENU.

  OR...

- CLICK THE CHART TYPE LIST ARROW ON THE CHART TOOLBAR.

TO CHART BY ROWS OR COLUMNS:

- SELECT THE CHART AND CLICK EITHER THE BY COLUMNS BUTTON OR THE BY ROWS BUTTON ON THE CHART TOOLBAR.

TO DRAG A PIECE FROM A PIE CHART:

1. CLICK THE CHART TO SELECT IT.
2. CLICK THE PIECE OF THE CHART YOU WANT TO MOVE.
3. CLICK AND DRAG THE PIECE AWAY FROM THE REST OF THE CHART.

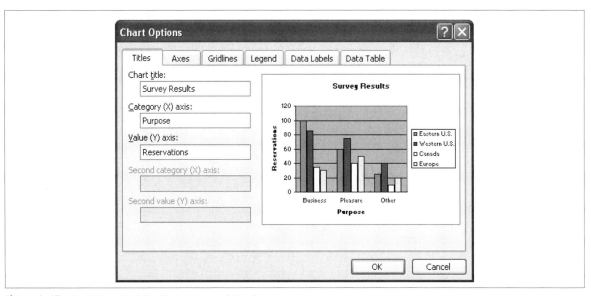

Figure 4-17. The Titles tab of the Chart Options dialog box.

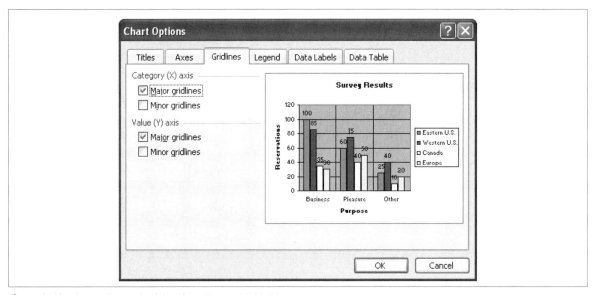

Figure 4-18. The Gridlines tab of the Chart Options dialog box.

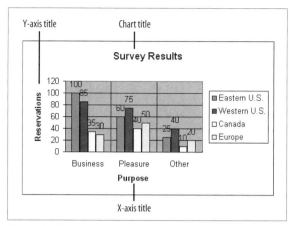

Figure 4-19. The Chart with value labels and gridlines added.

TIP *When you are changing Chart Types, checking the Default formatting check box removes any formatting you have applied to the chart and returns the chart to the default appearance.*

There are a lot of ways you can make a chart easier to read and understand. You can add titles to the chart's X-(horizontal) axis or Y-(vertical) axis, add gridlines, and add a legend. This lesson explains how to add and modify these items and how you can enhance your charts to make them easier to understand.

1 Make sure the chart is selected, then select Chart → Chart Type from the menu. Select the Column chart type from the Chart type list, click the Default formatting check box, and click OK.

The chart is changed from a pie chart to a column chart. Selecting the default formatting check box removes any previous formatting you've applied to the chart type and returns the chart to the default appearance. The selected chart changes from a pie chart to a column chart. Next, you need to change the data source for the chart.

2 Select Chart → Source Data from the menu, select the cell range A4:E7 (click the Collapse dialog button if you need to), and press Enter.

The column chart is updated to reflect the changes in the data source.

3 Select Chart → Chart Options from the menu and click the Titles tab.

The Titles tab of the Chart Options dialog box appears as shown in Figure 4-17. The chart title was removed when you applied the default formatting to the chart, so you will have to reenter it.

4 Click the Chart Title text box and type Survey Results.

Now add titles to the X- and Y-axis.

5 Click the Category (X) axis text box and type Purpose, then click the Value (Y) axis text box and type Reservations.

Next, add some data labels to the data series.

6 Click the Data Labels tab and check the Value option in the Labels Contains section.

The chart preview area displays a sample chart with the added data labels.

7 Click the Data Table tab and check both the Show data table and Show legend keys check boxes.

A data table displays the numbers on which the chart is based. Since you're working with an embedded chart (instead of a chart on a separate sheet) this information is already displayed in the worksheet, so you don't really need a data sheet. But, for practice's sake, try adding a data sheet.

8 Click OK.

The Chart Options dialog box closes and the chart is updated to reflect the changes you made. You can remove the data table since you don't need it.

Data Table button

9 Click the Data Table button on the Chart toolbar.

The data table disappears from the chart. Next, see how the chart will look if you add some gridlines.

10 Select Chart → Chart Options from the menu, click the Gridlines tab, and make sure the Major Gridlines check box is checked for the (Y) Axis and the (X) Axis (see Figure 4-18).

11 Click OK.

The Chart Options dialog box closes, and the chart reflects the changes you made, as shown in Figure 4-19.

QUICK REFERENCE

TO ADD OR REMOVE GRIDLINES FROM A CHART:

1. SELECT THE CHART, SELECT CHART → CHART OPTIONS FROM THE MENU, AND CLICK THE GRIDLINES TAB.

2. CHECK OR UNCHECK THE APPROPRIATE GRIDLINE CHECK BOXES.

TO ADD OR CHANGE TITLES OF A CHART:

1. SELECT THE CHART, SELECT CHART → CHART OPTIONS FROM THE MENU, AND CLICK THE TITLES TAB.

2. ENTER OR MODIFY THE TEXT IN THE TEXT BOXES THAT CORRESPOND TO THE DESIRED CHART TITLES.

TO ADD OR REMOVE A DATA TABLE:

1. CLICK THE DATA TABLE BUTTON ON THE CHART TOOLBAR.

    OR...

SELECT THE CHART, SELECT CHART → CHART OPTIONS FROM THE MENU, AND CLICK THE DATA TABLE TAB.

2. CHECK OR UNCHECK THE APPROPRIATE CHECK BOXES TO HIDE OR DISPLAY A DATA TABLE.

3. SELECT ONE OF THE PLACEMENT OPTIONS FOR THE LEGEND.

TO ADD OR REMOVE CHART DATA LABELS:

1. SELECT THE CHART, SELECT CHART → CHART OPTIONS FROM THE MENU, AND CLICK THE DATA LABELS TAB.

2. CHECK OR UNCHECK THE APPROPRIATE CHECK BOXES TO DISPLAY OR HIDE DATA LABELS.

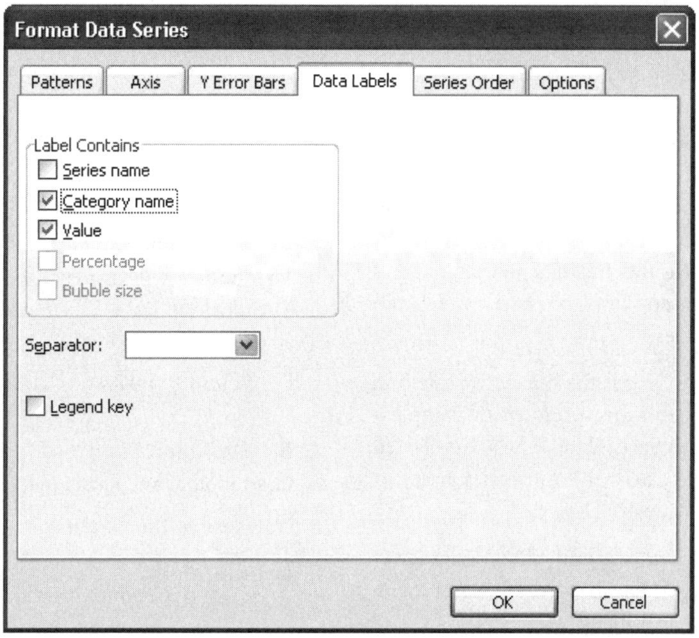

Figure 4-20. The Data Labels tab of the Format Data Series dialog box.

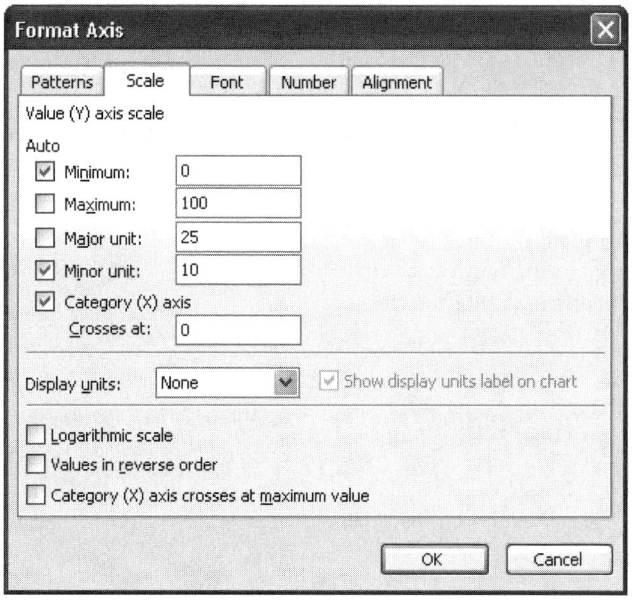

Figure 4-21. The Scale tab of the Format Axis dialog box.

You've already learned how to select and format objects in a chart—this lesson explores how to format two of the more tricky objects: a chart's data series and axis.

First, what exactly is a *data series*? A data series is a group on a chart that comes from the same row or column on a worksheet. Each data series in a chart has its own unique color or pattern. Most chart types can plot more than one data series in a chart at a time—such as the current column chart does, with the Business, Pleasure, and Other data series. One exception is pie charts, which can only plot a single data series.

So what is a chart *axis*? An axis is the line at the side of a chart that provides a scale of measurement or comparison in a chart. For most charts, data values are plotted along the value vertical (Y) axis, and categories are plotted along the horizontal category (X) axis.

Now that you (hopefully) understand what a data series and axis are, move to Step 1 to learn how to format them.

1 If necessary, open the workbook named Lesson 4C and save it as Survey Results.

2 Make sure the chart is selected, click the Chart Objects button list arrow on the Chart toolbar, and select Series "Eastern U.S."

Remember, if the Chart toolbar doesn't appear on your screen you can display it by selecting View → Toolbars → Chart from the menu.

Selection handles appear around each of the Eastern U.S. columns, indicating the series is selected. Once you select a chart element, you can format and change the element's settings.

Format Data Series button

3 Click the Format Data Series button on the Chart toolbar. Then click the Patterns tab.

The Format Data Series dialog box appears with the Patterns tab in front. Here you can change the color, texture, border, and other options of the selected data series.

4 Select a dark blue color.

This will format the columns in the Eastern U.S. data series with a dark blue color. You could also change the border or line color, style, and weight for the data series—or remove it altogether.

5 Click the Data Labels tab, check the Category name option, and click OK (see Figure 4-20).

This option will display a label above each category. The Format Data Series dialog box closes and the changes are made to the Eastern data series.

Here's how to format a chart's axis.

6 Click the Chart Objects button list arrow on the Chart toolbar and select the Value Axis.

Now format the Y-axis.

7 Click the Format Axis button and click the Scale tab.

When you create a chart, Excel automatically creates the scale of the chart. Ninety percent of the time you won't need to change a chart's default scale. For that other 10% of time, here's how you can enter your own values for the chart's scale:

8 Click in the Major unit text box and type 25. Click in the Maximum text box and type 100. Leave the Major unit and Maximum check boxes unchecked (see Figure 4-21).

This will adjust the scale of the chart.

9 Click OK.

The Format Axis dialog box closes and the changes are made to the Y-axis.

Since we looked only at a couple tabs in the Data Series dialog box, refer to Table 4-2 to see what those other tabs do.

Table 4-2. The Data Series Dialog Box Tabs

Tab	Description
Patterns	Changes a data series's colors, borders, and fill effects.
Axis	Allows you to plot the selected data series on a secondary axis—often used in combination charts.
Y Error Bars	Adds graphic bars that express the potential error (or degree of uncertainty) for each data marker in a series.
Data Labels	Adds value or data labels to the selected data series.
Series Order	Changes the order of the selected data series in the chart.
Options	Changes the width of all the data series in a chart and regulates whether the data series should overlap one another.

QUICK REFERENCE

TO ADD LABELS TO A DATA SERIES:

1. DOUBLE-CLICK THE DATA SERIES.

   OR...

   RIGHT-CLICK THE DATA SERIES AND SELECT SELECTED OBJECT FROM THE SHORTCUT MENU.

   OR...

   SELECT THE DATA SERIES AND SELECT FORMAT → SELECTED OBJECT FROM THE MENU.

2. CLICK THE DATA LABELS TAB AND SELECT THE APPROPRIATE OPTION.

TO CHANGE THE SCALE OF A CHART:

- DOUBLE-CLICK THE AXIS.

  OR...

- RIGHT-CLICK THE AXIS AND SELECT FORMAT AXIS FROM THE SHORTCUT MENU.

  OR...

- SELECT THE AXIS AND SELECT FORMAT → SELECTED OBJECT FROM THE MENU.

- CLICK THE SCALE TAB AND MAKE THE CHANGES TO THE SCALE.

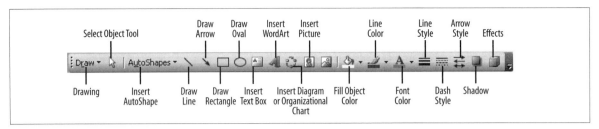

Figure 4-22. The Drawing toolbar.

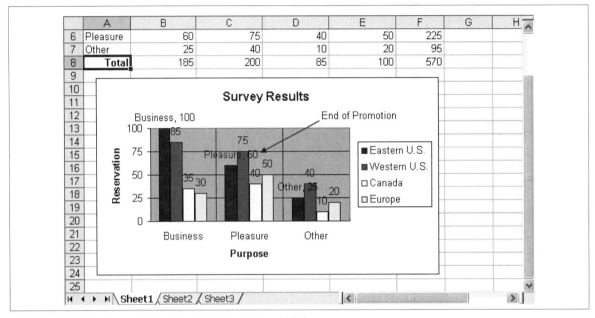

Figure 4-23. The chart with a text annotation and an arrow added.

Drawing button
Other Ways to View the Drawing Toolbar:
• Select **View→Toolbars→Drawing** from the menu.
• Right-click any toolbar and select **Drawing**

One of the best new features in Excel is the greatly improved drawing capabilities. You can easily annotate your charts and worksheets by adding lines, arrows, text boxes, and a huge variety of shapes. To use Excel's drawing capabilities, you need to use the Drawing toolbar which contains many tools for drawing shapes, lines, and arrows, and for formatting graphic objects with different coloring, shadow, and 3-D effect options.

Although we'll be using Excel's drawing features to annotate a chart in this lesson, you can also draw on worksheets to enhance them with arrows, text, and shapes.

1 Click the Drawing button on the Standard toolbar.

The Drawing toolbar appears, as shown in Figure 4-22. The Drawing toolbar gives you several tools you can use to add text, lines, and graphics to charts and worksheets.

Text Box button

2 Click the Text Box button on the Drawing toolbar.

The pointer changes to a ↓, indicating you can click and enter a caption or callout in the chart or worksheet.

3 Click to the right and slightly below the chart title with the ↓ pointer and type End of Promotion, as shown in Figure 4-23.

Go to the next step to add an arrow to the annotation.

Arrow button

4 Click the Arrow button on the Drawing toolbar.

This time the pointer changes to a +.

5 Move the + pointer to the left of the End of Promotion text, click and hold down the mouse button, drag the line to the Pleasure columns, and release the mouse button.

Compare your chart with the one in Figure 4-23. You won't need the drawing toolbar any more in this chapter, so here's how to get rid of it.

6 Click the Drawing button on the Standard toolbar.

The Drawing toolbar disappears.

7 Save your work.

Although we didn't cover every tool on the Drawing toolbar, the procedure for using each of them is the same. Remember that you can use the Drawing toolbar to add lines, arrows, shapes, and text boxes to both your charts *and* worksheets.

QUICK REFERENCE

TO VIEW THE DRAWING TOOLBAR:

- CLICK THE 🔲 DRAWING BUTTON ON THE STANDARD TOOLBAR.

  OR...

- SELECT VIEW → TOOLBARS → DRAWING FROM THE MENU.

TO DRAW AN OBJECT:

1. CLICK THE OBJECT YOU WANT TO DRAW ON THE DRAWING TOOLBAR (SUCH AS A LINE OR CIRCLE).
2. DRAG THE CROSSHAIR POINTER TO DRAW THE OBJECT.

TO RESIZE AN OBJECT:

1. CLICK THE OBJECT TO SELECT IT.
2. DRAG THE OBJECT'S SIZING HANDLES TO RESIZE IT.

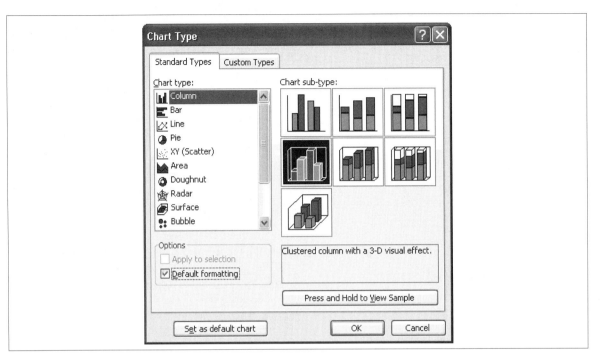

Figure 4-24. Selecting a 3-D column chart in the Chart Type dialog box.

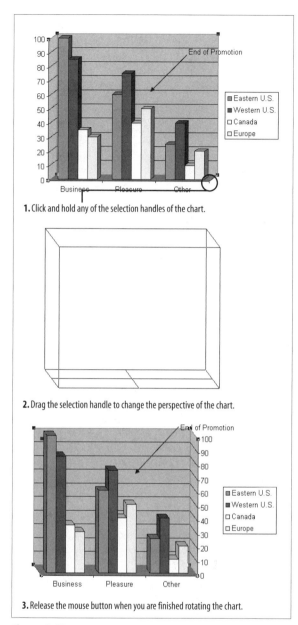

1. Click and hold any of the selection handles of the chart.

2. Drag the selection handle to change the perspective of the chart.

3. Release the mouse button when you are finished rotating the chart.

Figure 4-25. The steps in rotating a chart.

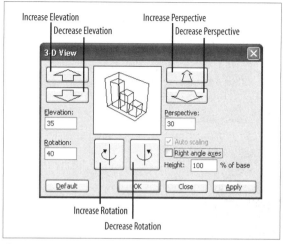

Figure 4-26. The 3-D View dialog box.

Three-dimensional (3-D) charts are some of the coolest-looking charts, but they don't always display their information correctly. The data in 3-D charts is often obscured by another data series. This lesson explains how you can rotate and elevate a 3-D chart to make sure everything is visible. There are two methods you can use to change the rotation and elevation of a 3-D chart:

- **Use the 3-D View Dialog box:** Using the 3-D View dialog box (which you can find by selecting Chart → 3-D View from the menu) lets you rotate a 3-D chart with a high degree of precision.

- **Use the Mouse:** Using the mouse is a quick method of rotating a 3-D chart, but it can be tricky and requires a lot of "mouse dexterity."

This lesson explains how to rotate a 3-D chart using both methods.

1 Make sure the chart is selected and select Chart → Chart Type from the menu.

The Chart Type dialog box appears, as shown in Figure 4-24.

2 Select the Clustered column with a 3-D visual effect, as shown in Figure 4-24, and then click the Default formatting check box to select it.

The Default formatting check box will remove any formatting you've applied to the chart and will return the chart to the default appearance.

3 Click OK.

The chart type is changed to a 3-D clustered column. Here's how to rotate the chart using the mouse:

4 Click the Chart Object list arrow on the Chart toolbar and select Corners.

Selection handles appear on the corners of the chart. Now you can rotate the 3-D chart by clicking and dragging any of the selection handles.

5 Position the pointer over the lower-right corner selection handle of the chart, click and hold the left mouse button, drag the chart down and to the right an inch, as shown in Figure 4-25, then release the mouse button.

Compare your chart with the one in Figure 4-25. Another way to rotate 3-D charts is with the 3-D View command on the Chart menu.

6 Select Chart → 3-D View from the menu.

The 3-D View dialog box appears, as shown in Figure 4-26. The 3-D View dialog box lets you rotate a 3-D chart with a high degree of precision. Before you rotate the chart, however, return it to its original position.

7 Click Default.

The chart is reset to its original position.

Increase Elevation button

8 Click the Increase Elevation button four times, until the Elevation textbox reads 35.

This will change the elevation of the chart. Notice how the preview section displays how the chart will look in the new position.

Increase Rotation button

9 Click the Increase Rotation button two times, until the Rotate textbox reads 40, then click Apply.

The charted is formatted with the new rotation and elevation settings.

10 Click Close and save your work.

QUICK REFERENCE

TO ROTATE A 3-D CHART:

1. SELECT THE CHART AND SELECT CHART → 3-D VIEW FROM THE MENU.

2. MAKE THE ROTATION AND PERSPECTIVE CHANGES IN THE 3-D VIEW DIALOG BY CLICKING THE APPROPRIATE CONTROLS AND CLICK OK.

OR...

1. SELECT THE CHART.

2. DRAG THE CHART'S SELECTION HANDLES.

Selecting and Saving a Custom Chart

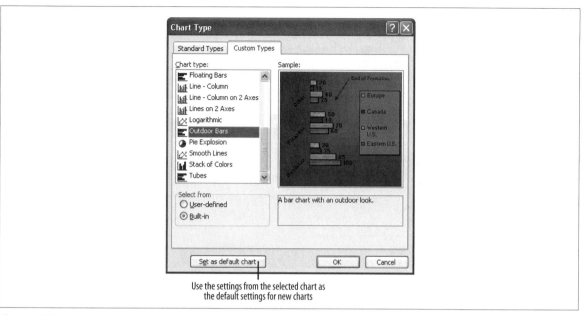

Use the settings from the selected chart as
the default settings for new charts

Figure 4-27. The Custom Types tab of the Chart Type dialog box.

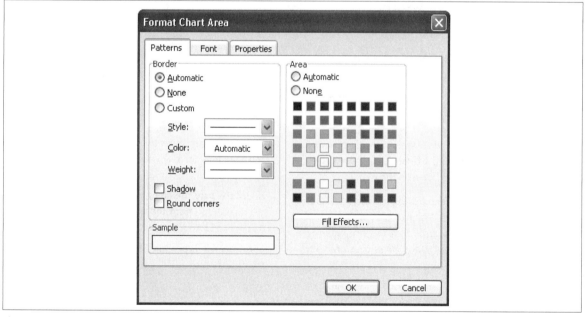

Figure 4-28. The Patterns tab of the Format Chart Area dialog box.

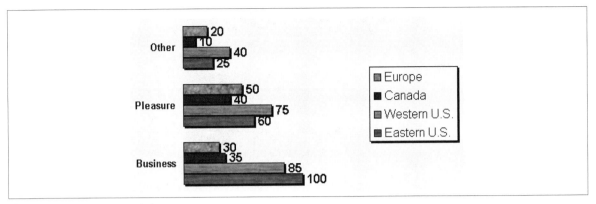

Figure 4-29. The reformatted chart.

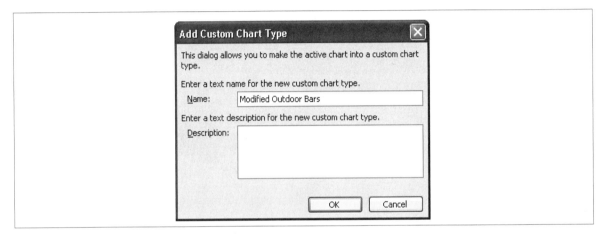

Figure 4-30. The Add Custom Chart Type dialog box.

So far in this chapter, you have worked with *standard charts*. You can also create and work with *custom charts*. Here are the basic differences between the two:

- **Standard Chart Type:** Standard charts include standard, simple formatting and chart options. You must add additional formatting and chart options, such as data labels and colors you want to appear in your chart. You can't save your own standard chart types.

- **Custom Chart Type:** A Custom chart is similar to a template or style and contains additional formatting and chart options, such as a legend, gridlines, data labels, colors, and patterns for various chart items. You can save custom charts, so you can create new charts based on a custom chart's formatting and options, saving a lot of time.

This lesson will give you practice creating and saving a custom chart type.

1 If necessary, open the workbook named Lesson 4D and save it as Survey Results.

2 Make sure the chart is selected, then select Chart → Chart Type from the menu and then click the Custom Types tab.

The Custom Types tab of the Chart Type dialog box appears, as shown in Figure 4-27.

Chart Objects list

3 Scroll down the Chart types list and select Outdoor Bars, as shown in Figure 4-27, and click OK.

The chart is updated with the Outdoor Bars custom chart settings. The green color of the chart is difficult to read, so you decide to change it.

4 Click the Chart Objects List Arrow on the Chart toolbar and select the Chart Area.

Now you can format the chart area.

Format Chart button

5 Click the Format Chart Area button on the Chart toolbar. Select the light yellow color from the Area section of the Patterns tab, as shown in Figure 4-28, and click OK.

The chart area is reformatted with the light yellow color you selected. Next, remove the green coloring from the chart's legend.

6 Double-click the chart's legend.

7 Select None from the Area section of the Patterns tab, and click OK.

The green fill color for the legend disappears.

8 Click the Chart Objects List Arrow on the Chart toolbar, select the Chart Area, and click the Format Chart Area button on the Chart toolbar.

You can also double-click the chart area to format it, it's sometimes tricky to know *where* exactly to double-click for some chart objects.

9 Click the Font tab, make sure Regular is selected from the Font style list and click OK.

The bold font formatting disappears from the chart title. Compare your chart with the one in Figure 4-29. You can save the current chart as a custom chart type, so you can quickly apply the formatting and options used in the current chart to other charts.

10 Select Chart → Chart Type from the menu, click the Custom Types tab, click the User-defined option under the Select from section, and click Add.

The Add Custom Chart Type dialog box appears, as shown in Figure 4-30. You must give your custom chart type a name, and if you want, a description.

11 In the Name text box, type Modified Outdoor Bars and click OK.

The formatting and options for the current chart have been saved as a user-defined custom chart named Modified Outdoor Bars. You can format a chart using the Modified Outdoor Bars settings by: selecting Chart → Chart Type from the menu; clicking the Custom Types tab and selecting the "User-defined" option under the "Select from" section; clicking the Modified Outdoors Bars; and then clicking OK.

12 Click OK.

The Chart Type dialog box closes. You can delete any custom charts you don't need.

13 Select Chart → Chart Type from the menu, click the Custom Types tab, and click the User-defined option under the "Select from" section.

14 Select the Modified Outdoor Bars custom chart, click Delete, and click OK to confirm the deletion. Click Cancel to close the dialog box.

To change the default chart type, select the chart you want to use as the default chart, select Chart → Chart Type from the menu, and click the "Set as default" chart button.

QUICK REFERENCE

TO CREATE A CUSTOM CHART:

1. EITHER CREATE OR OPEN A CHART THAT IS FORMATTED AND CUSTOMIZED THE WAY YOU WANT.

2. SELECT THE CHART, SELECT CHART → CHART TYPE FROM THE MENU, AND CLICK THE CUSTOM TAB.

3. CLICK THE USER-DEFINED OPTION AND CLICK ADD TO CREATE A CUSTOM CHART BASED ON THE CURRENT CHART.

4. ENTER A NAME AND DESCRIPTION FOR THE CUSTOM CHART AND CLICK OK.

TO CHANGE THE DEFAULT CHART TYPE:

1. EITHER CREATE OR OPEN A CHART THAT IS FORMATTED AND CUSTOMIZED THE WAY YOU WANT.

2. SELECT THE CHART, SELECT CHART → CHART TYPE FROM THE MENU, AND CLICK THE SET AS DEFAULT CHART BUTTON.

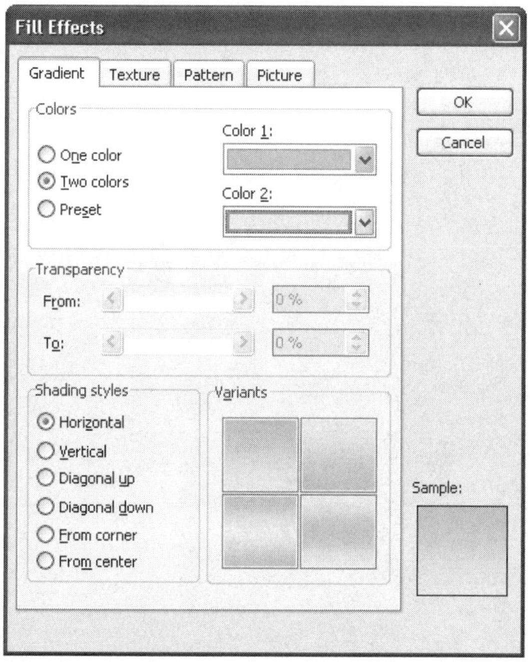

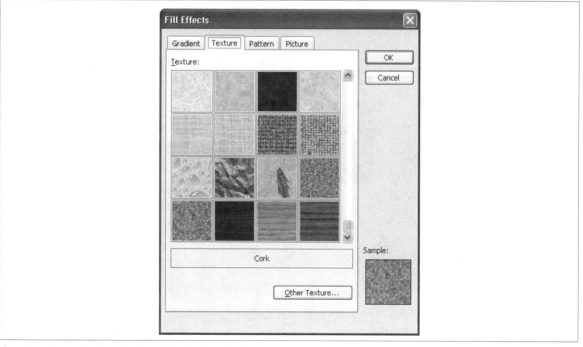

Figure 4-31. The Gradient tab of the Fill Effects dialog box.

Figure 4-32. The Texture tab of the Fill Effects dialog box.

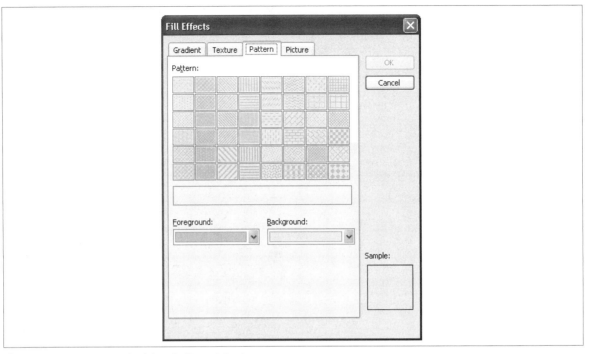

Figure 4–33. The Pattern tab of the Fill Effects dialog box.

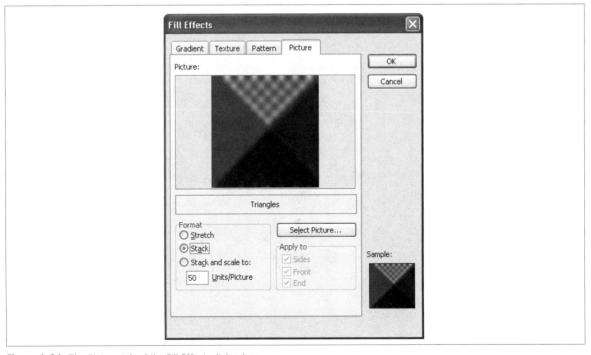

Figure 4–34. The Picture tab of the Fill Effects dialog box.

You can change the fill pattern used in chart objects to produce dramatic and eye-catching effects. You can change the fill patterns for the Chart Area, the Plot Area, and any columns, bars, or similar plot areas in a chart. This lesson explains how to do just that.

Format Object button
Other Ways to Format an Object:
• Double-click the object.
• Right-click the object and select **Format Object** from the shortcut menu.
• Click the object to select it and select **Format→ Selected Object** from the menu.

1 Make sure the chart is selected, click the Chart Objects List Arrow on the Chart toolbar, and select the Chart Area.

You can also double-click the chart area (if you know what it is!) to modify it. Now that you have selected the chart area, you can format it.

2 Click the Format Object button on the Chart toolbar and click the Patterns tab.

The Format Chart Area dialog box appears with the Patterns tab in front (Table 4-3 shows examples of types of fill patterns). Notice the area section contains a color palette that you can use to fill the selected object. When you want to use more dramatic fill effects to color an object than an ordinary color, click the Fill Effects button.

3 Click the Fill Effects and then click the Gradient tab.

The Fill Effects dialog box opens with the Gradient tab in front.

4 Click the Two colors option in the Colors section.

This indicates that you want to fill the background of the chart using a two-color gradient. You need to select the two colors you want to use in the fill pattern.

5 Click the Color 1 list arrow, select a bright green color, then click the Color 2 list and click the light green color, as shown in Figure 4-31.

Next, you need to select a shading style.

6 Select the Horizontal option under the Shading Styles section.

Notice the sample area in the lower right side of the dialog box previews how your gradient options will look.

7 Click OK to close the Fill Effect dialog box, then click OK to close the Format Chart Area dialog box.

The chart area is formatted with the two-color gradient you selected. Move on to the next step and format the Europe data series with another custom fill effect.

8 Click the Chart Objects list arrow on the Chart toolbar, select the Series "Europe" and click the Format button on the Chart toolbar. Click the Fill Effects button, then click the Picture tab.

The Fill Effects dialog box opens, with the Picture tab in front, as shown in Figure 4-34. The Picture tab lets you use a picture or graphic as the fill for the selected object.

9 Click Select Picture.

The Select Picture dialog box appears. You must specify the location and name of the picture or graphic you want to use to fill the data series.

10 Navigate to your practice folder or disk, select the Triangles file, and click Insert.

This will insert the Triangles graphic file as the fill object for the Europe data series. Notice the sample area in the lower right side of the dialog box, which previews what the picture or graphic looks like.

11 Under the Format section, select Stack and click OK to close the Fill Effect dialog box, then click OK again to close the Format Data Series dialog box.

The Europe data series is formatted with the Triangle pictures as the fill.

12 Save your changes and close the workbook.

Believe it or not, by learning how to use fill patterns, you've learned a formatting trick that probably less than five percent of all Excel users know. You should feel proud of yourself!

Table 4-3. Types of Fill Patterns

Fill Pattern Tab	Example	Description
Gradient		Fills objects with a two-color gradient
Texture		Fills objects with a texture
Pattern		Fills objects with a pattern
Picture		Fills objects with a graphic or picture file

QUICK REFERENCE

TO ADD FILL EFFECTS:

• DOUBLE-CLICK THE CHART OBJECT.

OR...

1. SELECT THE OBJECT AND CLICK THE FORMAT BUTTON ON THE CHART TOOLBAR.

2. CLICK THE PATTERNS TAB AND CLICK THE FILL EFFECTS BUTTON.

3. SELECT ONE OF THE FOUR TABS, SELECT A FILL EFFECT, AND CLICK OK.

Lesson Summary

Creating a Chart

To Create a Chart with the Chart Wizard: Select the cell range that contains the data you want to chart, and click the Chart Wizard button on the Standard toolbar or select Insert → Chart from the menu. Then, select the chart type and click Next. Next, verify (or change) the cell range used in the chart and click Next. Then, adjust the chart options by clicking the categorized tabs and selecting any options, then click Next. Finally, specify where you want to place the chart (as an embedded object or on a new sheet) and click Finish.

Moving and Resizing a Chart

To Resize a Chart: Click the chart to select it, then drag its sizing handles (located along the edges of the chart) until the chart is the size you want.

To Move a Chart: Click and hold down the mouse button on the blank area around a chart, drag the picture to a new location in the workbook, then release the mouse button.

Formatting and Editing Objects in a Chart

To Select a Chart Object: Click the object or click the [▾] Chart Objects list arrow on the Chart toolbar and select the object.

To Format a Chart Object: Double-click the object or select the object and click the Format Object button on the Chart toolbar. You can also format a chart object by right-clicking the object and selecting Format Object from the shortcut menu.

Changing a Chart's Source Data

To Change a Chart's Data Source: Select Chart → Source Data from the menu and click the Data Range tab. Click in the Data Range box and select the cell range on which you want to base the chart (click the Collapse Dialog box button if necessary), then click OK.

The [icon] Collapse Dialog button temporarily shrinks and moves the dialog box so that you enter a cell range by selecting cells in the worksheet. When you finish, you can click the button again or press Enter to display the entire dialog box.

To Use Nonadjacent Cell Ranges in a Chart: Press and hold the Ctrl key while you select additional cells.

Changing a Chart Type and Working with Pie Charts

The most common types of charts are column, bar, line, area, pie, and scatter.

To Change the Chart Type: Click the Chart Type list arrow on the Chart toolbar or select Chart → Chart Type from the menu.

To Chart by Rows or Columns: Click either the By Columns button or the By Rows button on the Chart toolbar.

To Drag a Piece from a Pie Chart: Click the chart to select it, click the piece of the chart you want to move, then drag the piece away from the rest of the chart.

Adding Titles, Gridlines, and a Data Table

To Add or Remove Gridlines from a Chart: Select Chart → Chart Options from the menu and click the Gridlines tab. Check or uncheck the appropriate gridline check boxes.

To Add or Change a Chart's Titles to a Chart: Select Chart → Chart Options from the menu and click the Titles tab. Enter or modify the text in the text boxes that correspond to the desired chart titles.

To Add or Remove a Data Table: Click the Data Table button on the Chart toolbar.

To Add or Remove Chart Data Labels: Select Chart → Chart Options from the menu, and click the Data Labels tab. Check or uncheck the appropriate check boxes to display or the chart hide data labels.

Formatting a Data Series and a Chart Axis

A data series is a group on a chart that comes from a row or column on a worksheet. An axis is a line that borders one side of a chart that provides a scale of measurement or comparison in a chart. For most charts, data values are plotted along the value (Y) axis, which is usually vertical, and categories are plotted along the category (X) axis, which is usually horizontal.

To Add Labels to a Data Series: Double-click the data series, or select the data series and select Format → Selected Object from the menu. Click the Data Labels tab and select the appropriate option.

To Change the Scale of a Chart: Double-click the axis; or right-click the axis and select Format Axis from the shortcut menu; or select the axis and select Format → Selected Object from the menu. Click the Scale tab and make the changes to the scale.

Annotating a Chart

To View the Drawing Toolbar: Click the Drawing button on the Standard toolbar or select View → Toolbars → Drawing from the menu.

To Draw an Object: Click the object you want to draw on the drawing toolbar, such as a line or circle, and drag the crosshair pointer to draw the object.

To Resize an Object: Select the object and drag its sizing handles to resize it.

Working with 3-D Charts

To Rotate a 3-D Chart: Select the chart and select Chart → 3-D View from the menu. Make the rotation and perspective changes in the 3-D View dialog by clicking the appropriate controls and then click OK.

Selecting and Saving a Custom Chart

A Custom chart contains formatting and options you specify, such as legends, gridlines, data labels, and formatting options. You can save custom charts, so you can create new charts based on a custom chart's formatting and options.

To Create a Custom Chart: Either create or open a chart that is formatted and customized the way you want. Select the chart, select Chart → Chart Type from the menu, and click the Custom tab. Click the User-defined option and click Add to create a custom chart based on the current chart. Enter a name and description for the custom chart and click OK.

To Change the Default Chart Type: Either create or open a chart that is formatted and customized the way you want; or select the chart, select Chart → Chart Type from the menu, and click the Set as default chart button.

Using Fill Effects

To Add Fill Effects: Double-click the chart object or select the object and click the Format button on the Chart toolbar. Click the Patterns tab and click the Fill Effects button. Select one of the four tabs, select a fill effect, and click OK.

Quiz

1. All of the following statements about charts are true except...

   A. You can place a chart on the same sheets as the data or on a new worksheet.

   B. To create a chart, select Tools → Chart from the menu.

   C. You can move a chart by clicking it and dragging it by the blank area around the chart to its new location.

   D. You can resize a chart by clicking it and dragging its sizing handles.

2. You want to track the progress of the stock market on a daily basis. Which type of chart should you use?

   A. Line chart

   B. Column chart

   C. Row chart

   D. Pie chart

3. All of the following are methods to edit or format a chart object except...

   A. Double-clicking the object.

   B. Right-clicking the object and selecting Format from the shortcut menu.

C. Selecting the object from the Chart Object list on the Chart toolbar and clicking the Format Object button.

D. Selecting Chart → Format from the menu, selecting the object from the Object list, and clicking Format.

4. Which of the following statements is NOT true?

A. You can change the cells that are plotted in a chart by selecting the new cells and clicking the Chart Wizard button on the Standard toolbar.

B. When you change the chart type, all its formatting options will always transfer perfectly to the new type of chart.

C. Holding down the Ctrl lets you select cell ranges that are not next to each other.

D. You can change the cells that are plotted in a chart by selecting Chart → Source Data from the menu and selecting the new cells.

5. The Drawing toolbar can only be used to annotate charts. (True or False?)

6. All of the following statements are true except…

A. You can change the perspective of 3-D charts by selecting Chart → 3-D View from the menu.

B. A Standard chart lets you save your chart formatting and settings, so you can create new charts using the same settings.

C. To add or remove a legend from a chart, click the Legend button on the Chart toolbar.

D. Many Excel dialog boxes have several Collapse Dialog box buttons, which you can use to temporarily shrink the dialog box to select cells.

7. The categories at the bottom of a chart are also called the…

A. X-axis

B. Y-axis

C. Z-axis

D. Category axis

8. Charts cannot be moved or resized once they have been created. (True or False?)

9. How can you open the Chart Options dialog box?

A. Click the Chart Options button on the Standard toolbar.

B. Quadruple-click any chart.

C. Select Chart → Chart Options from the menu.

D. Select Tools → Chart Options from the menu.

10. Which of the following are objects that you can add to an Excel chart? (Select all that apply.)

A. A legend

B. A data table

C. An category or x-axis title

D. Data labels

Homework

1. Open the Homework 4 workbook and save it as "Chart Practice."

2. What type of chart do you think would work best to present the information in this worksheet?

3. Use the Chart Wizard to create a chart that plots the cell range A3:E7. Give the chart the Chart Title "Package Sales" and place the chart in a separate sheet.

4. Click the legend to select it and change the font size used in the legend to 12 pt.

5. Make the legend taller by about 1/2 inch, and drag it to the bottom right of the chart.

6. Change the chart type to a 3-D Bar chart.

7. Change the color of the Vancouver color series to light green.

8. Use the drawing toolbar to add an arrow that points to the largest number in the chart (Montreal in the fourth quarter) and add a textbox at the other end of the arrow that says "Wow!"

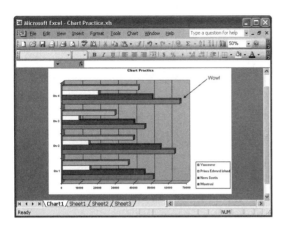

9. Change the chart's data source so that only the totals for each tour (cell range F4:F7) are plotted in the chart.

Quiz Answers

1. B. Create a chart by clicking the Chart Wizard button on the Standard toolbar or by selecting Insert → Chart from the menu.

2. A. Line charts are used to illustrate trends. If you used the other three chart types to track the stock market, there would be too many data points.

3. D. Format is not an option under the Chart menu.

4. A. Change a chart's source data by selecting the chart and selecting Chart → Source Data from the menu.

5. True. You can annotate charts and worksheets with the Drawing toolbar.

6. B. Custom charts, not Standard charts, allow you to save your chart formatting and settings so you can create new charts using the same settings.

7. A. The categories at the bottom of a chart are also known as the X-axis.

8. False. You can easily move or resize any chart in Excel.

9. C. Select Chart → Chart Options from the menu to open the Chart Options dialog box.

10. A, B, C, and D. All of these are types of objects that you can add to an Excel chart.

CHAPTER 5
MANAGING YOUR WORKBOOKS

CHAPTER OBJECTIVES:

Navigate between the sheets in a workbook

Insert, delete, rename, and move worksheets

Work with several worksheets and workbooks

Split and freeze a window

Add headers, footers, and page numbers to a worksheet

Specify what gets printed and where the page breaks

Adjust the margins, page size and orientation, and print scale

Protect and hide a worksheet

Create and use a template

Consolidate multiple worksheets

CHAPTER TASK: WORK WITH A WEEKLY SUMMARY REPORT

Prerequisites

- **Understand how to use menus, toolbars, dialog boxes, and shortcut keystrokes**
- **Understand how to open and save workbooks**
- **Understand how to enter values and labels**
- **Understand how to reference cells**

Financial and numeric information often does not fit on a single page. For example, a business's financial statement usually has several pages: an expense page, an income page, a cash-flow page, and so on. Similarly, Excel's workbooks contain several worksheets. New workbooks automatically contain three blank worksheets, but you can easily add more.

Up until now, you have only worked with a single *worksheet*. In this chapter, you will learn how to work with and manage *workbooks*. You'll learn how to move between the worksheets, add, rename, move, and delete worksheets, and create formulas that reference information from several different worksheets. Along the way, you'll learn a lot more about printing as well.

Switching Between Sheets in a Workbook

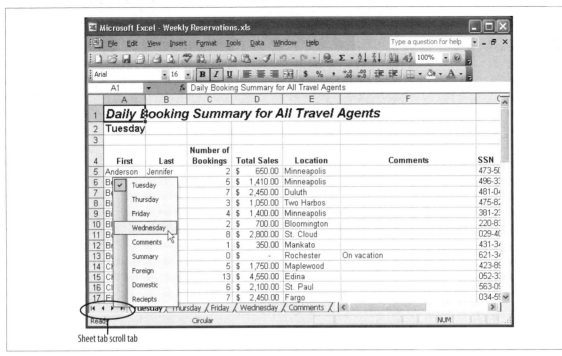

Figure 5-1. The sheet tab scroll buttons.

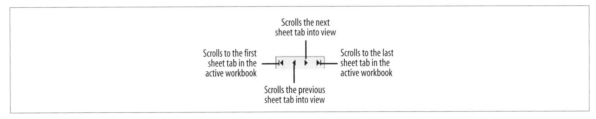

Figure 5-2. Right-click any of the tab scroll buttons to display a menu of sheets.

This lesson covers the basics of working with worksheets—namely how to move between them. Each worksheet has a tab that appears near the bottom of the workbook window. To switch to a different sheet, all you have to do is click its tab. Easy, huh? When there are too many tabs in a workbook to display them all, you can scroll through the worksheet tabs by clicking the scroll tab buttons, located at the bottom of the screen near the worksheet tabs.

1 Start Microsoft Excel.

2 Open the Lesson 5A workbook and save it as Weekly Reservations.

Excel saves the worksheet in a new file with the name "Weekly Reservations." This workbook contains several worksheets. It's easy to switch between the various worksheets in a workbook: simply click the worksheet's sheet tab. Move on to the next step and try it!

3 Click the Friday tab.

The Friday worksheet appears in front. You can tell the Friday worksheet is active because its sheet tab appears white. Once a worksheet is active, you can edit it using any of the techniques you already know.

4 Practice viewing the various worksheets in the workbook by clicking the worksheet tabs.

You may have noticed by now that there is not enough room to display all of the sheet tabs. Whenever this happens, you must use the tab scrolling buttons to scroll through the sheet tabs until the tab you want appears. Figure 5-2 describes the function of the various Tab Scrolling buttons.

5 Click the Next Tab Scroll button until the Summary tab appears.

6 Click the Summary tab.

The Summary sheet tab becomes active and its sheet tab changes from gray to white.

7 Click the First Tab Scroll button to move to the first sheet tab (Tuesday) in the workbook.

You can also switch between worksheets by using a right mouse button shortcut menu.

8 Right-click any of the Tab Scroll buttons.

Excel displays a shortcut menu listing the sheets in the current workbook, as shown in Figure 5-1.

9 Select Wednesday from the shortcut menu.

QUICK REFERENCE

TO ACTIVATE A WORKSHEET:

- CLICK THE SHEET TAB AT THE BOTTOM OF THE SCREEN.

   OR...

- RIGHT-CLICK THE SHEET TAB SCROLL BUTTONS AND SELECT THE WORKSHEET FROM THE SHORTCUT MENU.

TO SCROLL THROUGH WORKSHEETS IN A WORKBOOK:

- CLICK THE CORRESPONDING SCROLL SHEET TABS AT THE BOTTOM OF THE SCREEN.

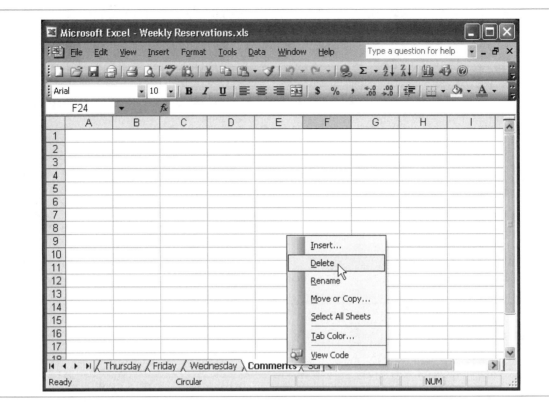

Figure 5-3. Deleting a selected worksheet.

Figure 5-4. Delete confirmation dialog box.

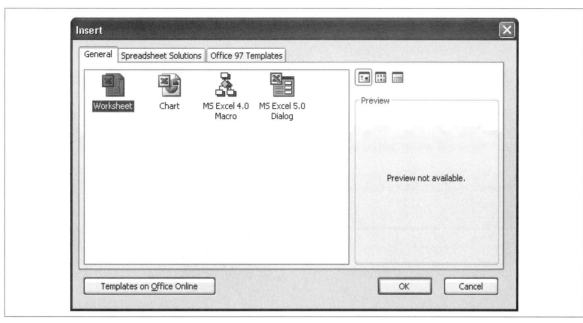

Figure 5-5. The Insert dialog box.

An Excel workbook contains three blank worksheets by default. You can easily add and delete worksheets to and from a workbook, which you'll learn how to do in this lesson.

1 Right-click the Comments tab.

A shortcut menu appears with commands to insert, delete, rename, move or copy, select all sheets, or view the Visual Basic code in a workbook, as shown in Figure 5-3.

2 Select Delete from the shortcut menu.

A dialog box appears warning you that the selected sheet will be permanently deleted, as shown in Figure 5-4.

3 Click Delete to confirm the worksheet deletion.

The Comments worksheet is deleted from the workbook.

4 Delete the Foreign, Domestic, Receipts, and Summary sheets from the workbook.

There are several worksheets that you need to add to the Weekly Reservations workbook—a worksheet for Monday's reservations and another to summarize the entire week. Inserting a new worksheet to a workbook is just as easy as deleting one.

5 Select Insert → Worksheet from the menu.

Excel inserts a new worksheet tab labeled Sheet1 to the left of the selected sheet. You can also insert worksheets using a right mouse button shortcut menu.

6 Right-click any of the sheet tabs and select Insert from the shortcut menu.

The Insert dialog box appears, as shown in Figure 5-5.

7 Verify that the Worksheet option is selected and click OK.

Excel inserts another worksheet tab labeled Sheet2 to the left of the Sheet1.

8 Save your work.

QUICK REFERENCE

TO ADD A NEW WORKSHEET:

*   RIGHT-CLICK ON A SHEET TAB, SELECT INSERT FROM THE SHORTCUT MENU, AND SELECT WORKSHEET FROM THE INSERT DIALOG BOX.

    OR...

*   SELECT INSERT → WORKSHEET FROM THE MENU.

TO DELETE A WORKSHEET:

*   RIGHT-CLICK ON THE SHEET TAB AND SELECT DELETE FROM THE SHORTCUT MENU.

    OR...

*   SELECT EDIT → DELETE SHEET FROM THE MENU.

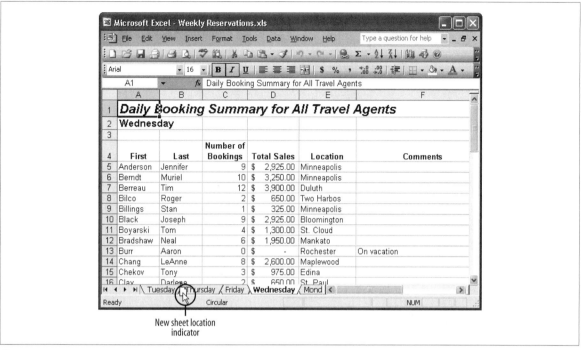

Figure 5-6. Moving a worksheet to a different location in a workbook.

Worksheets are given the rather boring and meaningless default names Sheet1, Sheet2, Sheet3, and so on. By the end of this lesson, you will know how to change a sheet's name to something more meaningful, such as "Budget" instead of "Sheet3".

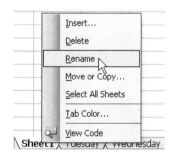

Renaming a Worksheet tab
Other Ways to Rename a Worksheet:
• Right-click the worksheet and select **Rename** from the shortcut menu.

Another important worksheet skill you'll learn in this lesson is how to move worksheets, so you can rearrange the order of worksheets in a workbook. Let's get started!

1 **Double-click the** Sheet1 tab.

The Sheet1 text is selected, indicating you can rename the worksheet. Worksheet names can contain up to 31 characters, including punctuation and spacing.

2 **Type** Monday **and press** Enter.

The name of the selected worksheet tab changes from Sheet1 to Monday. Move on to the next step to rename Sheet2.

3 **Rename the** Sheet2 **tab** Summary.

You have probably already noticed that the sheets in this workbook are out of order. Rearranging the order of sheets in a workbook is very easy and straightforward: simply drag and drop the sheets to a new location.

4 **Click and drag the** Wednesday tab **after the** Tuesday tab.

As you drag the Wednesday sheet, notice that the mouse pointer indicates where the sheet will be relocated, as shown in Figure 5-6.

TIP *You can copy a worksheet by holding down the Ctrl key while you drag the sheet to a new location.*

5 Drag the Summary sheet **after the** Friday sheet.

6 Drag the Monday sheet **in front of the** Tuesday sheet.

7 Save your work.

Working with worksheets is really quite easy isn't it? One more thing: instead of moving a worksheet, you can also copy it by pressing the Ctrl key as you drag the worksheet tab.

QUICK REFERENCE

TO RENAME A WORKSHEET:

- RIGHT-CLICK THE SHEET TAB, SELECT RENAME FROM THE SHORTCUT MENU, AND ENTER A NEW NAME FOR THE WORKSHEET.

    OR...

- DOUBLE-CLICK THE SHEET TAB AND ENTER A NEW NAME FOR THE WORKSHEET.

    OR...

- SELECT FORMAT → SHEET → RENAME FROM THE MENU, AND ENTER A NEW NAME FOR THE WORKSHEET.

TO MOVE A WORKSHEET:

- CLICK AND DRAG THE SHEET TAB TO THE DESIRED LOCATION.

    OR...

- SELECT EDIT → MOVE OR COPY SHEET FROM THE MENU, THEN SELECT THE WORKSHEET AND LOCATION WHERE YOU WANT TO MOVE THE WORKSHEET.

TO COPY A WORKSHEET:

- HOLD DOWN THE CTRL KEY WHILE YOU CLICK AND DRAG THE SHEET TAB TO ITS DESIRED LOCATION.

    OR...

- SELECT EDIT → MOVE OR COPY SHEET FROM THE MENU, THEN SELECT THE WORKSHEET AND LOCATION WHERE YOU WANT TO MOVE THE WORKSHEET.

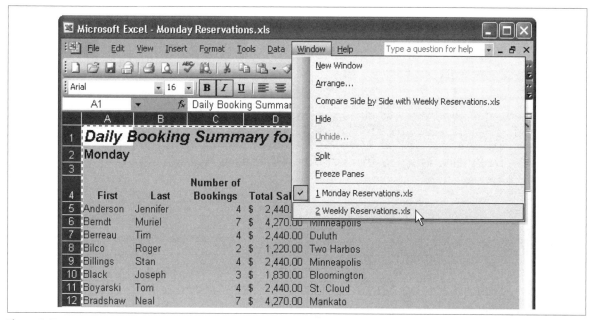

Figure 5-7. Moving between workbook files using the Window menu.

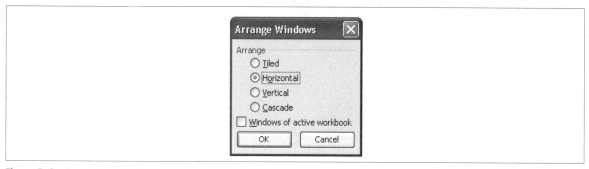

Figure 5-8. The Arrange Windows dialog box.

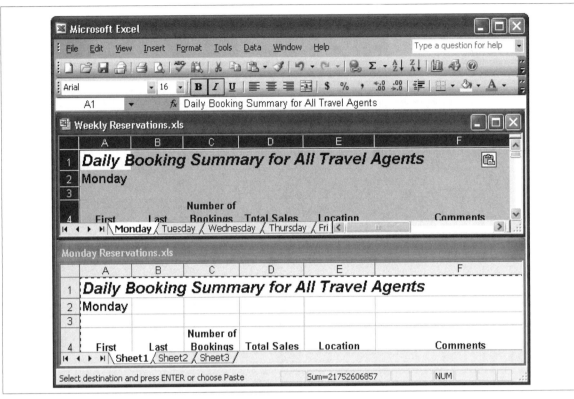

Figure 5-9. Viewing two workbook files in horizontal windows.

One of the benefits of Excel (and many other Windows programs) is that you can open and work with several files at once. Each workbook you open in Excel gets its own window. This lesson explains how to open and work with more than one workbook at a time. You will also learn some tricks on sizing and arranging windows.

1 If necessary, open the workbook named Lesson 5B and save it as Weekly Reservations.

2 Open the Monday Reservations workbook.

The workbook Monday Reservations appears. The Weekly Reservations workbook is also open, you just can't see it because the Monday Reservations workbook occupies the entire worksheet window area. To move back to the Weekly Reservations workbook, use the Window menu command. Before you return to the Weekly Reservations workbook, you need to copy the reservation information for Monday.

Click to select all the cells in a worksheet

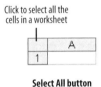

Select All button

3 Click the Select All button on Sheet1 to select the entire sheet, then click the Copy button on the Standard toolbar to copy the entire worksheet.

Now that the entire worksheet is copied, you need to move back to the Weekly Reservations file to paste the information.

Copy button

4 Select Window from the menu.

The Window menu appears, as shown in Figure 5-7. The Window menu contains a list of all the currently open workbooks, as well as several viewing commands.

5 Select Weekly Reservations from the Window menu.

You're back in the Weekly Reservations workbook. Now you can paste the information you copied from the Monday Reservations workbook.

NOTE *Don't confuse working with several Excel workbooks with working with several worksheets. Workbooks are the Excel files you open and save. Workbooks contain several worksheets within the same file.*

Paste button

6 Click the Monday tab, click cell A1 to make it active and click the Paste button on the Standard toolbar (or use any of the other paste methods you've learned) to paste the copied information.

The information you copied from Sheet1 of the Monday Reservations workbook is pasted into the Monday sheet of the Weekly Reservations workbook.

When you're working with two or more files, sometimes it's useful to view both workbooks at the same time.

7 Select Window → Arrange from the menu.

The Arrange Windows dialog box opens as shown in Figure 5-8.

8 Select Horizontal and click OK.

Excel displays both of the open files in two horizontally aligned windows, as shown in Figure 5-9. You need to copy a little more information from the Monday Reservations workbook into the Weekly Reservations workbook.

9 Click the Sheet2 tab in the Monday Reservations window, click cell A1, and click the Copy button on the Standard toolbar.

Now paste the copied label into the Weekly Reservations workbook.

10 Click the Summary tab in the Weekly Reservations window, click cell A1, and click the Paste button on the Standard toolbar.

The copied label is pasted into the Summary sheet of the Weekly Reservations workbook. You're done with the Monday Reservations worksheet.

11 Close the Monday Reservations window by clicking its close button.

The Monday Reservations workbook closes. Since you're working only with the Weekly Reservations workbook, you can maximize its window.

Maximize Button

12 Click the Weekly Reservations window's Maximize button.

The Weekly Reservations window maximizes to occupy the entire window area.

13 Save your work.

This lesson applies to other Windows programs as well. If you use Microsoft Word, you can work with and display several documents using the methods described in this lesson.

QUICK REFERENCE

TO SWITCH BETWEEN MULTIPLE OPEN WORKBOOKS:

- SELECT WINDOW FROM THE MENU AND SELECT THE NAME OF THE WORKBOOK YOU WANT TO VIEW.

TO VIEW MULTIPLE WINDOWS AT THE SAME TIME:

- SELECT WINDOW → ARRANGE ALL.

TO MAXIMIZE A WINDOW:

- CLICK THE WINDOW'S MAXIMIZE BUTTON.

TO RESTORE A WINDOW:

- CLICK THE WINDOW'S RESTORE BUTTON.

TO MANUALLY RESIZE A WINDOW:

1. POSITION THE MOUSE POINTER OVER THE EDGE OF THE WINDOW.

2. HOLD DOWN THE MOUSE BUTTON AND DRAG THE MOUSE TO RESIZE THE WINDOW.

3. RELEASE THE MOUSE BUTTON.

TO MOVE A WINDOW:

- DRAG THE WINDOW'S TITLE BAR TO THE LOCATION WHERE YOU WANT TO POSITION THE WINDOW.

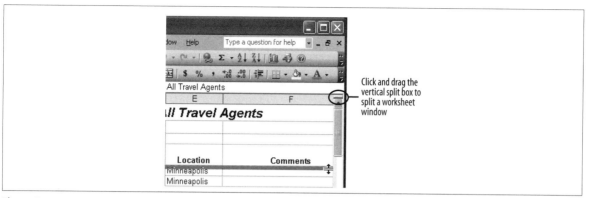

Figure 5-10. Splitting a window into two panes.

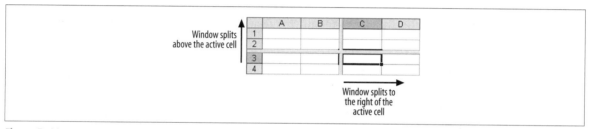

Figure 5-11. An example of using the Window → Split or Freeze Panes command.

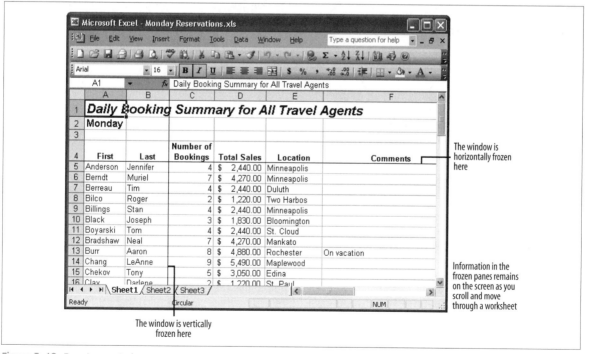

Figure 5-12. Freezing a window.

It doesn't take long to fill up a worksheet with so much data that it won't all fit on the same screen. When this happens, you have to scroll through the worksheet to add, delete, modify, and view information, skills you learned in a previous chapter. The problem with scrolling and viewing information in a large worksheet is that it can be confusing without the row or column labels.

To overcome this problem, you can *split* a window into two or four *panes*, which let you view multiple parts of the same worksheet. Once you create a pane, you can *freeze* it so it stays in the same place while you scroll around the rest of the worksheet.

1 Click the Monday tab and move the pointer over the vertical split box, located at the top of the vertical scroll bar. When the pointer changes to a ✛, drag the split box down directly beneath row 4, as shown in Figure 5-10.

Excel splits the worksheet window vertically into two separate panes. *Panes* are used to view different areas of a large worksheet at the same time. You can split a window into two panes either horizontally (as you've done) or vertically. Notice each of the panes contains its own vertical scroll bar, enabling you to scroll the pane to a different area of the worksheet.

2 Scroll down the worksheet in the lower pane until you reach row 60.

NOTE *Each pane has its own set of scroll boxes. Make sure you scroll down using the vertical scroll bar in the lower pane and not the upper pane.*

Notice that the worksheet scrolls down *only in the lower pane*. The upper pane stays in the same location in the worksheet, independent of the lower pane.

3 Move the pointer over the horizontal split box, located at the far right of the horizontal scroll bar. When the pointer changes to a ✛, drag the split box to the left, immediately after Column B.

Excel splits the worksheet window vertically, so it now contains four panes. Once you have split a window into several panes, you can *freeze* the panes so they stay in place.

4 Select Window → Freeze Panes from the menu.

Thin lines appear between the B and C columns, and the fourth and fifth rows as shown in Figure 5-12. When you *freeze* a window, data in the frozen panes (the left and/or top panes) will not scroll and remains visible as you move through the rest of the worksheet. Try scrolling the worksheet window to see for yourself.

5 Scroll the worksheet vertically and horizontally to view the data.

Notice how the frozen panes—Columns A through B, and rows 1 through 4, stay on the screen as you scroll the worksheet, allowing you to see the row and column labels. Now you're ready to unfreeze the panes.

6 Select Window → Unfreeze Panes from the menu.

The panes are now unfrozen. You can once more navigate in any of the four panes to view different areas of the worksheet at the same time. Since the exercise is almost over, you want to view the window in a single pane instead of four.

7 Select Window → Remove Split from the menu.

You are returned to a single pane view of the worksheet window.

Another way you can split and freeze panes is to place the active cell below the row you want to freeze and to the right of the column you want to freeze (as shown in Figure 5-11) and select Window → Split or Freeze Panes from the menu.

QUICK REFERENCE

TO SPLIT PANES:

- DRAG EITHER THE VERTICAL OR HORIZONTAL SPLIT BAR.

  OR...

- MOVE THE CELL POINTER TO THE CELL BELOW THE ROW YOU WANT AND TO THE RIGHT OF THE COLUMN YOU WANT TO SPLIT, AND SELECT WINDOW → SPLIT FROM THE MENU.

TO FREEZE PANES:

1. FOLLOW THE PREVIOUS INSTRUCTIONS TO SPLIT THE WINDOW INTO PANES.

2. SELECT WINDOW → FREEZE PANES FROM THE MENU.

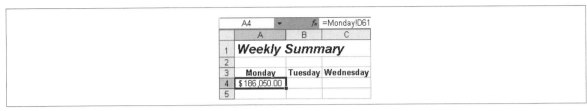

Figure 5-13. Referencing data in another sheet in the same workbook.

External reference indicator
┴
=Monday ! D61
┬   ┬
Sheet referenced   Cell referenced

Figure 5-14. An example of an external cell reference.

Figure 5-15. The Summary sheet with references to data in other sheets and in another workbook file.

You already know how to create references to cells in the same worksheet. This lesson explains how you can create references to cells in other worksheets, and even to cells in other workbook files altogether! References to cells or cell ranges on other sheets are called *external references* or *3-D references*. One of the most common reasons for using external references is to create a worksheet that summarizes the totals from other worksheets. For example, a workbook might contain 12 worksheets—1 for each month—and an annual summary worksheet that references and totals the data from each monthly worksheet.

1 Click the Summary tab.

2 Click cell A3, click the Bold button and the Center button on the Formatting toolbar, type Monday, and then click the Enter button on the Formula bar.

You need to need to add column headings for the remaining business days. Use the AutoFill feature to accomplish this task faster.

3 Position the pointer over the fill handle of cell A3, until it changes to a +, click and hold the mouse button, and drag the fill handle to select the cell range A3:E3.

The AutoFill function automatically fills the cell range with the days of the week. Now it's time to create a reference to a cell on another sheet in the workbook.

To refer to a cell in another sheet: type = (an equals sign) to enter a formula, click the sheet tab that contains the cell or cell range you want to use, click the cell or cell range you want to reference, and complete the entry by pressing Enter.

4 Click cell A4, type =, click the Monday sheet tab, click cell D61 (you will probably have to scroll the worksheet down), and press Tab.

Excel completes the entry and creates a reference to cell D61 on the Monday sheet, as shown in Figure 5-13. The Formula bar reads =Monday!D61. The *Monday* refers to the Monday sheet. The ! (exclamation point) is an *external reference indicator*—it means that the referenced cell is located outside the active sheet. D61 is the cell reference inside the external sheet. Figure 5-14 shows this external reference.

Complete the Summary sheet and reference the totals from the other sheets in the workbook.

TIP *You can create references to cells in other worksheets by clicking the sheet tab where the cell or cell range is located and then clicking the cell or cell range.*

5 Repeat Step 4 to add external references to the Total formula in cell D61 on the Tuesday, Wednesday, Thursday, and Friday sheets.

You can also reference data between different workbook files, just as you can reference data between sheets. This process of referencing data between different workbooks is called *linking*. Linking is dynamic, meaning that any changes made in one workbook are reflected in the other workbook. Try referencing a cell in a different workbook now: the first thing you'll need to do is open the workbook file that contains the data you want to reference.

6 Open the workbook Internet Reservations from your Practice folder.

To create a reference to a cell in this workbook, you first need to return to the Weekly Reservations workbook because it will contain the reference.

7 Select Window → Weekly Reservations from the menu.

You return to the Summary sheet of the Weekly Reservations workbook.

8 Click cell F3, click the Bold button and the Center button on the Formatting toolbar, and type Internet. Press Enter to move to cell F4, type = (an equals sign) to start creating the external reference.

Now you need to select the cell that contains the data you want to reference, or link.

9 Select Window → Internet Reservations from the menu.

You're back to the Internet Reservations workbook. All you need to do is click the cell containing the data you want to reference and complete the entry.

10 Click cell B8 and press Enter.

Complete the Summary sheet by totaling the information from the various external sources.

NOTE *There is one major problem with referencing data in other workbooks. If the workbook file you referenced or linked moves, or is deleted, you will get an error in the reference. Many people, especially those who email their workbooks, choose not to create references to data in other workbook files.*

11 Click cell G3, click the Bold button and Center button on the Formatting toolbar, type Total, and press Enter to complete the entry and move to cell G4.

AutoSum button

12 Click the AutoSum button on the Standard toolbar, notice that the cell range is correct (A4:F4), then press Enter.

Excel totals the cell range (A4:F4) containing the externally referenced data. Compare your worksheet with the one in Figure 5-15.

13 Save your work.

QUICK REFERENCE

TO CREATE AN EXTERNAL CELL REFERENCE:

1. CLICK THE CELL WHERE YOU WANT TO ENTER THE FORMULA.

2. TYPE = (AN EQUALS SIGN) AND ENTER ANY NECESSARY PARTS OF THE FORMULA.

3. CLICK THE TAB FOR THE WORKSHEET THAT CONTAINS THE CELL OR CELL RANGE YOU WANT TO REFERENCE. IF YOU WANT TO REFERENCE ANOTHER WORKBOOK FILE, OPEN THAT WORKBOOK AND SELECT THE APPROPRIATE WORKSHEET TAB.

4. SELECT THE CELL OR CELL RANGE YOU WANT TO REFERENCE AND COMPLETE THE FORMULA.

Select a preset header · Create a custom header or footer · Select a preset footer

Figure 5-16. The Header/Footer tab of the Page Setup dialog box.

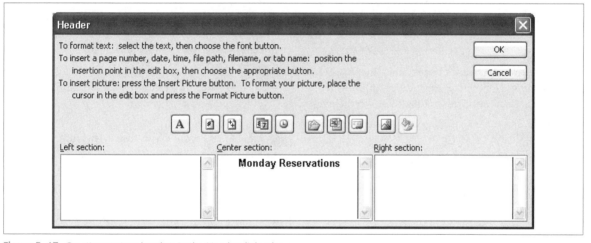

Figure 5-17. Creating custom headers in the Header dialog box.

Worksheets that are several pages long often have information such as the page number, the worksheet's title, or the date, located at the top or bottom of every page. Text that appears at the top of every page in a document is called a *header*, while text appearing at the bottom of each page is called a *footer*. In this lesson, you will learn how to use both headers and footers.

1 **If necessary, open the workbook named** Lesson 5C **and save it as** Weekly Reservations.

2 **Click the** Monday sheet tab **to make the Monday worksheet active.**

You need to specify the header and footer for the Monday worksheet.

3 **Select** File → Page Setup **from the menu and click the** Header/Footer tab.

The Header/Footer tab of the Page Setup dialog box appears, as shown in Figure 5-16. You can add a header and/or footer by selecting one of the preset headers and footers from the Header or Footer list, or you can create your own. The next few steps explain how to create a custom header.

4 Click the Custom Header button. (Table 5-1 shows examples of all the header and footer buttons.)

The Header dialog box appears, as shown in Figure 5-17. The Header dialog box lets you customize the header for the worksheet.

5 Click the Center section box.

Any text typed in the Center section box will appear centered across the top of the worksheet. You can format the text that appears in the header and footer by clicking the Font button.

Font button

6 Click the Font button, select Bold from the Font Style list, and click OK.

Now that you have formatted the header's font, type the text for the header in the Center section box.

7 Type Monday Reservations and click OK.

You return to the Header/Footer tab of the Page Setup dialog box. Notice that the header appears in the header preview area. Next, add a footer to the worksheet.

8 Click the Custom Footer button.

The Footer dialog box appears. You want to add the name of the workbook file in the left side of the footer.

File Name button

9 Click the Left Section box and click the File Name button to insert the file name code.

Excel inserts the file name code, "&[File]". This cryptic-looking code will display the name of the file, Weekly Reservations, in the footer. Since the file name code is in the Left Section box, it will appear left-aligned on the worksheet's footer. Now you want to add the page number to the right side of the footer.

Page Number button

10 Click the Right Section box, type Page, press the Spacebar, click the Page Number button to insert the page number code, and click OK to close the Footer dialog box.

You're back to the Header/Footer tab. Notice how the footer appears in the footer box.

11 Click Print Preview to preview your worksheet, then save it.

Table 5-1. Header and Footer Buttons

Button Icon	Button Name	Description	Button Icon	Button Name	Description
A	Font	Formats the font for the header and footer.		Total Pages	Inserts the total number of pages in the workbook.
	Time	Inserts the current time.		File Name	Inserts the workbook file name.
	Insert Picture	Allows you to choose a picture to place in the active worksheet.		Page Number	Inserts the current page number.
	Date	Inserts the current date.		Path & File	Inserts the path and file name of the active workbook.
	Sheet Name	Inserts the worksheet name.		Format Picture	Allows you to size, rotate, scale, crop and adjust the image in the header or footer.

QUICK REFERENCE

TO ADD OR CHANGE THE HEADER OR FOOTER:

1. SELECT FILE → PAGE SETUP FROM THE MENU AND CLICK THE HEADER/FOOTER TAB.

2. SELECT ONE OF THE PRESET HEADERS OR FOOTERS FROM THE HEADER OR FOOTER DROP-DOWN LIST.

TO ADD A CUSTOM HEADER OR FOOTER:

1. SELECT FILE → PAGE SETUP FROM THE MENU AND CLICK THE HEADER/FOOTER TAB.

2. CLICK THE CUSTOM HEADER OR CUSTOM FOOTER BUTTON.

3. ENTER THE HEADER OR FOOTER IN ANY OR ALL OF THE THREE SECTIONS. REFER TO TABLE 5-1.

Specifying a Print Area and Controlling Page Breaks

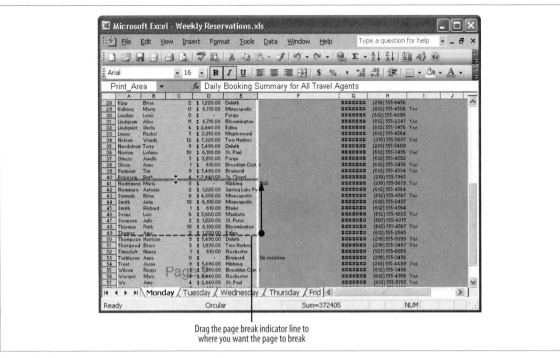

Drag the page break indicator line to
where you want the page to break

Figure 5-18. Adjusting page breaks in Page Break Preview mode.

Sometimes you may want to print only a particular area of a worksheet. You can specify an area of a worksheet to print using the File → Print Area → Set Print Area menu command. The Set Print Area command is especially useful when you're working with a huge worksheet. Instead of taking dozens of pages to print everything, you can use the Set Print Area command to print what is important, such as the worksheet totals.

Another topic covered in this lesson is how to force the page to break where you want when you print out a worksheet.

1 Press Ctrl + Home **to move to the beginning of the worksheet.**

2 Select the cell range A1:E61.

Yes, this is a very large cell range. You must hold down the mouse button and move the pointer down, below the Excel worksheet window to scroll down all select the cells. If you have trouble selecting this cell range using the mouse, click cell A1, press and hold down the Shift key, scroll down and click cell E61 and release the Shift key. The cell range you just selected is the part of the worksheet you want to print.

3 Select File → Print Area → Set Print Area **from the menu.**

Excel sets the currently selected cell range, A1:E61, as the print area. Unless you remove this print area, Excel will only print this cell range whenever you print the worksheet. Removing a print area is even easier than setting one.

4 Select File → Print Area → Clear Print Area **from the menu.**

The print area you selected, A1:E61, is cleared and Excel will now print the entire worksheet whenever you send it to the printer. For this exercise, however, you need to keep using the print range A1:E61, so undo the previous Clear Print Area command.

5 Click the Undo button **on the Standard toolbar.**

Excel undoes the Clear Print Area command.

When you print your worksheets, sometimes the page will break where you don't want it to. You can adjust where the page breaks with Excel's Page Break Preview feature.

6 Select View → Page Break Preview from the menu.

Excel changes the worksheet's window view from Normal to Page Break Preview mode, as shown in Figure 5-18. Print Break Preview mode shows you where the worksheet's pages will break when printed, as indicated by a dark blue line. The areas of the worksheet that are not included in the current print area appear in dark gray. You can adjust the page breaks by clicking and dragging the dark blue page break indicator line to where you want the page to break.

7 Scroll down the worksheet and click and drag the Page Break Indicator line until it appears immediately after row 40, as shown in Figure 5-18.

When you print the Monday worksheet, the page will break immediately after row 40. You're finished using

Page Break Preview mode, so change the view back to normal mode.

8 Select View → Normal from the menu.

You return to the Normal view of the workbook. Notice that a dotted line appears at the edge of the print area and after row 40. This dotted line indicates where the page will break when the worksheet is printed. Normally Excel automatically inserts a page break when the worksheet won't fit on the page, but you can manually insert your own page breaks as well.

9 Click cell A18, and then select Insert → Page Break from the menu.

A dashed page break indicator line appears between rows 17 and 18, indicating a horizontal page break.

Table 5-2 describes the different ways to page break.

Table 5-2. Inserting Page Breaks

To Break the Page This Way	Position the Cell Pointer Here
Horizontally	Select a cell in Column A that is in the row below where you want the page break.
Vertically	Select a cell in Row 1 that is in the column to the right of where you want the page break.
Both Horizontally and Vertically	Select the cell below and to the right of where you want the page break.

QUICK REFERENCE

TO SPECIFY A PRINT AREA:

1. SELECT THE CELL RANGE YOU WANT TO PRINT.

2. SELECT FILE → PRINT AREA → SET PRINT AREA FROM THE MENU.

TO CLEAR A PRINT AREA:

• SELECT FILE → PRINT AREA → CLEAR PRINT AREA FROM THE MENU.

TO INSERT A MANUAL PAGE BREAK:

1. MOVE THE CELL POINTER TO THE CELL WHERE THE NEXT PAGE SHOULD START, BUT MAKE SURE IT'S IN THE A COLUMN (OTHERWISE YOU WILL INSERT A HORIZONTAL PAGE BREAK AND A VERTICAL PAGE BREAK).

2. SELECT INSERT → PAGE BREAK FROM THE MENU.

TO ADJUST WHERE THE PAGE BREAKS:

1. SELECT VIEW → PAGE BREAK PREVIEW FROM THE MENU.

2. DRAG THE PAGE BREAK INDICATOR LINE TO WHERE YOU WANT THE PAGE BREAK TO OCCUR.

3. SELECT VIEW → NORMAL FROM THE MENU TO RETURN TO NORMAL VIEW.

Adjusting Page Margins and Orientation

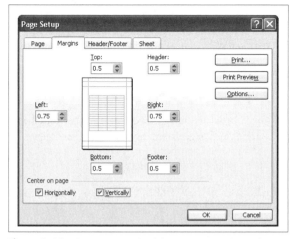

Figure 5-19. The Margins tab of the Page Setup dialog box.

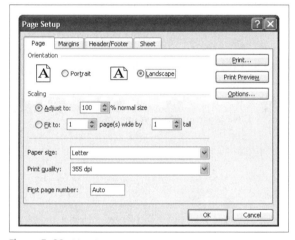

Figure 5-20. Margins on a page.

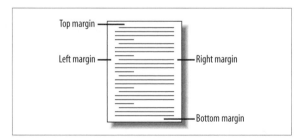

Figure 5-21. The Page tab of the Page Setup dialog box.

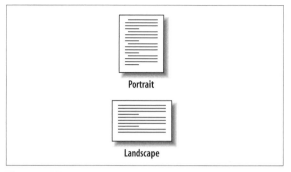

Figure 5-22. Comparison of portrait and landscape page orientations.

You're probably already aware that *margins* are the empty space between the text and the left, right, top, and bottom edges of a printed page. Excel's default margins are 1 inch at the top and bottom, and .75 inch margins to the left and right. There are many reasons to change the margins for a document: to make more room for text information on a page, to add some extra space if you're binding a document, or to leave a blank space to write in notes. If you don't already know how to adjust a page's margins, you will after this lesson.

This lesson also explains how to change the page orientation. Everything you print uses one of two different types of paper orientations: *Portrait* or *Landscape* (see Figure 5-22). In Portrait orientation, the paper is taller than it is wide—like a painting of a person's portrait. In Landscape orientation, the paper is wider than it is tall—like a painting of a landscape. Portrait orientation is the default setting for printing worksheets, but there are many times when you will want to use landscape orientation instead.

1 **Click** File → Page Setup **from the menu and click the** Margins tab **if it is not already in front.**

The Margins tab of the Page Setup dialog box appears, as shown in Figure 5-19. Here you can view and adjust the margin sizes for the current worksheet. Notice there are margins settings in the Top, Bottom, Left, Right, Header, and Footer boxes. See Figure 5-21 for examples of Top, Bottom, Left, and Right margins.

2 Click the Top Margin box down arrow until .5 appears in the box.

This will change the size of the top margin from 1.0 to 0.5. Notice that the Preview area of the Page Setup dialog box displays where the new margins for the worksheet will be.

3 Click the Bottom Margin box down arrow until .5 appears in the box.

In the same manner, you could adjust the left and right margins, and how far you want the worksheet's header and footer to print from the edge of the page. You can also specify if you want to center the worksheet horizontally or vertically on the page.

4 Click the Horizontally and Vertically check boxes in the Center on page section.

This will vertically and horizontally center the worksheet page when it is printed.

Do you think you have a handle on changing the margins of a worksheet? Good, because without further ado, we'll move on to page orientation.

5 Click the Page tab.

The Page tab appears, as shown in Figure 5-20.

6 In the Orientation area, click the Landscape option button.

This will change the worksheet's orientation to Landscape when it is printed.

7 Click OK.

The Page setup dialog box closes, and the worksheet's margins and page orientation settings are changed.

Print Preview button

8 Click the Print Preview button on the Standard toolbar to preview the Monday worksheet.

A print preview of the Monday worksheet appears on the screen. Unless you have eyes like a hawk (or a very large monitor), you probably won't notice the small changes you made to the worksheet's margins, but you can certainly tell that the page is using landscape orientation.

9 Click Close and save your work.

QUICK REFERENCE

TO ADJUST MARGINS:

1. SELECT FILE → PAGE SETUP FROM THE MENU AND CLICK THE MARGINS TAB.

2. ADJUST THE APPROPRIATE MARGINS.

TO CHANGE A PAGE'S ORIENTATION:

1. SELECT FILE → PAGE SETUP FROM THE MENU, AND CLICK THE PAGE TAB.

2. IN THE ORIENTATION SECTION, SELECT EITHER THE PORTRAIT OR LANDSCAPE OPTION.

Adding Print Titles and Gridlines

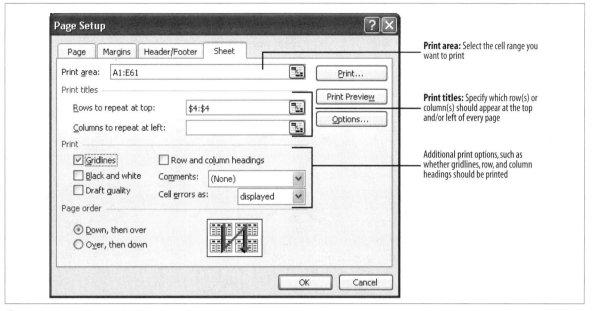

Print area: Select the cell range you want to print

Print titles: Specify which row(s) or column(s) should appear at the top and/or left of every page

Additional print options, such as whether gridlines, row, and column headings should be printed

Figure 5-23. The Sheet tab of the Page Setup dialog box.

If a worksheet requires more than one page to print, it can be confusing to read any subsequent pages because the column and row labels won't be printed. You can fix this problem by selecting File → Page Setup from the menu, clicking the Sheet tab, and telling Excel which row and column titles you want to appear at the top and/or left of every printed page.

This lesson will also show you how to make sure your worksheet's column and row labels appear on every printed page, and how to turn on and off the worksheet's gridlines when printing.

1 If necessary, open the workbook named Lesson 5D and save it as Weekly Reservations.

Print Preview button

2 Click the Print Preview button on the Standard toolbar.

Excel displays how the Monday worksheet will look when printed. Notice the status bar displays 1 of 3, indicating that the worksheet spreads across two pages.

3 Click Next to move to the next page and click near the top of the page with the 🔍 pointer.

Notice that the cells on pages 2 and 3 don't have column labels (First, Last, Number of Bookings, etc.), making the data on the second page difficult to read and understand. You want the column labels on the first page to appear at the top of every page.

4 Click Close to close the Print Preview window.

5 Select File → Page Setup from the menu and click the Sheet tab (see Figure 5-23).

The Sheet tab of the Page Setup dialog box is where you can specify which parts of the worksheet are printed. Notice the print area—the cell range A1:E61—appears in the Print area text box. You need to specify which rows you want to repeat at the top of every page. Move on to the next step to find out how to do this.

6 Click the Rows to repeat at top text box and click any cell in Row 4.

The **Collapse Dialog button** temporarily shrinks and moves the dialog box so that you enter a cell range by selecting cells in the worksheet. When you finish, you can click the button again or press <**Enter**> to display the entire dialog box.

You may have to click the Collapse Dialog button if the dialog box is in the way. When you click any cell in row 4, Excel inserts a reference to row 4 in the "Rows to repeat at top" text box. You aren't limited to repeating a single row across the top of a page—you can select several rows. You can also specify that you want a column(s) to repeat to the right side of every page.

By default, Excel does not print the horizontal and vertical cell gridlines on worksheets; however, you can elect to print a worksheet's gridlines. Printing a worksheet's gridlines can sometimes make them easier to read.

7 Check the Gridlines check box.

Now when you print the worksheet, the horizontal and vertical cell gridlines will also be printed.

8 Click Print Preview to display how the changes you've made to the worksheet will appear when printed.

9 Click Next to move to the next page and click near the top of the page with the 🔍 pointer.

Notice that the heading row now appears at the top of every page, and that gridlines appear on the worksheet.

10 Click Close and save your work.

QUICK REFERENCE

TO PRINT OR SUPPRESS GRIDLINES:

1. SELECT FILE → PAGE SETUP FROM THE MENU AND CLICK THE SHEET TAB.

2. ADD OR REMOVE THE CHECK MARK IN THE GRIDLINES CHECK BOX.

TO PRINT ROW OR COLUMN TITLES:

1. SELECT FILE → PAGE SETUP FROM THE MENU AND CLICK THE SHEET TAB.

2. SPECIFY WHICH ROW(S) OR COLUMN(S) SHOULD APPEAR AT THE TOP AND/OR LEFT OF EVERY PAGE IN THE APPROPRIATE BOXES UNDER THE TITLE SECTION.

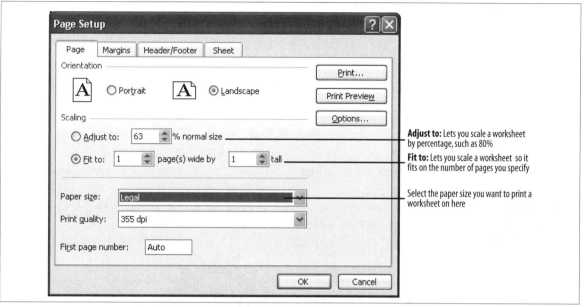

Figure 5-24. The Page tab of the Page Setup dialog box.

This lesson covers two important printing options: how to reduce the size of the printed worksheet so that it fits on a specified number of pages and how to print on different paper sizes. Most people normally print on standard letter-sized (8 × 11) paper, but Excel can also print on many other paper sizes, such as legal-sized (8 × 14).

1 Select File → Page Setup from the menu and click the Page tab.

The Page tab of the Page Setup dialog box appears, as shown in Figure 5-24. You want to scale the Monday worksheet so that it fits on a single page. Notice under the Scaling section that there are two different ways you can scale a worksheet:

- **Adjust to:** This option lets you scale a worksheet by a percentage. For example, you could scale a worksheet so that it is 80% of its normal size.

- **Fit to:** This option lets you scale the worksheet so that it fits on the number of pages you specify. You must specify how many pages wide by tall you want the worksheet to be printed on. This is usually the easiest and best way to scale a worksheet.

You want to scale the Monday worksheet so that it fits on a single page.

2 Click the Fit to option under the Scaling section, click the pages wide down arrow to select 1, and click the pages tall down arrow to select 1.

3 Click Print Preview to see how the newly scaled worksheet will look when printed.

Yikes! The data in the worksheet has become so small that it's almost unreadable.

4 Click Close to close the Print Preview window.

You return to the worksheet window. You decide using a larger sheet of paper—legal-sized—may help fit the entire worksheet on a single page.

5 Select File → Page Setup from the menu.

Now change the paper size from letter (the default setting) to legal.

6 Click the Paper size arrow and select Legal from the paper size list. In the Orientation area, click the Portrait option button.

Preview the worksheet to see how it will look if it is printed on legal-sized paper.

7 Click Print Preview to see how the worksheet will look when printed. Click Close when you're finished.

8 Save your work.

QUICK REFERENCE

TO CHANGE THE PRINT SCALE:

1. SELECT FILE → PAGE SETUP FROM THE MENU AND CLICK THE PAGE TAB.

2. ENTER THE PERCENT NUMBER IN THE % NORMAL SIZE TEXT BOX OR ENTER THE NUMBER OF PAGES YOU WANT THE WORKSHEET TO FIT ON.

TO CHANGE THE PAPER SIZE:

1. SELECT FILE → PAGE SETUP FROM THE MENU AND CLICK THE PAGE TAB.

2. CLICK THE PAPER SIZE LIST TO SELECT THE PAPER SIZE.

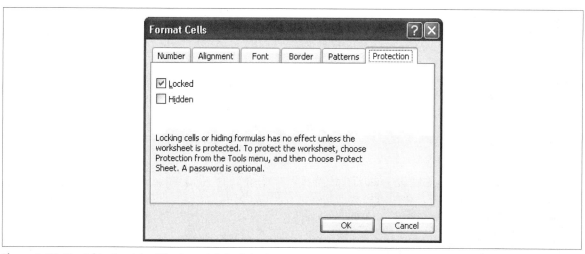

Figure 5-25. The Protection tab of the Format Cells dialog box.

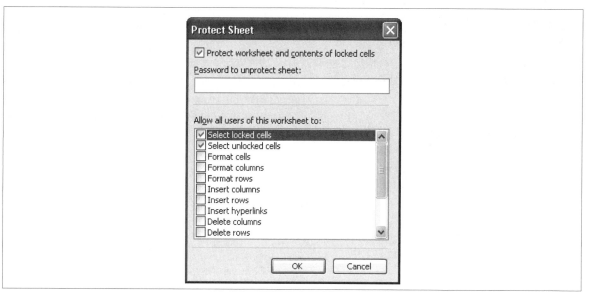

Figure 5-26. The Protect Sheet dialog box.

Figure 5-27. Message informing user that the current cell is protected.

Sometimes you may want to prevent other users from changing some of the contents in a worksheet. For example, you might want to allow users to enter information in a particular cell range, without being able to alter the labels or formulas in another cell range in the same worksheet. You can *protect* selected cells so that their contents cannot be altered, while still allowing the contents of *unprotected* cells in the same worksheet to be changed. You can protect cells by *locking* them on the Protection tab of the Format Cells dialog box.

Using a protected worksheet is useful if you want another user to enter or modify data in the worksheet without altering or damaging the worksheet's formulas and design. In this lesson, you will learn all about locking and unlocking cells and protecting worksheets.

1 Select the cell range D5:E60, select Format → Cells from the menu, and click the Protection tab.

TIP *Cells are protected by default.*

The Protection tab of the Format Cells dialog box appears, as shown in Figure 5-25. There are only two options on this tab:

- **Locked:** Prevents selected cells from being changed, moved, resized, or deleted. Notice the Locked box is checked. Excel locks all cells by default.

- **Hidden:** Hides a formula in a cell so that it does not appear in the Formula bar when the cell is selected.

Neither of these options has any effect unless the sheet is protected, which you'll learn how to do in a minute. Since you want users to be able to modify the cells in the selected cell range, you need to unlock them.

2 Uncheck the Locked check box and click OK.

The Format Cells dialog box closes and you return to the worksheet. At first, nothing appears to have changed. You need to protect the worksheet in order to see how cell protection works.

NOTE *By default, all cells are locked. Before you protect a worksheet, unlock the cells where you want a user to enter or modify information.*

3 Select Tools → Protection → Protect Sheet from the menu.

The Protect Sheet dialog box appears, as shown in Figure 5-26. You can specify which parts of the worksheet you want to protect, and you can assign a password that users must enter in order to unprotect the worksheet, once it has been protected.

4 Click OK.

The Protection Sheet dialog box closes and you return to the worksheet. Move on to the next step to see how the protected worksheet works.

5 Click cell A8 and press the Delete key.

When you try to delete or modify a locked cell, Excel displays a message informing you that the cell is protected, as shown in Figure 5-27. Go ahead and click OK. Now try modifying an unprotected cell.

6 Click cell D8 and press the Delete key.

Since you unlocked this cell in a previous step, Excel lets you clear its contents. Now that you have an understanding of cell protection, you can unprotect the worksheet.

7 Select Tools → Protection → Unprotect Sheet from the menu.

Excel unprotects the Monday sheet. Now you can modify all of the cells in the worksheet, whether they are locked or not.

Another way you can prevent unauthorized users from viewing or modifying restricted or confidential areas of your workbooks is to hide them. You can hide rows, columns, and entire worksheets. To prevent others from displaying hidden rows or columns, you can protect the workbook, as shown in Step 3.

8 Save your work.

QUICK REFERENCE

TO PROTECT A CELL OR CELL RANGE:

1. SELECT THE CELL OR CELL RANGE YOU WANT TO PROTECT OR HIDE.

2. SELECT FORMAT → CELLS FROM THE MENU AND CLICK THE PROTECTION TAB.

    OR...

    RIGHT-CLICK THE SELECTED CELL OR CELL RANGE AND SELECT FORMAT CELLS FROM THE SHORTCUT MENU.

3. ADD OR REMOVE CHECK MARKS IN THE LOCKED AND HIDDEN CHECK BOXES TO SPECIFY IF THE CELL OR CELL RANGE SHOULD BE LOCKED OR HIDDEN.

TO PROTECT A WORKSHEET:

1. SELECT TOOLS → PROTECTION → PROTECT SHEET FROM THE MENU.

2. SELECT THE APPROPRIATE OPTIONS FOR WHAT YOU WANT TO PROTECT.

3. (OPTIONAL) ENTER A PASSWORD.

TO UNPROTECT A WORKSHEET:

• SELECT TOOLS → PROTECTION → UNPROTECT SHEET FROM THE MENU.

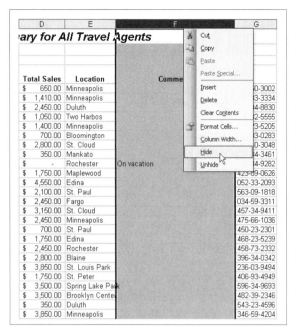

Figure 5-28. Selecting and hiding the F column.

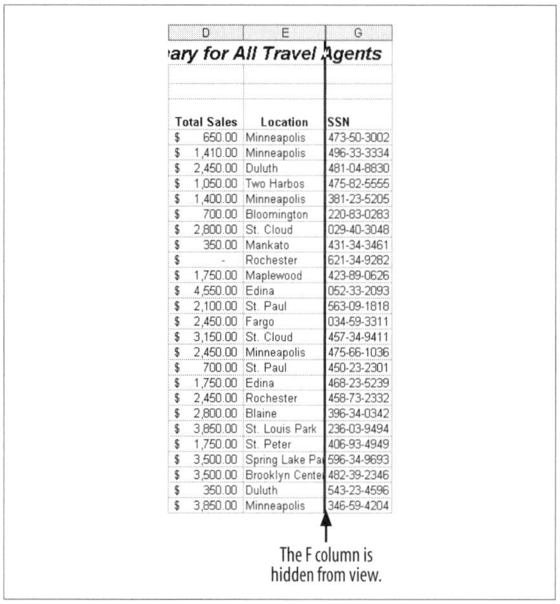

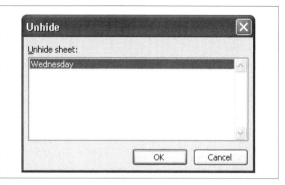

Figure 5-30. The Unhide dialog box.

In addition to protecting cells, Excel also gives you the ability to hide individual columns, rows, or sheets. Hiding a workbook's contents is the Excel equivalent of stuffing paperwork into your desk drawers: if you feel your screen is too cluttered with data, you can make part of your workbook disappear without actually deleting it.

Hiding data makes it easier to work with large, unwieldy workbooks. If you know you won't be working with a particular row or column, you can hide it while you enter data and then unhide it later. The same goes for individual sheets. If you know you will only be working with the Monday and Tuesday sheets, it makes sense to hide the Wednesday, Thursday and Friday sheets so you don't accidentally enter data there. If you know you will be printing a workbook or turning it into a presentation, you can hide sensitive data, such as a column that contains Social Security numbers. Let's try hiding a column.

1 If necessary, open the workbook named Lesson 5E and save it as Weekly Reservations.

2 Select the Tuesday sheet tab. **Right-click the** Column F heading **and select** Hide **from the shortcut menu.**

The F column disappears from the worksheet. It's not deleted, it's merely hidden from view. Notice how the column headings now go from E to G, skipping the F column.

NOTE *If a worksheet is protected, you cannot hide or unhide columns or rows.*

The F column is
hidden from view.

Figure 5-29. The F column is hidden from view.

3 Select the E and G columns by clicking and dragging the pointer across the column headings. Once the column headings are selected, right-click either of the column headings and select Unhide from the shortcut menu.

The F column reappears. You can also hide and unhide other columns or rows in the same manner. Hiding a sheet is a lot like hiding a column.

4 Select the Wednesday sheet tab and select Format → Sheet → Hide.

Excel hides the Wednesday sheet. You cannot hide a sheet by right-clicking a sheet's tab. Now let's unhide the sheet.

5 Select Format → Sheet → Unhide. In the Unhide dialog box, select Wednesday.

The Wednesday sheet reappears. You can hide more than one sheet at a time. Just repeat the method in Step 3.

NOTE *If you protect a sheet, you can still hide it. However, if your protect an entire workbook, you cannot hide or unhide an individual worksheet.*

TIP *Use the Format menu to hide or unhide a sheet.*

6 Save your work.

QUICK REFERENCE

TO HIDE A COLUMN OR ROW:

1. RIGHT-CLICK THE COLUMN HEADING OR THE ROW HEADING.

2. SELECT HIDE FROM THE SHORTCUT MENU.

   OR...

   SELECT THE COLUMN OR ROW AND SELECT FORMAT → COLUMNS (OR ROWS) → HIDE FROM THE MENU.

TO HIDE A SHEET:

1. SELECT THE SHEET YOU WANT TO HIDE.

2. SELECT FORMAT → SHEET → HIDE.

TO UNHIDE A SHEET

• SELECT FORMAT → SHEET → UNHIDE. IN THE UNHIDE DIALOG BOX, SELECT THE SHEET YOU WANT TO UNHIDE.

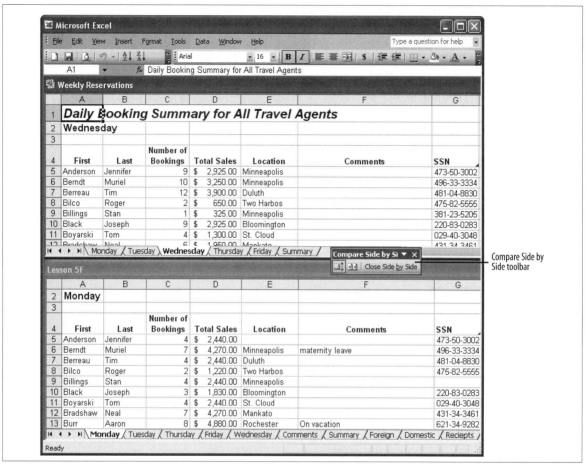

Figure 5-31. A side-by-side workbook comparison.

There are many different ways to view your worksheets and workbooks. This lesson explains how to zoom in (magnify) and out of a worksheet, how to view a worksheet in Full Screen mode, and how to use Excel 2003's new Compare Side by Side feature to view your workbooks. This feature opens the workbook windows one on top of the other so you can view and scroll through them at the same time and still make changes to each workbook individually.

First, let's learn how to zoom and use Full Screen mode.

1 Click the Zoom list arrow on the Standard toolbar and select 75%.

The worksheet appears on-screen at a magnification of 75%, allowing you to see more of the worksheet on the screen. However, the reduced magnification makes the worksheet difficult to read.

Zoom list

2 Click the Zoom list arrow on the Standard toolbar and select 100%.

The worksheet returns to the normal level of magnification. You can also see more of a worksheet by dedicating 100% of the screen to the worksheet in full screen mode. You've got zooming down; let's move on to Full Screen mode.

3 Select View → Full Screen from the menu.

All the familiar title bars, menus, and toolbars disappear and the worksheet appears in full screen mode. Full screen mode is useful because it devotes 100% of the screen real estate to viewing a worksheet. The disadvantage of full screen mode is all the Excel tools—the toolbars, status bar, etc.—are not as readily available. You can still access the menus, although you can no longer see them, by clicking the mouse at the very top of the screen.

4 Click the Close Full Screen button floating over the worksheet.

The full screen view closes and you are returned to the previous view.

Now, let's move on to the Compare Side by Side view that is new to Excel 2003.

5 Navigate to your Practice folder and open Lesson 5F.

The two workbooks you want to compare, Weekly Reservations and Lesson 5F, are open.

6 Select Window → Compare Side by Side with Weekly Reservations from the menu.

The two workbook windows appear side by side, as shown in Figure 5-31. You can easily see the differences between the two workbooks.

The Compare Side by Side toolbar has two buttons. The Synchronous Scrolling button is automatically selected and allows you to scroll through the documents at the same time. The Reset Window Position button resizes the windows for the best view.

7 Scroll down in the Lesson 5F workbook.

Notice that the Weekly Reservations workbook scrolls down at the same time.

8 Click the Close Side by Side button on the Compare Side by Side toolbar.

The windows are stacked on top of each other once again.

9 Close the Lesson 5F workbook.

QUICK REFERENCE

TO ZOOM:

- CLICK THE ZOOM LIST ARROW ON THE STANDARD TOOLBAR AND SELECT THE MAGNIFICATION LEVEL AT WHICH YOU WOULD LIKE TO VIEW YOUR WORKSHEET.

TO COMPARE WORKBOOKS SIDE BY SIDE:

1. OPEN THE TWO WORKBOOKS YOU WANT TO COMPARE.

2. SELECT WINDOW → COMPARE SIDE BY SIDE FROM THE MENU.

3. CLICK THE CLOSE SIDE BY SIDE BUTTON ON THE COMPARE SIDE BY SIDE TOOLBAR WHEN YOU'RE FINISHED.

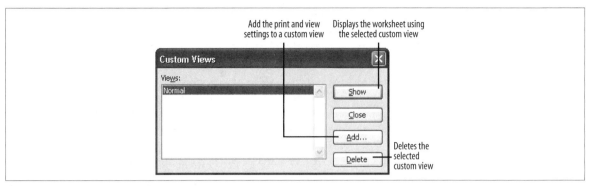

Figure 5-32. The Custom View dialog box.

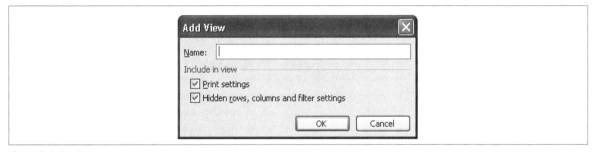

Figure 5-33. Adding a Custom View.

Changing the print settings, zoom level, and workbook appearance every time you view or print a workbook can get old. By creating a *custom view,* you can save the view and print settings so you don't have to manually change them. A custom view saves the following settings:

- Any print settings, including the print area, scale level, paper size and orientation.
- Any view settings, including the zoom level, if gridlines should be displayed, and any hidden worksheets, rows, or columns.
- Any filters and filter settings.

This lesson explains how to create and work with a custom view.

1 Select View → Custom Views **from the menu.**

The Custom Views dialog box appears, as shown in Figure 5-32. Any saved views for the current worksheet are listed here. You want to save the current, generic view of the Monday worksheet.

2 Click Add.

The Add View dialog box appears, as shown in Figure 5-33. You must enter a name for the current view, and select whether you want to include the worksheet's print settings and/or any hidden rows, columns, and filter settings.

3 Type Normal **in the Name box and click** OK.

Excel saves the custom view and closes the dialog box. Now you want to create another view of the worksheet—one that uses Portrait orientation and hides the Commissions column.

4 Right-click the Column I heading **and select** Hide **from the shortcut menu.**

Excel hides Column I.

5 Select File → Page Setup **from the menu, click the** Page tab, **select the** Landscape option **under the Orientation section, and click** OK.

Save the settings you made to the worksheet in a custom view.

6 Select View → Custom Views from the menu.

The Custom Views dialog box appears.

7 Click Add, type No Commission in the Name box, and click OK.

Excel saves the custom view and returns you to the worksheet. Now try retrieving one of your custom views.

8 Select View → Custom Views from the menu, select Normal, and click Show.

Excel displays the worksheet using the Normal custom view. Notice that Column I is no longer hidden.

9 Click the Print Preview button on the Standard toolbar to preview the worksheet.

Excel displays a preview of the Monday worksheet in Normal view.

10 Save and close the current workbook.

QUICK REFERENCE

TO CREATE A CUSTOM VIEW:

1. SET UP THE WORKSHEET'S APPEARANCE AND PRINT SETTINGS.

2. SELECT VIEW → CUSTOM VIEWS FROM THE MENU.

3. CLICK ADD AND GIVE THE VIEW A NAME.

TO USE A CUSTOM VIEW:

• SELECT VIEW → CUSTOM VIEWS FROM THE MENU, SELECT THE VIEW YOU WANT TO USE, AND CLICK SHOW.

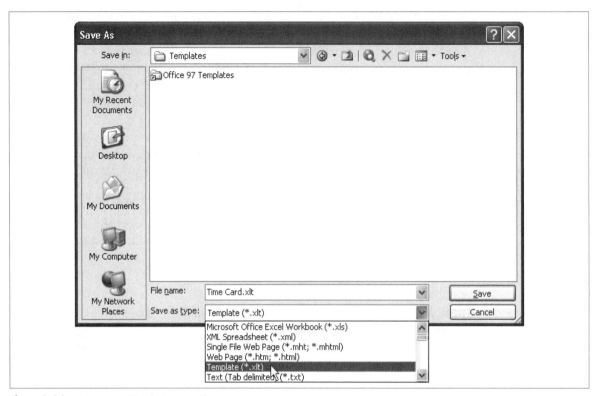

Figure 5-34. Saving a workbook as a Template.

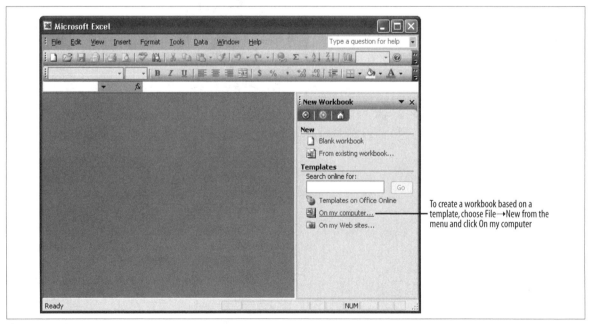

To create a workbook based on a template, choose File→New from the menu and click On my computer

Figure 5-35. The New Workbook task pane.

If you find yourself recreating the same type of workbook over and over, you can probably save yourself some time by using a template. A *template* is a workbook that contains standard data such as labels, formulas, formatting, and macros you use frequently. Once you have created a template, you can use it to create new workbooks, which saves you time since you don't have to enter the same information again and again. Creating a template is easy—you simply make the template, just like you would any other workbook, and then tell Excel you want to save the workbook as a template instead of as a standard workbook. To create a workbook from a template, you just select File → New from the menu and select the template you want to use. Excel comes with several built-in templates for common purposes such as invoices and expense reports.

In this lesson you will learn how to create a template and how to create a new workbook based on a template.

1 Navigate to your Practice folder and open the Time Card Form worksheet.

This worksheet tracks and totals the number of hours employees work in a week. You will be saving this worksheet as a template. But first you have to remove some information in the worksheet.

2 Select the cell range B6:H11 and press the Delete key.

Now you're ready to save the worksheet as a template.

3 Select File → Save As from the menu.

The Save As dialog box appears. Here you must specify that you want to save the current workbook as a template. Excel templates are stored with an .XLT extension instead of the normal .XLS extension (used for Excel workbooks).

4 Click the Save as type list arrow and select Template from the list, as shown in Figure 5-34.

Templates are normally kept in a special template folder (usually something such as *C:\Program-Files\Microsoft Office\Templates*). When you select the Template file format, Excel automatically changes the file location to save the template in this folder. The file list window is updated to show the contents of the Template folder.

NOTE *If the file location doesn't change when you select the Template file type, you'll have to move the Template folder manually.*

5 In the File Name box, type Time Card and click the Save button.

Excel saves the workbook as a template.

6 Close all open workbooks.

Now that you have created a template, you can use the template to create a new workbook. Try it!

7 Select File → New from the menu.

The New Workbook task pane appears as shown in Figure 5-35.

8 Select On my computer from the New Workbook task pane.

Here you can select the template you want to use to create your new workbook.

Time Card.xlt

A Workbook Template

9 Select the Time Card template and click OK.

A new workbook based on the Time Card template appears in the document window.

10 Fill out the time card worksheet by entering various hours for the employees (use your imagination).

Once you have finished filling out the time card, you can save it as a normal workbook file.

11 Click the Save button on the Standard toolbar.

The Save As dialog box appears.

12 Save the workbook as Week 1 Timecard.

The workbook is saved as a normal Excel workbook.

13 Close the Week 1 Timecard worksheet.

You don't want to leave the Time Card template on this computer, so delete it.

14 Select File → New from the menu, select On my computer from the New Workbook task pane. Right-click the Time Card template in the Templates dialog box and select Delete from the shortcut menu. Close the dialog box and the task pane when you're finished.

QUICK REFERENCE

TO CREATE A TEMPLATE:

1. EITHER CREATE OR OPEN A WORKBOOK THAT YOU WANT TO USE FOR THE TEMPLATE.

2. SELECT FILE → SAVE AS FROM THE MENU.

3. SELECT TEMPLATE FROM THE SAVE AS TYPE LIST, GIVE THE TEMPLATE A NAME, AND CLICK OK TO SAVE THE TEMPLATE.

TO CREATE A WORKBOOK BASED ON A TEMPLATE:

1. SELECT FILE → NEW FROM THE MENU.

2. CLICK GENERAL TEMPLATE IN THE NEW WORKBOOK TASK PANE.

3. DOUBLE-CLICK THE TEMPLATE YOU WANT TO USE (YOU MAY HAVE TO SELECT IT FROM ONE OF THE TABBED CATEGORIES).

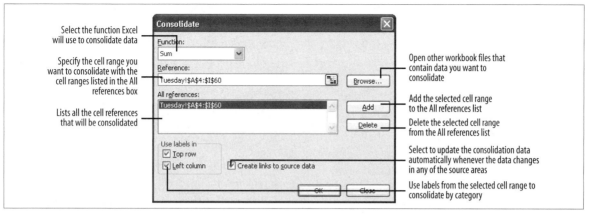

Figure 5-36. The Consolidate dialog box.

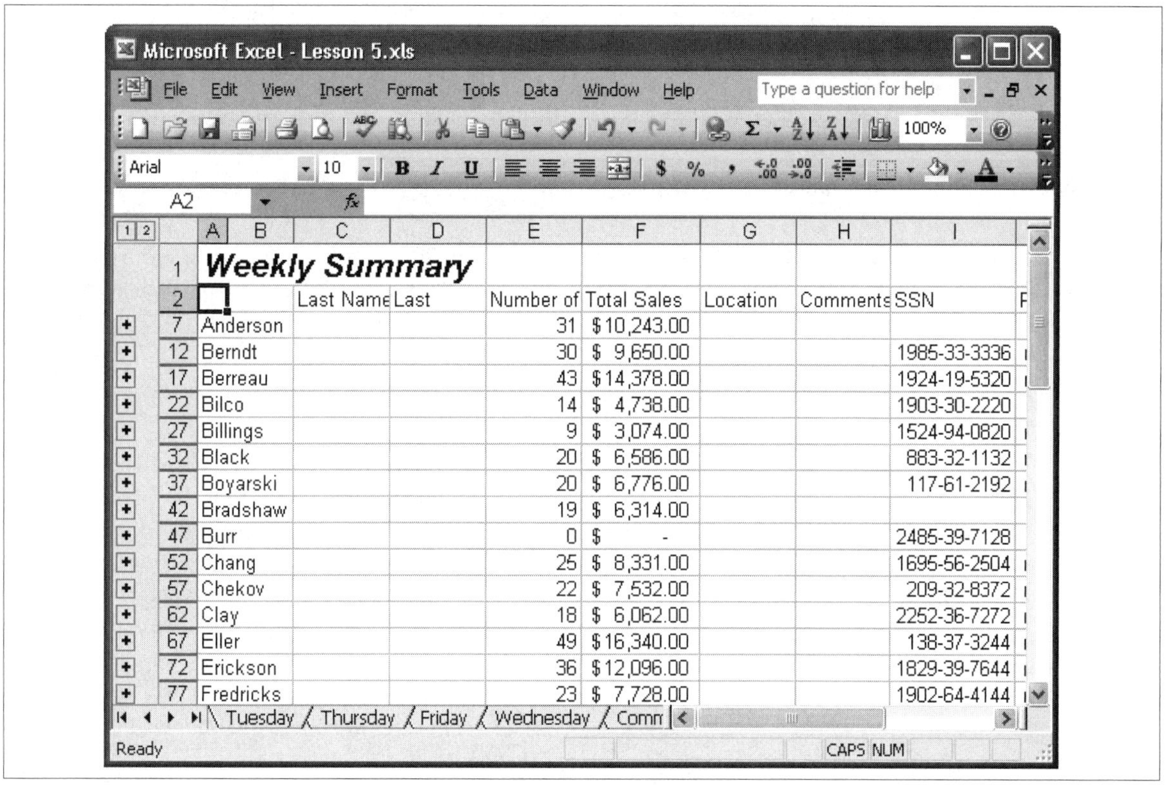

Select the function Excel will use to consolidate data

Specify the cell range you want to consolidate with the cell ranges listed in the All references box

Lists all the cell references that will be consolidated

Open other workbook files that contain data you want to consolidate

Add the selected cell range to the All references list

Delete the selected cell range from the All references list

Select to update the consolidation data automatically whenever the data changes in any of the source areas

Use labels from the selected cell range to consolidate by category

Figure 5-37. The Consolidate command has summarized the information from each of the daily worksheets.

Earlier in this chapter, you manually created a summary worksheet that summarized information on other worksheets. You can have Excel automatically summarize or *consolidate* information from up to 255 worksheets into a single master worksheet using the Data → Consolidate command. This lesson will give you some practice consolidating data.

1 Open the Lesson 5A workbook.

You should remember this workbook; it's the one you've already worked on that contains worksheets for each weekday. The first step in consolidating several worksheets it to select the *destination area*: the worksheet and cells where the consolidated data will go.

2 Activate the Summary worksheet by clicking the Summary tab, and then click cell A2.

Cell A2 is the first cell in the destination range—where the consolidated information will go.

3 Select Data → Consolidate from the menu.

The Consolidate dialog box appears, as shown in Figure 5-36. You can consolidate data in two ways:

- **By Position:** Data is gathered and summarized from the same cell location in each worksheet.
- **By Category:** Data is gathered and summarized by its column or row headings. For example, if your January column is Column A in one worksheet and Column C in another, you can still gather and summarize January when you consolidate by category. Make sure the Top row and/or Left column check boxes in the "Use labels in" section of the Consolidate dialog box are selected to consolidate by category.

For this exercise, you will consolidate by category.

4 Make sure the insertion point is in the Reference text box, then click the Tuesday tab and select the cell range A4:I60.

The absolute reference Tuesday!$A$4:$I$60 appears in the reference text box. Now you need to add the selected cell range to the list of information you want to consolidate.

5 Click Add to add the selected cell range to the "All references" list.

The selected cell reference, Monday!$A$4:$I$60, appears in the "All references" list. Next, you have to add the next cell range or worksheet you want to consolidate.

6 Click the Wednesday tab.

When you click the Wednesday tab, Excel assumes the cell range for this worksheet will be the same as the previously selected Tuesday worksheet, and enters the absolute Wednesday!$A$4:$I$60 in the reference text box for you. Excel has guessed correctly; this is the information you want to add to the consolidation list, so you can click the Add button.

7 Click Add to add the selected cell range to the "All references" list.

Now that you know how to add references to the All references list, you can finish adding the remaining worksheets.

8 Finish adding the remaining worksheets (Thursday, and Friday) to the "All references" list by repeating Steps 6 and 7.

Once you've finished adding the cell ranges that contain the information you want to consolidate, you need to tell Excel you want to consolidate by category.

9 Check both the Top row and Left column check boxes to consolidate by category.

If these check boxes were empty, Excel would consolidate the information by position. There's just one more thing to do before you consolidate the selected information.

10 Check the Create links to source data check box.

This will link the consolidated data, ensuring that it is updated automatically if the data changes in any of the source areas.

11 Click OK to consolidate the information from the selected worksheets.

The dialog box closes and Excel consolidates the information, totaling the sales for all the worksheets. You will probably have to adjust the width of any columns that display ######## so they properly display their contents. Notice Excel also now displays the outline symbols to the left of the worksheet, as shown in Figure 5-37. We'll explain outlining for another lesson.

12 Exit Excel without saving your work to finish the lesson.

For more on consolidating and summarizing information, see Chapter 11.

QUICK REFERENCE

TO CONSOLIDATE DATA:

1. IF POSSIBLE, START WITH A NEW WORKBOOK AND SELECT A CELL IN THAT WORKBOOK AS THE DESTINATION FOR THE CONSOLIDATED INFORMATION.

2. SELECT DATA → CONSOLIDATE FROM THE MENU.

3. SELECT A CONSOLIDATION FUNCTION (SUM IS THE MOST COMMONLY USED FUNCTION).

4. SELECT THE CELL RANGE FOR THE FIRST WORKSHEET (CLICK THE BROWSE BUTTON IF YOU WANT TO REFERENCE ANOTHER WORKBOOK FILE) AND CLICK ADD.

5. REPEAT STEP 4 FOR EACH WORKSHEET YOU WANT TO CONSOLIDATE.

6. SELECT THE LEFT COLUMN AND/OR TOP ROW CHECK BOXES TO CONSOLIDATE BY CATEGORY. LEAVE THESE CHECK BOXES BLANK TO CONSOLIDATE BY POSITION.

7. CHECK THE CREATE LINKS TO SOURCE DATA CHECK BOX IF YOU WANT THE CONSOLIDATED DATA TO BE UPDATED.

8. CLICK OK.

Chapter Five Review

Lesson Summary

Switching Between Sheets in a Workbook

Switch to a worksheet by clicking its sheet tab at the bottom of the screen.

Right-clicking the sheet tab scroll buttons lists all the worksheets in a shortcut menu.

The sheet scroll tab buttons, located at the bottom of the screen, scroll through the worksheet tabs in a workbook.

Inserting and Deleting Worksheets

To Add a New Worksheet: Select Insert → Worksheet from the menu or right-click on a sheet tab, select Insert from the shortcut menu, and select Worksheet from the Insert dialog box.

To Delete a Worksheet: Select Edit → Delete Sheet from the menu or right-click on the sheet tab and select Delete from the shortcut menu.

Renaming and Moving Worksheets

By default, worksheets are named Sheet1, Sheet2, Sheet3, and so on.

To Rename a Worksheet: There are three methods:

- Double-click the sheet tab and enter a new name for the worksheet.
- Right-click the sheet tab, select Rename from the shortcut menu, and enter a new name for the worksheet.
- Select Format → Sheet → Rename from the menu, and enter a new name for the worksheet.

Move a worksheet by dragging its sheet tab to the desired location.

Copy a worksheet by holding down the Ctrl key while dragging the worksheet's tab to a new location.

Working with Several Workbooks and Windows

Click the Select All button to select all the cells in a worksheet.

Switch between open workbooks by selecting Window from the menu and selecting the name of the workbook you want to view.

Select Window → Arrange All to view multiple windows at the same time.

Click a window's Maximize button to maximize a window, and click the window's Restore button to return the window to its original size.

To Manually Resize a Window: Restore the window, then drag the edge of the window until the window is the size you want.

To Move a Window: Drag the window by its title bar to the location where you want to position the window.

Splitting and Freezing a Window

To Split Panes: Drag either the vertical or horizontal split bar or move the cell pointer to the cell below the row and to the right of the column you want to split and select Window → Split from the menu.

To Freeze Panes: Split the window into panes, then select Window → Freeze Panes from the menu.

Referencing External Data

You can include references to values in other worksheets and workbooks by simply selecting the worksheet or workbook (open it if necessary) and clicking the cell that you want to reference.

Creating Headers, Footers, and Page Numbers

Add headers and footers to your worksheet by selecting File → Page Setup from the menu and clicking the Header/Footer tab. Select a preset header or footer from the Header or Footer drop-down list or create your own by clicking the Custom Header or Custom Footer button.

Specifying a Print Area and Controlling Page Breaks

To Select a Print Area: Select the cell range you want to print and select File → Print Area → Set Print Area from the menu.

To Clear a Print Area: Select File → Print Area → Clear Print Area from the menu.

To Insert a Manual Page Break: Move the cell pointer to the cell where the page should start and select Insert → Page Break from the menu.

To Adjust Where the Page Breaks: Select View → Page Break Preview from the menu and drag the Page Break Indicator line to where you want the page break to occur. Select View → Normal from the menu when you're finished.

Adjusting Page Margins and Orientation

To Adjust Margins: Select File → Page Setup from the menu and click the Margins tab. Adjust the appropriate margins.

To Change a Page's Orientation: Select File → Page Setup from the menu, and click the Page tab. In the Orientation section, select either the Portrait or Landscape option.

Adding Print Titles and Gridlines

To Print or Suppress Gridlines: Select File → Page Setup from the menu and click the Sheet tab. Add or remove the check mark in the Gridlines check box.

To Print Row or Column Titles: Select File → Page Setup from the menu and click the Sheet tab. Specify which row(s) or column(s) should appear at the top and/or left of every page in the appropriate boxes under the Title section.

Changing the Paper Size and Print Scale

To Change the Print Scale: Select File → Page Setup from the menu and click the Page tab. Enter a percent number in the "% normal size" text box or enter the number of pages you want the worksheet to fit on.

To Change the Paper Size: Select File → Page Setup from the menu and click the Page tab. Click the Paper size list to select the paper size.

Protecting a Worksheet

To Protect a Cell or Cell Range: Select the cell or cell range you want to protect, select Format → Cells from the menu, and click the Protection tab. Check the Locked check box. By default, all cells are locked.

You must protect a worksheet to prevent changes to be made to any locked cells. Protect a worksheet by selecting Tools → Protection → Protect Sheet from the menu and specifying the areas you want protected.

Select Tools → Protection → Unprotect Sheet from the menu to unprotect a worksheet.

Hiding Columns, Rows, and Sheets

- **To Hide a Column or Row:** Right-click the column heading or the row heading. Select Hide from the shortcut menu.
- **To Hide a Sheet:** Select the sheet you want to hide. Select Format → Sheet → Hide.
- **To Unhide a Sheet:** Select Format → Sheet → Unhide. Select the worksheet you want to unhide.

Viewing a Worksheet and Comparing a Workbook Side by Side

To Zoom: Click the Zoom list arrow on the Standard toolbar and select the magnification level at which you would like to view your worksheet.

To Compare workbooks Side by Side: Open the two workbooks you want to compare and select Window → Compare Side by Side from the menu. Click the Close Side by Side button on the Compare Side by Side toolbar when you're finished.

Viewing a Worksheet and Saving a Custom View

A custom view saves the current appearance of a workbook so that you don't have to change the settings every time you view or print the workbook.

To Create a Custom View: Set up the worksheet's appearance and print settings and select View → Custom Views from the menu.

To Use a Custom View: Select View → Custom Views from the menu, select the view you want to use, and click Show.

Working with Templates

To Create a Template: Create a new workbook or open an existing workbook you want to use for the template and select File → Save As from the menu. Select Template from the "Save as type" list, give the template a name, and click OK to save the template.

To Create a Workbook Based on a Template: Select File → New from the menu. In the Templates area, click the On my computer… option button and select the template you want to use.

Consolidating Worksheets

You can summarize or consolidate information from multiple worksheets into a single master sheet with the Data → Consolidate command.

To Consolidate Data: If possible, start with a new workbook and select a cell in that workbook as the destination for the consolidated information. Select Data →

Consolidate from the menu and select a consolidation function (SUM is the most commonly used function). Select the cell range for the first worksheet (click the Browse button if you want to reference another workbook file) and click Add. Select the other worksheets you want to consolidate, clicking Add after each one. Select the Create links to source data check box if you want the consolidated data to be updated.

Quiz

1. All of the following statements are true except…

    A. You can change the order of worksheets in a workbook by dragging their sheet tabs to new positions.

    B. You can rename a sheet by double-clicking its sheet tab.

    C. You can switch between worksheets by selecting Window from the menu and selecting the name of the sheet from the Window menu.

    D. You can add and delete worksheets from the workbook.

2. How can you switch between worksheets when there isn't enough room on the screen to display all the sheet tabs? (Select all that apply):

    A. Click the Sheet Tab Scroll buttons until the sheet tab you want appears, then click that sheet tab.

    B. Select Window from the menu and select the name of the sheet from the Window menu.

    C. Right-click any sheet tab and select the name of the sheet from the shortcut menu.

    D. Press Ctrl + → or Ctrl + ← to move between the sheets.

3. Formulas can contain references to cells in other worksheets and even in other workbooks. (True or False?)

4. Which of the following statements is NOT true?

    A. You can delete a sheet by right-clicking its sheet tab and selecting Delete from the shortcut menu.

    B. The Select All button, located to in the upper-left corner of the worksheet window, selects the entire worksheet.

    C. You can split a window into several panes by clicking the Panes button on the Standard toolbar.

    D. You can freeze a pane so that it stays in place.

5. You're trying to print a worksheet that has just a few columns that won't fit on a single page. Which of the following methods is the easiest way to get this worksheet to fit on a single page?

    A. Open the Print dialog box (File → Page Setup), click the Page tab, select the "Fit to" option and specify that you want the worksheet to fit on 1 page wide by 1 page tall.

    B. Open the Print dialog box (File → Page Setup), click the Margins tab, and adjust the worksheet's margins.

    C. Click the Preview button on the Standard toolbar and click the Shrink to Fit button.

    D. Adjust the size of the fonts and the width of the columns in the worksheet.

6. Cells in a worksheet are unlocked by default. (True or False?)

7. Which of the following statements is NOT true?

    A. You must protect a document to prevent changes being made to any locked cell.

    B. You can lock or unlock a cell or cell range by clicking the Lock button on the Standard toolbar.

    C. You can switch between open workbooks by selecting Window from the menu and selecting the name of the workbook from the Window menu.

    D. Excel normally prints the column and row-heading labels on every page of worksheet.

8. Which of the following options is NOT located in the Page Setup dialog box?

   A. Page Orientation

   B. Margins

   C. Headers and Footers

   D. Page Break Preview

9. How do you add a new worksheet to a workbook?

   A. Click the New Worksheet button on the Standard toolbar.

   B. New worksheets must be purchased from Microsoft for $.25 a piece.

   C. Right-click any worksheet tab and select Insert from the shortcut menu.

   D. Select New → Worksheet from the menu.

10. How do you set a print area, so that Excel only prints part of a worksheet?

    A. Select area you want to print and select File → Print Area → Set Print Area from the menu.

    B. Select area you want to print and click the Print Preview button on the Standard toolbar.

    C. Select the area you want to print and click the Print button on the Standard toolbar.

    D. There's isn't a way of doing this.

11. How can you view and/or add a page header to a worksheet?

    A. Click the Header button on the Formatting toolbar.

    B. Select File → Page Setup from the menu and click the Header/Footer tab.

    C. Select area you want to print and click the Print button on the Standard toolbar.

    D. There is no way to do this.

12. The page isn't breaking where you want it to when you print a worksheet. How can you change this?

    A. Click the Break Page button on the Standard toolbar, and then click where you want the page to break several times with the hammer cursor.

    B. Click the cell where you want the page to break and select Window → Freeze Panes from the menu.

    C. Click the Print Preview button on the Standard toolbar and click the Fit to Print button on the toolbar.

    D. Select View → Page Break Preview from the menu and drag the page break indicator line to where you want the page to break.

13. How can you hide a row or column?

    A. Right-click the row or column heading and select Hide from the shortcut menu.

    B. Select the row or column heading and select Tools → Hide from the menu.

    C. Cover the row or column with a piece of masking tape.

    D. Select the row or column heading and click the Hide button on the Formatting toolbar.

14. You want to print a worksheet on legal-sized paper. How can you do this?

    A. Select Format → Paper from the menu and select Legal from the Paper Size list.

    B. Right-click the Select All button on the worksheet and select Legal Size from the shortcut menu.

    C. Select File → Page Setup from the menu, click the Paper Size tab, and select Legal from the Paper Size list.

    D. You need to purchase a legal-sized printer and the legal version of Microsoft Excel.

Homework

1. Open the Homework 5A workbook and save it as "Regional Expenses."

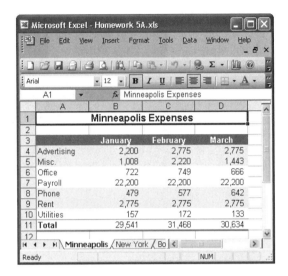

2. Move the Boston sheet tab in front of the Minneapolis tab.

3. Rename the "Minneapolis" tab "Twin Cities".

4. Insert two new worksheets with the names "Dallas" and "Totals"

5. Open the Homework 5B workbook. Copy its information to the Dallas worksheet in your Regional Expenses workbook. Close the Homework 5B workbook when you're finished.

6. Go to the Totals worksheet and create a worksheet that summarizes the monthly expenses for all four regional offices. (Hint: You'll have to create external references to do this).

7. Go to the Twin Cities worksheet, select the range A3:C11 and set it as a Print Area.

8. Add a header to the worksheet that says "Regional Expenses, First Quarter".

9. Split any worksheet into two panes, freeze the panes, and then remove the split.

Quiz Answers

1. C. You switch to a worksheet by clicking its sheet tab. You switch between open workbooks by selecting them from the Window menu.

2. A and C. Clicking the Sheet Tab Scroll buttons displays new sheet tabs, which you can then click. Right-clicking a sheet tab displays a shortcut menu that lists all the worksheets in a workbook.

3. True. You can create references to cells in other worksheets and workbooks by viewing the worksheet or workbook and selecting the cell(s) you want to reference.

4. C. There isn't a Panes button on the Standard toolbar.

5. A. Using the "Fit to" scaling option is by far the easiest method to force the worksheet to fit on a single page. B and D might work, but they take a lot more time and effort.

6. False. Cells are locked by default. You must unlock them by selecting Format → Cells from the menu, clicking the Protection tab, and removing the check from the Locked check box.

7. B. There isn't a Lock button on the Standard toolbar (although adding a Lock button might not be a bad idea).

8. D. Page Break Preview is located under View → Page Break Preview.

9. C. To add a new worksheet to a workbook, right-click any worksheet tab and select Insert from the shortcut menu.

10. A. To set a print area, select an area you want to print and select File → Print Area → Set Print Area from the menu.

11. B. You can add and/or view the page header by selecting File → Page Setup from the menu and clicking the Header/Footer tab.

12. D. You can change where the page breaks are by selecting View → Page Break Preview from the menu and dragging the page break indicator line to where you want the page to break.

13. A. You can hide a row or column by right-clicking the row or column heading and selecting Hide from the shortcut menu.

14. C. To print on legal-sized paper, select File → Page Setup from the menu, click the Paper Size tab, and select Legal from the Paper Size list.

CHAPTER 6

MORE FUNCTIONS AND FORMULAS

CHAPTER OBJECTIVES:

Create a formula with several operators and cell ranges

Use the Insert Function feature to enter and edit formulas

Create and use range names

Select nonadjacent cell ranges

Use the AutoCalculate feature

Create a conditional formula with the IF function

Use the PMT function

Display and print formulas in a worksheet

Identify and fix formula errors

CHAPTER TASK: CREATE PAYROLL AND MORTGAGE WORKSHEETS

Prerequisites

- **Understand how to use menus, toolbars, dialog boxes, and shortcut keystrokes**
- **Understand how to select cell ranges**
- **Understand how to enter values, labels, and formulas into a cell**
- **Understand how to reference cells**

Formulas are the heart and soul of a spreadsheet. Without formulas, Excel would be nothing more than a grid you could use to enter numbers and text. As you will see in this chapter, formulas can do a lot more than just adding, subtracting, multiplying, and dividing. Excel has hundreds of different formulas you can use to create complex statistical, financial, and scientific calculations. The most expensive calculator in the world couldn't come close to matching all the functions Excel has.

This chapter is somewhat different from the others in this book: it's broken into two different parts. In the first part of this chapter, you will become an expert at creating formulas and using different types of functions. The second part of this chapter is a reference of the most commonly used functions, organized by category.

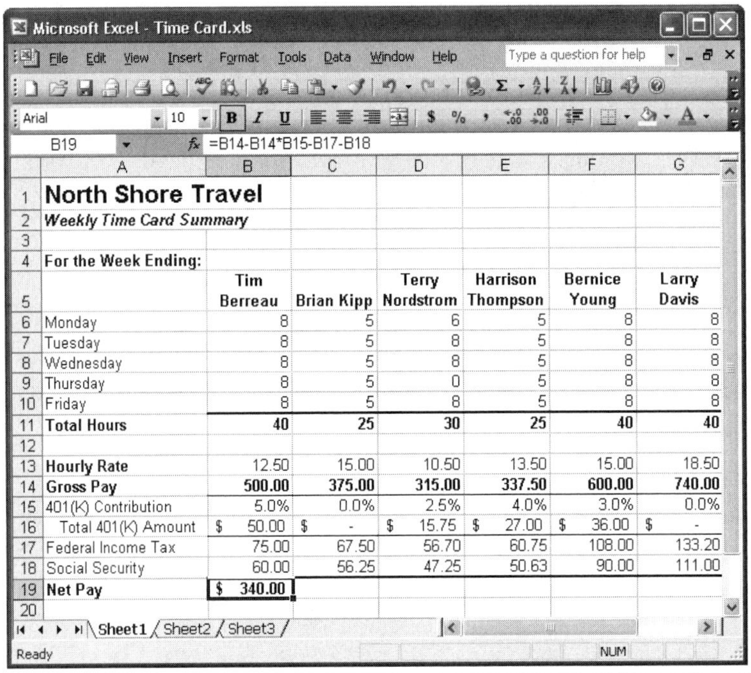

Formulas with Several Operators and Cell Ranges

Figure 6-1. Entering a formula with several operators and cell ranges.

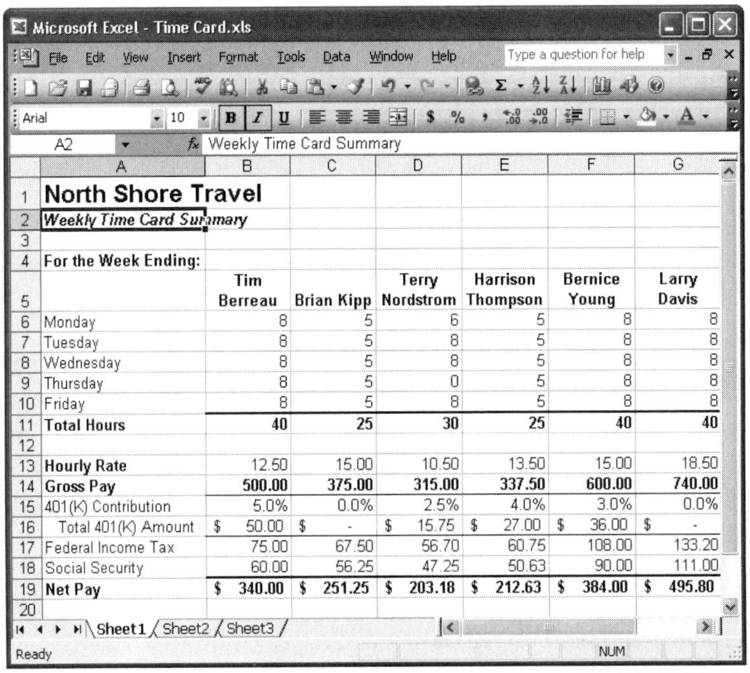

Figure 6-2. The completed worksheet.

We'll start this chapter by creating some more complicated formulas. First let's review: formulas can contain several values, such as 81 and 3.5; cell references, such as B5 and C1:D11; operators, such as * (multiplication) and + (addition); and functions, such as SUM and AVERAGE. When you combine several operations and functions into a single formula (see Figure 6-1), Excel performs the operations in the order shown in Table 6-1. When a formula contains several operators with the same precedence, Excel calculates the formula from left to right. You can change the order Excel calculates a formula by enclosing the part of the formula you want Excel to calculate first in parentheses.

You'll get some practice creating formulas with several references and operators in this lesson by creating formulas to compute employee 401(K)contributions and net pay.

1 Start Microsoft Excel. If necessary, open the workbook Lesson 6A and save it as Time Card.

This time card calculates the employees weekly payroll for the Duluth North Shore Travel office. All the information and *almost* all of the formulas are already here; you just need to add a few more formulas to complete the timecard workbook. First, you need to create a formula to calculate how much to deposit to each employee's 401K account. North Shore Travel matches the employee's 401K contribution, so this formula will be a little trickier than what you're used to.

2 Click cell B16 and type =.

Typing an equals sign tells Excel that you want to enter a formula.

3 Click cell B14, type *, and click cell B15 (or you can type B14*B15). *Don't press Enter after entering the formula!*

This part of the formula multiplies gross pay (in cell B14) with the percentage the employees want to deduct for their 401K contribution (in cell B15). You're not finished with the formula yet—remember that North Shore Travel matches any 401K contributions made by their employees.

4 Type *2 and press Enter.

Excel calculates the total 401K amount, $50. Copy the formula you just created to the rest of the row.

5 Copy the formula in cell B16 to the cell range C16:H16.

The worksheet needs one more formula: one to calculate the net pay.

6 Click cell B19, type =, click cell B14, and type – (a minus sign).

Here's where the formula gets tricky. You can't directly subtract the 401K amount from cell B16 since it includes both the employee *and* company contribution. You will have to calculate the amount of the employee's 401K contribution and then subtract it from the gross pay.

7 Click cell B14 (that's right, click cell B14 again) type *, click cell B15, and press Enter.

The formula subtracts the amount of the employee deduction (5% of $500, or $25) from the gross pay. The formula isn't finished yet—you have to go back and subtract the Federal Income Tax and Social Security amounts.

8 Click cell B19, click the Formula bar, and type –B17-B18 at the end of the formula. The complete formula should now read =B14-B14*B15-B17-B18. Complete the formula by pressing Enter.

Your formula is finished and Excel calculates the net pay for the employee. Wow! There's not much money left over, is there?

9 Copy the formula in cell B19 to the cell range C19:H19.

Compare your worksheet with the one in Figure 6-2.

When you use several operators in a formula, Excel performs the operations in the order shown in Table 6-1. When a formula contains operators with the same precedence—for example, if a formula contains both a multiplication and division operator—Excel calculates them from left to right. To change the order of evaluation, enclose the part of the formula to be calculated first in parentheses. For example, the formula =(10-5)+(4/2) would subtract 5 from 10, then divide 4 by 2, and then add the results.

Table 6-1. Order in Which Excel Performs Operations in Formulas (the order is displayed from top to bottom)

Operator	Description
( )	Parentheses change the order of evaluation. For example:
	=(20+5) / (10-5) would add 20 and 5 (25), subtract 10 by 5 (5) and then divide the results to equal 5.
	But...
	=20+5/10-5 would divide 5 by 10 (0.5), add the result to 20 (20.5) and then subtract 5 to equal 15.5.
:	Reference Operator
%	Percent
^	Exponentiation
* and /	Multiplication and division
+ and -	Addition and subtraction
= = =	Comparison

QUICK REFERENCE

**TO CHANGE THE ORDER IN WHICH EXCEL
PERFORMS OPERATIONS IN FORMULAS:**

- ENCLOSE THE PART OF THE FORMULA YOU WANT
  TO CALCULATE FIRST IN PARENTHESES.

Using the Insert Function Feature

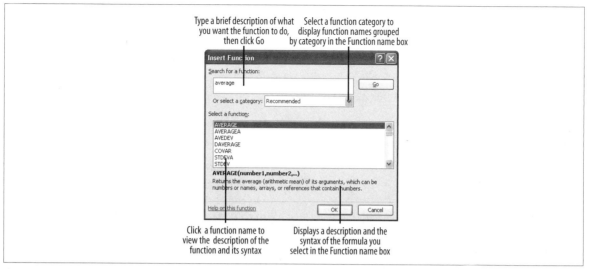

Type a brief description of what you want the function to do, then click Go

Select a function category to display function names grouped by category in the Function name box

Click a function name to view the description of the function and its syntax

Displays a description and the syntax of the formula you select in the Function name box

Figure 6-3. The Insert Function dialog box.

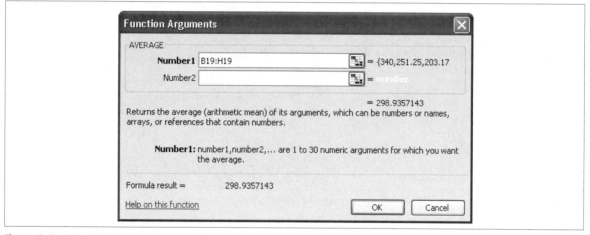

Figure 6-4. The Function Arguments dialog box helps you enter a formula.

There are several hundred functions available in Excel. Some functions are rather easy to enter, such as the SUM function, while others are much more difficult. For example, the syntax for the DB function, used to depreciate an asset, is "DB(cost,salvage,life,period,month)". Yikes! How are you supposed to remember that? Luckily, if you use Excel's Insert Function feature you don't have to.

The Insert Function feature helps you select, enter, and edit worksheet functions. To use the Insert Function feature all you have to do is click the Insert Function button on the Formula bar.

In this lesson, you will use the Insert Function feature to create a simple AVERAGE formula.

1 Click cell A20, click the Bold button on the Formatting toolbar, type Average Net Pay, and press Tab.

In cell B20, you will use the Insert Function button to help you create a formula that calculates the Average Net Pay.

Insert Function button

2 **Click the** Insert Function button **on the Formula bar.**

The Insert Function dialog box appears, as shown in Figure 6-3. Simply type a brief description of what you want a function to do, then click Go. Excel will display a list of functions likely to fit your needs.

3 **In the** Search for a function box **type** average **and click** Go.

Excel displays a list of functions that are somehow related to the world "average."

4 **Select** AVERAGE **from the Function list.**

Notice the bottom of the Insert Function dialog box displays a description and the syntax of the selected function.

The **Collapse Dialog button** temporarily shrinks and moves the dialog box so that you enter a cell range by selecting cells in the worksheet. When you finish, you can click the button again or press <Enter> to display the entire dialog box.

5 **Click** OK.

The Insert Function dialog box closes, and the Function Arguments dialog box appears, as shown in Figure 6-4. The AVERAGE function is actually a very simple function—the only arguments (parts or values of a formula) it requires are the numbers you that you want to average.

6 **Select the cell range** B19:H19.

This range contains the Net Pay for all the employees.

NOTE *If the Insert Function dialog box is in the way when you want to select a cell or cell range, you can click any text box's Collapse Dialog button to collapse the function palette and select the cell or cell range.*

7 **Press** Enter.

The Function palette completes the formula for you and closes. Cell A22 calculates and displays the average Net Pay amount.

8 **Save your work.**

The Insertion Function dialog box organizes formulas by categories. Table 6-2 lists and describes the different types of function categories that are available.

Table 6-2. Function Categories

Category	Description
Most Recently Used	Lists the functions you've used most recently.
All	Lists every function available in Excel.
Financial	Lists financial functions to calculate interest, payments, loans, etc.
Date & Time	Lists functions to calculate date and time values.
Math & Trig	Lists math and trigonometry functions, such as SUM, COS, and TAN.
Statistical	Lists statistical functions, to calculate averages, standard deviations, etc.
Lookup & Reference	Lists functions that look up or reference values.
Database	Lists functions that look up or calculate values in a list or database.
Text	Lists functions that can be used with text or labels.
Logical	Lists IF…THEN functions.
Information	Lists functions that return information about values and the worksheet itself.
User Defined	Lists custom functions that you (or another use) have created.

QUICK REFERENCE

TO USE THE INSERT FUNCTION BUTTON TO ENTER OR EDIT A FORMULA:

1. SELECT THE CELL WHERE YOU WANT TO ENTER OR EDIT A FORMULA AND CLICK THE INSERT FUNCTION BUTTON ON THE FORMULA BAR.

2. SELECT THE CATEGORY OF THE TYPE OF FUNCTION YOU WANT TO USE FROM THE "OR SELECT A CATEGORY" DROP-DOWN LIST.

OR...

1. TYPE A BRIEF DESCRIPTION OF THE FUNCTION OR FORMULA YOU WANT TO CREATE AND CLICK GO.

2. SELECT THE FUNCTION YOU WANT TO USE FROM THE "SELECT A FUNCTION" LIST AND CLICK OK.

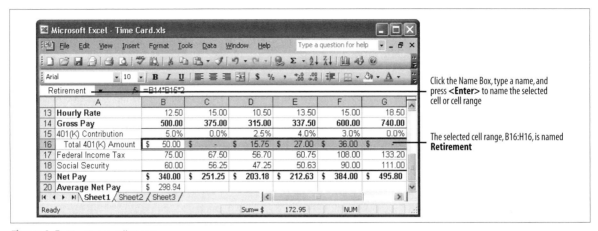

Figure 6-5. Naming a cell range.

Figure 6-6. The Create Names dialog box.

You can create a range name by selecting a cell range and then giving it a name in the **Name box** in the Formula bar.

References for cells and cell ranges can sometimes be difficult to read and remember. In the current workbook, what does the cell range B16:H16 refer to? It's the cell range that contains the total 401K contributions (both the employee's and employer's) for each employee. Assigning a name to a cell or cell range makes it easier to read, remember, and use in formulas. So instead of totaling the 401K contributions with the formula, =SUM(B16:H16), you could use a range name to create the more legible formula, =SUM(Total401K).

This lesson will show you how to create range names and use them in your formulas. This lesson also explains how to use column and row heading labels in your formulas, and how Excel can automatically create range names for you.

1 Select the cell range B16:H16.

The selected cell range contains the employer and employee contributions to each employee's 401K account. Here's how to give the selected cell range a meaningful name, instead of referring to it as B16:H16.

2 With the cell range B16:H16 still selected, click the Name box in the Formula bar, type Retirement (as shown in Figure 6-5), and press Enter.

Now when you need to reference the 401(K) amounts, you can use the Range Name "Retirement" instead of the obscure and hard-to-remember cell reference B16:H16.

3 Click cell A21, click the Bold button on the Formatting toolbar, type Total 401K, and press Tab.

4 In cell B21, type =SUM(Retirement) and press Enter.

Excel calculates the sum of the Retirement range, B16:H16.

Once you create a Named Range you can quickly select it by picking it from the Name box in the Formula bar.

Name Box List

5 Click the Name box arrow and select Retirement.

Excel selects the Retirement range. You don't have to manually create names; you can have Excel automatically create them for you.

6 Select the cell range A5:H11, and select Insert → Name from the menu.

Here's a brief summary of what each of the items in the Name submenu does:

- **Define:** Creates a name for a cell, a cell range, or constant or computed value that you can use to refer to the cell, range, or value. (This is the same as typing it directly in the Name box.) You can also delete any existing names.

- **Paste:** Inserts the selected name into the Formula bar. If the Formula bar is active and you begin a formula by typing an equals sign (=), clicking Paste will paste the selected name at the insertion point. If the Formula bar is not active, double-clicking a name in the Paste Name box pastes an equal sign (=) followed by the selected name into the Formula bar.

- **Create:** Creates names by using labels in a selected range.

- **Apply:** Searches formulas in the selected cells and replaces references with names defined for them, if they exist.

- **Label:** Creates names for formulas by using text labels from the rows or columns of a selected range.

7 Select Create from the Name menu.

The Create Names dialog box appears, as shown in Figure 6-6. The Create Names will automatically create range names based on the current selection.

8 Verify that the Top row and Left column check boxes are checked and click OK.

The Create Names dialog box closes, and Excel automatically creates names for the selected cell range. You can verify that Excel created the correct names by clicking the Name box arrow.

9 Click the Name Box List arrow.

The column heading names should appear in the Name Box list.

10 Click anywhere in the worksheet window to close the Name Box list.

You can also use column and row labels in the worksheet to refer to data in formulas—without having to create any names at all!

11 Click cell A22, click the Bold button on the Formatting toolbar, type Max Hourly Rate, and press Tab.

12 In cell B22, type =MAX(Hourly Rate) and press Enter.

Excel returns the maximum value in the Hourly Rate row, 18.50.

13 Save your work.

QUICK REFERENCE

TO NAME A CELL OR CELL RANGE:

1. SELECT THE CELL OR CELL RANGE YOU WANT TO NAME.

2. CLICK THE NAME BOX ON THE FORMULA BAR, TYPE THE NAME, AND PRESS ENTER.

TO AUTOMATICALLY CREATE NAMES:

1. SELECT THE CELL OR CELL RANGE YOU WANT TO NAME.

2. SELECT INSERT → NAME → CREATE FROM THE MENU.

3. IF NECESSARY, CHANGE THE CHECK BOXES IN THE CREATE NAMES DIALOG BOX.

4. CLICK OK.

TO CHANGE THE CELL REFERENCE OF A NAME:

1. SELECT THE NEW CELL OR CELL RANGE YOU WANT TO USE AS THE REFERENCE.

2. SELECT INSERT → NAME → APPLY FROM THE MENU.

3. SELECT THE NAME YOU WANT TO USE ON THE SELECTED REFERENCE AND CLICK OK.

TO DELETE NAMES:

• SELECT INSERT → NAME → CREATE FROM THE MENU, SELECT THE NAME YOU WANT TO DELETE, AND CLICK DELETE.

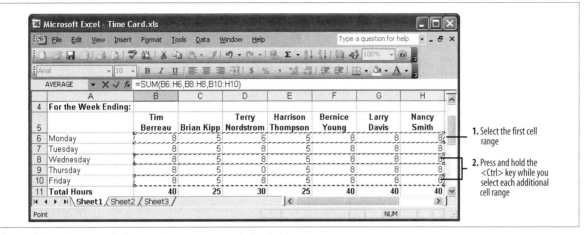

Figure 6-7. Selecting multiple nonadjacent ranges with the Ctrl key.

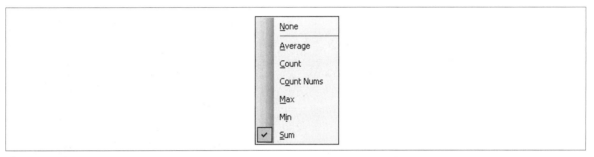

Figure 6-8. Shortcut menu list of AutoCalculate options.

If you've gotten this far in the book you obviously know how to select and use cell ranges in your formulas. But, how do you select cell ranges that aren't next to each other? That's the first topic explained in this lesson.

Also covered in this lesson is Excel's nifty *AutoCalculate* feature, used to calculate a total or average of a cell range without entering a formula.

1 If necessary, open the workbook Lesson 6B and save it as Time Card.

2 Click cell A24, click the Bold button on the Formatting toolbar, type M-W-F, and press Tab.

Next you want to total the hours from the Monday, Wednesday, and Friday rows only. You can select several nonadjacent cell ranges by holding down the Ctrl key when you select the ranges.

AutoSum button

3 Make sure cell B24 is active and click the AutoSum button on the Standard toolbar.

Excel selects the closest cell with data in it (B22) as the argument for the SUM function. This isn't the cell range you want to use in your formula—you want to find the totals of the Monday, Wednesday, and Friday rows.

4 Select Monday's cell range, B6:H6, press and hold the Ctrl key, select Wednesday's cell range, B8:H8, and then select Friday's cell range, B10:H10. Release the Ctrl button when you're finished.

The nonadjacent ranges in the Monday, Wednesday, and Friday rows are all selected, as indicated by the shimmering dotted line around each of the columns (see Figure 6-7). Notice the Formula bar displays the cell ranges: =SUM(B6:H6,B8:H8,B10:H10).

5 Press Enter.

Excel calculates the total hours for the Monday, Wednesday, and Friday rows.

On to the second topic covered in this lesson—Auto-Calculate. Sometimes you may want to calculate the total of several cells without actually creating a formula. Excel's AutoCalculate makes this incredibly easy—simply select the cell range you want to total, and the calculation is displayed on the status bar.

Sum=240

AutoCalculate, found in the Status Bar

6 Select the cell range B6:H10.

The AutoCalculate area of the status bar displays the total of the selected cell range: Sum=240. You can also use AutoCalculate to do other simple and quick calculations. To change the calculation type, right-click the AutoCalculate area of the status bar.

7 Right-click the AutoCalculate area of the Status bar.

A shortcut menu appears with a list of the AutoCalculate options (see Figure 6-8):

* **None:** Disables AutoCalculate.
* **Average:** Calculates the average of the selected cells.
* **Count:** Counts the number of nonempty cells.
* **Count Nums:** Counts the number of cells that contain numbers.
* **Max:** Returns the largest value in a range of cells.
* **Min:** Returns the smallest value in a range of cells.
* **Sum:** Adds all the numbers in a range of cells (the default setting).

You want AutoCalculate to display the average of any selected cells.

8 Select Average from the AutoCalculate shortcut menu.

AutoCalculate calculates the average for the selected cell range. Return AutoCorrect back to the default Sum setting.

9 Right-click the AutoCalculate area of the Status bar and select Sum.

10 Save your work.

QUICK REFERENCE

TO SELECT NONADJACENT CELL RANGES:

* SELECT THE FIRST CELL RANGE, THEN PRESS AND HOLD THE CTRL KEY WHILE YOU SELECT ADDITIONAL CELL RANGES.

TO USE AUTOCALCULATE:

* SELECT THE CELL RANGE YOU WANT TO TOTAL OR CALCULATE. THE STATUS BAR WILL DISPLAY THE RESULTS.

TO CHANGE THE AUTOCALCULATE FUNCTION:

* RIGHT-CLICK THE AUTOCALCULATE AREA OF THE STATUS BAR AND SELECT THE FUNCTION YOU WANT AUTOCALCULATE TO USE FROM THE SHORTCUT MENU.

Using the IF Function to Create Conditional Formulas

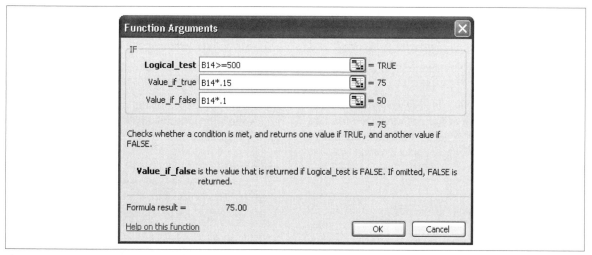

Figure 6-9. Creating a conditional formula using the IF function and the Function Arguments dialog box.

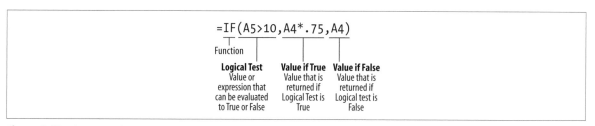

Figure 6-10. The syntax for the IF function.

This lesson introduces a very useful function: the *IF* function. The IF function is a *conditional function* or *logical function* because it will evaluate a condition you specify, return one value if the condition is true and another value if the condition is false. For example, you could use the IF function in an invoice to create a formula that would subtract a 5% discount from the invoice if the total was more than $500.00; otherwise, it wouldn't subtract anything.

The IF function contains three parts or arguments, as shown in Figure 6-10. Since you can use the Insert Function button to help you create IF function formulas, you really don't need to memorize the syntax of the IF function.

1 Click cell B17 and press Delete to clear the cell contents.

The Federal Income tax rate changes at different income levels. You have determined that employees who earn $500 or more in a week are subject to a 15%

tax rate, while employees who earn less than $500 in a week are subject to a 10% tax rate. You can create a formula using the IF function to evaluate the employee's earnings and then multiply it by the appropriate tax rate. The IF function is a little more difficult than other functions, so use the Insert Function tool to help you enter it.

Insert Function button

2 Click the Insert Function button on the Formula bar.

The Function Arguments dialog box appears.

3 Select Logical in the Function category list, select IF in the Function name list, and click OK.

The Function Arguments dialog box appears, as shown in Figure 6-9. You're ready to start entering the IF formula.

4 Type B14>=500 in the in Logical_test **text box.**

You just entered the first argument of the IF function, which evaluates a statement as true or false (see Figure 6-10). Here you want to evaluate if the value in B14 is equal to or greater than $500.

NOTE *Remember, you can also create cell references by clicking the cell or cell range you want to reference. Click the Collapse Dialog Box button to collapse the function palette and select the cell range if the Function Arguments dialog box is in the way.*

The next step is entering true argument of the IF function.

5 Select the Value_if_true **text box by clicking it or pressing the Tab key, and type** B14*.15.

If the value in B14 is equal to or greater than 500, the IF function will multiply it by 0.15. Move on to the next step to complete the IF function by entering the Value if false argument—what the function should do if the value is *not* equal to or greater than $500.

6 Move to the Value_if_false **text box by clicking it or pressing the Tab key, and type** B14*.1.

If the value in B14 is less than $500, the IF function will multiply the value in cell B14 by 0.10. Compare your screen with the one shown in Figure 6-9.

7 Click OK **to complete the formula.**

The Function Arguments dialog box closes. The IF function in B17 multiplies the Gross Pay by 15%, since it is equal to or greater than $500.

8 Copy the formula in cell B17 to the remaining cells in row 17.

After copying the IF formula, notice that those columns with Gross Pay less than $500 are multiplied by 10% instead of 15%.

9 Save your work and close the current workbook.

The IF function is one of the more difficult functions, but it's also very powerful and is well worth the effort of learning how to use it.

QUICK REFERENCE

TO USE THE IF FUNCTION IN A FORMULA:

* WRITE THE FORMULA USING THE SYNTAX =IF(LOGICAL_TEST,VALUE_IF_TRUE,VALUE_IF_FALSE).

OR...

1. CLICK THE INSERT FUNCTION BUTTON ON THE FORMULA BAR TO OPEN THE INSERT FORMULA DIALOG BOX.

2. SELECT LOGICAL IN THE FUNCTION CATEGORY LIST, SELECT IF IN THE FUNCTION NAME LIST, AND CLICK OK.

3. ENTER THE REQUIRED ARGUMENTS FOR THE IF FUNCTION.

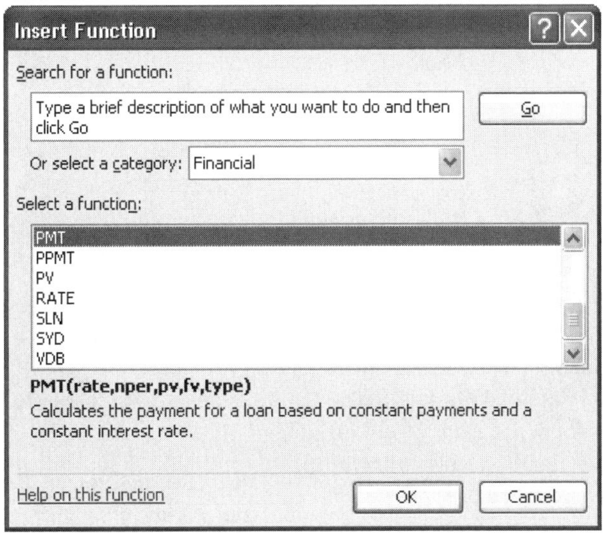

Using the PMT Function

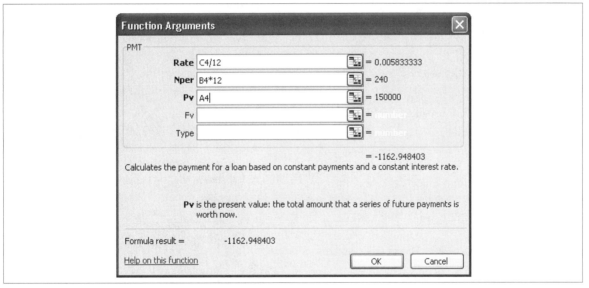

Figure 6-11. The Insert Function dialog box.

Figure 6-12. The Function Arguments dialog box.

	A	B	C	D	E	F
1	**Mortgage Payment Table**					
2						
3	**Loan Amount**	**Loan Length (in years)**	**Interest Rate**	**Monthly Payment**	**Total Payments**	**Interest Paid**
4	$ 150,000	20	7.0%	$1,162.95	$279,107.62	$129,107.62
5	$ 150,000	20	7.5%	$1,208.39	$290,013.55	$140,013.55
6	$ 150,000	30	7.5%	$1,048.82	$377,575.83	$227,575.83

Figure 6-13. Using the PMT function to calculate monthly loan payments.

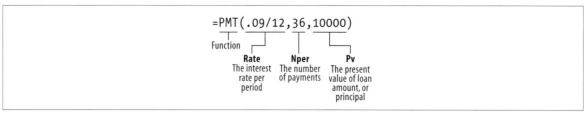

$$=PMT(.09/12, 36, 10000)$$

Function

Rate
The interest rate per period

Nper
The number of payments

Pv
The present value of loan amount, or principal

Figure 6-14. The PMT Function.

The PMT function is a very valuable function if you work with real estate, investments, or are considering taking out a loan. The PMT function calculates the payment for a loan based on periodic payments and a constant interest rate. For example, say you want to take out a $10,000 car loan at 8% interest and will pay the loan off in four years. You can use the PMT function to calculate that the monthly payments for such a loan would be $244.13. You can also use the PMT function to determine payments to annuities or investments. For example, if you want to save $50,000 in 20 years by saving the same amount each month, you can use PMT to determine how much you must save.

Insert Function button

1 Open the workbook named Lesson 6C and save it as Mortgage Table.

All of the information you need to find the monthly payments has already been entered. All you have to do is use the PMT function to calculate the monthly payment. The PMT function is a little complicated, so use the Insert Function feature to help you enter it.

2 Click cell D4 and click the Insert Function button on the Formula bar.

3 Select Financial from the Or Select a Category list, scroll down the Select a Function list, select PMT, and then click OK (see Figure 6-11).

The Function Arguments dialog box appears, as shown in Figure 6-12. You're ready to start entering the PMT formula to calculate the monthly mortgage payments. (See Figure 6-13 for the PMT syntax.) Look at Figure 6-12: the first argument of the PMT function is the interest rate. Since the Function Arguments dialog box is in the way, you'll have to click the

Collapse Dialog button to see and reference the cells on the worksheet.

Collapse Dialog Box button

4 Click the Rate Collapse Dialog Box button, click cell C4, and press Enter.

Because you want to calculate monthly payments instead of annual payments, you will need to divide the annual interest rates by 12.

5 Type /12 to divide the annual interest rate.

C4/12 should appear in the Rate text box. The next argument in the PMT function is the *Nper*—the total number of payments for the loan.

6 Click the Nper box and type B4*12.

Again, you want to calculate monthly payments so you need to multiply the total number of years by 12. The last step in the PMT formula is entering the *Pv*—the principal.

Enter Button

7 Click the Pv Collapse Dialog Box button, click cell A4, and press Enter.

You're finished entering the PMT formula so you can close the Function Arguments dialog box.

8 Click OK.

The Function Arguments dialog box closes, and the monthly payment ($1,162.95) appears in cell D4.

Hey! Why does the monthly payment appear red (a negative number)? It's because the PMT formula shows the borrower's point of view, and therefore the payments are calculated as a negative cash flow. You can easily change the formula so that it shows a positive number by editing the formula and placing a minus sign in front of the Pv value.

9 Edit the formula in cell D4 by clicking the Formula bar, and adding a - (minus sign) immediately after the = sign so that the formula reads =-PMT(C4/12,B4*12,A4), then click the Enter button on the Formula bar.

The PMT formula now displays the monthly payments as a positive number. Copy the formula to find the monthly payments for the other loans.

10 Copy the formula you just created to the cell range D4:D6.

The PMT formula is copied. Cell D5 displays a monthly payment of $1,208.39 and cell D6 displays a monthly payment of $1,048.82. Now that you have calculated the monthly payments for each of the three loans, you can easily calculate even more information, such as the total interest paid and total amount paid on each loan.

11 Click cell E4, type =, click cell D4, type *, click cell B4, type *12 so that the formula reads =D4*B4*12, and click the Enter button on the Formula bar.

Now that you know the total amount of all the loan payments, you can find how much the total interest will be.

12 Click cell F4, type =, click cell E4, type -, click cell A, and click the Enter button on the Formula bar.

Wow! That interest really adds up, doesn't it?

13 Copy the formula in cell E4 into cells E5:E6. Copy the formula in cell F4 into cells F5:F6. Compare your workbook with the one in Figure 6-13.

14 Try experimenting with different loan amounts, interest rates, and loan lengths for the different loans, then save your work and close the Mortgage table worksheet.

QUICK REFERENCE

TO USE THE IF FUNCTION IN A FORMULA:

- WRITE THE FORMULA USING THE SYNTAX PMT(RATE,NPER,PV).

OR...

1. CLICK THE INSERT FUNCTION BUTTON ON THE FORMULA BAR TO OPEN THE INSERT FORMULA DIALOG BOX.

2. SELECT FINANCIAL IN THE OR SELECT A CATEGORY LIST, SELECT PMT IN THE SELECT A FUNCTION LIST, AND CLICK OK.

3. ENTER THE REQUIRED ARGUMENTS FOR THE PMT FUNCTION.

Click to display
formulas

Figure 6-15. The View tab of the Options dialog box.

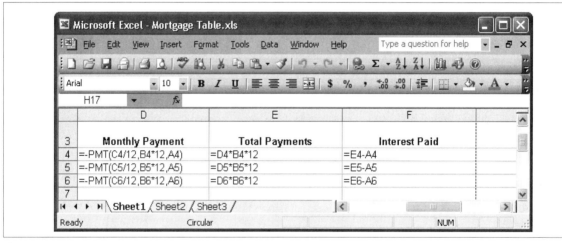

Figure 6-16. A worksheet with formulas displayed.

Excel normally displays the results of formulas in the worksheet, but not the actual formula. You can choose to have Excel display the actual formulas in the worksheet cells instead of their results, however, and learning how to do that is the topic of this lesson. Once you display a worksheet's formulas, you can print them for documentation purposes.

1 Select Tools → Options from the menu and click the View tab.

The View tab of the Options dialog box appears, as shown in Figure 6-15.

2 In the Window options section, check the Formulas check box, then click OK.

The Options dialog box closes. Notice that the worksheet columns are expanded, and instead of displaying the results of formulas, they now display the actual formulas, as shown in Figure 6-16. Since the worksheet columns are so wide, you will have to scroll through the worksheet to see all of the formulas.

3 Scroll the worksheet horizontally, until you can see the F column.

You can also print the worksheet with the formulas displayed. For the formulas to be meaningful when they are printed, however, you need to tell Excel to print the worksheet row number and column letter headings.

4 Select File → Page Setup **from the menu and click the** Sheet tab.

Now specify that you want the row and column headings to be printed.

5 **Check the** Row and Column Headings check box **and click** OK.

Now preview your worksheet to see how it will look when printed.

Print Preview button

6 Click the Print Preview button **on the Standard toolbar. Use the** 🔍 **pointer to zoom in and out of the worksheet.**

The worksheet will be printed with the formulas and row and column headings displayed.

7 Click Close.

8 Select Tools → Options **from the menu, make sure the View tab is selected, click the** Formulas check box **to deselect it, and then click** OK.

Excel displays the results of the formulas instead of the formulas themselves.

9 Close the workbook without saving it.

QUICK REFERENCE

TO DISPLAY OR HIDE WORKSHEET FORMULAS:

1. SELECT TOOLS → OPTIONS FROM THE MENU AND CLICK THE VIEW TAB.

2. CHECK OR UNCHECK THE FORMULAS CHECK BOX.

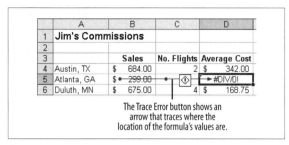

Figure 6-17. A worksheet with a Traced Error arrow.

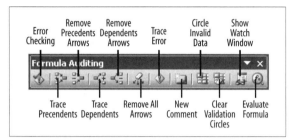

Figure 6-18. The Formula Auditing toolbar.

TIP *Excel displays #### when numerical informa-tion is too large to be displayed in a cell. Adjust the column width to fix the problem.*

Sometimes Excel comes across a formula that it cannot calculate. When this happens, it displays an error value. Error values occur because of incorrectly written formulas, referencing cells or data that doesn't exist, or breaking the fundamental laws of mathematics.

1 Navigate to your Practice folder and open the workbook Lesson 6D.

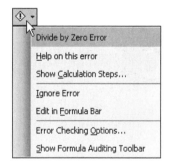

Trace Error button list

This workbook (created by a user who is not as proficient in Excel as you are) contains several common errors that you will likely encounter. Notice that cells B7, B8, B10, and B12 all have a string of #####s in

them. Technically, this isn't an error—the numerical information in the cells is just too large to be displayed in the current cell width. To fix the problem you simply need to widen the column.

2 Double-click the line between the B and C column headers.

Excel automatically adjusts the width of the selected column so that it can display the widest cell entry and the #####s disappear.

Excel 2003 includes a useful new feature that checks for errors in your formulas—think of it as spell check for math. Errors are always indicated by a green triangle in the upper left corner of the cell. This indicates that there is an error in the formula.

A green triangle appears in a cell when an error is found.

3 Click cell D5 to select it.

This cell displays #DIV/0!. This error code results when Excel tries to divide a number by zero. Notice that a Trace Error button appears next to the cell. The button offers a drop-down list of things you can do to correct the cell.

4 Click the Trace Error button drop-down list and select Show Formula Auditing Toolbar from the list.

The Formula Auditing toolbar appears, as shown in Figure 6-18. The Formula Auditing toolbar helps you find cells that have a relationship to a formula, displays formulas affected by changes made to the cell, and tracks down the sources of errors.

Trace Error button

5 Click cell D5, and then click the Trace Error button on the Formula Auditing toolbar.

An arrow appears from the active cell, D5, to the cells that caused the error, as shown in Figure 6-17. Notice cell B5 contains a value, while cell C5 is blank—the source of the #DIV/0! error in cell D5. To fix the error, you must enter a value in cell C5.

Remove All Arrows button

6 Click cell C5, type 1, and press Enter. Click the Remove All Arrows button on the Formula Auditing toolbar to remove the tracer arrow.

The error value in cell D5 is replaced by the correct calculation of the formula. Next, look at cell B12, which calculates the agent's commission. The commission rate at North Shore travel is 5%, so this commission amount seems too large. You can investigate this value by tracing the cell precedents.

Trace Precedents button

7 Click cell B12 and click the Trace Precedents button on the Formula Auditing toolbar.

Arrows appear from the cell range B4:B10 to cell B12. You can now easily see the source of the problem: the cell range includes both the sales totals *and* the sum of the sales totals, doubling the value used to calculate commission. Fix the error.

8 Edit the formula in cell B12 so it reads =B10*0.05 and press Enter.

The formula now calculates a more reasonable commission amount, $731.70. You can close the Formula Auditing toolbar since you're finished using it.

9 Click the Formula Auditing toolbar's close button to close it.

Table 6-3 lists the error values Excel displays when it encounters an error and what these rather cryptic-looking error values mean.

Table 6-3. Excel Error Values

Error Value	Description
#####	The numeric value is too wide to display within the cell. You can resize the column by dragging the boundary between the column headings.
#VALUE!	You entered a mathematical formula that references a text entry instead of a numerical entry.
#DIV/0!	You tried to divide a number by zero. This error often occurs when you create a formula that refers to a blank cell as a divisor.
#NAME?	You entered text in a formula that Excel doesn't recognize. You may have misspelled the name or function or typed a deleted name. You also may have entered text in a formula without enclosing the text in double quotation marks.
#N/A	This error occurs when a value is not available to a function or a formula. If certain cells on your worksheet contain data that is not yet available, enter #N/A in those cells. Formulas that refer to those cells will then return #N/A instead of attempting to calculate a value.
#REF!	The #REF! error value occurs when a cell reference is not valid. You probably deleted the cell range referenced to in a formula.
#NUM!	The #NUM! error value occurs when you used an invalid argument in a worksheet function.
#NULL!	You specified an intersection of two ranges in a formula that do not intersect.

QUICK REFERENCE

TO DISPLAY OR HIDE THE AUDITING TOOLBAR:

• SELECT TOOLS → AUDITING → SHOW AUDITING TOOLBAR.

Mathematical Functions

You can find any of Excel's mathematical functions on a typical scientific calculator. If you still remember your algebra classes, many of these functions, such as SIN, COS, and LOG should be familiar to you.

Function	Syntax	Description
ABS	=ABS(number)	Determines the absolute value of a number. The absolute value of a number is the number without its sign.
ACOS	=ACOS(number)	Returns the arccosine of an angle. ACOS is the inverse of the COS function.
ASIN	=ASIN(number)	Returns the arcsine of an angle. ASIN is the inverse of the SIN function.
COMBIN	=COMBIN(number, number_chosen)	Calculates the number of possible combinations from a given number of items. **Example:** You want to form a two-person team from five candidates, and you want to know how many possible teams can be formed. COMBIN(5, 2) equals 10 teams.
COS	=COS(number)	Returns the cosine of an angle.
DEGREES	=DEGREES(angle)	Converts radians into degrees.
EVEN ODD	=EVEN(number)	Rounds a number up to the nearest even or odd integer.
EXP	=EXP(number)	Calculates the value of the constant e (approximately 2.71828182845904) raised to the power specified by its argument. **Example:** EXP(2) equals e2, or 7.389056
FACT	=FACT(number)	Calculates the factorial of a number. The factorial of a number is the product of all the positive integers from one up to the specified number. **Example:** FACT(5) equals 1*2*3*4*5 equals 120
LN	=LN(number)	Calculates the natural (base e) logarithm of a positive number.
LOG	=LOG(number, base)	Calculates the logarithm of a positive number using a specified base.
LOG10	=LOG(number)	Calculates the base 10 logarithm of a number.
MOD	=MOD(number, divisor)	Returns the remainder after a number is divided by divisor. **Example:** MOD(3, 2) equals 1, the remainder of dividing 3 by 2.
PI	=PI( )	Returns the value of the constant pi (π), accurate to 14 decimal places.
POWER	=POWER(number, power)	Raises a number to the specified power.
PRODUCT	=PRODUCT(number1, number2…)	Multiplies all the numbers in a range of cells
RADIANS	=DEGREES(angle)	Converts degrees to radians.
RAND	=RAND()	Generates a random number between 0 and 1.

Function	Syntax	Description
RANDBETWEEN	=RANDBETWEEN (bottom, top)	Generates a random number between the bottom and top arguments.
ROUND ROUNDDOWN ROUNDUP	=ROUND(number, num_digits)	Rounds a number to a specified number of digits. The ROUNDDOWN and ROUNDUP function take the same form as the ROUND function, and as their name implies, always round either up or down.
SIGN	=SIGN(number)	Determines the sign of a number. Results in 1 if the number is positive, zero (0) if the number is 0, and -1 if the number is negative.
SIN	=SIN(number)	Returns the sine of an angle.
SQRT	=SQRT(number)	Returns a positive square root of a number.
SUM	=SUM(number1, number2...)	Adds all the numbers in a range of cells. You can enter the SUM function by clicking the AutoSum button on the Standard toolbar.
TAN	=TAN(number)	Returns the tangent of an angle.

Financial Functions

Excel's financial functions are vital if you work with investments or real estate. Financial functions help determine loan payment amounts, calculate the future value of investments, and find rates of return.

Function	Syntax	Description
FV	=FV(rate, number of periods, payment, present value*, type*)[a]	Calculates the future value of an investment based on periodic, constant payments and a constant interest rate. **Example:** You plan to deposit $2,000 a year for 35 into an IRA, and you expect a 10% average rate of return: =FV(10%,35,-2000) equals $542,048.74
IMPT	=PMT(rate, period, number of periods, present value, future value*, type*)	Calculates the interest payment for over a specified period of time, with constant periodic payments and a constant interest rate. **Example:** The following formula calculates the interest due in the first month of a three-year $8000 loan at 10% annual interest: IPMT(0.1/12, 1, 36, 8000) equals -$66.67
IRR	=IRR(values, guess)	Calculates the internal rate of return of investment. The investments do not have to be equal, but they must occur at regular intervals. The internal rate of return is the interest rate received for an investment consisting of payments (negative values) and income (positive values) that occur at regular periods. **Example:** You want to start a business. It will cost $40,000 to start the business, and you expect to net the following income in the first three years: $10,000, $15,000, and $20,000. Enter the four values in the cells A1:A4 of the worksheet, making sure to enter the initial $40,000 investment as a negative value: IRR(A1:A4) equals 5%
NPV	=NPV(rate, value1, value2, ...)	Calculates the net present value of an investment by using a discount rate and a series of future payments (negative values) and income (positive values).
PMT	=PMT(rate, number of periods, present value, future value*, type*)	Calculates the payment for a loan based on constant payments and a constant interest rate. **Example:** The following formula calculates the monthly payment on a $20,000 loan with an annual interest rate of 9% that must be paid in 36 months: PMT(9%/12, 36, 20000) equals ($635.99)

Function	Syntax	Description
PV	=PV(rate, number of periods, payment, future value*, type*)	Returns the present value of an investment. **Example:** An annuity that pays $600 every month for the next 20 years costs $50,000, and the money paid out will earn 7%. You want to determine whether this would be a good investment. Using the PV function, you find that the present value of the annuity is: PV(0.07/12, 12*20, 600, , 0) equals ($77,389.50)
RATE	=RATE(total number of payments, payment, present value)	Determines the interest rate per period of an annuity. **Example:** You want to calculate the rate of a four-year (48-month) $8,000 loan with monthly payments of $200. Using the RATE function you find: RATE(48, -200, 8000) equals 0.77 percent This is the monthly rate, because the period is monthly. The annual rate is 0.77%*12, which equals 9.24 percent.

a. * signifies an optional argument

Date and Time Functions

You can use dates and time in your formulas just like any other value. For example, if cell A1 contained the entry 5/1/99 you could use the formula =A1+100 to calculate the date 100 days later, which is 8/9/99.

One very important thing to know about working with date and time functions: while Excel can display dates and times using just about any format, it actually stores dates as chronological numbers called *serial values*. So while you think of dates as months, days, and years, such as May 1, 1999, Excel thinks of dates in terms of serial numbers, such as 36281.

> **NOTE** *Since the following date and time formulas often return serial number values, you should format any cells with date or time formulas with data and time formats that you can easily understand. You can also create custom number formats to display the results of date formulas. For example, the custom format dddd would display only the day, Monday, instead of the entire date, 8/9/99.*

Function	Syntax	Description
DATE	=DATE(year, month, day)	Enters a date in the cell. **Example:** DATE(99,5,1) equals May 1, 1999.
TODAY	=TODAY( )	A special version of the DATE function. While the DATE function can return the value of any date, the TODAY function always returns the value of the current date.
TIME	=TIME(hour, minute, second)	Enters a time in the cell. Uses a 24-hour (military) time system. **Example:** TIME(14,30) equals 2:30 P.M.
TODAY	=NOW( )	A special version of the TIME function. While the TIME function can return the value of any time, the NOW function always returns the value of the current time.
WEEK-DAY	=WEEKDATE (serial_number, return_type)	Returns a day of the week for a specific date. The serial_number argument is a date value (or reference to one). **Example:** WEEKDAY("2/14/90") equals Wednesday.
YEAR	=YEAR (serial_number, return_type)	Returns a value of the year for a specific date. The serial_number argument is a date value (or reference to one). **Example:** YEAR("3/15/1998") equals 1998.
MONTH	=MONTH (serial_number, return_type)	Returns a value of the month for a specific date. The serial_number argument is a date value (or reference to one). **Example:** MONTH("3/15/1998") equals 3.
DAY	=DAY(serial_number, return_type)	Returns a value of the day for a specific date. The serial_number argument is a date value (or reference to one). **Example:** DAY("3/15/1998") equals 15.
HOUR	=HOUR (serial_number)	Returns hour value for a specific time. The serial_number argument is a time value (or reference to one). Uses a 24-hour time format. **Example:** HOUR("12:15:45") equals 12.

Function	Syntax	Description
MINUTE	=MINUTE (serial_number)	Returns the minute value for a specific time. The serial_number argument is a time value (or reference to one). Uses a 24-hour time format. **Example:** MINUTE("12:15:45") equals 15.
SECOND	=SECOND (serial_number)	Returns a value of a second for a specific time. The serial_number argument is a time value (or reference to one). Uses a 24-hour time format. **Example:** SECOND("12:15:45") equals 45.
HOUR	=HOUR(number, number_chosen)	Calculates the number of possible combinations from a given number of items. **Example:** You want to form a two-person team from five candidates, and you want to know how many possible teams can be formed: COMBIN(5, 2) equals 10 teams.
DAYS360	=DAYS360(start_date,end_date)	Returns the number of days between 2 dates based on a 360-day year (12 30-day months), which is used in some accounting calculations. **Example:** DAYS360("1/30/93", "2/1/93") equals 1

Statistical Functions

Excel offers a large number of functions to help you analyze statistical data. If they're not enough you can also use the *Analysis Toolpak*, found under Tools → Data Analysis.

Function	Syntax	Description
AVERAGE	=AVERAGE(number1, number2…)	Calculates the average, or arithmetic mean, of the numbers in the range or arguments.
COUNT	=COUNT(number1, number2…)	Counts the number of cells that contain numbers, including dates and formulas. Ignores all blank cells and cells that contain text or errors.
COUNTA	=COUNTA(number1, number2…)	Counts the number of all nonblank cells, regardless of what they contain.
COUNTIF	=COUNTIF(range,criteria, sum_range)	Counts the cells only if they meet the specified criteria. Similar to SUMIF.
MAX	=MAX(number1, number2…)	Returns the largest value in a range.
MEDIAN	=MEDIAN(number1, number2…)	Calculates the median of the numbers in the range or arguments. The median is the number in the middle of a set of numbers—half the numbers have values that are greater than the median, and half have values that are less.
MIN	=MIN(number1, number2…)	Returns the smallest value in a range.
MODE	=MODE(number1, number2…)	Determines which value occurs most frequently in a set of numbers.
STDEV	=STDEV(number1, number2…)	Estimates standard deviation based on a sample. The standard deviation is a measure of how widely values are dispersed from the average value.
STDEVP	=STDEVP(number1, number2…)	Estimates standard deviation based on an entire population.
SUMIF	=SUMIF(range,criteria, sum_range)	Adds the cells only if they meet the specified criteria. **Example:** You want to total the cell range B1:B5 only if the value in cellA1 is greater than 500: SUMIF(A1,">500",B1:B5)
VAR	=VAR(number1, number2…)	Estimates variance based on a sample.
VARP	=VARP(number1, number2…)	Estimates variance based on an entire population.

Database Functions

Database functions return results based on filtered criteria. All the database functions use the same basic syntax "=Function(*database, field, criteria*)"". The arguments include:

- **Database:** The cell range that makes up the list or database.

	A
1	**Destination**
2	New York
3	Boston

Using this criteria range (A1:A3) in a database function would only calculate records with New York or Boston in the Destination field.

- **Field:** Indicates which column is used in the function. You can refer to fields by their column label enclosed with double quotation marks, such as "Name" or as a number that represents the position of the column in the list: 1 for the first column, 2 for the second, and so on—not the column heading numbers!

- **Criteria:** Is a reference to the cell or cell range that specifies the criteria for the function. For example, you might only want to total records from a certain region.

Function	Syntax	Description
DAVERAGE	=DAVERAGE(database, field, criteria)	Find the average of values in a column in a list or database that match the criteria you specify.
DCOUNT	=DCOUNT(database, field, criteria)	Counts the number of cells that contain numbers from a list or database that match the criteria you specify.
DGET	=DGET(database, field, criteria)	Extracts a single record from a database that matches the criteria you specify.
DMAX	=DMAX(database, field, criteria)	Returns the largest value from a database that matches the criteria you specify.
DMIN	=DMIN(database, field, criteria)	Returns the smallest value from a database that matches the criteria you specify.
DSTDEV	=DSTDEVP(database, field, criteria)	Estimates standard deviation based on a sample. The standard deviation is a measure of how widely values are dispersed from the average value.
DSUM	=DSUM(database, field, criteria)	Adds the values in a column in a list or database that match the criteria you specify.
DVAR	=DVAR(database, field, criteria)	Estimates variance based on a sample from selected list or database entries.

Lesson Summary

Formulas with Several Operators and Cell Ranges

If you combine several operators in a single formula, Microsoft Excel performs the operations in this order: ( ), :, %, ^, * and /, + and -, = = =.

Change the order of precedence by enclosing the part of the formula you want to calculate first in parentheses.

Using Insert Function to Enter and Edit Formulas

The Insert Function tool assists you in selecting, entering, and editing worksheet functions.

To Use the Insert Function Tool to Enter or Edit a Formula: Select the cell where you want to enter or edit a formula and click the Insert Function button on the Formula bar. Select the category of the type of function you want to use from the list.

Creating and Using Range Names

You can create a range name by selecting a cell range and then giving it a name in the Name box in the Formula bar.

You can refer to names in your formulas—for example, =SUM(Expenses) instead of =SUM(B3:B35). You can also refer to column and row headings in your formulas.

To Automatically Create Names: Select the cell or cell range you want to name and select Insert → Name → Create from the menu. Change the check boxes in the Create Names dialog box and click OK.

To Change the Cell Reference of a Name: Select the new cell or cell range you want to use as the reference and Select Insert → Name → Apply from the menu. Select the name you want to use in the selected reference and click OK.

To Delete Names: Select Insert → Name → Create from the menu, select the name you want to delete, and click Delete.

Selecting Nonadjacent Ranges and Using AutoCalculate

Select cell ranges that aren't next to each other by selecting the first range, and press and hold the Ctrl key while you select additional cells.

The Status bar displays the total (or other selected calculation) of the selected cell range.

To Change the AutoCalculate Function: Right-click the AutoCalculate area of the Status bar and select the function you want AutoCalculate to use from the shortcut menu.

Using the IF Function to Create Conditional Formulas

The IF function evaluates a condition you specify and returns one value if the condition is true and another value if the condition is false.

The syntax for the IF function is "=IF(logical_test,value_if_true,value_if_false)". It's much easier to create IF formulas using the Insert Function tool.

Using the PMT Function

The PMT function calculates the payment for a loan based on periodic payments and a constant interest rate.

The syntax for the PMT function is =PMT(rate,nper,pv). It's much easier to create PMT formulas using the Insert Function tool.

Displaying and Previewing Formulas

To Display or Hide Worksheet Formulas: Select Tools → Options from the menu, click the View tab, and check or uncheck the Formulas check box.

To Preview Formulas: Click the Print Preview button on the Standard toolbar.

Fixing Errors in Your Formulas

Be able to identify and correct any error values.

The Auditing toolbar helps track the cause of an error. Display it by selecting Tools → Auditing → Show Auditing Toolbar.

Quiz

1. Excel always calculates formulas from left to right. (True or False?)

2. Which of the following formulas will Excel NOT be able to calculate? (Trick Question!)

   A. =SUM(A1:A5)-10

   B. =SUM(Sales)-A3

   C. =SUM(A1:A5)/(10-10)

   D. =SUM(A1:A5)*.5

3. Which of the following statements is NOT true?

   A. The Insert Function button on the Formula bar helps you select, enter, and edit formulas.

   B. Range names can contain up to 255 characters, including spaces.

   C. You can create a range name by selecting a cell range and entering the range name in the Name box in the Formula bar.

   D. You can refer to range names when you reference cells in your formulas.

4. Which of the following statements is NOT true?

   A. You can select cell ranges that aren't next to each other by selecting the first cell range, pressing and holding the Ctrl key, and selecting any additional cell ranges.

   B. =IF(A4 >10, 0.5, 0) is a example of a properly entered formula using the IF function.

   C. If the Insert Function tool obscures the cells you want to reference in a formula you can click the Collapse Dialog box to temporarily shrink the Insert Function tool.

   D. Excel displays the error value "######" when it doesn't recognize the text you've entered into a formula.

5. Which is the fastest method to find the total of a cell range?

   A. Select a blank cell, click the AutoSum button on the Standard toolbar, select the cell range and click Enter.

   B. Select a blank cell, type "=SUM", select the cell range, type ")", and click Enter.

   C. Select the cell range and the status bar will display its total.

   D. Select the cell range, click the AutoSum button, and the Name box in the Formula bar will display the total.

6. What does the error #DIV/0! mean?

   A. That a number value is too wide to display within the cell.

   B. That a formula is divided by zero or an empty cell.

   C. That a formula is divided by the letter O.

   D. That you won't be receiving any stock dividends this year.

7. You are thinking about buying a $250,000 house. What function can help you calculate your monthly payments?

   A. SUM

   B. IF

   C. PMT

   D. COUNT

8. Which of the following statements is NOT true?

   A. Range names can make it to reference cells. For example, instead of typing (A1:B10), you could refer to the same cell range by its name, Expenses.

   B. You can create a range name by selecting a cell range and then entering its name in the Name box in the Formula bar.

   C. You can't use range names in a formula.

   D. You can use column and row labels in a worksheet to refer to data in formulas.

9. Which of the following formulas would find the smallest number in the cell range B10 to E25?

   A. =COUNT(B10:E25)

   B. =MIN(B10:E25)

   C. =FIND(B10:E25)

   D. =SMALL(B10:E25)

Homework

1. Open the Homework 6 workbook and save it as "Commission Bonus."

2. Add formulas in the Total column and Total row that total the appropriate column or row.

3. Create a formula in cell B10 that calculates the average of the cell range B4:F8.

4. Use AutoCalculate to find the totals sales to W Europe and E Europe. (Hint: select cell range B4:C8 and look at the status bar.)

5. In cell B14, create a formula that calculates how much of a commission bonus each agent receives. If an agent's sales were more than $30,000, they receive a $500 bonus; otherwise, they receive nothing. (Hint: You'll have to use the IF function.) Copy the formula to the remaining travel agents when you've completed the formula.

6. Display the formulas used in the Commission Bonus worksheet instead of their results. Change the display back to results when you're finished.

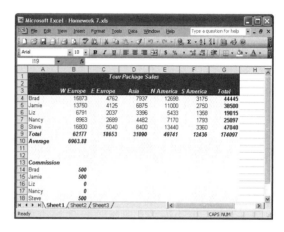

7. Create a range name: select the cell range A14:B18 click in the Name box, and type "Commissions."

Quiz Answers

1. False. If you combine several operators in a single formula, Microsoft Excel performs the operations in this order: ( ), :, %, ^, * and /, + and -, = = =.

2. C. The (10-10) portion of the formula would result in 0, causing the formula to divide by 0, which, if you remember your math classes, is impossible.

3. B. Range names cannot have spaces in them.

4. D. The error value "######" means a numeric value is too wide to display within the cell. You can resize the column by dragging the boundary between the column headings.

5. C. Selecting the cell range will display its total in the status bar and is the fastest and easiest way to find the total of a cell range.

6. B. #DIV/0! is the division by zero error.

7. C. The PMT function calculates the payment for a loan based on periodic payments and a constant interest rate.

8. C. You can use range names in a formula—for example, =SUM(Income).

9. B. =MIN(B10:E25) would find the smallest number.

CHAPTER 7
WORKING WITH LISTS

CHAPTER OBJECTIVES:

Create a list

Add, find, edit, and delete records

Sort a list

Use the AutoFilter to filter a list

Create a custom AutoFilter

Create and use an advanced filter

Use data validation when entering records to a list

CHAPTER TASK: CREATE A LIST THAT TRACKS CUSTOMERS AND FLIGHTS

Prerequisites

- **Understand how to use menus, toolbars, dialog boxes, and shortcut keystrokes**
- **Understand how to enter values and labels**

Another task Excel can perform is keeping track of information in *lists* or *databases*. Some examples of things you might track in a list include telephone numbers, clients, and employee rosters. Once you create a list in Excel, you can easily find, organize, and analyze its information with Excel's rich set of list-management features.

Working with lists in Excel 2003 is a breeze compared to earlier versions of the program. Microsoft added six major enhancements to list functionality that make the process much more user-friendly. When you create a list using Excel 2003, the following features are engaged automatically: AutoFilter; a list border; an Insert row; resize handles; a Total row; and the List toolbar.

In this chapter, you will learn how to create a list, and then add, modify, delete, and find information in it. You'll also learn how you can use Excel's filter commands to display specific information, such as records from a specific Zip Code.

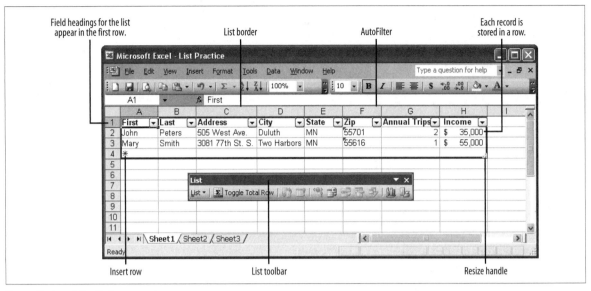

Field headings for the list appear in the first row.   List border   AutoFilter   Each record is stored in a row.

Insert row   List toolbar   Resize handle

Figure 7-1. A list with two records.

We'll start this chapter by creating a list. Microsoft has made creating lists easier in Excel 2003 by adding six major enhancements to list functionality. When you designate a range of cells as a list, it automatically has:

- **AutoFilter:** The AutoFilter feature is now the default setting for lists. It appears in each column header row and allows you to sort your data faster.

- **Borders:** When you create a list, a dark blue list border outlines the range of cells, separating it from the data in the rest of the worksheet.

- **Insert row:** A blank row with an asterisk (*) in the first cell appears at the bottom of a created list. Any information typed in this row will automatically be added to the list.

- **Resize handles:** You can make your list bigger or smaller by clicking on and dragging the handle found on the bottom-righthand corner of the list border.

- **Total row:** You can easily add a total row to your list by clicking on the Toggle Total Row button on the List toolbar. If you click on any cell in this row, a drop-down menu of aggregate functions appears.

- **List toolbar:** To aid in making changes to your list quickly, a List toolbar appears whenever a cell is selected within the list range.

Now that we've established the new list enhancements for Excel 2003, let's learn more about them.

1 Start Microsoft Excel, navigate to your practice folder, open the workbook named Lesson 7A, and save it as List Practice.

The List Practice workbook appears on your screen. There are two main components of a list:

- **Records:** Each record contains information about a thing or person, just like a listing in a phone book. The two records in this list are John Peters and Mary Smith.

- **Fields:** Records are broken up into fields, which store specific pieces of information. Examples of field names in this set of data are First (first names), Last (last names), and Income (yearly income per person).

In Excel, the columns contain the list's fields, and the rows contain the list's records. See Figure 7-1 for an example of how information is stored in columns and rows.

NOTE   *The Zip Codes in this list are entered as values, not numbers. When you want to enter a number as a label rather than a value, type an apostrophe (') before the number. If you didn't add this apostrophe, Excel would remove the leading zeros (0) from any Zip Codes beginning with (0), such as 01586.*

Now that you know the basics about list data, let's create one. Table 7-1 offers a set of guidelines for creating lists.

2 Select the cell range A1:H3 and select Data → List → Create List from the menu.

The Create List dialog box appears. Since you selected the cell range before you started the process, it automatically appears in the box.

This set of data already has field names that you want to use as the list's headers.

3 Make sure the My list has headers check box is checked and click OK.

Your data has been turned into a list.

4 Click cell A1 to deselect the cell range.

Compare your list to the one in Figure 7-1.

Take notice of the changes: a dark blue border appears around the list; arrows appear in each of the column headings, showing you that AutoFilter is enabled; the column headings are now bold; Resize handles appear; an Insert row is added; and the List toolbar appears.

Table 7-1. Guidelines for Creating Lists

Guideline	Why?
Have one list on a worksheet only.	Some list management features, such as filtering, can be used on only one list at a time.
Avoid putting blank rows and columns in the list.	So that Microsoft Excel can more easily detect and select the list.
Create column labels in the first row of the list.	Excel uses the labels to create reports and to find and organize data.
Design the list so that all rows have similar items in the same column.	This makes the list more meaningful and organized.
Try to break up information as much as possible.	This gives you more power to sort, filter, and manipulate the list.
Each column should contain the same type of information.	This will make the list easier to read and understand.
Don't use duplicate field names.	Duplicate field names can cause problems when entering and sorting information.

QUICK REFERENCE

TO CREATE A LIST IN EXCEL:

1. ENTER THE FIELD NAMES AS COLUMN HEADERS.

2. ENTER RECORDS AS ROWS.

3. SELECT THE CELL RANGE.

4. SELECT DATA → LIST → CREATE LIST FROM THE MENU.

OR...

PRESS CTRL + L.

5. IF YOU HAVE FIELD HEADINGS, MAKE SURE THE MY LIST HAS HEADERS CHECK BOX IS CHECKED.

6. CLICK OK.

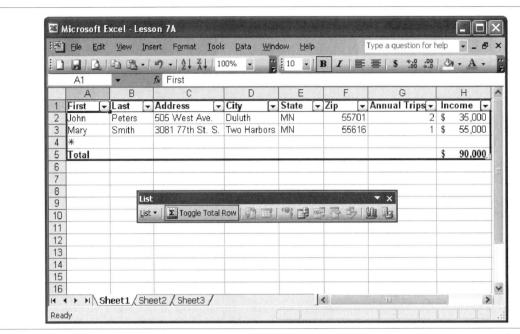

Figure 7-2. The list with split and frozen panes and a visible Total row.

Creating a list using Excel 2003 is easy enough, but working with them can be another story. This lesson will guide you through a few things that you can do to make working with your lists a little less stressful: splitting and freezing the worksheet so that the field headings always remain visible and using the Total row.

> **TIP** *When working with lists, especially longer ones, it is usually also a good idea to split and freeze the worksheet window so the field headings remain visible as you move through the rest of the worksheet.*

Vertical Split Box

1 Move the pointer over the vertical split box, located at the top of the vertical scroll bar. When the pointer changes to a ⭞, drag the split box down directly beneath row 1.

Excel splits the worksheet window vertically into two separate panes.

2 Select Window → Freeze Panes from the menu.

The frozen heading row will always be visible at the top of the worksheet, even if the list contains thousands of records.

Now, let's learn how to use the Total row.

3 Click cell A2 to ensure that the active cell is located inside the list (the cell range A1:H3).

The list must be activated in order to use the List toolbar.

4 Click the Toggle Total Row button on the List toolbar.

The Total row appears right below the Insert row in your list, as shown in Figure 7-2.

When the Total row is active, the word "Total" can be seen in the first cell of the row and a suitable Subtotal formula in the last cell of the row. The Total row allows you to calculate some sort of total for every one of the columns in your list.

5 Click on cell H5 and click the drop-down list arrow.

A list of aggregate functions appears.

6 Select the Average **option.**

Excel inserts the Average subtotal function into cell H5. The average income of John Peters and Mary Smith is $45,000.

Hiding the Total row is just as easy as displaying it.

7 Click the Toggle Total Row button **on the List toolbar.**

The Total row is hidden from your view.

See Table 7-2 for a complete list of the Total row functions along with a brief explanation of each one.

Table 7-2. Total Row Function Options

Function	Description
None	No function is inserted.
Average	Calculates the average, or arithmetic mean, of the numbers in the column.
Count	Counts the number of all nonblank cells, regardless of what they contain.
Count Nums	Counts the number of cells that contain numbers, including dates and formulas. Ignores all blank cells and cells that contain text or errors.
Max	Returns the largest value in a column.
Min	Returns the smallest value in a column.
Sum	Adds all of the numbers in a column.
StdDev	Estimates standard deviation based on a sample. The standard deviation is a measure of how widely values are dispersed from the average value.
Var	Estimates variance based on a sample.

QUICK REFERENCE

TO FREEZE THE FIELD HEADINGS:

1. MOVE THE POINTER OVER THE VERTICAL SPLIT BOX UNTIL IT CHANGES TO A ╪ .

2. DRAG THE SPLIT BOX UNTIL IT LIES DIRECTLY BENEATH THE ROW CONTAINING THE FIELD HEADINGS.

3. SELECT WINDOW → FREEZE PANES FROM THE MENU.

TO SHOW OR HIDE THE TOTAL ROW:

• CLICK THE TOGGLE TOTAL ROW BUTTON ON THE LIST TOOLBAR.

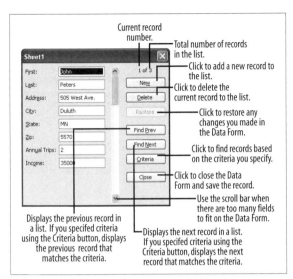

Current record number.
Total number of records in the list.
Click to add a new record to the list.
Click to delete the current record to the list.
Click to restore any changes you made in the Data Form.
Click to find records based on the criteria you specify.
Click to close the Data Form and save the record.
Use the scroll bar when there are too many fields to fit on the Data Form.
Displays the next record in a list. If you specifed criteria using the Criteria button, displays the next record that matches the criteria.
Displays the previous record in a list. If you specifed criteria using the Criteria button, displays the previous record that matches the criteria.

Figure 7-3. The Data Form dialog box.

Once you have created a list, you can add records to a list with Excel's Data Form dialog box, which you can find under the Data → Form menu. Actually, the Data Form can do a lot of things, including:

- Add records
- Display and scroll through records
- Edit existing records
- Delete records
- Find specific records

This lesson focuses on using both the Data Form dialog box and the Insert row to add records to the current list.

First, let's use the Insert Row to add a record to the list.

1 Click cell A4 to make it the active cell.

You know that this is the Insert row because there is an asterisk (*) in the leftmost cell. Notice that it does not disappear when you click cell A4.

TIP *Tab moves the insertion point forward one field or cell. Shift + Tab moves the insertion point back one field or cell.*

2 Type Susan and press Tab to move to the next cell.

The asterisk (*) moves to cell A5. This means that row 5 is the new Insert row.

Go ahead and enter the rest of the information for this record in Row 4, as shown in the next step.

3 Enter the rest of the information for Susan Ratcliff in the fields as follows:

First	Last	Address	City
Susan	Ratcliff	Rt. 8, Box 109	Duluth
State	**Zip**	**Annual Trips**	**Income**
MN	55801	4	$40,000

That's all there is to entering records using the Insert row. Now, let's use the Data Form dialog box.

4 Select Data → Form from the menu.

The Data Form dialog box appears, with the first record in the list, John Peters, as shown in Figure 7-3. One of the benefits of the Data Form is that it makes it easy to display and navigate through the various records in a list.

5 Click the Find Next button to move to the next record in the list.

The next record in the list, Mary Smith, appears in the Data Form.

6 Click the Find Prev button to move to the previous record in the list.

The previous record, John Peters, appears in the Data Form. You can also use the Data Form to add new records.

7 Click the New button.

A blank data form appears. Notice the text "New Record" appears where the record number counter was, indicating you are adding a new record to the list. The insertion point appears in the first field of the Data Form.

8 Type Harold in the First box and press Tab to move the insertion point to the next field.

Finish entering the rest of the information for this record.

9 Enter the rest of the information for Harold Williams in the fields as follows:

First	Last	Address	City
Harold	Williams	55 Sugar Lane	Duluth
State	Zip	Annual Trips	Income
MN	55701	2	$25,000

10 Click Close when you have finished entering the information for Harold Williams.

The Data Form dialog box closes. Notice the records you added are placed at the end of the list.

11 Save your workbook and close it.

QUICK REFERENCE

TO ADD RECORDS USING THE INSERT ROW:

1. CLICK THE LEFTMOST CELL OF THE INSERT ROW.

2. ENTER THE INFORMATION FOR THE RECORD IN THE APPROPRIATE CELLS.

TO ADD RECORDS USING THE DATA FORM DIALOG BOX:

1. MAKE SURE THE ACTIVE CELL IS LOCATED SOMEWHERE IN THE LIST AND SELECT DATA → FORM FROM THE MENU.

2. CLICK NEW AND ENTER THE INFORMATION FOR THE RECORD IN THE APPROPRIATE TEXT BOXES.

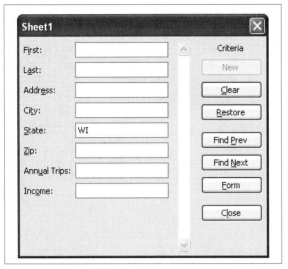

Figure 7-4. The Criteria Data Form.

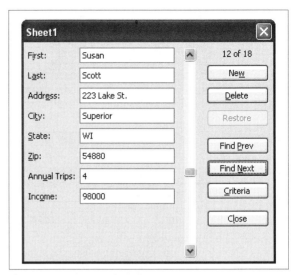

Figure 7-5. Finding a record with the Data Form.

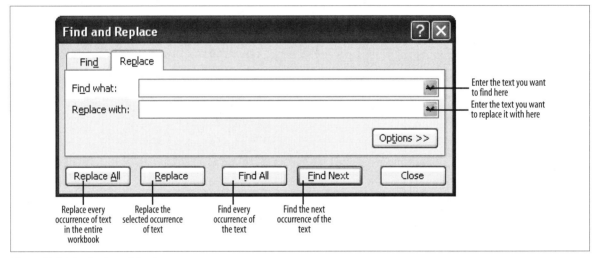

Figure 7-6. The Replace dialog box.

A task you will undoubtedly want to do if you work with a list is look up or find a specific record or records, such as a record for a particular client. Like so many other procedures in Excel, there are two different ways to search for records in your lists:

- Using the Edit → Find Command
- Using the Data Form dialog box

This lesson examines both methods; plus, you'll also learn how you can find and replace information. For example, if you misspell a city's name throughout a list, you can use the Find and Replace command to replace every occurrence of the incorrect spelling with the correct spelling.

1 Open the workbook named Lesson 7B and save it as Database List.

One method of finding a specific record in a list is to use the Data Form.

2 Make sure the active cell is located inside the list and select Data → Form from the menu.

The Data Form appears.

3 Click the Criteria button.

A blank data form appears,. Notice the text Criteria appears where the record number counter was, indicating you are working with a Criteria Data Form. To use the Criteria Data Form, simply type what you want to look for in the appropriate fields and click the Find Next button.

4 Click the State field, type WI, as shown in Figure 7-4, and click Find Next.

The Data Form displays the first record it finds in the list that is from WI, as shown in Figure 7-5.

5 Click Find Next to move to the next record that matches the WI criteria.

The Data Form moves to the next WI record.

6 Click Close.

You can also find information in a list using Excel's standard Find function, located under Edit → Find. You can also find and replace information. There is a mistake in the list: the Zip Code for Chekov, MN 55411 should be 55414. Use Replace to fix the mistake.

7 Select Edit → Replace from the menu.

The Replace dialog box appears, as shown in Figure 7-6. Enter the incorrect Zip Code you want to replace—55411, and the Zip Code you want to replace it with—55414.

8 In the Find what box, type 55411, click the Replace with box, and type 55414.

Now you can replace all the incorrect Zip Codes with the correct Zip Codes.

9 Click Replace All.

All of the 55411 Zip Codes are changed to 55414.

NOTE *Think before using the Replace All button—you might not want it to replace every instance of a word or value! You can find and replace each individual occurrence of a word, phrase, or value by clicking Find Next and then Replace.*

10 Click Close on the Replace dialog box and save your work.

QUICK REFERENCE

TO FIND RECORDS USING THE DATA FORM:

1. MAKE SURE THE ACTIVE CELL IS LOCATED INSIDE THE LIST AND SELECT DATA → FORM FROM THE MENU.

2. CLICK THE CRITERIA BUTTON, ENTER THE INFORMATION YOU WANT TO SEARCH FOR IN THE APPROPRIATE FIELDS, AND CLICK EITHER THE FIND NEXT OR FIND PREV BUTTON.

TO FIND RECORDS USING THE EDIT → FIND COMMAND:

1. SELECT EDIT → FIND FROM THE MENU.

2. ENTER THE INFORMATION YOU WANT TO SEARCH FOR AND CLICK THE FIND NEXT BUTTON.

TO FIND AND REPLACE INFORMATION:

1. SELECT EDIT → REPLACE FROM THE MENU.

2. ENTER THE TEXT YOU WANT TO SEARCH FOR IN THE FIND WHAT BOX AND ENTER THE TEXT YOU WANT TO REPLACE IT WITH IN THE REPLACE WITH BOX.

3. CLICK REPLACE ALL TO FIND AND REPLACE EVERY OCCURRENCE OF THE TEXT OR CLICK THE FIND NEXT BUTTON TO VERIFY EACH REPLACEMENT.

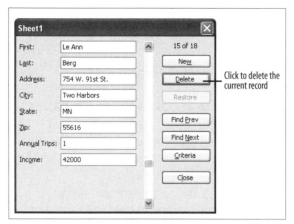

Figure 7-7. You can easily delete selected records in the Data Form dialog box.

Figure 7-8. Confirm a record deletion.

Deleting records is another basic list or database skill you need to know. For example, if you use a list to track membership, you keep the list up-to-date by deleting people that are no longer members. There are two ways to delete records:

• By using the Data Form dialog box (see Figure 7-7).
• By deleting the row on which the record is stored.

This lesson will give you some practice using each method.

1 Make sure the active cell is located inside the list and select Data → Form from the menu.

You need to delete the record for Nancy Pauls. First, you need to find her record.

2 Click the Criteria button.

The Criteria Data Form appears.

3 In the First field box type Nancy, click the Last field box, type Pauls, and click the Find Next button.

The record for Nancy Pauls appears in the Data Form.

4 Click the Delete button.

A dialog box appears, asking you to confirm the deletion, as shown in Figure 7-8.

5 Click OK to confirm the deletion of the record.

The record for Nancy Pauls is deleted, and the next record, Susan Scott, appears in the data form.

6 Click Close to return to the worksheet.

Notice that there are no blank rows where the previously deleted records were. When you delete a record using the Data Form dialog box, Excel automatically moves the following rows up to replace the deleted record.

You can also delete records by deleting the record's row.

7 Right-click the Row 12 Heading and select Delete from the shortcut menu.

The entire row is deleted, and the remaining rows move up to replace the deleted row.

You're doing great! Believe it or not, you've already made it halfway through the chapter and are well on your way to learning everything there is to know about lists.

QUICK REFERENCE

TO DELETE A RECORD:

1. MAKE SURE THE ACTIVE CELL IS LOCATED INSIDE THE LIST AND SELECT DATA → FORM FROM THE MENU.

2. FIND THE RECORD YOU WANT TO DELETE USING THE FIND NEXT, FIND PREV, OR CRITERIA BUTTONS.

3. CLICK DELETE AND CONFIRM THE DELETION OF THE RECORD.

   OR...

   DELETE THE RECORD'S ROWS OR CELLS.

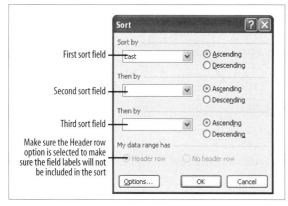

Figure 7-9. An unsorted list.

Figure 7-10. List sorted in ascending order by last name.

Figure 7-11. The Sort dialog box.

Normally, when you enter new records to a list, you add them to the end of the list, in the order you receive them. That's fine, but what if you want the list's records to appear in alphabetical order? Excel also has great ability to sort information. It can sort records alphabetically, numerically, or chronologically (by date). Additionally, Excel can sort information in ascending (A to Z) or descending (Z to A) order. Table 7-3 shows examples of this. You can sort an entire list or any portion of a list by selecting it. This lesson will show you several techniques you can use to sort information in your lists.

1 Click cell B1 to make it active.

Figure 7-9 shows an unsorted list. You want to sort the list by the last name, so you select the Last field.

Sort Ascending button

2 Click the Sort Ascending button on the Standard toolbar.

Excel sorts this list, ordering the records in ascending (A–Z) order by last name, as shown in Figure 7-10. You can also sort a list in descending (Z–A) order.

Sort Descending button

3 Click cell A1 to make it active, then click the Sort Descending button on the Standard toolbar.

The list is sorted in descending (Z–A) order by the First field.

So far, you have sorted the list by a single field. You can sort lists by up to three fields by using the Sort dialog box found under Data → Sort.

4 Select Data → Sort from the menu.

The Sort dialog box appears, as shown in Figure 7-11. You want to sort the list by the last name and then by the first name.

5 Select Last from the Sort by arrow and make sure the Ascending option is selected.

The list will be sorted in ascending order (A–Z) by the last name. Next, specify the second field you want to sort the list by.

6 Click the first Then by arrow, select First, and make sure the Ascending option is selected.

You're ready to sort the list.

7 Click OK.

The Sort dialog box closes and the list is sorted in ascending order, first by the last names and then by first names.

8 Save your work.

The information you sorted in this lesson was in a list, but you can use the same sorting techniques to sort information anywhere in a worksheet, whether it is in a list or not.

Table 7-3. Sort Examples

Order	Alphabetic	Numeric	Date
Ascending	A, B, C	1, 2, 3	1/1/99, 1/15/99, 2/1/99
Descending	C, B, A	3, 2, 1,	2/1/99, 1/15/99, 1/1/99

QUICK REFERENCE

TO SORT A LIST BY ONE FIELD:

1. MOVE THE CELL POINTER TO THE COLUMN YOU WANT TO USE TO SORT THE LIST.

2. CLICK EITHER THE SORT ASCENDING BUTTON OR SORT DESCENDING BUTTON ON THE STANDARD TOOLBAR.

   OR...

1. CLICK THE DROP-DOWN LIST ARROW ON ANY OF THE FIELD HEADINGS.

2. SELECT THE SORT ASCENDING OR SORT DESCENDING OPTION.

TO SORT A LIST BY MORE THAN ONE FIELD:

1. MAKE SURE THE CELL POINTER IS LOCATED WITHIN THE LIST AND SELECT DATA → SORT FROM THE MENU.

2. SELECT THE FIRST FIELD YOU WANT TO SORT BY FROM THE DROP-DOWN LIST AND SPECIFY ASCENDING OR DESCENDING ORDER.

3. REPEAT STEP 2 FOR THE SECOND AND THIRD FIELDS YOU WANT TO SORT BY (IF DESIRED).

Filtering a List with the AutoFilter

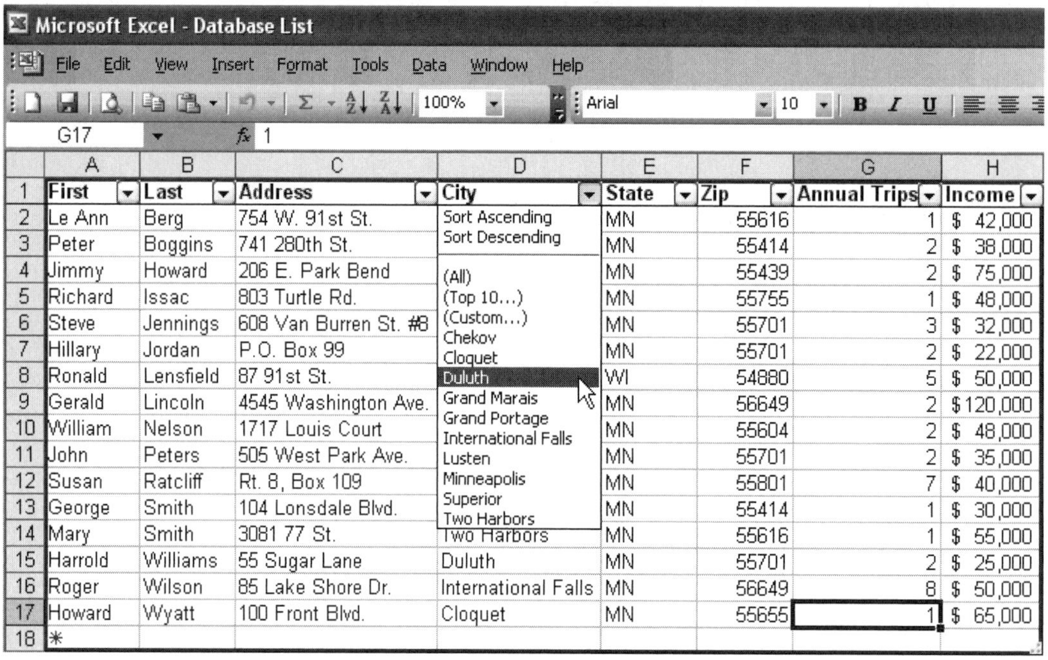

Figure 7-12. Using the AutoFilter on a worksheet.

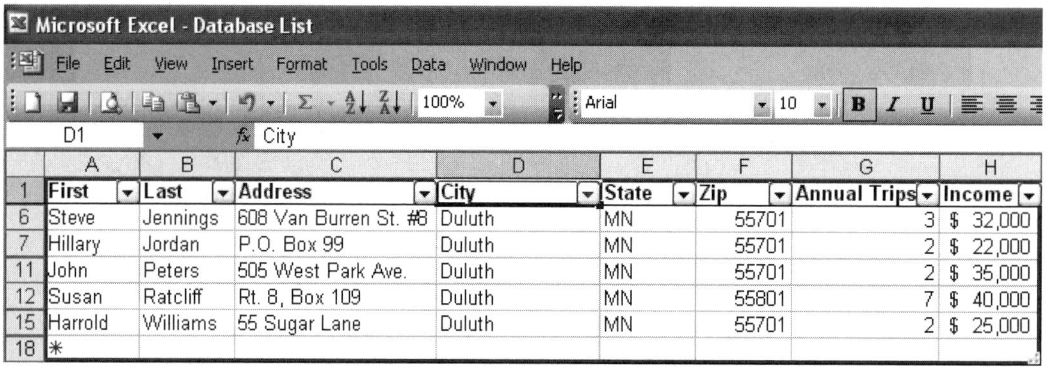

Figure 7-13. A list filtered by AutoFilter.

Sometimes, you may want to see only certain records in your lists. By *filtering* a list, you display only the records that meet your criteria and hide the records that do not. For example, you could filter a client list to display only clients who live in California. There are several ways to filter your lists. In this lesson, you will learn the fastest and easiest way to filter a list with Excel's nifty *AutoFilter* feature.

Due to the enhancements that Microsoft made to list functionality in Excel 2003, AutoFilter is enabled by default whenever a group of cells is designated as a list. You may not always want this feature to be active, so first let's learn how to turn it off.

1 **If necessary, open the workbook named** Lesson 7C **and save it as** Database List.

2 Make sure the active cell is located inside the list and select Data → Filter → AutoFilter from the menu.

AutoFilter is turned off, all of the records are listed, and the AutoFilter arrows disappear from the right of the field headings.

To turn AutoFilter back on, simply repeat Step 2.

3 Make sure the active cell is located inside the list and select Data → Filter → AutoFilter from the menu.

List arrows reappear to the right of each of the field names.

4 Click the City list arrow.

An AutoFilter list containing all the cities in the column appears beneath the City field (see Figure 7-12).

5 Select Duluth from the AutoFilter list.

Excel filters the list so that only records that contain Duluth in the City field are displayed, as shown in Figure 7-13. Notice the status bar indicates the number of records that matched the filter and that the AutoFilter list arrow for the City field changes colors,

indicating it is filtering the worksheet. You can filter a list by more than one field at a time.

Number of Filtered Records

6 Click the Annual Trips list arrow and select 2 from the AutoFilter list.

Excel narrows the filter so that only those records that contain "Duluth" in the City field and "2" in the Annual Trips field are displayed. Notice that the colors of the AutoFilter list arrows for both the City field and Annual Trip field are different, indicating they are filtering the worksheet. Here's how to remove the current filter criteria and display all the records.

7 Select Data → Filter → Show All from the menu.

All the records are displayed again.

Table 7-4 describes those other confusing items that appear in a field's AutoFilter list.

Table 7-4. AutoFilter Options

Options	Description
(All)	Display all rows.
(Top 10…)	Display all rows that fall within the upper or lower limits you specify, either by item or percentage; for example, the amounts within the top 10% of income.
(Custom…)	Apply two criteria values within the current column, or use comparison operators other than AND (the default operator). See the next lesson for more information on this option.
Sort Ascending	Sort this column, ordering the records in ascending (A–Z) order.
Sort Descending	Sort this column, ordering the records in descending (Z–A) order.

QUICK REFERENCE

TO FILTER A LIST WITH AUTOFILTER:

- CLICK ONE OF THE DROP-DOWN ARROWS IN THE FIELD NAMES OF THE HEADER ROW AND SELECT AN ITEM YOU WANT TO USE TO FILTER THE LIST.

TO REMOVE AN AUTOFILTER:

- SELECT DATA → FILTER → AUTOFILTER FROM THE MENU.

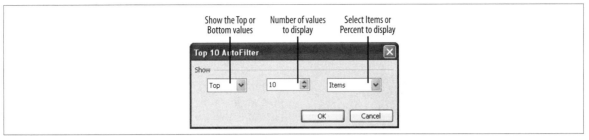

Show the Top or Bottom values   Number of values to display   Select Items or Percent to display

Figure 7-14. The Top 10 AutoFilter dialog box.

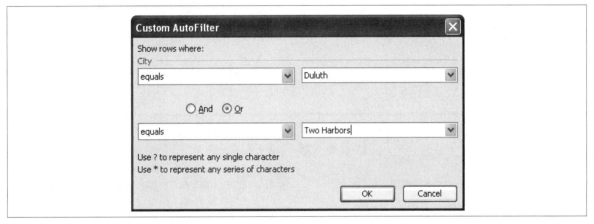

Figure 7-15. The Custom AutoFilter dialog box.

In the previous lesson, you learned how to use the Auto-Filter feature to filter records by selecting a single value for one or more columns. When you need to filter using more complicated criteria, you have to use a *Custom AutoFilter*. Custom AutoFilters are more difficult to set up and create than ordinary AutoFilters, but they're much more flexible and powerful. Custom AutoFilter can filter records based on more than one value—such as clients in a list that live in California *or* Oregon—and can filter records based on ranges—such as clients with an income greater than $40,000.

This lesson explains how to create and use a Custom AutoFilter. First, though, we need to cover one more ordinary AutoFilter topic—how to use the Top 10 option to filter records with the highest (top) or lowest (bottom) values in a list:

1 Click the Income list arrow and select (Top 10...) from the AutoFilter list.

The Top 10 AutoFilter dialog box appears, as shown in Figure 7-14.

2 Replace the 10 in the middle box with a 5 and click OK.

The records for the clients with the highest five incomes are displayed. Now that you know which clients have the highest incomes, you can remove the filter.

3 Click the Income list arrow and select (All) from the AutoFilter list.

The filter is removed and all the records are displayed.

4 Click the City list arrow and select (Custom...) from the AutoFilter list.

The Custom AutoFilter dialog box appears, as shown in Figure 7-15.

5 Make sure equals appears in the City list, then click the top comparison list arrow (adjacent to the equals option) and select Duluth.

In the next step, you'll specify that you want to filter any records from Two Harbors as well.

6 Click the Or option, click the bottom City list arrow, select equals, click the bottom comparison list arrow, and select Two Harbors.

Compare your dialog box to Figure 7-15. The custom AutoFilter will now display records in which the City field equals Duluth *or* Two Harbors. This type of search criteria is called a *Logical Condition*. You could also specify the logical condition criteria in a way so that only records from Duluth *and* those with incomes greater than $30,000 are filtered.

7 Click OK.

The dialog box closes, and only the records from the city of Duluth or Two Harbors are displayed.

8 Select Data → Filter → AutoFilter from the menu to deselect it.

The AutoFilter is turned off and all the records are displayed.

Custom AutoFilters are much more flexible and powerful than ordinary AutoFilters, but they still have some limitations. For example, you can't filter lists based on more than two values (such as clients from California, Oregon, or Washington). For really complicated filtering tasks, you'll need to use an *advanced filter*, which is covered in the next lesson.

QUICK REFERENCE

TO USE A CUSTOM AUTOFILTER:

1. CLICK ONE OF THE DROP-DOWN ARROWS IN THE FIELD NAMES OF THE HEADER ROW AND SELECT CUSTOM FROM THE LIST.

2. SPECIFY YOUR FILTER CRITERIA IN THE CUSTOM AUTOFILTER DIALOG BOX.

Filtering a List with an Advanced Filter

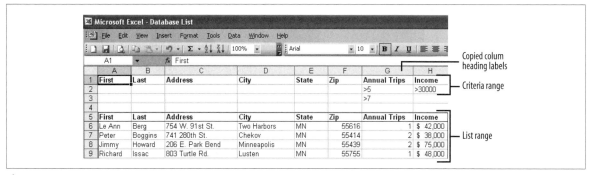

Figure 7-16. Creating the criteria range for an advanced filter.

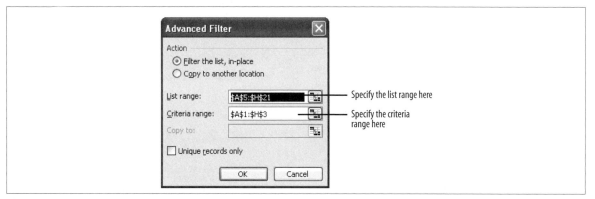

Figure 7-17. The Advanced Filter dialog box.

Advanced filtering is by far the most powerful and flexible way to filter your lists. It's also by far the most difficult method and requires more work to set up and use. Advanced Filters do have several capabilities their simpler AutoFilter cousins lack, including:

- **More complex filtering criteria:** You can filter a list based on as many values in as many columns as you want.

- **The ability to extract the filtered records:** Once you have created an Advanced Filter, you can copy the filtered records to a new location. This is the main reason most people use Advanced Filters.

To create an Advanced Filter you must start by defining a *criteria range*. A criteria range is a cell range, located at the top of your list, which contains the filter criteria. Figure 7-16 shows an example of a worksheet with a criteria range.

1 Select rows 1 through 4, right-click any of the selected row number headings, and select Insert from the shortcut menu.

Excel inserts four blank rows above the list. These blank rows will be the *Criteria Range*—the cell range that contains a set of search conditions you will use in your advanced filter. (See Table 7-5 for descriptions of operators and wildcards to use in an advanced filter.) The next step in creating an Advanced Filter is to copy the column labels from the list you want to filter.

2 Select the cell range A5:H5, click the Copy button on the Standard toolbar, click cell A1, and click the Paste button on the Standard toolbar to paste the copied cells.

Next, you need to specify the criteria for the advanced filter. You want to display only those clients with incomes greater than $30,000 *and* that have taken more than five trips *or* those clients that have taken more than seven trips.

3 Click cell G2, type >5, click cell H2, type >30000, and press Enter.

This will filter clients that have taken more than five annual trips *and* have incomes greater than $30,000. Next, you want to add a logical condition so that any clients who have taken more than seven annual trips are also selected, regardless of their income.

4 Type >7 in cell G3 and press Enter.

Compare your worksheet to the one in Figure 7-16. You're ready to filter the data.

5 Click any of the cells in the list range and select Data → Filter → Advanced Filter from the menu.

The Advanced Filter dialog box appears, as shown in Figure 7-17. Since you opened the Advanced Filter with the active cell in the list, the list range is already selected. You still have to specify what the criteria range is, however.

6 Click the Criteria range box and select the Criteria range—A1:H3.

You're ready to apply the advanced filter.

NOTE *Make sure you don't select the blank row between the criteria range and the list range, or the Advanced Filter won't work!*

7 Verify that the Filter the list, in-place option is selected and click OK.

The list range is filtered to match the criteria you specified in the criteria range. Notice the Status bar displays how many records were found. You remove Advanced Filters just the same as AutoFilters.

8 Select Data → Filter → Show All from the menu.

All the records are again displayed.

Table 7-5. Comparison Operators and Wildcards

Options	Description
=	Equal to
<>	Not equal to
>	Greater than
<	Less than
>=	Greater than or equal to
<=	Less than or equal to
*	Any number of characters in the same position as the asterisk **Example:** *east finds "Northeast" and "Southeast"
?	Any single character in the same position as the question mark. **Example:** sm?th finds "smith" and "smyth"

QUICK REFERENCE

TO CREATE AN ADVANCED FILTER:

1. YOUR WORKSHEET SHOULD HAVE AT LEAST THREE BLANK ROWS THAT CAN BE USED AS A CRITERIA RANGE ABOVE THE LIST.

2. COPY THE COLUMN LABELS FROM THE LIST AND PASTE THEM IN THE FIRST BLANK ROW OF THE CRITERIA RANGE.

3. IN THE ROWS BELOW THE CRITERIA LABELS, TYPE THE CRITERIA YOU WANT TO MATCH. MAKE SURE THERE IS AT LEAST ONE BLANK ROW BETWEEN THE CRITERIA VALUES AND THE LIST.

4. SELECT DATA → FILTER → ADVANCED FILTER FROM THE MENU.

5. IN THE ADVANCED FILTER DIALOG BOX, SPECIFY THE LIST RANGE AND THE CRITERIA RANGE.

6. MAKE SURE THE FILTER LIST IN-PLACE OPTION IS SELECTED AND CLICK OK.

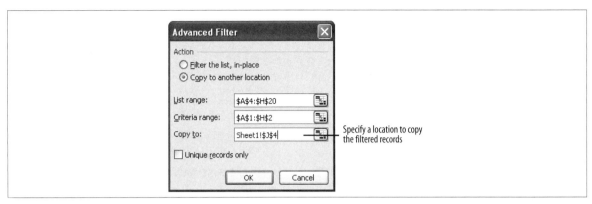

Figure 7-18. Copying filtered records in the Advanced Filter dialog box.

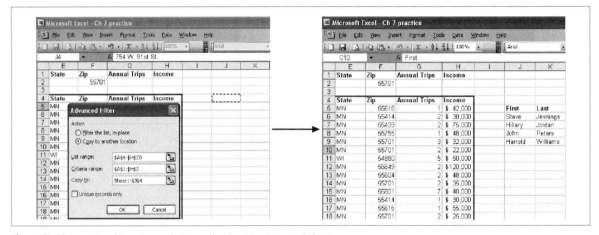

Figure 7-19. Copying filtered records to another location in a worksheet.

When you filter a list, you may want to copy or extract the records that meet your search criteria. You must use an Advanced Filter to copy filtered records to a new location. (Microsoft really should have let you copy filtered records with the much simpler AutoFilter as well, but they didn't, so there's no use complaining about it.)

1 Clear the current criteria in the Criteria Range by selecting the cell range G2:H3 and pressing the Delete key.

Since you will only need one row for your criteria you'll need to delete one of the rows in the criteria range.

2 Right-click the Row 2 heading and select Delete from the shortcut menu.

Next you need to enter a new set of search criteria. This time you want to find and then extract all the records that are in the 55701 Zip Code.

3 Click cell F2, type 55701, and press Enter.

You're ready to filter the list, only instead of filtering the list in-place, you want to copy the filtered records to a new location in the workbook.

4 Click any cell in the list range (A4:H20) and select Data → Filter → Advanced Filter from the menu.

The Advanced Filter dialog box appears, as shown in Figure 7-18. This time, instead of Filtering the list in place, you want to copy it to a new location in the worksheet.

5 Verify that the List Range and Criteria Range match what is shown in Figure 7-18, then select the Copy to another location **option in the Action section.**

The last step in extracting the records from the 55701 Zip Code is to specify where you want to paste the filtered records.

6 Click the Copy to box **and click cell** J4.

This is where the filtered records—those that meet the 55701 zip code criteria you specified in the Advanced Filter—will be copied.

NOTE *You can only copy filtered records to the same worksheet when you use the Advanced Filter copy to new location option. If you want to copy the filtered records to a different sheet in the workbook, or to a different workbook altogether, you have to copy the filtered records to a location on the current sheet; and either cut or copy the filtered records to the desired location in a different worksheet or workbook.*

7 Click OK.

The Advanced Filter dialog box closes and Excel copies the records that meet the search criteria with the 55701 Zip Code to the new location.

8 Save your work.

You deserve a medal if you've made it through the last couple of lessons in one piece. Creating and working with advanced filters are one of the most difficult procedures you can perform in Excel.

QUICK REFERENCE

TO COPY OR EXTRACT FILTERED RECORDS:

1. YOUR WORKSHEET SHOULD HAVE AT LEAST THREE BLANK ROWS THAT CAN BE USED AS A CRITERIA RANGE ABOVE THE LIST.

2. COPY THE COLUMN LABELS FROM THE LIST AND PASTE THEM IN THE FIRST BLANK ROW OF THE CRITERIA RANGE.

3. IN THE ROWS BELOW THE CRITERIA LABELS, TYPE THE CRITERIA YOU WANT TO MATCH. MAKE SURE THERE IS AT LEAST ONE BLANK ROW BETWEEN THE CRITERIA VALUES AND THE LIST.

4. SELECT DATA → FILTER → ADVANCED FILTER FROM THE MENU.

5. IN THE ADVANCED FILTER DIALOG BOX, SPECIFY THE LIST RANGE AND THE CRITERIA RANGE.

6. SELECT THE COPY TO ANOTHER LOCATION OPTION.

7. SELECT THE COPY TO BOX, SELECT THE CELL WHERE YOU WANT TO COPY THE FILTERED RECORDS AND CLICK OK.

Using Data Validation

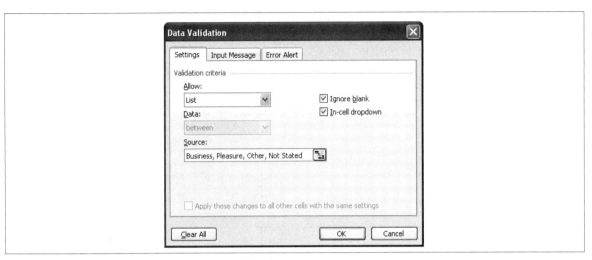

Figure 7-20. The Settings tab of the Data Validation dialog box.

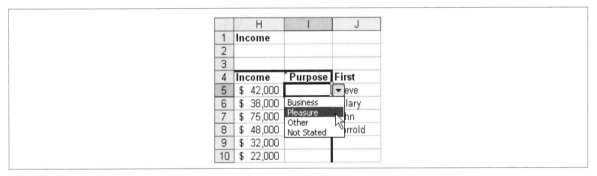

Figure 7-21. A drop-down list appears when you select a restricted cell.

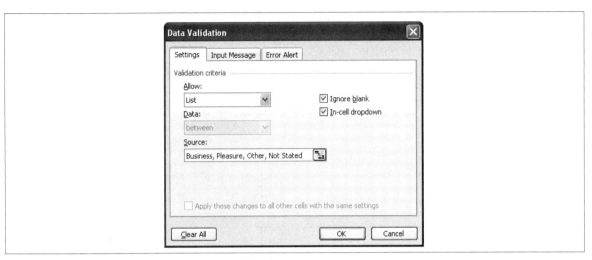

Figure 7-22. The Input Message tab of the Data Validation dialog box.

Figure 7-23. A pop-up message appears when you select the restricted cell.

You can help users enter accurate and appropriate information into your worksheets with Excel's *Data Validation* feature. Data validation restricts the type of information that can be entered in a cell and can provide the user with instructions on entering information in a cell.

1 Click cell I4 to select it, click the Bold button and the Center button **on the Formatting toolbar, type** Purpose, **and press** Enter.

You have just entered a new field heading for your list. Notice that the border extends to include this column in your list.

2 Click the Column I header **to select the entire column.**

You want to restrict any entries to the Purpose field to a list of specific options.

3 Select Data → Validation **from the menu and click the** Settings tab **if necessary.**

The Data Validation dialog box appears, as shown in Figure 7-20. You want to provide the user with a list of entries they can select from for the Purpose field.

4 Click the Allow list arrow, **select** List, **then click the** Source box **and type** Business, Pleasure, Other, Not Stated, **as shown in Figure 7-20. Make sure the** In-cell drop-down check box **is checked to display the list of valid entries whenever a cell in the Purpose column is selected.**

You're ready to test your data validation rules.

5 Click OK, **then click cell** I5.

Notice a drop-down list arrow appears to the right of the cell, as shown in Figure 7-21.

6 Click the drop-down list arrow **and select** Pleasure **from the list.**

Excel enters the Pleasure option from the list. Move on to the next step to see what happens if you type an invalid entry.

7 Make sure cell I5 is selected, type Unknown, **and press** Enter.

A warning dialog box appears, preventing you from entering invalid information.

8 Click Cancel **to close the dialog box.**

A list is just one way of validating data—there are many other ways to restrict data entry. In the next step, you will use the Validation feature to verify that entries made to the State column use two-digit state abbreviations.

9 Click the Column E column header **to select the entire column, then select** Data → Validation **from the menu.**

The Data Validation dialog box appears. You must specify that any entries in the selected cells must contain no more or no less than two digits.

10 Click the Allow list arrow, **select** Text Length, **click the** Minimum textbox **and type** 2, **and then click the** Maximum textbox **and type** 2.

You can also use the Data Validation dialog box to provide a user filling out your form with helpful information or feedback.

11 **Click the** Input Message tab.

The Input Message tab appears, as shown in Figure 7-22.

12 **Click the** Input Message textbox, **type** Enter the client's state of residence, **and click** OK.

The dialog closes. Test out the data validation options for the state column.

13 **Click cell** E6.

The message "Enter the client's state of residence" you entered in the Data Validation dialog box appears next to the cell, as shown in Figure 7-23.

14 **Save your work and exit Excel.**

QUICK REFERENCE

TO USE DATA VALIDATION:

1. SELECT THE CELL OR CELL RANGE YOU WANT TO VALIDATE.

2. SELECT DATA → VALIDATION FROM THE MENU.

3. CLICK ONE OR MORE OF THE FOLLOWING THREE TABS AND CHANGE THE NECESSARY SETTINGS.

SETTING: SPECIFY THE TYPE OF DATA THE CELL WILL ACCEPT.

INPUT MESSAGE: SPECIFY A MESSAGE TO APPEAR WHEN THE CELL IS SELECTED.

ERROR ALERT: SPECIFY A MESSAGE THAT APPEARS IF INVALID DATA IS ENTERED.

Chapter Seven Review

Lesson Summary

Creating a List

To Create a List in Excel: Enter the field names as column headers and records as rows. Select the cell range, select Data → List → Create List from the menu or press Ctrl + L, make sure the My list has headers check box is checked, and click OK.

Using the Total Row

To Show or Hide the Total Row: Click the Toggle Total Row button on the List toolbar.

Using the Data Form to Add Records

To Add Records to a List Using the Data Form: Make sure the active cell is located somewhere in the list and select Data → Form from the menu. Click New and enter the information for the record in the appropriate text boxes.

Finding Records

To Find Records Using the Data Form: Make sure the active cell is located inside the list and select Data → Form from the menu. Click the Criteria button, enter the information you want to search for in the appropriate fields, and click either the Find Next or Find Prev button.

To Find Records Using the Edit → Find Command: Select Edit → Find from the menu. Enter the information you want to search for and click the Find Next button.

To Find and Replace Information: Select Edit → Replace from the menu. Enter the text you want to search for in the Find what box and enter the text you want to replace it with in the Replace with box. Click Replace All to search and replace every occurrence of the text, or click the Find Next box.

Deleting Records

To Delete a Record with the Data Form: Make sure the active cell is located inside the list and select Data → Form from the menu. Find the record you want to delete using the Find Next, Find Prev, or Criteria buttons, click Delete, and confirm the deletion of the record.

To Delete a Record Directly in the Worksheet: Delete the record's rows or cells.

Sorting a List

To Sort a List by One Field: Move the cell pointer to the column you want to use to sort the list and click either the Sort Ascending button or Sort Descending button on the Standard toolbar. Or, click the drop-down list arrow on any of the field headings and select either the Sort Ascending or Sort Descending option.

To Sort a List by More than One Field: Make sure the cell pointer is located within the list and select Data → Sort from the menu. Select the first field you want to sort by from the drop-down list and specify Ascending or Descending order. Select the second and third fields you want to sort by (if desired).

Filtering a List with the AutoFilter

AutoFilter displays only the records that meet your criteria, and hides the records that do not.

To Filter a List with AutoFilter: Select the filter criteria from the drop-down arrows in the field names of the header row.

To Remove an AutoFilter: Select Data → Filter → AutoFilter from the menu.

Creating a Custom AutoFilter

A Custom AutoFilter allows you to filter records based on more than one value or a range.

To Use a Custom AutoFilter: Move the cell pointer anywhere within the list, make sure AutoFilter is active, click one of the drop-down arrows in the field names of the header row, and select Custom from the list. Specify your filter criteria in the Custom AutoFilter dialog box.

Filtering a List with an Advanced Filter

Advanced filters are difficult to set up, but they enable you to filter a list based on as many values in as many columns as you want and copy the filtered records to a new location.

To Create an Advanced Filter: Your worksheet should have at least three blank rows that can be used as a criteria range above the list. Copy the column labels from the list and paste them in the first blank row of the criteria range. In the rows below the criteria labels, type the criteria you want to match. Make sure AutoFilter is active, specify the list range and the criteria range, make sure the Filter list in-place option is selected, and click OK.

Copying Filtered Records

To Copy or Extract Filtered Records: Set up an Advanced Filter and enter the filter criteria. Select Data → Filter → Advanced Filter from the menu and specify the list range and the criteria range. Select the Copy to another location option, select the Copy to box, select the cell where you want to copy the filtered records, and click OK.

Using Data Validation

Data Validation restricts the type of information that is entered in a cell and provides the user with feedback and instructions.

To Use Data Validation: Select the cell or cell range you want to validate and select Data → Validation from the menu. Click any or all of the tabs (Settings, Input Messages, and Error Alert) and change the settings.

Quiz

1. Which of the following statements is NOT true?

   A. Field names appear in the first row of a list.

   B. Each record in a list is stored in a column.

   C. Selecting Data → Form from the menu opens the Data Form dialog box, which you can use to add, modify, find, and delete list records.

   D. You can add a new record to the database by entering the data as a new row in the worksheet, or by selecting Data → Form from the menu, clicking the New button, and filling out the New Record form.

2. How can you find specific information in a list? (Select all that apply.)

   A. Click the Find button on the Standard toolbar.

   B. Select Edit → Find from the menu.

   C. Select Tools → Finder from the menu.

   D. Select Data → Form from the menu to open the Data Form dialog box and click the Criteria button.

3. How can you delete a record? (Select all that apply.)

   A. Select Data → Form from the menu to open the Data Form dialog box, find the record, and click the Delete button.

   B. Click the Delete button on the Standard toolbar.

   C. Delete the cells or row that contain the record from the worksheet.

   D. Select Data → Delete Record from the menu.

4. Which of the following statements is NOT true?

   A. You can quickly sort a list by placing the cell pointer in the column/field you want to sort by and clicking either the Sort Ascending or Sort Descending button on the Standard toolbar.

   B. You can sort by up to three fields at a time by selecting Data → Sort from the menu.

   C. To display only records that meet your criteria, select Data → AutoFilter from the menu.

   D. To display only records that meet your criteria, click the AutoFilter button on the Standard toolbar.

5. You can extract filtered records from a Custom Auto-Filter. (True or False?)

6. Which of the following is NOT a step in creating an Advanced filter?

   A. Add a criteria range above the list. Make sure it contains the list's column labels.

   B. Add the criteria to the criteria range. Make sure you leave a blank row between the criteria range and the list.

C. Select Data → Filter from the menu and specify the list and criteria ranges.

D. Select the data you want to use to filter the list by the field's drop-down lists.

7. Which of the following statements is NOT true?

A. You must protect the worksheet in order to use Excel's data validation feature.

B. Data Validation lets you restrict which type of information is entered in a cell.

C. You can provide users with information and feedback using Data Validation.

D. To use Data Validation, select Data → Validation from the menu.

8. How can you apply an AutoFilter to a list?

A. Move the cell pointer anywhere within the list and select Data → Filter → AutoFilter from the menu.

B. Right-click any column heading in the worksheet and select AutoFilter from the shortcut menu.

C. Click the AutoFilter button on the Standard toolbar.

D. Add the formula =AUTOFILTER(LIST) somewhere in the list.

Homework

1. Open the Lesson 11A workbook and save it as "Sales Data."

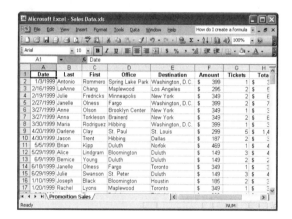

2. Turn this data into a list.

3. Use the AutoFilter to display only records that are from the Minneapolis office.

4. Display all the records, then use the AutoFilter to display the top 10 total amounts.

5. Use the Data Form to add a new record with the following information:

- Date: 5/3/2000
- Last: Schmidt
- First: Jamie
- Office: St. Paul
- Destination: New York
- Amount: $700
- Tickets:1
- Commission: Yes

6. Sort the list alphabetically by destination.

7. For the cells in Row 2, use Excel's Data Validation feature to enter helpful Input Messages, such as "Enter your last name" and "Enter the travel agent's office". Try selecting the cells when you're finished and see if your Input Messages appear.

Quiz Answers

1. B. Records in a list are stored in rows, not columns.

2. B and D. You can find information in a list by selecting Edit → Find from the menu or by selecting Data → Form from the menu to open the Data Form dialog box and click the Criteria button.

3. A and C. You can delete a record by selecting Data → Form from the menu to open the Data Form dialog box, find the record, and click the Delete button. You can also delete a record by deleting the cells or row that contain the record from the worksheet.

4. D. There isn't an AutoFilter button on the Standard toolbar (although it would make a nice addition).

5. False. You can only extract filtered records from an Advanced filter.

6. D. You specify the criteria for an Advanced filter in the criteria range, so there's no need to select the criteria from drop-down lists.

7. A. You don't have to protect a worksheet to use data validation.

8. A. To apply an AutoFilter to a list, move the cell pointer anywhere within the list and select Data → Filter → AutoFilter from the menu.

CHAPTER 8
AUTOMATING TASKS WITH MACROS

CHAPTER OBJECTIVES:

Record a macro

Play a macro

Assign a shortcut key and toolbar button to a macro

Edit a macro's Visual Basic code

Insert code into an existing macro

Declare variables using the DIM statement

Prompt for user input

Use If...Then statements

CHAPTER TASK: CREATE AND EDIT SEVERAL MACROS

Prerequisites

• **Understand how to use menus, toolbars, dialog boxes, and shortcut keystrokes**

• **Understand how to enter text and values into cells**

• **Understand how to edit, cut, copy, and paste text**

If you find yourself performing the same task over and over again, you might want to consider creating a macro to complete the task for you. A *macro* helps you perform routine tasks by automating them. Instead of manually performing a series of time-consuming, repetitive actions, you can record a single macro that does the entire task all at once for you.

This entire chapter is devoted to macros. We start with the basics and discuss how to record and play a macro. Next, you will learn how to assign shortcut keys and toolbar buttons to your macros. Finally, you'll move into some advanced topics: how to write and edit macros using the Visual Basic programming language.

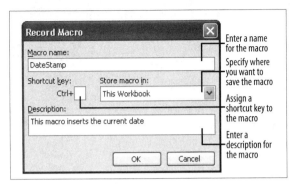

Figure 8-1. The Record Macro dialog box.

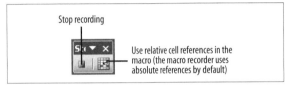

Figure 8-2. The Macro Recorder toolbar.

A macro is a series of Excel commands and instructions that are grouped together and executed as a single command. Instead of manually performing a series of time-consuming, repetitive actions in Excel yourself, you can create a macro to perform the task for you. There are two ways to create a macro: by recording it or by writing it in Excel's built-in Visual Basic programming language. This lesson explains the easy way to create a macro—by recording the task(s) you want the macro to execute for you.

When you record a macro, imagine you're being video-taped. *Everything* is recorded—all your commands, the data you enter, even any mistakes you make! Before you record a macro, you should write down a script that contains all the steps you want the macro to record. Practice or rehearse your script a couple times, to make sure it works, before you actually record it. If you do make a mistake while recording a macro, don't worry—you can delete the existing macro and try again or you can edit the macro's Visual Basic source code and fix the mistake (more on that later). Let's get started!

1 **Open the workbook named** Lesson 8A **and save it as** Macro Practice.

In this exercise, you'll create a macro that inserts the current data into a cell. You can do this by entering the =TODAY() function (which inserts the current date) into a cell and then copying the formula. Use the Paste Special command to paste only the formula's resulting value, because the =TODAY() function displays whatever the *current* date is, and would keep changing. Writing a formula and using the Paste Special command is a time-consuming process, however, so record a macro to perform this repetitive task for you.

2 **Click cell** B3.

This is where you want to insert the current date. You're ready to start recording your macro.

3 **Select** Tools → Macro → Record New Macro **from the menu.**

The Record Macro dialog box opens, as shown in Figure 8-1. You must give your new macro a name, and if you want, assign a shortcut key to it. Notice the store macro list box—you can store macros in one of three locations:

- **Personal Macro Workbook:** If you want a macro to be available whenever you use Microsoft Excel, store the macro in your Personal Macro Workbook.
- **New Workbook:** Stores the macro in a new workbook.
- **This Workbook:** Stores the macro in the active or current workbook.

4 **In the Macro name box, type** DateStamp, **then in the Description box, type** This macro inserts the current date.

Macro names can be no longer than 25 characters and cannot include spaces.

5 **Click** OK.

The Record Macro dialog disappears and you return to the worksheet. Notice the Macro toolbar appears in the document window, as shown in Figure 8-2. The Macro toolbar indicates that Excel is currently recording everything you type and every command into the DateStamp macro. Do the next several steps *very carefully*—you don't want to make a mistake and have it recorded in your macro!

6 Type =Today() **and click the** Enter button **on the Formula bar.**

The TODAY() function will display the current date in the active cell. That's OK for today, but not for any day after, when the date changes. You need to copy the formula and then paste the resulting value using the Paste Special command.

7 **Make sure cell B3 is selected and click the** Copy button **on the Standard toolbar.**

Next, use the Paste Special command to paste the resulting value of the TODAY() formula in the cell.

8 **Make sure cell B3 is selected and select** Edit → Paste Special **from the menu.**

The Paste Special dialog box appears.

9 **Select the** Values **option under the Paste section and click** OK.

The Paste Special dialog box closes, and Excel pastes the value of the TODAY() formula in cell B3. Next, format the cell.

10 **Click the** Bold button **and then the** Center button **on the Formatting toolbar.**

The active cell is now boldfaced and centered. This is the last step you want in the macro, so you can stop the macro recorder.

Stop button

11 **Click the** Stop button **on the Macro Record tool-bar.**

The Macro toolbar closes indicating that you are no longer recording a macro.

NOTE *If the Macro Record toolbar is no longer on your screen at this step, just select Tools → Macro → Stop Recording from the menu.*

In the next lesson, you will learn how to play the macro you just recorded.

QUICK REFERENCE

TO RECORD A MACRO:

1. SELECT TOOLS → MACRO → RECORD NEW MACRO FROM THE MENU.

2. ENTER A NAME AND DESCRIPTION FOR THE MACRO.

3. IF YOU WANT, ASSIGN A SHORTCUT KEYSTROKE TO YOUR MACRO AND SPECIFY WHERE YOU WANT YOUR MACRO TO BE SAVED.

4. CLICK OK AND CAREFULLY PERFORM THE ACTIONS YOU WANT TO INCLUDE IN YOUR MACRO.

5. CLICK THE STOP BUTTON ON THE MACRO RECORD TOOLBAR WHEN YOU'RE FINISHED RECORDING YOUR MACRO.

OR...

SELECT TOOLS → MACRO → STOP RECORDING FROM THE MENU.

Figure 8-3. The Macro dialog box.

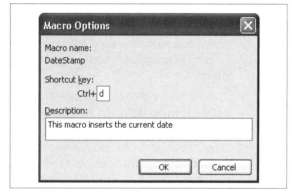

Figure 8-4. Assigning a shortcut key to a macro in the Macro Options dialog box.

In this lesson, you get to play the DateStamp macro you recorded in the previous lesson. Once you have created a macro, you can assign a keystroke shortcut to it, such as Ctrl + D, to make it faster and easier to access. You'll learn in this in this lesson.

1 Click cell C3.

You want to enter the current date in this cell. Watch how your DateStamp macro saves you time.

2 Select Tools → Macro → Macros from the menu.

The Macro dialog box appears, as shown in Figure 8-3. The Macro dialog box displays the available macros you can run.

3 Click the DateStamp from the Macro Name list macro and click Run.

The DateStamp macro you recorded in the previous lesson runs, automatically entering the TODAY() function, then copying and pasting its resulting value, and finally formatting it.

If you use a particular macro frequently, you can assign it a keyboard shortcut. For example, instead of selecting Tools → Macro → Macro from the menu, selecting the macro and clicking the Run button, you could run the macro by pressing a keystroke shortcut, such as Ctrl + D.

4 Select Tools → Macro → Macros from the menu.

The Macro dialog box appears.

5 Select the DateStamp macro and click the Options button.

The Macro Options dialog box appears, as shown in Figure 8-4. The following explains how you can assign a shortcut key to the macro.

6 Click the Shortcut key box, type d, and click OK.

Close the Macro dialog box and try running the macro using your new Ctrl + D shortcut key.

7 Click the Macro dialog box's close button.

The Macro dialog box closes.

8 Click cell D3 and press Ctrl + D.

Excel executes the DateStamp macro and inserts today's date in the active cell.

Well done! You've already learned how to record a macro, how to play a macro, and how to assign a shortcut key-stroke to a macro. Not bad for only two lessons.

QUICK REFERENCE

TO PLAY A MACRO:

1. SELECT TOOLS → MACRO → MACROS FROM THE MENU.

2. SELECT THE MACRO YOU WANT TO PLAY AND CLICK RUN.

TO ASSIGN A SHORTCUT KEY TO A MACRO:

1. SELECT TOOLS → MACRO → MACROS FROM THE MENU.

2. SELECT THE MACRO YOU WANT TO ASSIGN A SHORTCUT KEYSTROKE TO AND CLICK OPTIONS.

3. ENTER THE KEYSTROKE IN THE SHORTCUT KEY BOX.

TO DELETE A MACRO:

1. SELECT TOOLS → MACRO → MACROS FROM THE MENU.

2. SELECT THE MACRO AND CLICK DELETE.

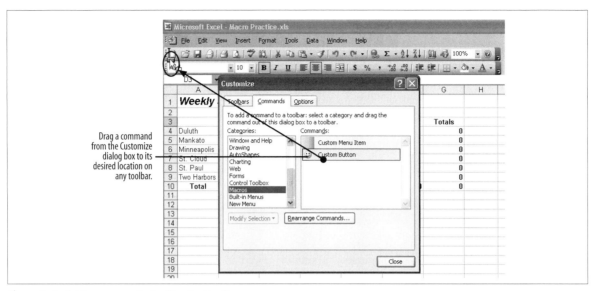

Figure 8-5. Adding a macro to the Standard toolbar.

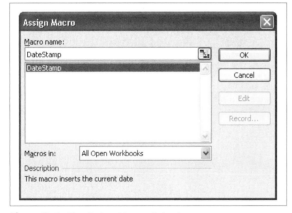

Figure 8-6. The Assign Macro dialog box.

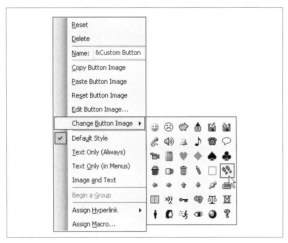

Figure 8-7. Selecting a button image.

Another way to make macros fast and easy to access is by adding them as buttons to a toolbar. In this lesson, you will add the DateStamp macro you've created to a button on the Standard toolbar.

1 Select View → Toolbars → Customize from the menu and click the Commands tab.

The Customize dialog box appears, as shown in Figure 8-5. The Commands tab lets you select commands and macros you want to add on your toolbars. The commands are organized by categories, just like Excel's menus.

2 In the Categories list, scroll to and click the Macros category.

Notice the Commands list is updated and lists a custom menu item and a custom button, as shown in Figure 8-5.

Custom button

3 Drag the Custom button to the very beginning of the Standard toolbar, as shown in Figure 8-5.

Now you need to assign a macro to the button.

4 With the Customize dialog box still open, right-click the custom button you just added to the Standard toolbar and select Assign Macro from the Shortcut menu.

The Assign Macro dialog box appears, as shown in Figure 8-6.

5 Select the DateStamp macro and click OK.

The DateStamp macro is assigned to the selected button. Follow the next step to give the DateStamp button a more meaningful name and image.

6 With the Customize dialog box still open, right-click the Custom button you just added to the Standard toolbar.

The button shortcut menu appears.

7 Select the Name textbox from the Shortcut menu and replace the text &Custom Button with Date Stamp.

Don't press Enter yet. You still need the shortcut menu open in order to change the image on the button.

8 Select Change Button Image from the Shortcut menu and select ✎ from the list of pictures, as shown in Figure 8-7.

You're finished adding the DateStamp macro to a button on the Standard toolbar, so you can close the Customize dialog box.

9 Click Close to close the Customize dialog box.

The Customize dialog closes. Now test the new toolbar button.

10 Move the pointer over the DateStamp button on the Standard toolbar.

After a moment, a Screen Tip appears by the button with its name—DateStamp.

11 Click cell E3 and click the DateStamp button on the Standard toolbar.

Excel executes the DateStamp macro and inserts today's date in the active cell.

12 Select View → Toolbars → Customize from the menu.

Now that the Customize dialog is displayed, you can remove the DateStamp button from the Standard toolbar.

13 Drag the DateStamp button off the Standard toolbar into the Customize dialog box.

The DateStamp button is deleted from the Standard toolbar.

14 Click Close to close the Customize dialog box.

QUICK REFERENCE

TO ADD A MACRO TO A TOOLBAR:

1. SELECT VIEW → TOOLBARS → CUSTOMIZE FROM THE MENU.

   OR...

   RIGHT-CLICK ANY TOOLBAR OR THE MENU AND SELECT CUSTOMIZE FROM THE SHORTCUT MENU.

2. CLICK THE COMMANDS TAB.

3. SELECT THE MACROS CATEGORY FROM THE CATEGORIES LIST AND DRAG THE CUSTOM BUTTON TO THE DESIRED TOOLBAR.

4. RIGHT-CLICK THE CUSTOM BUTTON, SELECT ASSIGN MACRO FROM THE SHORTCUT MENU, AND SELECT THE MACRO YOU WANT TO ASSIGN.

TO REMOVE A BUTTON FROM A TOOLBAR:

1. SELECT VIEW → TOOLBARS → CUSTOMIZE FROM THE MENU.

2. DRAG THE BUTTON OFF THE TOOLBAR INTO THE CUSTOMIZE DIALOG BOX.

Editing a Macro's Visual Basic Code

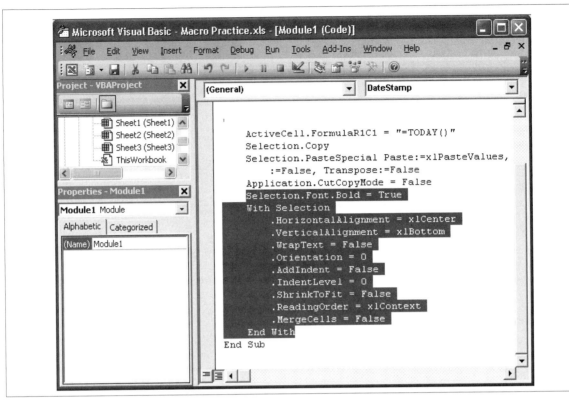

Figure 8-8. The Microsoft Visual Basic Editor.

This lesson introduces you to the Visual Basic (also called VB or VBA) programming language. Visual Basic is the code Excel uses to record macros. Okay, you're probably thinking, "You can't be serious! I can't program my VCR!" Relax. This lesson is meant to help you become familiar with the Visual Basic language and the Visual Basic editor so you can make *minor* changes to your macros once you have recorded them. Just imagine you're learning several words in a foreign language so that when you're presented with a menu you'll recognize some of the entrées. Let's get started, and don't worry—it's not going to be nearly as bad as you probably think it will be.

The best way to learn about Visual Basic is to view existing code. In this lesson, we'll view and edit the Date-Stamp macro.

1 Select Tools → Macro → Macros from the menu.

The Macros dialog box appears.

2 Select the DateStamp macro from the Macro Name list and click Edit.

The Microsoft Visual Basic Editor program appears, as shown in Figure 8-8. Yikes! You're probably thinking, "What is all of that complex programming code doing on my screen?" Those funny-looking words aren't Hungarian, they're *Visual Basic*—the code or language in which the macro you recorded is written. Whenever you record a macro, Excel writes and saves it in *Visual Basic*.

You don't have to learn Visual Basic to be proficient at Excel, but knowing the basics can be helpful if you ever want to modify an existing macro. Take a closer look at the code for the DateStamp macro. Some of the procedures should make a little sense to you. For example, the line "Selection.Copy" is the copy procedure, and the "Selection.Paste" is the paste procedure.

You decide that you no longer want the DateStamp macro to center and bold the current cell's contents.

Before you move on to the next step, look at the macro's code and see if you can guess which lines of code apply the bold and center formatting.

3 **Find the line of code that says** With Selection.

Believe it or not, the portion of code beginning with "Selection.Font.Bold = True" and ending with "End Selection" is the part of the macro that centersand boldfaces the current selection. The line of code after "End Selection, *Selection.Font.Bold = True* is what applies bold formatting to the current selection. Since you no longer want the macro to format or align the selected cell, you can delete all of this code.

4 **Select the block of code beginning with** Selection.Font.Bold = True **and ending with** End With, **as shown in Figure 8-8.**

Delete the selected text.

5 **Press** Delete **to delete the selected code.**

That's it! You've made the necessary modifications so that the DateStamp macro still enters the current date but will no longer perform any formatting functions.

6 **Click the** Save button **on the Visual Basic Standard toolbar to save the code.**

Now that you've finished editing the macro's code, you can close the Visual Basic Editor.

7 **Close the Visual Basic Editor by clicking the** close button **or selecting** File → Close and return to Microsoft Excel **from the menu.**

The Visual Basic Editor window closes and you return to Excel. Try out your newly modified macro to see if it works.

8 **Click cell** A3, **then select** Tools → Macro → Macros **from the menu.**

The Macro dialog box appears.

9 **In the Macro Name list, click the** DateStamp macro, **then click** Run.

The modified DateStamp macro runs, this time entering the current date without formatting the cell.

10 **Save your work.**

QUICK REFERENCE

TO EDIT A MACRO'S VISUAL BASIC CODE:

1. SELECT TOOLS → MACRO → MACROS FROM THE MENU.

2. SELECT THE MACRO AND CLICK EDIT.

3. WHEN YOU'RE FINISHED EDITING THE MACRO'S CODE, CLICK THE SAVE BUTTON AND THEN CLOSE THE VISUAL BASIC EDITOR WINDOW.

Figure 8-9. The Macro dialog box.

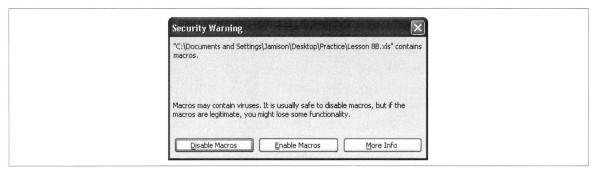

Figure 8-10. Because of the risk of viruses, you must enable any macros in a workbook when you open it.

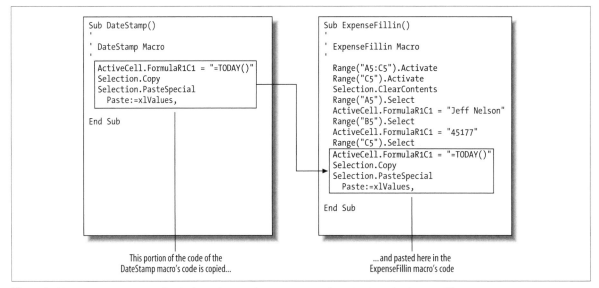

Figure 8-11. Copying a portion of code from the DateStamp macro and pasting it in the ExpenseFillin macro.

Let's face it—unless you're a programmer, it's unlikely that you will ever learn any of Visual Basic's hundreds of functions, statements, and expressions, and that's okay. You have already learned how you can view and even edit Visual Basic code created by Excel's macro recorder. A very useful technique you can use to edit and create macros is to insert code that has been copied, or plagiarized, from another macro. This technique lets you add steps to your existing macros by recording the steps you want to add in new macros, copying the appropriate code and inserting it in the existing macro.

1 Open the Lesson 8B workbook and save it as Employee Expenses (leave the current Macro Practice workbook open).

When you open the Lesson 8B file a frightening-looking dialog box like the one shown Figure 8-10 might appear. Macros are like miniature programs, so there is an almost infinitesimally small chance that a macro in an Excel worksheet could in fact be a virus created by some disgruntled, malicious loser. If you know where the workbook came from, it's probably safe to enable the macros it contains.

2 If necessary, click Enable Macros.

Imagine this is an employee expense report you have to fill out once a week. Since you enter the same information in this workbook on a regular basis, you have recorded a macro to perform some of the repetitive work of filling out the form for you.

3 Select Tools → Macro → Macros from the menu.

The Macro dialog box opens, as shown in Figure 8-9. The name of the macro that fills in the basic, repetitive information is ExpenseFillin.

4 Select the macro ExpenseFillin and click Run.

The Macro dialog box closes, and Excel runs the ExpenseFillin macro, which fills in the employee name and number. It would be nice if the ExpenseFillin macro also added the date you completed the Expense Report. You can do this by copying the procedure from the DateStamp macro you created in the Macro Practice workbook and pasting it in the code of the ExpenseFillin macro.

5 Select Tools → Macro → Macros from the menu.

The Macro dialog box appears. First, you need to copy the code from the DateStamp macro, located in the Macro Practice workbook.

6 Select the macro 'Macro Practice.xls'!DateStamp and click Edit.

The Microsoft Visual Basic editor appears with the DateStamp macro code. You need to copy only the portion of code that inserts today's date into the active cell.

7 Select the block of code beginning with ActiveCell.FormulaR1C1 = "=TODAY()" and ending with Selection.PasteSpecial Paste:=xlPasteValues, as shown in Figure 8-11, and click the Copy button on the Visual Basic toolbar.

Now that you've copied the procedure that inserts the current date, you must insert, or paste it into the appropriate place in the ExpenseFillin macro.

8 Close the Visual Basic Editor by clicking the close button or selecting File → Close from the menu.

The Visual Basic Editor window closes and you return to Excel.

9 Select Tools → Macro → Macros from the menu, select the macro ExpenseFillin, and click Edit.

The Microsoft Visual Basic editor appears with code for the ExpenseFillin macro. You need to paste the copied DateStamp code into the appropriate place in the ExpenseFillin macro code.

10 Move the insertion point to the end of the line Range("C5").Select, press Enter to add a blank line, then click the Paste button on the Visual Basic toolbar.

The copied code from the DateStamp macro is inserted into the ExpenseFillin macro. Compare your macro to the one shown in Figure 8-11. (Don't worry if your code is spaced differently and has different tabs.)

11 Close the Visual Basic Editor by clicking the close button or selecting File → Close from the menu.

It's time to test your macro.

12 Select Tools → Macro → Macros from the menu, select the ExpenseFillin macro, and click Run.

Excel runs the ExpenseFillin macro, which now also adds the current date in cell C5. Clear the information the macro entered and save the workbook to finish this lesson.

13 Select the cell range A5:C5, press the Delete key, and then save the workbook.

QUICK REFERENCE

TO INSERT VISUAL BASIC CODE INTO AN EXISTING MACRO:

1. OPEN THE WORKBOOK THAT CONTAINS THE MACRO WITH THE CODE YOU WANT TO COPY.

   OR...

   RECORD A NEW MACRO WITH THE STEPS YOU WANT TO ADD TO AN EXISTING MACRO.

2. SELECT TOOLS → MACRO → MACROS FROM THE MENU.

3. SELECT THE MACRO THAT CONTAINS THE CODE YOU WANT TO COPY AND CLICK EDIT.

4. COPY THE NECESSARY PORTION OF CODE USING STANDARD TEXT COPY PROCEDURE.

5. CLOSE THE VISUAL BASIC EDITOR AND REPEAT STEP 2.

6. SELECT THE EXISTING MACRO WHERE YOU WANT TO PASTE THE COPIED CODE AND CLICK EDIT.

7. PLACE THE INSERTION POINT WHERE YOU WANT TO PASTE THE COPIED CODE, ADD A BLANK LINE BY PRESSING ENTER, AND CLICK THE PASTE BUTTON ON THE VISUAL BASIC STANDARD TOOLBAR.

8. IF NECESSARY, EDIT THE PASTED CODE.

9. CLICK THE SAVE BUTTON AND EXIT THE VISUAL BASIC EDITOR.

   YOU MAY WANT TO DELETE THE OTHER MACRO IF IT IS NO LONGER NEEDED.

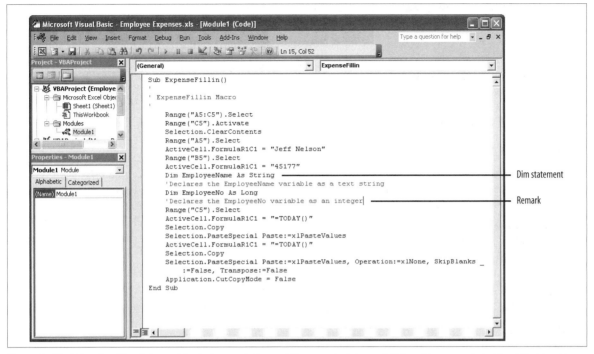

Figure 8-12. Using the Dim statement to declare variables and the remark statement (') to add comments to Visual Basic code.

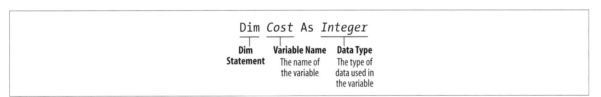

Figure 8-13. The syntax for the Dim statement.

You've probably heard that programming is a lot like algebra. In algebra you use *variables*, like the r in the equation πr^2. Programming uses variables too. You should always *declare* any variables when you use them in code. Declaring a variable is like telling Excel "I'm going to be using a variable named 'r' in my code." In Visual Basic, you use the DIM statement to declare variables, using the syntax "DIM *variablename* As *datatype*", as shown in Figure 8-13. This lesson explains how to declare variables using the Dim statement. (You'll actually get to *use* the variables you declare in the next lesson.)

Another topic covered in this lesson is how to add remarks to your code. Code can be confusing—you can make it easier to understand by adding explanatory remarks via REM statements. A REM statement doesn't do anything as far as the code is concerned—it's just a way to add notes explaining the function of the code. You

can add a REM statement by typing an apostrophe before the comment. For example: 'Adds the current date.

1 Make sure the Employee Expenses is the active workbook, then select Tools → Macro → Macros from the menu, select the macro ExpenseFillin and click Edit.

The Microsoft Visual Basic editor appears with the code for the ExpenseFillin macro (see Figure 8-12). Since several other users occasionally use this report, you decide you want to edit the macro so it prompts the user for their name and employee number. You'll learn how to prompt the user for information or *Input* in the next lesson. For now, you have to declare the variables for the employee name and number.

2 Add a blank line immediately above the line Range("A5").Select. **Place the insertion point in the blank line, type** Dim EmployeeName As String, **and press** Enter.

Remember, a variable is any piece of information that changes, like the *x* in an algebra problem. In the case of the ExpenseFillin macro, the employee's name will be the variable. Variables must have a name, like the *x* in the algebra problem. You name a variable a name *declaring* it with the *Dim* statement. The Dim statement must be entered in the following syntax: "Dim *variablename* as *datatype*". Here's what the arguments of the Dim statement mean:

- **Variablename:** The name of the variable—for example, EmployeeName.
- **Datatype:** The type of data you want to use in the variable, such as a number, date, or text. See Table 8-1 for a list of data types. Make sure you add an *As* between the variable name and the data type—for example, As String.

Since the line of code "Dim EmployeeName As String" you just entered is a little confusing, you can add a REM statement after it to explain what it does. The following explains how.

3 Type 'Declares the EmployeeName variable as a text string **and press** Enter.

Next, you'll need to declare the Employee Number.

NOTE *Don't forget the apostrophe (') at the beginning of the remark! Otherwise Visual Basic will try to recognize the text as a value.*

4 Type Dim EmployeeNo as Long **and press** Enter.

Notice as you enter code, the Visual Basic editor displays a list of words that can be used in the current statement. To accept a word, select the word from the list and press Tab. You declare the EmployeeNo as a Long integer, since it will always be a numeric value. Add a remark explaining what the preceding line of code does.

5 Type 'Declares the EmployeeNo variable as an integer **and press** Enter.

Save the updated macro.

6 Click the Save button **on the Visual Basic toolbar.**

In the next lesson you will get a chance to use the variables you declared with the DIM statement. Table 8-1 lists the more common data types that can be used with the DIM statement.

Table 8-1. Data Types Used in Variables

Date Type	Size	Range
Byte	1 byte	0 to 255
Boolean	2 bytes	True or False
Integer	2 bytes	-32,768 to 32,767
Long (Long Integer)	4 bytes	2,147,483,648 to 2,147,483,647
Date	8 bytes	January 1, 1000 to December 31, 9999
String (Text)	Varies	Approximately 2 billion characters

QUICK REFERENCE

TO DECLARE A VARIABLE:

- ADD A DIM STATEMENT AT THE BEGINNING OF THE PROCEDURE, USING THE SYNTAX DIM VARIABLENAME AS DATATYPE.

TO ADD A REMARK TO A PROCEDURE:

- ADD AN APOSTROPHE (') BEFORE THE REMARK.

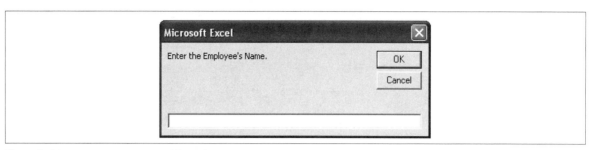

Figure 8-14. An Input Box generated from the InputBox statement.

```
Sub ExpenseFillin()
'
' ExpenseFillin Macro
'
    Dim EmployeeName As String
    'Decleares the EmployeeName as a text string
    Dim EmployeeNo As Long
    'Declares the EmployeeNo as an Integer
    EmployeeName = InputBox("Enter the Employee's Name.")————— The InputBox function
    EmployeeNo = InputBox("Enter the Employee Number.")
    Range("A5:C5").Select
    Range("C5").Activate
    Selection.ClearContents
    Range("A5").Select
    ActiveCell.FormulaR1C1 = EmployeeName
    Range("B5").Select
    ActiveCell.FormulaR1C1 = EmployeeNo
    Worksheets("Sheet1").PageSetup.CenterFooter = "Expense Report for: " &
        EmployeeName
    Range("C5").Select
    ActiveCell.FormulaR1C1 = "=TODAY()"
    Selection.Copy
    Selection.PasteSpecial Paste:=xlValues, Operation:=xlNone, SkipBlanks:=False,
        Transpose:=False
End Sub
```

Figure 8-15. The edited ExpenseFillin VBA code.

When creating macros and code, it is often useful to prompt the user for information. You can then use this information in any number of ways—place it in a cell, use it in a calculation, or print it in a header or footer.

This lesson explains one of the easiest methods of prompting the user for information—using the *InputBox* function. The InputBox function prompts the user for information by displaying a dialog box like the one shown in Figure 8-14. The syntax for the InputBox function is "*InputBox(Prompt)*" where *Prompt* is the message you want to display (usually enclosed in quotation marks (" ").

1 Make sure the Visual Basic editor is still open and that it displays the ExpenseFillin code (see Figure 8-15).

2 Place the insertion point immediately after the 'Declares the EmployeeNo as an Integer statement, press Enter, type EmployeeName = Input-Box("Enter the Employee's Name."), and press Enter.

As you type, Visual Basic displays a small window that displays information about the function you're entering and its parameters. This statement will display an InputBox, as shown in Figure 8-14, which will ask the user to enter the EmployeeName variable.

3 Type EmployeeNo = InputBox("Enter the Employee Number.") and press Enter.

This will display another dialog box, which will ask the user to enter the EmployeeNumber variable. Once the user has entered the EmployeeName and EmployeeNo variables in the Input Boxes, you can place EmployeeName and EmployeeNo variables in the appropriate cells.

4 **Find the** ActiveCell.FormulaR1C1 = "Jeff Nelson" **statement and edit it so it reads** Active-Cell.FormulaR1C1 = EmployeeName.

Make sure you remove the quotation marks! Now the macro will insert the EmployeeName variable the user enters in the Input Box instead of the name "Jeff Nelson."

5 **Find the** ActiveCell.FormulaR1C1 = "45177" **statement and edit it so it reads** ActiveCell.FormulaR1C1 = EmployeeNo **and press** Enter.

TIP *You can combine, or "concatenate," two pieces of information using the ampersand (&) symbol. For example, you can create the message "Expense Report for: Bill Smith" by combining a text string* "Expense Report for" *with a variable, such as* EmployeeName.

You decide to enter the text from the EmployeeName variable in the page footer for the worksheet as well.

6 **Type** Worksheets("Sheet1").PageSetup.CenterFooter = "Expense Report for: " & EmployeeName.

That last statement was a bit confusing—here's what it does. We'll start from the end of the code and work our way to the beginning. EmployeeName is the variable you declared and it equals whatever the user enters in the InputBox. Before that is the ampersand symbol (&), which combines the EmployeeName variable with the text message "Expense Report for: ". Note that the text message (or text string) must be enclosed in quotation marks (" "). The first part of the statement, *Worksheets("Sheet1").PageSetup.CenterFooter,* refers to the center footer of the Sheet1 worksheet. So the line of code tells Excel you want the center footer of Sheet1 to equal, or display the message "Expense Report for: *EmployeeName variable*" or whatever name the user enters in the InputBox.

You're ready to test your macro.

7 **Click the** Save button **on the Visual Basic toolbar to save the macro, then close the Visual Basic Editor by clicking the** close button **or selecting** File → Close **from the menu.**

The Visual Basic editor closes and you return to the Excel program screen.

8 **Select** Tools → Macro → Macros **from the menu, select** ExpenseFillin, **and click** Run.

An Input Box appears asking you to input the employee's name, as shown in Figure 8-14.

9 **Type in your name, click** OK, **type** 7000 **in the second Input Box, and click** OK.

The ExpenseFillin macro fills in the Expense report with the EmployeeName and EmployeeNo variables you entered in the two Input Boxes. Preview the workbook to verify that the EmployeeName also appears in the workbook footer.

10 **Click the** Print Preview **button on the Standard toolbar.**

The workbook appears in Print Preview mode. Notice that the ExpenseFillin macro has entered the employee name at the center footer.

11 **Click** Close **to close the Print Preview window.**

Clear the information entered by the ExpenseFillin macro.

12 **Select the cell range** A5:C5 **and press the** Delete **key, then save your work.**

QUICK REFERENCE

TO USE THE INPUTBOX STATEMENT:

• ADD AN INPUT STATEMENT USING THE SYNTAX INPUTBOX(PROMPT).

Using the If...Then...Else Statement

```
If condition Then
    statement ———— If the stated condition is true
                    then this action will happen.
Else
    elsestatement ———— Otherwse, this action will happen.
End If
```

Figure 8-16. The Syntax for the If...Then statement.

```
Dim EmployeeName As String
    'Decleares the EmployeeName as a text string
    'Declares the EmployeeNo as an Integer
    Dim EmployeeNo As Long
    EmployeeName = InputBox("Enter the Employee's Name.")
    If EmployeeName = "Jeff Nelson" Then
        EmployeeNo = 45177
    Else
        EmployeeNo = InputBox("Enter the Employee Number.")
    End If
```

Figure 8-17. The If...Then statement in a VBA macro's code.

The If...Then statement takes action based on a certain condition. For example, *if* an employee's weekly sales are more than $2,500, *then* calculate a 5% commission bonus for the employee, *else* don't calculate a bonus. The syntax for the If...Then statement is shown in Figure 8-16.

In this lesson you will use the If...Then statement to enter the employee number 45177 *if* the employee is Jeff Nelson, *else* the user will have to enter their employee number.

1 Make sure Employee Expenses is the active workbook, select Tools → Macro → Macros from the menu, select the macro ExpenseFillin, and click Edit.

The Microsoft Visual Basic editor appears with the ExpenseFillin macro code. Jeff Nelson is normally the only person that uses the Employee Expense workbook. To save time, you decide to add a conditional statement to the ExpenseFillin macro, so if the EmployeeName is "Jeff Nelson," the macro will automatically enter Jeff's Employee Number. Otherwise, if the EmployeeName is not "Jeff Nelson," the macro will prompt the user to enter their Employee Number.

2 Place the insertion point immediately after the statement EmployeeName = InputBox("Enter the Employee's Name"), press Enter, enter the statement If EmployeeName = "Jeff Nelson" THEN and press Enter.

This is the beginning of your IF...THEN...ELSE statement. IF the EmployeeName equals "Jeff Nelson" THEN you want to set the EmployeeNo variable to equal Jeff's employee number, 45177.

3 Press Tab, type EmployeeNo = 45177, and press Enter.

You don't have to add a Tab before the statement—it just makes your code easier to read and is a standard practice in programming. The next step in the IF...THEN...ELSE statement is adding the ELSE statement.

4 Type Else.

The next step is entering the ELSE statement—what to do if the EmployeeName does not equal "Jeff Nelson." If the EmployeeName does not equal "Jeff Nelson," you want Excel to display the InputBox to prompt the user for their Employee Number. You've already written this statement, so you can include it as the ELSE statement.

5 Place the insertion point at the beginning of the statement EmployeeNo = InputBox("Enter the Employee Number"), press Tab, press End to move to the end of the line, and press Enter.

Finish the IF...THEN...ELSE statement by adding the closing statement: End If.

6 Type End If.

Compare your code with the code shown in Figure 8-17. You're ready to save and test your new macro code.

7 Click the Save button on the Standard toolbar to save the macro, then close the Visual Basic Editor by clicking the close button or selecting File → Close from the menu.

The Visual Basic editor closes and you return to the Excel program screen.

8 Select Tools → Macro → Macros from the menu, select the macro ExpenseFillin, and click Run.

9 Type Jeff Nelson **in the InputBox and press** Enter.

The macro enters "Jeff Nelson" in cell A5 and his employee number "45177" in cell B5.

10 **Select** Tools → Macro → Macros **from the menu, select the macro** ExpenseFillin, **and click** Run.

See what happens when you enter a name other than "Jeff Nelson."

11 **Enter your own name in the InputBox and click** OK.

Since the EmployeeName variable wasn't "Jeff Nelson" another InputBox appears, asking for the employee number.

12 **Type** 55555, **press** Enter, **save your work, and exit Microsoft Excel.**

Give yourself a pat on the back if you've gotten this far. You've just finished what is arguably the most difficult task in Excel—working with code.

QUICK REFERENCE

TO USE AN IF...THEN STATEMENT:

• ADD AN IF...THEN STATEMENT USING THE FOLLOWING SYNTAX:

IF CONDITION THEN

    STATEMENT IF TRUE

ELSE

    STATEMENT IF FALSE

END IF

Chapter Eight Review

Lesson Summary

Recording a Macro

To Record a Macro: Select Tools → Macro → Record New Macro from the menu. Enter a name, description, and shortcut keystroke (optional) for the macro. Click OK and carefully perform the actions you want to include in your macro. Click the Stop button on the Macro Record toolbar when you're finished recording your macro.

When you record a macro, everything is recorded—including any mistakes you make. You should create a script that contains the steps you want the macro to record to minimize the amount of mistakes.

Playing a Macro and Assigning a Macro a Shortcut Key

To Play a Macro: Select Tools → Macro → Macros from the menu, select the macro you want to play, and click Run.

To Assign a Shortcut Key to a Macro: Select Tools → Macro → Macros from the menu, select the macro you want to assign a shortcut keystroke to, and click Options. Enter the keystroke in Shortcut key box.

To Delete a Macro: Select Tools → Macro → Macros from the menu, select the macro you want to delete, and click Delete.

Adding a Macro to a Toolbar

To Add a Macro to a Toolbar: Select View → Toolbars → Customize from the menu and click the Commands tab. Select the Macros category from the Categories list and drag the Custom button to the desired toolbar. Right-click the custom button, select Assign Macro from the shortcut menu, and select the macro you want to assign.

To Remove a Button from a Toolbar: Select View → Toolbars → Customize from the menu and drag the button off the toolbar.

Editing a Macro's Visual Basic Code

To Edit a Macro's Visual Basic Code: Select Tools → Macro → Macros from the menu, select the macro, and click Edit. When you've finished editing the macro's code, click the Save button and then close the Visual Basic Editor window.

Inserting Code in an Existing Macro

You can create macros that are more complex by copying sections of code from one macro to another macro.

Declaring Variables and Adding Remarks to VBA Code

You must declare any variables using the DIM statement, which uses the syntax Dim VariableName As DataType.

You can add a REM statement or comment to your code by typing an apostrophe (') before the comment.

Prompting for User Input

The Input statement prompts the user for information. The syntax for the InputBox statement is Input-Box(Prompt).

Using the If...Then...Else Statement

The If...Then statement takes action based on one condition and another action based on another condition.

The syntax for the IF...THEN...ELSE statement is:

```
If Condition Then
    Statement If True
Else
    Statement If False
End If
```

Quiz

1. Only menu and toolbar commands are recorded when you record a macro. (True or False?)

2. Which of the following statements is NOT true?

   A. Excel records macros in Visual Basic language.

   B. Macros names can be up to 25 characters long, including spaces.

   C. You start the macro recorder by selecting Tools → Macro → Record New Macro from the menu.

   D. You can assign a keystroke shortcut to a macro to make it quicker to access.

3. Which of the following statements declares a variable?

   A. REM HireDate as Date

   B. InputBox(HireDate) = Date

   C. Dim HireDate as Date

   D. Sub HireDate() = Date

4. Which of the following statements is NOT true?

   A. You can edit a macro's Visual Basic source code by selecting Tools → Macro → Macros from the menu, selecting the macro, and clicking the Edit button.

   B. You can edit, cut, copy, and paste Visual Basic code just like ordinary text.

   C. The InputBox function lets you add remarks to your code.

   D. The IF…THEN…ELSE statement takes an action based on a certain condition.

5. How can you play a macro?

   A. Select Tools → Macro → Macros from the menu and select the macro.

   B. Select Tools → Play Macro from the menu and select the macro.

   C. Click the Play Macro button on the toolbar and select the macro.

   D. Take music lessons from a professional macro player to learn how to do this.

6. You can assign a macro to which of the following? (Select all that apply.)

   A. The Office Assistant, to punish it for appearing unexpectedly.

   B. A keystroke shortcut, such as Ctrl + D.

   C. A button on any toolbar.

   D. A button on the Status bar.

Homework

1. Create a new workbook and save it as "My Macros."

2. Select Tools → Macro → Record New Macro from the menu. In the Macro name box type "Enter-Address," click the Store macro, and select This Workbook, then click OK to start recording.

3. Type your name, address, and phone number in the following format:

	A	B	C
1	Jeff Nelson		
2	500 Pine Street, Suite #301		
3	Minneapolis, MN 55431		
4	Tel. (612) 555-8181		

4. Click the cell that contains your name and apply bold formatting.

5. Click the Stop button.

6. Clear the address information you just entered and try running your macro.

7. Edit the macro's Visual Basic code so that it enters "Nancy Gordon" instead of your name.

8. Assign the shortcut key Ctrl + E to the macro.

Quiz Answers

1. False. Everything is recorded: every menu you select, every button you click, everything you type, even any mistakes you make!

2. B. Macros can't have spaces in them.

3. C. The Dim statement declares a variable, so the statement "Dim HireDate as Date" would declare the "HireDate" variable as a date data type variable.

4. C. The InputBox allows you to accept input from a user.

5. A. You can play a macro by selecting Tools → Macro → Macros from the menu and selecting the macro.

6. B and C. You can assign a macro to either a keystroke shortcut or to a button on any toolbar.

CHAPTER 9

WORKING WITH OTHER PROGRAMS

CHAPTER OBJECTIVES:

Insert an Excel worksheet into a Word document

Modify an embedded worksheet

Link an Excel chart into a Word document

Insert a graphic into a worksheet

Open and save files in different formats

CHAPTER TASK: INSERT INFORMATION BETWEEN DIFFERENT PROGRAMS

Prerequisites

- **Understand how to start and operate Microsoft Word**
- **Understand how to edit and work with Excel worksheets and charts**
- **Understand how to open and save files**

One of the great benefits of working with Microsoft Windows is that you can share information between different programs. This chapter explains how you can use Excel with other programs. You'll learn how to insert an Excel worksheet and chart into a Microsoft Word document. You'll also learn the subtle differences between *embedding* and *linking* files into other programs. This chapter also explains how to open and save different file formats, such as Lotus 1-2-3 or text files, in Excel.

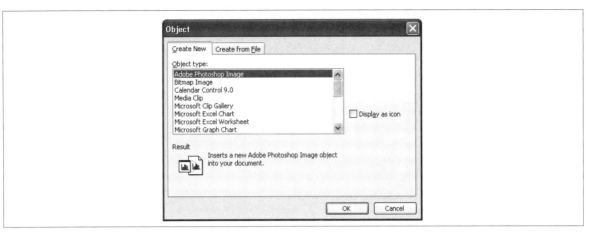

Figure 9-1. The Create New tab of the Object dialog box.

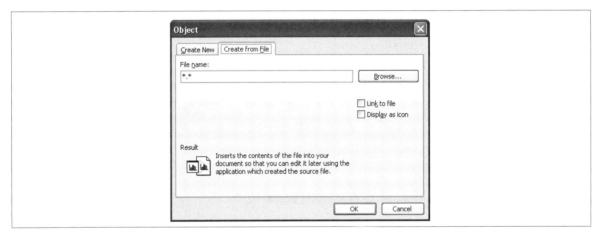

Figure 9-2. The Create from File tab of the Object dialog box.

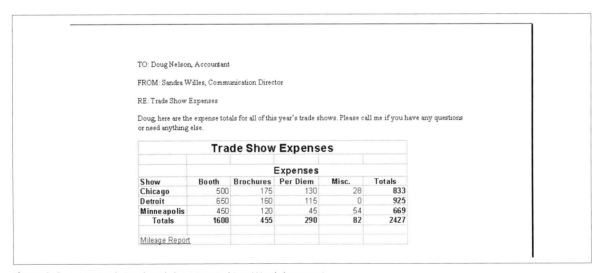

Figure 9-3. A Microsoft Excel worksheet inserted in a Word document.

Microsoft Word is a powerful word-processing program that can create professional-looking documents. Since Word is part of the Microsoft Office Suite, it makes sense that more people use Excel together with Word than any other program. In this lesson, you will learn how to *embed* an Excel worksheet into a Word document.

1 Start the Microsoft Word program.

2 Navigate to your Excel 2003 Practice folder and open the document named Interoffice Memo.

The procedure for opening a file in Word is identical to opening a file in Excel. Click the Open button on the Standard toolbar or select File → Open from the menu. The Interoffice Memo document appears in Word's main document window.

3 Move the insertion point (⌶) to the end of the document by pressing the down arrow key (↓), or by clicking to the end of the document with the mouse.

This is where you want to insert an Excel worksheet.

4 Select Insert → Object from the menu.

The Object dialog box appears with the Create New tab in front, as shown in Figure 9-1. You can create and insert new objects with the Create New tab, or you can insert an existing file with the Create from File tab. You have already created and saved a worksheet in Excel, so you need to insert the worksheet from an existing file.

5 Click the Create from File tab.

The Create from File tab appears in front, as shown in Figure 9-2. You need to specify the name and location of the file you want to insert into the document.

6 Click the Browse button.

The Browse dialog box appears, allowing you to find and locate the file you want to insert into your document.

7 Navigate to your practice folder or disk and select the Expenses file.

Notice that the icon for the Expenses file indicates that it is a Microsoft Excel file.

8 Click OK.

The Browse dialog box closes and you return to the Create from File tab of the Object dialog box. Notice the Expenses file name and location appear in the File name box.

There are several other options on this page you should know about:

- **Link to file:** Inserted objects are normally *embedded*, or saved inside the documents in which they are inserted. If you check the "Link to file" option the object will still be inserted in the document, but Word will only create a link to the original file instead of saving a copy of it inside the document. You should use the "Link to file" option when you want to ensure that any changes made in the original file are updated and reflected in the document in which it is inserted.

- **Display as icon:** Inserted objects are normally viewable directly from the Word document window. Checking the "Display as icon" option causes the inserted objects to appear only as icons. You must double-click the object in order to view it.

9 Click OK.

Word accesses the Excel file and then inserts it into the document at the insertion point.

10 Compare your document with the one in Figure 9-3.

11 Save the changes you've made to the Word document by clicking the Save button on the Standard toolbar.

QUICK REFERENCE

TO INSERT AN EMBEDDED EXCEL WORKSHEET INTO A WORD DOCUMENT:

1. PLACE THE INSERTION POINT WHERE YOU WANT THE WORKSHEET TO BE INSERTED.

2. SELECT INSERT → OBJECT FROM THE MENU.

3. CLICK THE CREATE FROM FILE TAB TO USE AN EXISTING WORKSHEET FILE OR CLICK THE CREATE NEW TAB TO CREATE A NEW WORKSHEET.

4. SPECIFY THE EXCEL WORKSHEET FILE YOU WANT TO INSERT (IF YOU SELECTED CREATE FROM FILE) OR ELSE CREATE THE WORKSHEET FROM SCRATCH (IF YOU SELECTED CREATE NEW).

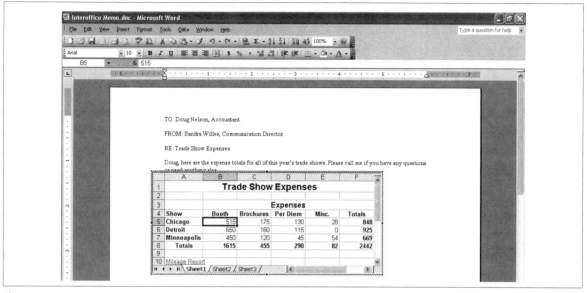

Figure 9-4. Modifying an Excel Worksheet object.

Trade Show Expenses					
		Expenses			
Show	Booth	Brochures	Per Diem	Misc.	Totals
Chicago	515	175	130	28	848
Milwaukee	470	135	110	25	740
Detroit	650	160	115	0	925
Minneapolis	450	120	45	54	669
Totals	2085	590	400	107	3182

Figure 9-5. The modified worksheet.

After you insert an Excel worksheet, you can make changes to the worksheet simply by double-clicking it. Double-clicking any embedded or linked object opens the source program the object was created in, or, in the case of this lesson, Microsoft Excel. If the program the object was created with isn't installed on your computer, you can still view and print the object, but you can't make changes to it.

TIP *Double-click an object to edit or modify it.*

1 Double-click the inserted worksheet object in the document.

The Excel program opens inside of the Word document, as shown in Figure 9-4. Notice that Excel menus and toolbars replace the Word toolbars and menus. Now you can make changes to the worksheet object.

2 Select cell B5.

With the cell selected, you can replace the cell's data simply by typing.

3 Type 515 and press Tab.

The number 515 replaces the number 500 and Excel moves to the next cell.

4 Select the entire Detroit row by clicking the Row 6 heading.

The entire row is selected.

5 Select Insert → Rows from the menu.

A new row is inserted immediately above the Detroit row. Now enter the data for the new row.

6 Click cell A6, type Milwaukee, and press Tab to move to the next cell.

7 Type the following, pressing Tab after making each entry:

470 135 110 25

Now that you have entered the data you must calculate the total for the row.

AutoSum button

8 Click the AutoSum button on the Standard toolbar.

Excel makes an educated guess regarding which cells you want to use to calculate the total and selects them—in your case, Excel guesses correctly.

9 Press Enter to accept the formula.

Excel calculates the row total and moves to the next cell. Notice that after you inserted a new row, the bottom total row is no longer displayed. Here's how to resize the Excel worksheet object so that the entire worksheet is displayed.

10 Position the pointer over the lower-right sizing handle, until the pointer changes to a ↖, then click and hold the left mouse button and drag the mouse down until you can see the bottom row of the worksheet, and then release the mouse button.

The entire worksheet object should be visible in the document window.

11 Click anywhere outside the worksheet object to stop modifying the worksheet and return to Word.

The standard Word menu and toolbars replace the Excel menu and toolbars. Compare your document to the one in Figure 9-5.

12 Save your work.

It can be confusing knowing what the differences are between linked and embedded objects. Table 9-1 compares each of these methods for inserting information created with other programs into Word documents.

Table 9-1. Embedded Versus Linked Objects

Object	Description
Embedded	An embedded object is actually saved within the file. Files with embedded objects are larger than files with linked objects. The advantage of using embedded objects is that the objects are actually saved inside the file, so you don't have to worry about any attached files becoming erased or lost.
Linked	A linked object is not saved in the file. Instead, a link contains information on where to find the source data file. The advantage of using linked objects is that when the source file is changed, the linked object in the file is automatically updated to reflect the changes.

QUICK REFERENCE

TO MODIFY AN EMBEDDED OR LINKED OBJECT:

1. DOUBLE-CLICK THE EMBEDDED OBJECT.

2. WHEN YOU HAVE FINISHED EDITING THE OBJECT, CLICK ANYWHERE OUTSIDE THE OBJECT TO RETURN TO THE HOST PROGRAM.

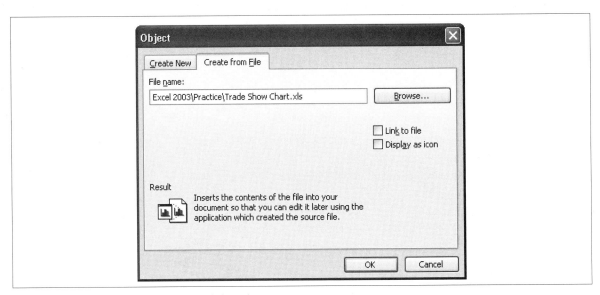

Figure 9-6. Inserting a linked Microsoft Excel chart object.

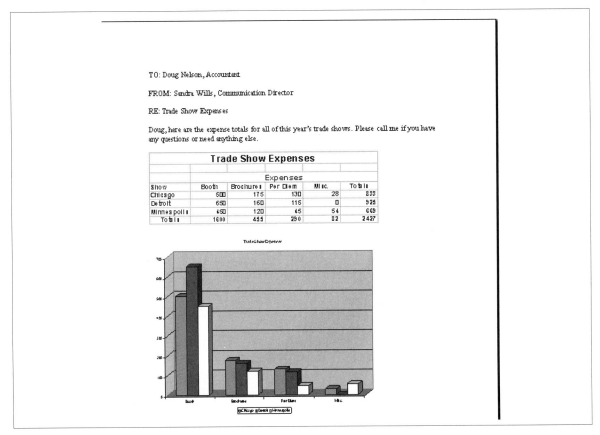

Figure 9-7. A linked Excel chart.

So far you have been inserting and working with an *embedded* Excel worksheet. This lesson mixes things up a bit. You will still be inserting information created in Excel, but in this lesson you will be inserting a *linked* Excel chart. Remember, when you insert an *embedded* object, you are actually storing and saving the object inside the file. A *linked* file is not stored and saved in a Word document but is connected to it. So if you make changes to the linked source file, it will be automatically updated in the Word document.

1 Press Ctrl + End **to move to the end of the document.**

Just like in Excel, Ctrl + End moves you to the end of a document in Word.

2 Press Enter **twice to add two blank lines.**

Now insert the linked chart object.

3 Select Insert → Object **from the menu and click the** Create from File tab **if it does not appear in front.**

The Create from File tab appears in front, as shown in Figure 9-6. You need to specify the name and location of the file you want to insert into your document.

4 Click the Browse button.

The Browse dialog box appears, allowing you to find and locate the file you want to insert into your document.

5 Navigate to your Practice folder or disk and select the Trade Show Chart **file.**

Notice the icon for the Trade Show Chart file indicates that it is a Microsoft Excel file.

6 Click Insert.

The Browse dialog box closes and you return to the Create from File tab of the Object dialog box. Notice the "Trade Show Chart" file name and location now appears in the File name text box.

7 Click the Link to file check box.

Checking the "Link to file" check box only inserts a link to the specified file in the Word document instead of inserting an embedded copy of the file. You should use "Link to file" if you want to display any changes made to the original file in your document.

8 Click OK.

Word accesses the Excel chart and then inserts a link to it in the document at the insertion point.

9 Resize the Chart object so it is similar in size to the one shown in Figure 9-7.

10 Save your work.

11 Select File → Exit **from the menu to close the Microsoft Word program.**

QUICK REFERENCE

TO INSERT A LINKED OBJECT FILE:

1. PLACE THE INSERTION POINT WHERE YOU WANT TO INSERT THE LINKED OBJECT.

2. SELECT INSERT → OBJECT FROM THE MENU AND CLICK THE CREATE FROM FILE TAB.

3. MAKE SURE THE LINK TO FILE CHECK BOX IS SELECTED, AND THEN SPECIFY THE FILE YOU WANT TO INSERT.

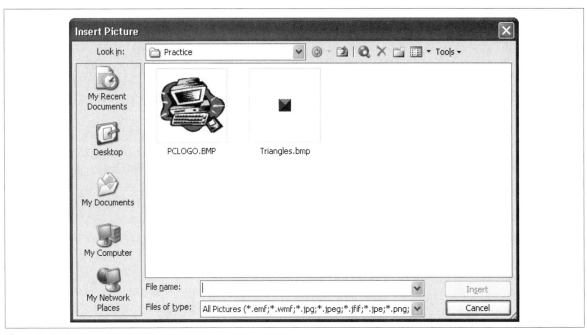

Figure 9-8. The Insert Picture dialog box.

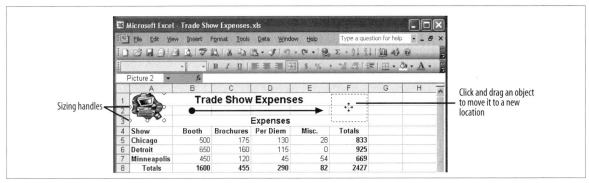

Figure 9-9. Move an object by dragging and dropping it.

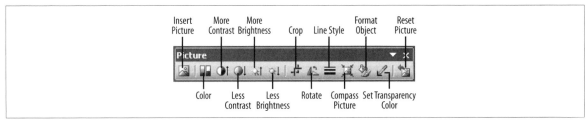

Figure 9-10. The Picture toolbar.

Pictures, graphics, and illustrations can make your worksheets more professional looking. This lesson explains how to insert clip art and graphics into your worksheets. You can insert graphics and pictures created with graphics programs such as Microsoft Paint (which comes with Windows), scanned pictures, or graphics from a clip art library.

1 Start Microsoft Excel, open the Expenses workbook, and save it as Trade Show Expenses.

2 Click cell A1.

This is where you want to insert the graphic.

3 Select Insert → Picture → From File from the menu.

The Insert Picture dialog box appears, as shown in Figure 9-8. You need to specify the name and location of the graphic file to be inserted into your Excel worksheet.

4 Navigate to your Practice folder or disk and select the PCLogo file.

Excel displays a preview of the graphic in the left side panel of the Insert Picture dialog box.

5 Click the Insert button to insert the PCLogo graphic.

Excel inserts the picture file PCLogo in the worksheet.

6 Select the picture (if necessary) of the PCLogo by clicking it.

See the boxes along the edges of the picture? Those are *sizing handles* and are used to resize or crop objects. Go ahead and resize the picture.

7 Position the pointer over the lower-right sizing handle, until the pointer changes to a ↘, then click and hold the left mouse button, drag the mouse diagonally down and to the right until the bottom of the picture is flush with the top of Row 4, then release the mouse button.

8 With the picture still selected, click and hold the left mouse button and drag the picture to the right side of the page, as shown in Figure 9-9. Release the left mouse button to drop the picture.

9 Save your work and close the Trade Show Expenses workbook.

You probably noticed several other options listed under the Insert → Picture menu. Table 9-2 lists what they are and what they do.

Table 9-2. The Insert Picture Menu

Insert	Description
🖼	Opens the Clip Gallery where you can select a clip art image to insert.
🖼	Inserts a graphic file in the active cell.
🔷	Inserts a ready-made shape, such as a circle, rectangle, star, arrow, etc.
🔲	Inserts a Microsoft Organization Chart object into worksheet.
🔺	Creates spectacular text effects, such as **WordArt**.
📷	Scans an image and inserts it at the insertion point.

QUICK REFERENCE

TO INSERT A GRAPHIC:

1. CLICK THE CELL WHERE YOU WANT TO INSERT THE GRAPHIC AND SELECT INSERT → PICTURE → FROM FILE FROM THE MENU.

2. SELECT THE FILE LOCATION AND NAME AND CLICK OK.

TO RESIZE A GRAPHIC:

• CLICK THE OBJECT TO SELECT IT, THEN DRAG ITS SIZING HANDLES UNTIL THE OBJECT IS THE SIZE YOU WANT.

TO MOVE A GRAPHIC:

• CLICK THE PICTURE AND HOLD MOUSE BUTTON, DRAG THE PICTURE TO A NEW LOCATION IN THE DOCUMENT, THEN RELEASE THE MOUSE BUTTON.

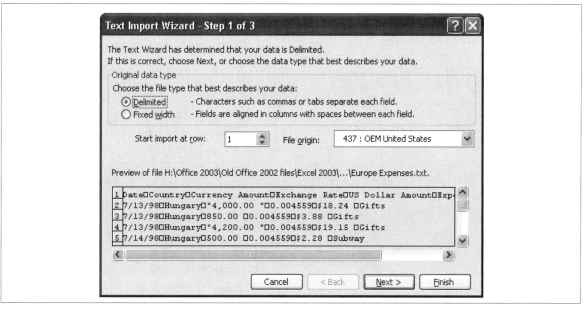

Figure 9-11. The Text Import Wizard dialog box.

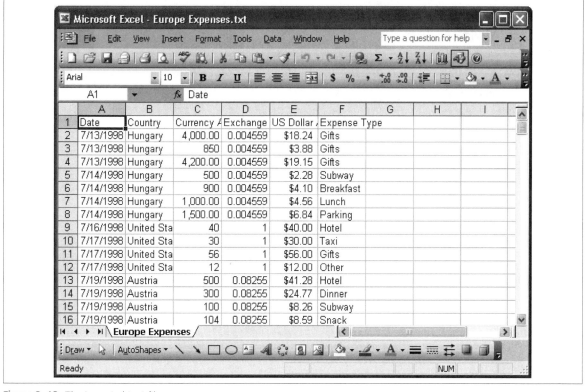

Figure 9-12. The imported text file.

People from different countries speak different languages. Likewise, computer programs save files in different formats that other programs sometimes can't read. Fortunately, just as some people can speak several languages, Excel can read and write in other file formats. (See Table 9-3 for a list of the various file formats and extensions that Excel can import and export.)

This lesson shows how you can open one of the most common file formats in Excel—a tab-delimited text file.

1 Click the Open button on the Standard toolbar and navigate to your Practice folder or disk.

Normally the Open dialog box displays only files created with Microsoft Excel. To open files created with other programs, you need to select the file type you want from the "Files of type" list arrow—in this case, Text files.

2 Click the Files of type list arrow, select Text Files, select the Europe Expenses file, and click Open.

The Text Import Wizard dialog box appears, as shown in Figure 9-11. You must specify how the information is stored in the text file. There are two options:

- **Delimited:** Tabs, colons, semicolons, or other characters separate items in your text file. This is the most common (and default) option.
- **Fixed Width:** All the items in your text file are the same length.

The Europe Expenses is a *tab-delimited* text file—that is, tabs separate its fields, so you don't need to make any changes and can continue on to the next step.

3 Click Next.

The second step of the Text Import Wizard appears. Notice the tab box is checked under Delimiters (what separates the text). No changes needed here.

4 Click Next.

The third step of the Text Import Wizard allows specifying formatting options for any of the columns of data. For example, you could specify that a particular column be formatted as a data or number field. It isn't important to format any of the columns here, however, so you can complete the Text Import Wizard.

5 Click Finish.

The Text Import Wizard closes and the imported text file appears in the Excel worksheet window.

The following explains how to save a workbook in a different format.

6 Select File → Save As from the menu.

The Save As dialog box appears.

7 Click the Save as type list arrow, scroll down the list and select WKS (1-2-3).

This will save the file in Lotus 1-2-3 format.

8 Click Save to save the Europe Expenses workbook as a Lotus 1-2-3 file, then close it (but leave Microsoft Excel open!).

Table 9-3. Importable and Exportable File Formats and Extensions

File Format	Extensions
Microsoft Excel 97/2000/2002	.xls, .xlt
Microsoft Excel 5.0/95	.xls, .xlt
Microsoft Excel 4.0, 3.0, 2.0	.xls, .xlw, .wlc, .xlm
Lotus 1-2-3	.wk4, .wk3, .fm3, .fmt, .all, .wk1, .wks
Quattro Pro	.wb1, .wbi
Text (Both tab- and comma-delimited)	.txt, .csv
Dbase 2, 3, 4	.dbf
Microsoft Access 2.0, 95, 97	.mdb

QUICK REFERENCE

TO OPEN A NON-EXCEL FILE IN EXCEL:

1. CLICK THE OPEN BUTTON ON THE STANDARD TOOLBAR.

2. CLICK THE FILES OF TYPE LIST ARROW AND SELECT ALL FILES TO DISPLAY ALL FILES.

3. FIND AND DOUBLE-CLICK THE FILE YOU WANT TO OPEN.

TO SAVE A FILE IN A DIFFERENT FILE FORMAT:

1. SELECT FILE → SAVE AS FROM THE MENU.

2. CLICK THE SAVE AS TYPE LIST ARROW AND SELECT THE FILE FORMAT YOU WANT TO SAVE THE FILE IN.

3. ENTER A NEW NAME FOR THE FILE, IF YOU WANT, AND CLICK SAVE.

Chapter Nine Review

Lesson Summary

Inserting an Excel Worksheet into a Word Document

To Insert an Embedded Excel Worksheet into a Word Document: Place the insertion point where you want the worksheet to be inserted and select Insert → Object from the menu. Click the Create from File tab to use an existing worksheet file or click the Create New tab to create a new worksheet. Select the worksheet you want to insert (if you selected Create from File) or create the worksheet from scratch (if you selected Create New).

Modifying an Inserted Excel Worksheet

Double-click any embedded or linked object to edit it. Click anywhere outside the object when you're finished.

An embedded object is saved within the file. Files with embedded objects are larger than files with linked objects. The advantage of using embedded objects is that the objects are actually saved inside the file, so you don't have to worry about any attached files becoming erased or lost.

A linked object is not saved in the file. Instead, a link contains information on where to find the source data file. The advantage of using linked objects is that if the source file is changed, the linked object in the file is automatically updated to reflect the changes.

Inserting a Linked Excel Chart in a Word Document

To Insert a Linked Object File: Place the insertion point where you want the worksheet to be inserted, select Insert → Object from the menu, and click the Create from File tab. Make sure the Link to File check box is selected and specify the file you want to insert.

Inserting a Graphic into a Worksheet

To Insert a Graphic: Click the cell where you want to insert the graphic and Select Insert → Picture → From File from the menu. Select the file location and name and click OK.

Resize an object by dragging its sizing handles until the object is the size you want.

Move an object by clicking and dragging it to a new location and releasing the mouse button.

Opening and Saving Files in Different Formats

To Open a Non-Excel File in Excel: Click the Open button on the Standard toolbar and select All Files from the Files of type list. Find and open the file.

To Save a File in a Different File Format: Select File → Save As from the menu and select the file format from the Save as type list.

Quiz

1. What is the difference between an embedded and linked object?

   A. An embedded object is saved within the file, a linked object is a hyperlink to another file.

   B. An embedded object is saved within the file, a linked object is not saved in the file. Instead, a connection to the file is inserted.

   C. An embedded object can be inserted on the same page as other text or information, a linked file must be placed on its own separate page.

   D. An embedded object is saved in a separate file, a linked object is saved with the file it was inserted into.

2. Double-click an embedded or linked object to modify it. (True or False?)

3. Which of the following statements is NOT true?

   A. When you insert an object, you can either insert an existing file or you can create a new file.

   B. Clicking the "Link to file" check box inserts a link to the file instead of embedding the file.

   C. You can only insert graphics or pictures into Excel charts.

   D. You insert graphics by selecting Insert → Picture → From File from the menu.

Homework

1. Open the workbook Lesson 2A and save it as a .CSV (Comma Delimited) text file named "Mileage".

2. Create a new workbook, select Insert → Picture → ClipArt from the menu, and insert a picture of a turtle into the workbook.

3. Resize the turtle picture so that it is about 50% of the original size, then move it down about an inch.

4. Open the Homework 5 workbook and save it as "Web Practice."

5. Click cell A10, type "Expenses," and press Enter. Click cell A10, click the Insert Hyperlink button on the Standard toolbar, and create a hyperlink to the Expenses workbook.

6. Exit Microsoft Excel and start Microsoft Word. Type "Here are the results of last month's survey:" and press Enter.

7. Insert the Lesson 7A workbook into the Word document at the insertion point.

Quiz Answers

1. B. An embedded object is saved within a file. A linked object is not actually saved within a file, but points to the inserted file.

2. True. Double-clicking an object lets you modify it.

3. C. You can insert graphics or pictures into worksheets or charts.

CHAPTER 10
USING EXCEL WITH THE INTERNET

CHAPTER OBJECTIVES:

Add hyperlinks to a worksheet

Browse hyperlinks and using the web toolbar

Save a workbook as a non-Interactive web page

Save a workbook as an interactive web page

Retrieve information from a web page

CHAPTER TASK: PUBLISH AN EXCEL WORKSHEET TO THE WEB

Prerequisites

- **Understand how to use menus, toolbars, dialog boxes, and shortcut keystrokes**
- **Have a basic familiarity with the Internet and the World Wide Web**

In a few years, the Internet has changed how most businesses and computers work, so it's no surprise that the biggest changes and improvements in Excel 2003 have to do with how it works and interacts with the Internet.

Excel's Internet features let you add hyperlinks to your workbooks to link them to another workbook, a file created in another program, or even a Web page. You can also save your worksheets and charts as a Web page and place them on your corporate Intranet or the World Wide Web so that other users can view them. In addition, you can create *interactive Web pages* that allow users to add, change, and calculate your worksheet's information from Microsoft Internet Explorer 4.01 or later. Finally, you can retrieve information stored on a Web page and place it on your worksheets.

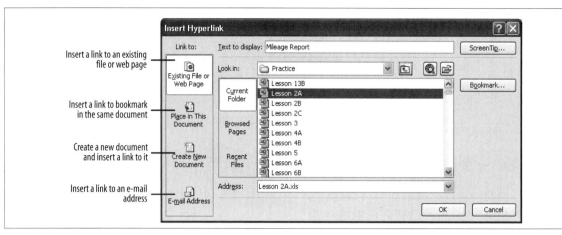

Figure 10-1. The Insert Hyperlink dialog box.

Hyperlink

In this lesson, you will learn how to use hyperlinks in Excel. A *hyperlink* points to a file, a specific location in a file, or a Web page on the Internet or on an Intranet. Whenever you click on a hyperlink, you jump to the hyperlink's destination (if it's available). A hyperlink is usually indicated by colored and underlined text. If you have ever been on the World Wide Web, you've used hyperlinks all the time to move between different Web pages.

1 Open the workbook named Lesson 10 and save it as Trade Show Expenses.

You may need to click the Files of Type list and select Microsoft Excel Files if you can't find it.

2 Click cell A10, type Mileage Report and press Enter.

This is the text for the hyperlink. The next step is to create the destination for the hyperlink. A hyperlink's destination can be any file on your computer, on the network, or even on the Internet.

Insert Hyperlink button
Other Ways to insert a Hyperlink:
• Select **Insert→Hyperlink** from the menu.

3 Click cell A10 and click the Insert Hyperlink button on the Standard toolbar.

The Insert Hyperlink dialog box appears, as shown in Figure 10-1. Here you can specify a Web address or name and location of a file you want to add as a hyperlink. If you know the location and name of the file or Web address, you can type it directly in the dialog box; otherwise, you can navigate to the file. There are three different buttons in the Insert Hyperlink dialog box that let you browse for four different types of hyperlink destinations. These buttons are:

• **Existing File or Web Page:** Creates a link that takes you to another Excel workbook or to a file created in another program, such as a Microsoft Excel worksheet, or to a web page on the Internet.

• **Place in This Document:** Takes you to a bookmark in the same document.

• **Create New Document:** Creates a new Microsoft Excel workbook and then inserts a hyperlink into it.

• **E-mail Address:** Creates a clickable e-mail address.

4 Click the Existing File or Web Page button.

The "Look in:" list appears, which displays a list of files that you can use as the destination for your hyperlink. The file you want is in the Practice folder, however, so you will have to navigate to its location.

5 Navigate to your Practice folder or disk. Select the Lesson 2A workbook file and click OK.

The Insert Hyperlink dialog box closes and you return to the worksheet window. Notice the text "Mileage

Report" appears blue and underlined, signifying it's a hyperlink. For now, *don't click the Mileage Report Hyperlink!* We'll cover that in the next lesson.

Once you create a hyperlink, you can easily edit it to change its title or target, copy it, or delete it by clicking by right-clicking the hyperlink. Try it!

6 Right-click the hyperlink to view the shortcut menu.

A shortcut menu with the most frequently used hyperlink commands appears. Here, you could select Edit Hyperlink to change the hyperlink's target or edit the hyperlink's title; you could select Open Hyperlink to open the hyperlink's target; or you could select

Remove Hyperlink to unlink the text to its destination. Your hyperlink is fine the way it is, so close the shortcut menu.

7 Click anywhere in the worksheet window to close the shortcut menu.

8 Save your work.

In the next lesson, you will get a chance to actually use the hyperlink you just created and see how you can browse Excel's files using the Web toolbar.

QUICK REFERENCE

TO INSERT A HYPERLINK:

1. SELECT THE CELL YOU WANT TO USE FOR THE HYPERLINK AND CLICK THE INSERT HYPERLINK BUTTON FROM THE STANDARD TOOLBAR.

   OR...

   SELECT THE TEXT YOU WANT TO USE FOR THE HYPERLINK AND SELECT INSERT → HYPERLINK FROM THE MENU.

2. EITHER SELECT A FILE YOU WANT (USE THE BROWSE BUTTONS TO HELP YOU LOCATE THE FILE) OR TYPE A WEB ADDRESS FOR THE HYPERLINK'S DESTINATION AND CLICK OK.

TO EDIT A HYPERLINK:

- RIGHT-CLICK THE HYPERLINK AND SELECT EDIT HYPERLINK FROM THE SHORTCUT MENU.

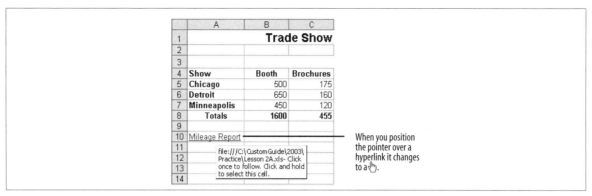

Figure 10-2. Click a hyperlink...

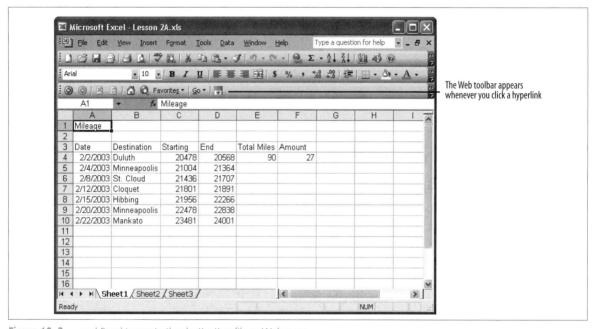

Figure 10-3. ...and Excel jumps to the destination file or Web page.

If an Excel workbook contains one or more hyperlinks, you can navigate or browse between the files connected by the hyperlinks. In this lesson you will test the hyperlinks you created earlier to make sure they work. Chances are, browsing between two files will be nothing new to you, because browsing hyperlinks in Microsoft Excel is no different than browsing the Web.

1 Click the hyperlink Mileage Report in cell A10 (see Figure 10-2).

Two things happen whenever you click a hyperlink in Excel: First, you immediately jump to the hyperlink's destination—in this case Lesson 2A, the Mileage

Report workbook, as shown in Figure 10-3. Second, Excel displays the Web toolbar (if it isn't there already) so you can easily navigate between your files just like you would if you were surfing the Internet.

Move on to the next step, and we'll create a hyperlink to the first workbook, Trade Show Expenses, so that the user can easily return to it.

2 Click cell A14, type Return to Trade Show Expenses and press Enter.

This text will contain the hyperlink to the workbook "Trade Show Expenses."

Insert Hyperlink button
Other Ways to insert a Hyperlink:
• Select **Insert**→**Hyperlink** from the menu.

3 Click cell A14 and click the Insert Hyperlink button on the Standard toolbar.

The Insert Hyperlink dialog box appears.

4 Make sure your Practice folder appears as the Current Folder.

If it isn't the current folder, navigate to it in the "Look in:" list.

5 Scroll down the list, select the Trade Show Expenses workbook file, and click OK.

The Link to File dialog box closes and the name and location of the Trade Show Expenses is added to the Link to file or URL text box.

6 Click the hyperlink Return to Trade Show Expenses in cell A14.

Back button

The Trade Show Expenses workbook appears in the worksheet window. Use the Web toolbar to jump back to the previously viewed document. (Table 10-1 describes the various Web toolbar buttons.)

7 Click the Back button on the Web toolbar.

You're back to the Lesson 2A workbook. Now jump forward to the Trade Show Expenses workbook.

Forward button

8 Click the Forward button on the Web toolbar.

The Trade Show Expenses workbook appears in the worksheet window. Excel can browse and navigate Web pages on the Internet just as easily as it can browse workbooks. In the next lesson, you'll learn how to save an Excel workbook as a Web page, so it can be viewed on the Internet.

You don't need the Web toolbar anymore, so go ahead and close it.

9 Right-click the Web toolbar and select Web to close the Web toolbar.

Table 10-1. The Web toolbar buttons

Button Icon	Button Name	Description
	Back	Brings you back to the previously viewed Web page.
	Forward	Brings to forward to the next viewed Web page.
	Stop Current Jump	Stops loading a Web page.
	Refresh Current Page	Reloads or refreshes the current Web page.
	Start Page	Brings you to your home page.
	Search the Web	Search the Web for specified information.

Table 10-1. The Web toolbar buttons (Continued)

Button Icon	Button Name	Description
Favorites ▾	Favorites	Quickly brings you to Web pages that you have bookmarked and use frequently.
Go ▾	Go	Displays a list of Web commands that also appear on the Web toolbar.
▣	Show Only Web Toolbar	Toggles whether toolbars other than the Web toolbar should be displayed or hidden.

QUICK REFERENCE

TO JUMP TO A HYPERLINK'S DESTINATION:

• CLICK THE HYPERLINK.

TO BROWSE FILES WITH EXCEL:

• USE THE WEB TOOLBAR (SEE TABLE 10-1) TO NAVIGATE BETWEEN FILES JUST LIKE YOU WOULD BROWSE THE INTERNET.

TO HIDE THE WEB TOOLBAR:

• RIGHT-CLICK THE WEB TOOLBAR AND SELECT WEB.

OR...

• SELECT VIEW → TOOLBARS → WEB FROM THE MENU.

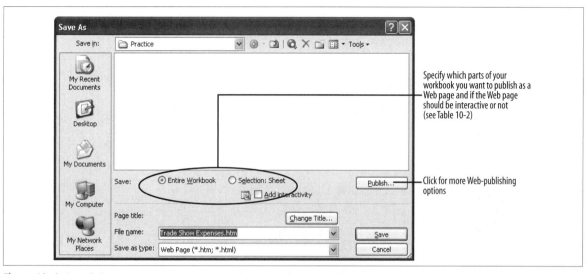

Figure 10-4. Specify how you want to save your Web Page in the Save As dialog box.

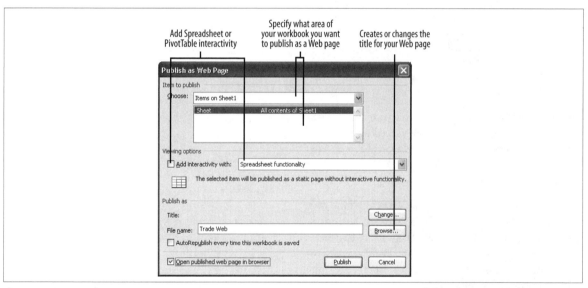

Figure 10-5. The Publish as Web Page dialog box.

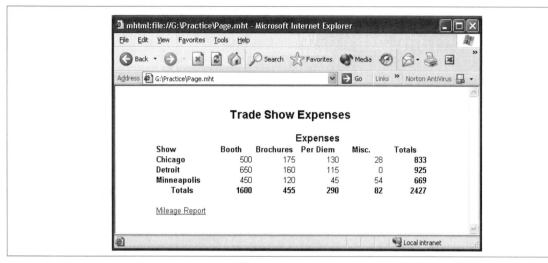

Figure 10-6. Displaying a non-interactive Web page in a Web browser.

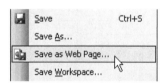

Save as Web page

This lesson explains how you can save your Excel worksheets as Web pages so they can be viewed on the Internet. You can save any existing Excel worksheets as Web page files (also known as HTML files) by selecting File → Save as Web Page from the menu.

Saving Excel workbooks as Web pages isn't anything new. What is new, however, is that Excel 2003 can save workbooks as Interactive Web pages. This means that users can interact with the data on your Web page because they have basic spreadsheet functionality. Interactive Web Pages lets your users enter data, format it, calculate it, and sort and filter it. There is one major drawback to Interactive Web pages, however—only users who have Microsoft's Internet Explorer 4.01 or later Web-browsing software (surprise!) can use Office 2003's Interactive Web pages, so any Netscape Navigator users are left in the dark. If your Web audience includes Netscape Navigator users, you can still save your workbooks as static non-interactive Web pages. Table 10-2 explains some of the differences between the two.

This lesson explains how to save a non-interactive Web page.

1 Make sure Trade Show Expenses is the active workbook, then select File → Save as Web Page from the menu.

The Save As dialog box appears, as shown in Figure 10-4. You can save an Excel workbook as several different types of Web pages:

TIP *By default, Excel 2003 saves Web pages as a single file Web page (MHTML) that saves all the elements of a worksheet, including text and graphics into a single file. You can still save worksheets as ordinary HTML files by selecting Single File Web page from the Save as type list.*

* **Entire Workbook (Non-Interactive):** Saves everything in the workbook—all your worksheets and charts—as non-interactive web pages. To save the entire workbook, check the Entire Workbook check box.

* **Sheet or Selection (Interactive or Non-Interactive):** Saves a worksheet or selected cell range. To save a sheet or selection, click the Publish button and specify the area of the workbook you want to save. You can add interactivity by checking the "Add Interactivity with" box and selecting "Spreadsheet functionality" from the drop-down list.

- **PivotTable (Interactive):** Saves a worksheet or selected cell range as an Interactive PivotTable on the Web, which users can use to pivot, filter, and sort data. To save a sheet or selection as a PivotTable, click the Publish button, specify the area of the workbook you want to save, check the "Add Interactivity with" box and select "PivotTable functionality" from the drop-down list.

2 Click the Publish button.

The Publish as Web Page dialog box appears, as shown in Figure 10-5. Here you have to specify which areas of your workbook you want to save and how to save them.

3 Select Items on Sheet1 from the Choose list, then select Sheet All Contents of Sheet1 from the box under the Choose list.

4 Type Trade Web in the File name box, check the Open published web page in browser box, and click the Publish button.

Of course, you can also click the Browse button and Navigate to the drive and folder where you want to save your Web page. Excel saves Sheet1 of the Trade Show Expenses workbook as a non-interactive Web page and then opens the Web page in your computer's Web browser. Since the Web page isn't interactive, you can only view its information. We'll create an interactive Web page in the next lesson.

Table 10-2. Interactive vs. Non-Interactive Web Pages

Web Page Type	Description
Interactive Web Pages	Interactive Web pages let users interact with the data on your Web page because they include basic spreadsheet functionality. Interactive Web Pages let your users enter data, format data, calculate data, and sort and filter. Interactive Web pages require Microsoft Internet Explorer 4.01 or greater so not everyone can use them.
Non-Interactive Web Pages	Non-interactive Web pages allow users to view worksheet data but not interact with it. Users can view non-interactive Web pages in any Web browser, unlike when they view interactive pages, which requires Microsoft Internet Explorer version 4.01 or later.

QUICK REFERENCE

TO SAVE A WORKBOOK AS A NON-INTERACTIVE WEB PAGE:

1. OPEN THE WORKBOOK AND SELECT FILE → SAVE AS WEB PAGE FROM THE MENU.

2. CLICK PUBLISH.

3. SPECIFY WHAT YOU WANT TO PUBLISH ON YOUR WEB PAGE FROM THE CHOOSE LIST AND TYPE A NAME FOR YOUR WEB PAGE FILE IN THE FILE NAME BOX.

4. CLICK PUBLISH.

Figure 10-7. Interactive web page with basic spreadsheet functionality.

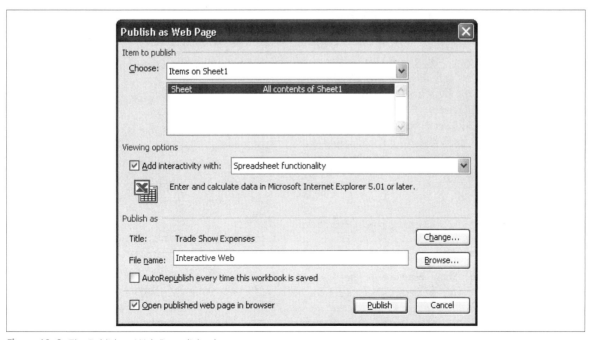

Figure 10-8. The Publish as Web Page dialog box.

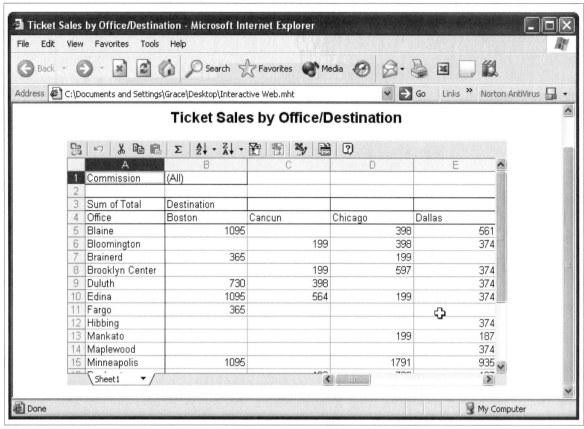

Figure 10-9. Workbooks saved as Interactive PivotTables.

In the previous lesson, you learned how to save a workbook as a non-interactive Web page. Non-interactive Web pages are great if you want only to present information and/or if you don't know which Web browser your audience has. If you're publishing to a corporate Intranet and/or you know your audience uses Microsoft Internet Explorer 4.01 or later, you can save your workbooks as interactive Web pages, which allow users to add, change, sort, filter, and calculate the data presented on a Web page.

1 If necessary, open the workbook named Lesson 10 and save it as Trade Show Expenses.

2 Make sure Trade Show Expenses is the active workbook, then select File → Save as Web Page from the menu.

The Save As dialog box appears.

3 Click the Publish button.

The Publish as Web Page dialog box appears, as shown in Figure 10-8. First you have to specify which areas of the workbook you want to publish.

4 Select Items on Sheet1 from the Choose list, then select Sheet   All Contents of Sheet1 from the box under the Choose list.

Next you have to tell Excel that you want to save the Web page with interactivity. When you save a worksheet as a Web page you can add interactivity with:

- **Spreadsheet functionality:** Enables users to enter, change, and calculate data like they're using an Excel worksheet.

- **PivotTable functionality:** Enables users to pivot, filter, sort, and analyze data like they would using an Excel PivotTable report (see Chapter 11 if you're a little unclear about what a PivotTable report is).

5 Add a check to the Add Interactivity with box and verify that Spreadsheet functionality appears in the drop-down list to the right.

You can also create or change the title that appears at the top of your Web page, whether your Web page is interactive or not.

6 Click the Change button.

The Set Title dialog box appears.

7 Type TradeShowExpenses in the Title box and click OK.

Lastly you have to specify a file name for the Web page and where you want to save it.

8 Type InteractiveWeb in the File name box, add a check to the Open published web page in browser box, and click the Publish button.

Excel saves Sheet1 of the TradeShowExpenses workbook as an interactive Web page and opens the Web page in Microsoft Internet Explorer, as shown in Figure 10-7. Let's test the interactive Web page.

9 Click cell B5, type 400 and press Enter.

Wow! The Web page let's you change the worksheet's number and recalculates it, just like Microsoft Excel! By no means do Interactive Web pages have all of Excel's bells and whistles features, but they have enough functionality for you to perform basic calculations. Notice the Web page even has an Excel toolbar, which contains buttons for the basic worksheet functions, such as cut, copy, paste, AutoSum, and sort.

Sort Descending button

10 Select the cell range A5:F7 and click the Sort Descending button on the toolbar.

Excel sorts the selected cell range alphabetically in descending order.

11 Close Microsoft Internet Explorer and close all open workbooks in Excel.

QUICK REFERENCE

TO SAVE A WORKBOOK AS AN INTERACTIVE WEB PAGE:

1. OPEN THE WORKBOOK AND SELECT FILE → SAVE AS WEB PAGE FROM THE MENU.

2. CLICK PUBLISH.

3. SPECIFY WHAT YOU WANT TO PUBLISH ON YOUR WEB PAGE FROM THE CHOOSE LIST AND TYPE A NAME FOR YOUR WEB PAGE FILE IN THE FILE NAME BOX.

4. CHECK THE ADD INTERACTIVITY WITH BOX.

5. CLICK PUBLISH.

Import an External Data Source

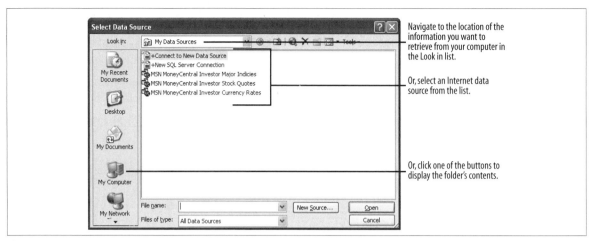

Figure 10-10. The Select Data Source dialog box.

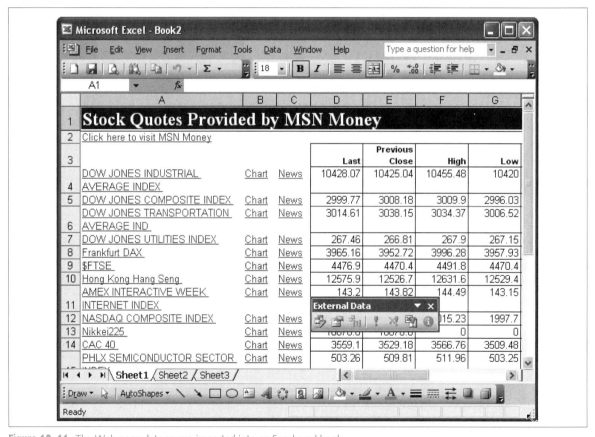

Figure 10-11. The Web page data source imported into an Excel workbook.

This lesson explains how to import external data into your Excel worksheet. You can import information that is currently on your computer or information that is on the Internet, which saves you a lot of typing. Better yet, you can update the data you import with any new information that might appear in the original source. For example, you need a data sheet of the Dow Jones stock quotes every day. Instead of re-importing that information every day, you can simply refresh the original Dow Jones data source you imported in Excel, and the information will automatically be updated. Ready to try it?

1 Create a new workbook. Make sure you are connected to the Internet.

This lesson will require a connection to the Internet to import the data source in this lesson.

2 Select Data → Import External Data → Import Data from the menu.

The Select Source Data dialog box appears, as shown in Figure 10-10.

A list of data sources appears in the window. These are queries that Microsoft has already created for your convenience. As you can see, almost all of these data sources are online stock quotes, which many Excel users would find useful.

3 Click MSN MoneyCentral Investor Major Indicies to select it.

This data source compiles a list of Dow Jones stock quotes daily on the Internet.

4 Click Open.

The Import Data dialog box appears, asking where you want to import the information on your worksheet. A line like marching ants should appear around cell A1, where the information will be imported. If you want the information to be imported into another area of the worksheet, just click the cell.

5 Click OK to close the Import Data dialog box.

Excel imports the data source into the worksheet and the External Data toolbar appears, as shown in Figure 10-11. You can use these buttons to refresh the imported data source.

You can also import data that is already on your computer or company Intranet.

6 Click Sheet 2 of the workbook to start a new page.

You will import a data source from your Practice folder.

7 Select Data → Import External Data → Import Data from the menu.

The process is a bit different from importing a data source on the Internet.

Notice that the left side of the dialog box includes five buttons. You can use these buttons to navigate to different areas of your computer. The "Look in" list is your best bet to find your Practice folder, however.

8 Navigate to your Practice folder in the Look in list of the Select Source Data dialog box.

The Practice folder contains the data source you want to import to Sheet 2.

9 Select Office Expenses in the Practice folder and click Open.

The New Web Query dialog box appears, asking which tables you want to import.

10 Click Import to import the entire table.

The Import Data dialog box appears, asking where you want to insert the imported information in your worksheet.

11 Click cell A1 in the worksheet.

A line that looks like marching ants surrounds the cell, indicating that the imported data source will be inserted there.

12 Click OK.

Excel imports the Office Expenses Sheet 1 into the worksheet.

That's all there is to importing an external data source!

QUICK REFERENCE

TO IMPORT EXTERNAL DATA:

1. SELECT DATA → IMPORT EXTERNAL DATA → IMPORT DATA FROM THE MENU.

2. NAVIGATE TO AND SELECT THE DATA SOURCE YOU WANT TO IMPORT.

3. CLICK OPEN.

4. SELECT WHERE YOU WANT THE DATA SOURCE TO APPEAR IN THE WORKSHEET AND CLICK OK.

Figure 10-12. The External Data Range Properties dialog box.

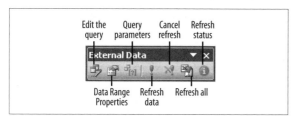

Figure 10-13. External Data toolbar.

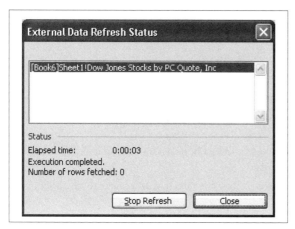

Figure 10-14. The External Data Refresh Status dialog box.

Just because a data source was imported does not mean its properties or formatting are set in stone forever. Once you have inserted a data source, you may find that you want to change its properties. This lesson is a brief overview of how to change your data source's properties.

Data Range Properties button

1 Make sure you have your worksheet from Lesson 10.5 open and click Sheet. Click the Data Range Properties button on the External Data toolbar.

The External Data Range Properties dialog box appears. as shown in Figure 10-12. You can set how you want Excel to import the information into your worksheet here.

2 Click OK.

Refer to Table 10-3 to find out more information on what these options and other commands in the Properties dialog box do.

Refresh Data button

3 Click the Refresh Data button on the External Data toolbar (see Figure 10-13).

The Refresh Data dialog box appears to ask if the file is secure.

4 The file is secure, so click OK.

Excel updates the data source to include the most recent information available from its location on the Internet. Pretty neat, eh?

If there is more than one data source in your workbook, you can refresh all data sources at one time.

Refresh All button

5 Click the Refresh All button on the External Data toolbar.

This refreshes all of the data sources in the workbook.

Notice that the cursor changes into an hourglass when you refresh the data source. This indicates that Excel is updating the information in the data source. If you find that this action is taking a while, you can click the Refresh Status button to see how the refresh process is going.

Refresh Status button

6 Click the Refresh Status button on the External Data toolbar.

The External Data Refresh Status dialog box appears, as shown in Figure 10-14. The dialog box tells you how much information has been downloaded, how much time has elapsed, and other information.

Refer to Table 10-3 for more information on the properties you can set in a data source.

Table 10-3. Data Range Properties

Command	Description
Save query definition	Check this option so your worksheet remembers where to go when it refreshes the data. Uncheck it so the data source can not be refreshed again.
Save password	Check this option so that Excel automatically enters the password when the data source is refreshed.
Enable background refresh	Check this option so that when you refresh the data source you can continue working in Microsoft Excel. Otherwise, you must wait until Excel is completely finished refreshing the data source to work with the program.
Refresh every	Check this option to refresh the data source at specific intervals and then enter the number of minutes you want between refreshes in the minutes box.
Refresh data on file open	Check this option so that the data source automatically refreshes when you open the workbook. The Save query definition check box must be selected to refresh the data.
Remove external data from worksheet before saving	Check this option so that Excel deletes the data source information when you save the worksheet.
Include field names	Check this option so that Excel automatically inserts the data source's field names as column labels for the data source.
Preserve column sort/filter/layout	Check this option to preserve any sort order, filtering, or column order changes you make in a data source when it is refreshed.
Include row numbers	Check this option to allow the data source to use its own row numbering.
Preserve cell formatting	Check this option to retain cell formatting that you apply in Microsoft Excel when you refresh the data source.
Adjust column width	Check this option so that Excel automatically adjusts its column width to display the imported data source information.
Fill down formulas in columns adjacent to data	Check this option if you want Excel to copy formulas in a data source to new columns when it is refreshed.

QUICK REFERENCE

TO SET EXTERNAL DATA SOURCE PROPERTIES:

- CLICK THE DATA RANGE PROPERTIES BUTTON FROM THE EXTERNAL DATA TOOLBAR.

    OR...

1. SELECT DATA → IMPORT EXTERNAL DATA → DATA RANGE PROPERTIES FROM THE MENU.

2. SELECT THE PROPERTIES YOU WANT TO APPLY TO THE DATA SOURCE.

TO REFRESH A DATA SOURCE:

- CLICK THE REFRESH DATA BUTTON ON THE EXTERNAL DATA TOOLBAR.

    OR...

- CLICK THE REFRESH ALL BUTTON ON THE EXTERNAL DATA TOOLBAR.

TO VIEW THE REFRESH STATUS:

- CLICK THE REFRESH STATUS BUTTON ON THE EXTERNAL DATA TOOLBAR.

TO CANCEL A REFRESH:

- CLICK THE CANCEL REFRESH BUTTON ON THE EXTERNAL DATA TOOLBAR.

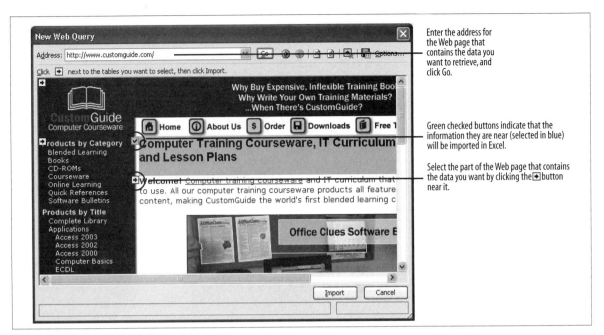

Enter the address for the Web page that contains the data you want to retrieve, and click Go.

Green checked buttons indicate that the information they are near (selected in blue) will be imported in Excel.

Select the part of the Web page that contains the data you want by clicking the ☀ button near it.

Figure 10-15. The New Web Query dialog box.

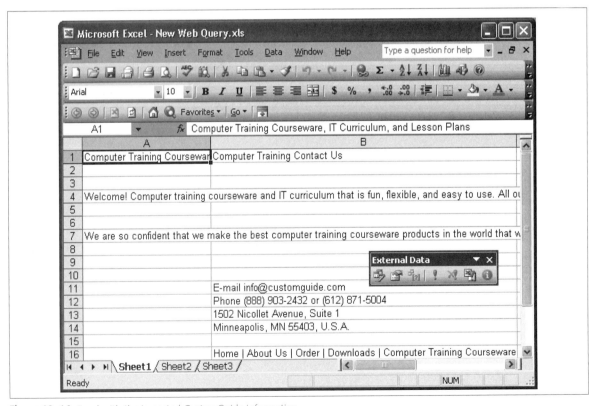

Figure 10-16. Excel with the imported CustomGuide information.

For the most part, any information you may want to add to an Excel worksheet can be done with the Import Data command. Sometimes, however, you may want to specialize the information you import, which requires a more advanced procedure. For example, you might want to import only a specific part of a Web page. You would create a new query to perform this procedure.

1 Create a new workbook.

2 Select Data → Import External Data → New Web Query from the menu.

The New Web Query dialog box appears with the MSN web site in the window (how shameless). In case you want to import the contents of a different Web page, you have to type the address of the Web page you want to import in the text box.

3 Type www.customguide.com in the Address text box and click Go.

As shown in Figure 10-15, the CustomGuide Web page appears in the New Web Query dialog box (how shameless). Notice that there are little yellow boxes with arrows in them spread out over the page. Each button is attached to a different table or section of the page. When you see a section of the page you want to import, all you have to do is click the yellow button near it.

4 Click any three ➔ buttons on the CustomGuide page.

Notice that the ➔ yellow arrow buttons turn into ☑ green check buttons after they are clicked. Only the

checked boxes will return information from their respective tables in the Web page. This is a great improvement from Excel 2000, where you had no choice; you had to import entire Web pages at a time.

NOTE *If you will need to retrieve or query the Web page again in the future, you can save the Web query by clicking the Save Query button. The query will then appear in the Select Data Source dialog box, along with the queries that are already created for Excel.*

5 Click Import.

Excel asks where you want to put the queried information. You can place the data in a location on any existing worksheet, or you can place the data on a new worksheet.

6 Click OK to place the queried data in cell A1 of the current worksheet.

Excel retrieves the data from the CustomGuide Web page and puts it in cell A1 of the current worksheet, as shown in Figure 10-16. The External Data toolbar also appears, which you can later use to refresh the data to make sure you have the most recent numbers.

7 Exit Microsoft Excel without saving any of your work.

Well done! You've finished another chapter and have learned a new set of skills. Move on to the "Chapter Ten Review" and see how much you've retained.

Table 10-4. New Web Query Dialog Box Toolbar

Button Icon	Button Name	Function
	Back	Click to go back to the Web page where you previously were.
	Forward	Click to go forward to the Web page where you previously were.
	Stop	Click to stop downloading a Web page.
	Refresh	Click to Refresh a Web page.
	Hide Icons	Click to hide the icons on the Web pages in the New Web Query dialog box.
	Save Query	Click to save the query in the Select Data Source dialog box.

QUICK REFERENCE

TO CREATE A NEW WEB QUERY:

1. SELECT DATA → IMPORT EXTERNAL DATA → NEW WEB QUERY FROM THE MENU.

2. TYPE THE ADDRESS OF THE WEB PAGE FROM WHICH YOU WANT TO IMPORT INFORMATION AND CLICK GO.

3. CLICK THE ICONS NEAR THE INFORMATION YOU WANT TO IMPORT AND CLICK IMPORT.

4. SPECIFY WHERE IN THE WORKBOOK YOU WANT TO INSERT THE RESULTS OF THE QUERY AND CLICK OK.

Chapter Ten Review

Lesson Summary

Adding Hyperlinks to a Worksheet

A hyperlink is a link that points to a file, a specific location in a file, or a Web page on the Internet or on an intranet.

To Insert a Hyperlink: Select the cell you want to use for the hyperlink and click the Insert Hyperlink button from the Standard toolbar or select Insert → Hyperlink from the menu. Either select a file you want (use the browse button to help you locate the file) or type a Web address for the hyperlink's destination and click OK.

To Edit a Hyperlink: Right-click the hyperlink and select Edit Hyperlink from the shortcut menu.

Browsing Hyperlinks and using the Web Toolbar

Click a hyperlink to jump to its destination (the file or Website it's linked to). The Web toolbar will appear whenever you click a hyperlink in Excel.

To Browse Files with Excel: Use the Web toolbar to navigate between files just like you would browse the Internet.

To Hide the Web Toolbar: Right-click the Web toolbar and select Web or select View → Toolbars → Web from the menu.

Saving a Workbook as a Non-Interactive Web Page

Non-Interactive Web Pages allow users to view worksheet data but not interact with it. Users can view non-interactive Web pages in any Web browser, unlike when they view interactive pages, which requires Microsoft Internet Explorer version 4.01 or later.

To Save a Workbook as a Non-Interactive Web Page: Open the workbook and select File → Save as Web Page from the menu and click Publish. Specify what you want to publish on your Web page from the Choose list, type a name for your Web page file in the File name box, and click Publish.

Saving a Workbook as an Interactive Web Page

- Interactive Web Pages let users interact with the data on your Web page because they include basic spreadsheet functionality. Interactive Web pages let your

users enter data, format data, calculate data, and sort and filter. Interactive Web pages require Microsoft Internet Explorer 4.01 or greater, so not everyone can use them.

- **To Save a Workbook as an Interactive Web Page:** Open the workbook, select File → Save as Web Page from the menu, and click Publish. Specify what you want to publish on your Web page from the Choose list, type a name for your Web page file in the File name box, check the Add interactivity with box, and click Publish.

Import External Data

Select Data → Import External Data → Import Data from the menu. Navigate to and select the data source you want to import. Click Open. Select where you want the data source to appear in the worksheet and click OK.

Refresh a Data Source and Set Data Source Properties

To Set External Data Source Properties: Click the Data Range Properties button from the External Data toolbar. Or, select Data → Import External Data → Data Range Properties from the menu. Then, select the properties you want to apply to the data source.

To Refresh a Data Source: Click the Refresh Data button on the External Data toolbar. Or, click the Refresh All button on the External Data toolbar.

To View the Refresh Status: Click the Refresh Status button on the External Data toolbar.

To Cancel a Refresh: Click the Cancel Refresh button on the External Data toolbar.

Create a New Web Query

To Create a Web Query: Select Data → Import External Data → New Web Query from the menu, click the Browse button, and navigate to the Web page that contains the data you want to query (or type the URL of the Web page if you know it). Select the part of the Web page you want to query (usually just the tables), click OK, specify where in the workbook you want to insert the results of the query, and click OK.

Quiz

1. A hyperlink can point to which of the following items? (Select all that apply.)

   A. A location in the same Excel workbook.

   B. A different Excel workbook.

   C. A Microsoft Word document.

   D. A Web page on the Internet.

2. The Web toolbar automatically appears whenever you click a hyperlink in an Excel workbook. (True or False?)

3. Which of the following statements is NOT true?

   A. Interactive Web pages allow users to enter, format, calculate, and sort Excel worksheet data using a Web browser.

   B. Non-interactive Web pages allow users to view Excel worksheet data using a Web browser but not to change it.

   C. Interactive PivotTables allow users to pivot, filter, and sort an Excel PivotTable using a Web browser.

   D. Users must have Version 4.0 or later of either Microsoft Internet Explorer or Netscape Navigator in order to work with an Interactive Web page.

4. When you save an Excel workbook as a HTML file, some of the workbook's formatting may be lost. (True or False?)

5. You can edit a hyperlink by right-clicking it and selecting Hyperlink → Edit Hyperlink from the shortcut menu. (True or False?)

Homework

1. Open the Lesson 4A workbook and save it as "Web Practice."

2. Click cell A10 type "Expenses" and press Enter. Click cell A10, click the Insert Hyperlink button on the Standard toolbar, and create a hyperlink to the Expenses workbook.

3. Save the Web Practice workbook as a Web page.

4. Try running several of Excel's built-in Web queries.

Quiz Answers

1. A, B, C, and D. A hyperlink can point to any of these items and more.

2. True. The Web toolbar always appears whenever you click a hyperlink in any Microsoft Office application.

3. D. Netscape Navigator cannot view Excel's Interactive Web pages.

4. True. An HTML file doesn't have as many formatting options as an Excel worksheet.

5. True. To edit a hyperlink, right-click it and select Hyperlink → Edit Hyperlink from the shortcut menu.

CHAPTER 11

DATA ANALYSIS AND PIVOTTABLES

CHAPTER OBJECTIVES:

Create a PivotTable

Change or "pivot" a PivotTable

Use the page field to filter what data is displayed in a PivotTable

How to group information in a PivotTable by date

Create and work with subtotals

Use Database functions (DSUM)

Use Lookup functions (VLOOKUP)

Group and outline a worksheet

CHAPTER TASK: ANALYZE TICKET SALES

Prerequisites

- **Understand how to use menus, toolbars, dialog boxes, and shortcut keystrokes**
- **Understand how to create and work with a list**
- **Understand how to enter formulas**

Once you have created a list, there are many ways to analyze its data. You should already know some basic ways to analyze information, such as filtering records. This chapter explains more advanced and powerful methods of analyzing list information.

Creating a PivotTable feature is usually the best way to summarize and analyze list data—which is why we'll spend more than half of the chapter discussing it. A *PivotTable* is a way to summarize list information. Peek at Figures 11-1 and 11-2 to see how much easier it is to make sense of numbers in a list with a PivotTable. This chapter explains the ins and outs of PivotTables—how to create them, modify their structure, and edit the data a PivotTable is based on.

This chapter also includes lessons on several other ways to summarize and analyze worksheet information, such as how use Excel's subtotal function, how to create database-specific formulas, and how to outline your worksheets.

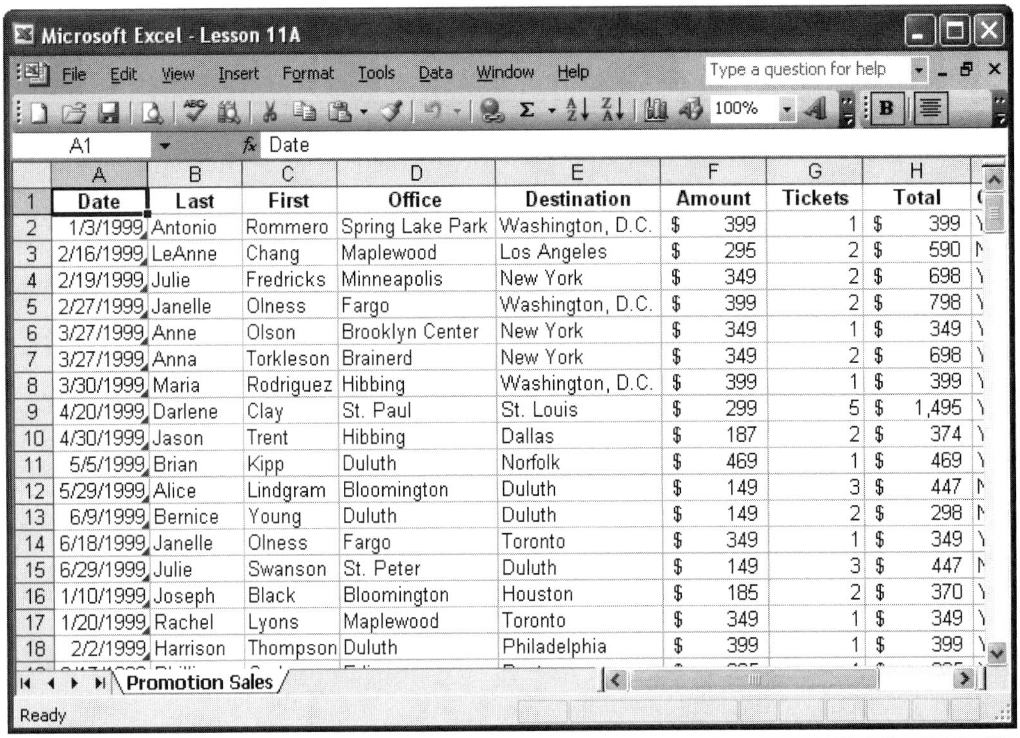

	A	B	C	D	E	F	G	H
1	Date	Last	First	Office	Destination	Amount	Tickets	Total
2	1/3/1999	Antonio	Rommero	Spring Lake Park	Washington, D.C.	$ 399	1	$ 399
3	2/16/1999	LeAnne	Chang	Maplewood	Los Angeles	$ 295	2	$ 590
4	2/19/1999	Julie	Fredricks	Minneapolis	New York	$ 349	2	$ 698
5	2/27/1999	Janelle	Olness	Fargo	Washington, D.C.	$ 399	2	$ 798
6	3/27/1999	Anne	Olson	Brooklyn Center	New York	$ 349	1	$ 349
7	3/27/1999	Anna	Torkleson	Brainerd	New York	$ 349	2	$ 698
8	3/30/1999	Maria	Rodriguez	Hibbing	Washington, D.C.	$ 399	1	$ 399
9	4/20/1999	Darlene	Clay	St. Paul	St. Louis	$ 299	5	$ 1,495
10	4/30/1999	Jason	Trent	Hibbing	Dallas	$ 187	2	$ 374
11	5/5/1999	Brian	Kipp	Duluth	Norfolk	$ 469	1	$ 469
12	5/29/1999	Alice	Lindgram	Bloomington	Duluth	$ 149	3	$ 447
13	6/9/1999	Bernice	Young	Duluth	Duluth	$ 149	2	$ 298
14	6/18/1999	Janelle	Olness	Fargo	Toronto	$ 349	1	$ 349
15	6/29/1999	Julie	Swanson	St. Peter	Duluth	$ 149	3	$ 447
16	1/10/1999	Joseph	Black	Bloomington	Houston	$ 185	2	$ 370
17	1/20/1999	Rachel	Lyons	Maplewood	Toronto	$ 349	1	$ 349
18	2/2/1999	Harrison	Thompson	Duluth	Philadelphia	$ 399	1	$ 399

Figure 11-1. It's difficult to see the bottom line in a long list like this.

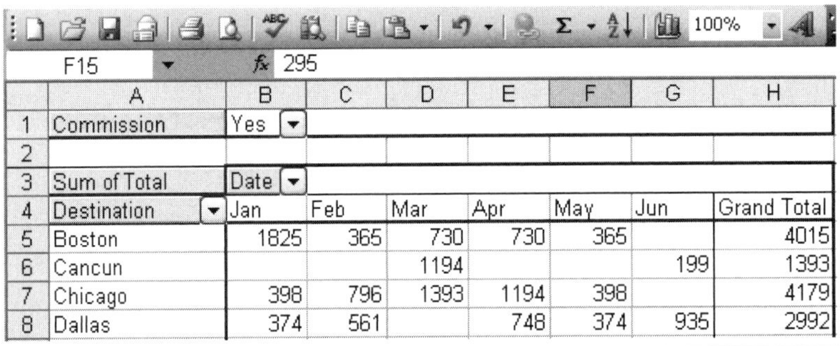

	A	B	C	D	E	F	G	H
1	Commission	Yes						
2								
3	Sum of Total	Date						
4	Destination	Jan	Feb	Mar	Apr	May	Jun	Grand Total
5	Boston	1825	365	730	730	365		4015
6	Cancun			1194			199	1393
7	Chicago	398	796	1393	1194	398		4179
8	Dallas	374	561		748	374	935	2992

Figure 11-2. This Pivot Table displays a summary view of Figure 1-11's information.

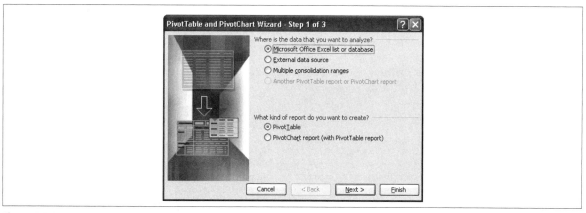

Figure 11-3. Step 1 of 3 of the PivotTable Wizard.

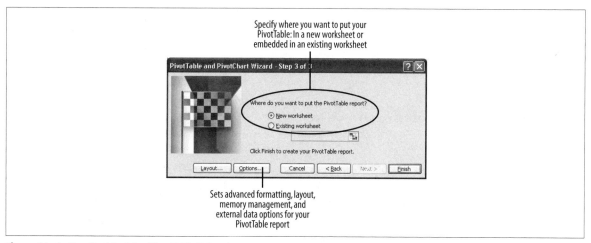

Figure 11-4. Step 3 of 3 of the PivotTable Wizard.

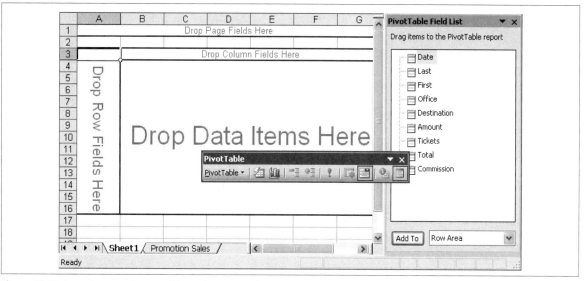

Figure 11-5. A newly created PivotTable (without any information yet).

Creating a PivotTable is remarkably easy. Create Pivot-Tables using the PivotTable Wizard, which asks which fields you want to include in the PivotTable, how you want your PivotTable organized, and which types of calculations your PivotTable should perform. PivotTables may sound confusing, but they will make a lot more sense when you've actually created one.

1 **Open the workbook named** Lesson 11A **and save it as** PivotTable.

This workbook contains figures for ticket sales from a recent promotion. The list contains flight dates, agents, offices that sold the tickets, destinations, sales amounts, and if the agents received a commission or not. It's difficult to see the bottom line in a large list like this. For example, how many tickets did the Blaine office sell, or how many tickets were sold to London? The PivotTable Wizard can help you summarize the list and provide you with meaningful information.

2 **Make sure the cell pointer is located in the list (A1:I200) and select** Data → PivotTable and Pivot-Chart Report **from the menu.**

The Step 1 of the PivotTable Wizard dialog box appears (see Figure 11-3). Here you must specify the location of the data you want to use in your PivotTable. There are four options:

- **Microsoft Excel list or database:** Creates a PivotTable from data in columns on your worksheet (the most commonly used option).
- **External data source:** Creates a PivotTable from data stored in a file or database outside of the current workbook or Microsoft Excel.

- **Multiple consolidation ranges:** Creates one Pivot-Table from multiple cell ranges in different worksheets.
- **Another PivotTable:** Creates a PivotTable from another PivotTable in the same workbook.

You also have to specify if you want to create just a PivotTable Report or a PivotTable Report along with a corresponding PivotChart report.

3 **Verify that the** Microsoft Excel list or database **and the** PivotTable **options are both selected and click** Next.

Step 2 of the PivotTable Wizard appears. You need to tell the PivotTable Wizard where the data you want to use in the PivotTable is located. Because the cell pointer was located inside the list when you started the PivotTable Wizard, the cell range of the list (A1:I200) is already selected.

4 **Click** Next.

The third and last step of the PivotTable Wizard appears, as shown in Figure 11-4. Here's where you tell Excel to put your PivotTable report. You can place your PivotTable report in:

- A new worksheet
- Embedded in an existing worksheet.

5 **Verify that the** New worksheet **option is selected and click** Finish.

The PivotTable Wizard dialog box closes and the Pivot-Table appears on a new worksheet, as shown in 11-5. Notice that the PivotTable is empty—that's because we haven't specified the data we want to analyze yet—something you'll learn in the next lesson.

QUICK REFERENCE

TO CREATE A PIVOTTABLE:

1. MAKE SURE THE CELL POINTER IS LOCATED IN THE LIST.

2. SELECT DATA → PIVOT TABLE AND PIVOTCHART REPORT FROM THE MENU.

3. SELECT THE LOCATION OF THE DATA YOU WANT TO INCLUDE IN YOUR PIVOTTABLE REPORT AND THE TYPE OF REPORT (PIVOTTABLE REPORT OR PIVOTTABLE WITH PIVOTCHART REPORT) AND CLICK NEXT.

4. IN STEP 2 MAKE SURE THE LIST RANGE IS SELECTED AND CLICK NEXT.

5. IN STEP 3, SPECIFY A LOCATION FOR THE PIVOTTABLE (A NEW WORKSHEET OR AN EXISTING WORKSHEET).

6. CLICK FINISH.

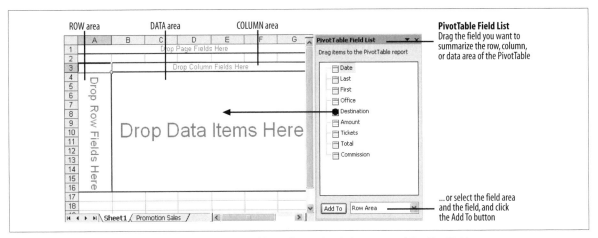

Figure 11-6. Dragging the Office field from the PivotTable toolbar to the Column area of the PivotTable.

Figure 11-7. The PivotTable summarizing the total tickets sold by Destination and Office.

Once you've created your PivotTable report, you have to specify the data you want to analyze with the PivotTable. It's easy to specify which data you want to analyze—simply drag it from the PivotTable toolbar and onto the Row, Column, or Data area on the PivotTable report. You're not going to understand how to do this unless you try it—so let's get started!

1 Drag the Destination field button from the Pivot-Table Field List to the ROW area of the PivotTable diagram.

The Destination field appears at the top of the ROW area in the PivotTable. Next, make the Office field the column heading for the PivotTable.

2 Drag the Office field button from the PivotTable Field List to the COLUMN area of the PivotTable diagram, as shown in Figure 11-6.

You have selected the Destination field to be the row heading and the Office field to be the column heading for your PivotTable. Now you need to select the field you want to summarize.

3 Drag the Number of Tickets field button from the PivotTable Field List to the DATA area of the PivotTable diagram.

Compare your dialog box with the one shown in Figure 11-7.

The neat thing about PivotTables is that their information is *dynamic*. This means that once you've created a PivotTable, you can rearrange or "pivot" it to view its data in different ways. For example, you could rearrange the PivotTable you just created so that it summarizes the amount of the total ticket sales instead of the total number of tickets sold.

4 Drag the Sum of Tickets field button **(located in cell A3) off the PivotTable diagram.**

The PivotTable will no longer total the number of tickets sold. You can easily summarize another field by dragging it onto the DATA area of the PivotTable diagram.

5 Drag the Total field button **to the** DATA **area of the PivotTable diagram.**

You can also rearrange a PivotTable's headings.

6 Drag the Destination field button **from the ROW area of the PivotTable diagram to the** COLUMN **area and drag the** Office field button **from the COLUMN area of the PivotTable diagram to the** ROW **area.**

Hopefully, you're starting to understand the true power of PivotTables. PivotTables can usually make information stored in even the longest lists easy to understand. Once you make a PivotTable you can change the information it summarizes in an instant, simply by dropping and dragging.

QUICK REFERENCE

TO SPECIFY PIVOTTABLE DATA:

1. MAKE SURE THE CELL POINTER IS LOCATED IN THE LIST.

2. DRAG THE FIELD NAMES YOU WANT TO SUMMARIZE TO THE APPROPRIATE SECTION OF THE PIVOTTABLE DIAGRAM (PAGE, COLUMN, ROW, OR DATA).

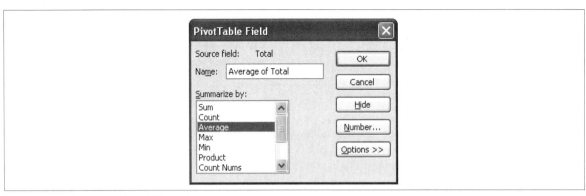

Figure 11-8. The PivotTable Field dialog box.

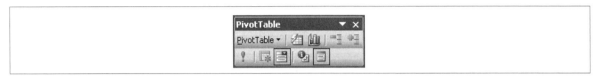

Figure 11-9. The PivotTable toolbar.

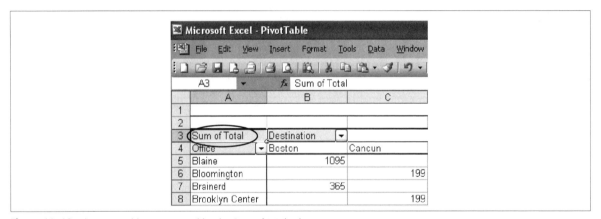

Figure 11-10. The PivotTable summarized by the Sum of total sales.

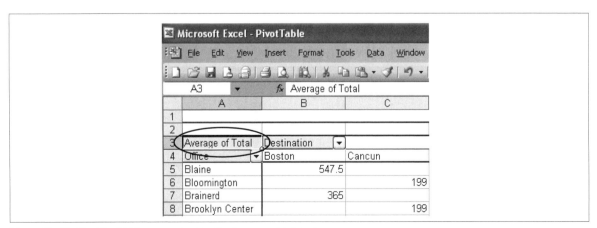

Figure 11-11. The PivotTable summarized by the Average of total sales.

In the previous lesson, you learned how to change the data you want included in the PivotTable report. You can also change how a PivotTable summarizes its information. For example, you might want a PivotTable to display averages instead of totals.

1 Click cell B5 and select Window → Freeze Panes from the menu.

Now the column and row headings to the left and above the active cell (B3) will always be visible as you scroll through the worksheet.

2 Scroll down to Row 23.

The PivotTable has created column totals, which calculate the total number of reservations made at each office.

3 Scroll to the T column.

The PivotTable has also calculated the total number of reservations made to each destination.

Field Settings button

4 Click the Field Settings button on the PivotTable toolbar (see Figure 11-9).

The PivotTable Field dialog box appears, as shown in Figure 11-8. This lets you change how a PivotTable is calculated. For example, instead of totaling the total sales made, you could find the average.

5 Select Average from the Summarize by list and click OK.

The PivotTable Field dialog box closes and the PivotTable displays the average total sales (see Figure 11-11).

QUICK REFERENCE

TO SPECIFY PIVOTTABLE DATA:

1. MAKE SURE THE CELL POINTER IS LOCATED IN THE LIST.

2. DRAG THE FIELD NAMES YOU WANT TO SUMMARIZE TO THE APPROPRIATE SECTION OF THE PIVOTTABLE DIAGRAM (PAGE, COLUMN, ROW, OR DATA).

Selecting What Appears in a PivotTable

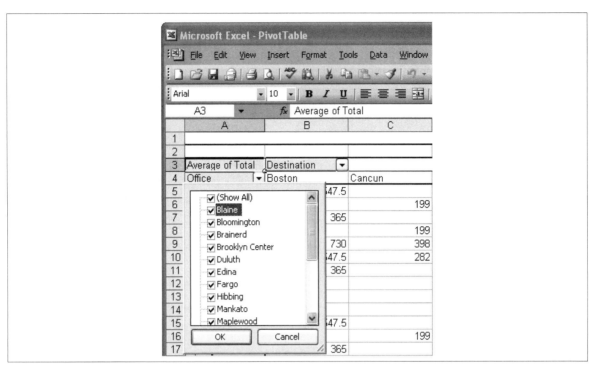

Figure 11-12. Using a page field to filter summary information in a PivotTable.

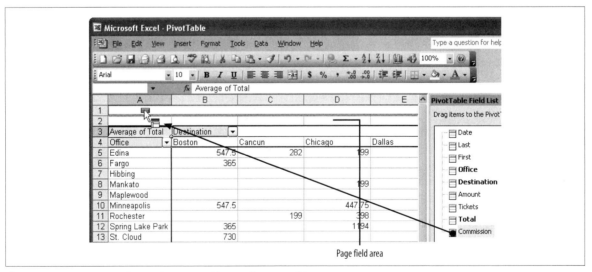

Figure 11-13. Dragging a field to the Page Field area of a PivotTable report.

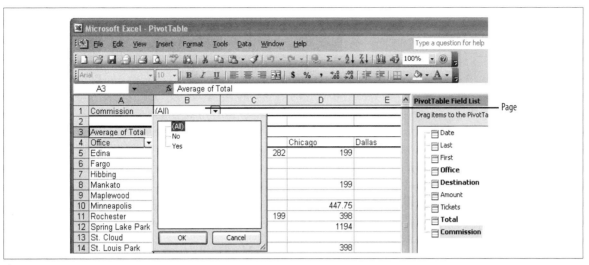

Figure 11-14. Using a page field to filter summary information in a PivotTable.

You can filter which information is summarized in a PivotTable either by clicking a row or column field's drop-down arrows and selecting the items you want to include in the PivotTable report, or by adding a *page field* to the PivotTable. In this lesson, you'll learn how to filter the information that is included in a PivotTable Report using both methods.

1 If necessary, find and open the Lesson 11B workbook and save it as PivotTable.

2 Click the Office field drop-down list located in cell A4.

A drop-down list appears beneath the Office field, as shown in Figure 11-12. Check the values that you want in your PivotTable and uncheck those you don't.

3 Remove the checkmark from the Blaine, Bloomington, Brainerd, Brooklyn Center, and Duluth boxes and click OK.

These offices no longer appear in the PivotTable report. You can also filter the information that appears in a PivotTable report by adding a Page Field to the PivotTable.

4 Drag the Commission field button to the PAGE area of the PivotTable diagram (see Figure 11-13).

Now you will be able to filter the PivotTable using the commission field and display data for sales with commissions, sales without commissions, or both.

5 Click the Commission list arrow, select Yes, and click OK (see Figure 11-14).

The PivotTable displays only information for commissioned sales.

QUICK REFERENCE

TO ADD A PAGE FIELD TO A PIVOTTABLE:

1. MAKE SURE THE CELL POINTER IS LOCATED IN THE PIVOTTABLE AND CLICK THE PIVOTTABLE WIZARD BUTTON ON THE PIVOTTABLE TOOLBAR.

2. DRAG THE FIELD NAME YOU WANT TO USE TO FILTER THE PIVOTTABLE TO THE PAGE SECTION OF THE PIVOTTABLE DIAGRAM AND CLICK FINISH.

TO FILTER A PIVOTTABLE'S SUMMARY INFORMATION:

- SELECT WHAT YOU'D LIKE TO SEE ON THE PIVOTTABLE REPORT FROM THE ROW HEADING, COLUMN HEADING, OR PAGE FIELD DROP-DOWN LIST.

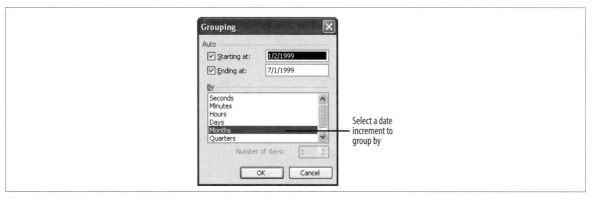

	A	B	C	D	E
1	Commission	Yes ▼			
2					
3	Average of Total	Date ▼			
4	Destination ▼	1/2/1999	1/3/1999	1/4/1999	1/5/1999
5	Boston	730			
6	Cancun				
7	Chicago				
8	Dallas				374

Figure 11-15. Summarizing ticket sales by date.

Grouping ✕

Auto

☑ Starting at: 1/2/1999

☑ Ending at: 7/1/1999

By

Seconds
Minutes
Hours
Days
Months
Quarters

Number of days: 1

OK   Cancel

Select a date increment to group by

Figure 11-16. The Grouping dialog box.

	A	B	C	D	E
1	Commission	Yes ▼			
2					
3	Average of Total	Date ▼			
4	Destination ▼	Jan	Feb	Mar	Apr
5	Boston	608.3333333	365	730	730
6	Cancun			597	
7	Chicago	398	398	696.5	1194
8	Dallas	374	561		374

Figure 11-17. Grouping the dates in the PivotTable by months.

PivotTables can usually summarize information without any outside help from you. When you want to summarize a list by dates, however, you will probably need to coach Excel and tell it how you want to group the information in the PivotTable: by days, months, quarters, or years. In this lesson, we'll rearrange our PivotTable and summarize its information by month. First, you need to rearrange your PivotTable to summarize it by date.

1 Drag the Office field button off the PivotTable diagram and drag the Destination field button from the Column area of the PivotTable to the Row area.

Next, you need to add the Date field to the PivotTable's Column area.

2 Drag the Date field button to the Column area of the PivotTable.

Now the PivotTable summarizes ticket sales by destination and date as shown in Figure 11-15. The only problem is that the PivotTable summarizes the dates by day—making the summary information rather meaningless. You can make the PivotTable more useful by grouping the days into months using the Group command. First you need to specify what information you want to group by—the dates.

3 Click the Date button located in cell B3 then select Data → Group and Outline → Group from the menu.

The Grouping dialog box appears, as shown in Figure 11-16. You need to select a date or time interval by which to group.

4 Select Months from the By list and click OK.

The Group dialog box closes and the PivotTable groups the dates by month, as shown in Figure 11-17.

QUICK REFERENCE

TO GROUP INFORMATION BY DATE OR TIME:

1. SELECT THE ROW OR COLUMN HEADING THAT CONTAINS THE DATE OR TIME VALUE YOU WANT TO GROUP BY AND CLICK THE GROUP BUTTON ON THE PIVOTTABLE TOOLBAR.

   OR...

   SELECT ANY ROW OR COLUMN HEADING THAT CONTAINS THE DATE OR TIME VALUE YOU WANT TO GROUP BY AND SELECT DATA → GROUP AND OUTLINE → GROUP FROM THE MENU.

2. SPECIFY THE STARTING AND ENDING DATES AND THE INTERVAL YOU WANT TO GROUP THE DATES OR TIME BY, THEN CLICK OK.

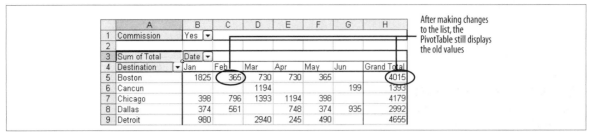

Figure 11-18. A PivotTable that needs to be refreshed.

Figure 11-19. The Refreshed PivotTable.

If you modify the source data a PivotTable is based on, the PivotTable isn't automatically updated. Instead you must manually *refresh* the PivotTable anytime you change its underlying source data. This lesson explains how to do just that.

1 Click cell A3 and then click the Field Settings button on the PivotTable toolbar. Select Sum from the dialog box and click OK.

Now the PivotTable will display the Sum of the total, instead of the Average.

2 Click the Promotion Sales tab. Click cell G19, type 100, and press Enter.

Obviously, Philip Grahams didn't sell 100 tickets to Boston, but this is a big enough number that you will be able see the changes in the PivotTable's February column when you update it.

3 Click the Sheet1 tab to return to the PivotTable.

Look at cell C5, the February column. The PivotTable does not reflect the increased ticket sales you made to the list, as shown in Figure 11-18.

Refresh Data button
Other Ways to Refresh a Pivot Table:
• Select **Data→Refresh Data** from the menu.

4 Click anywhere in the PivotTable and click the Refresh Data button on the PivotTable toolbar.

The PivotTable is refreshed and correctly displays the current list data, as shown in Figure 11-19.

5 Go back and change cell G19 on the Promotion Sales tab back to 1, and press Enter. Click the Sheet1 tab to return to the PivotTable and click the Refresh Data button on the PivotTable toolbar.

That's it—we're finished working with PivotTables! PivotTables are the most powerful way to summarize information in a list, but they're not the only method you can use. The remainder of this chapter explores some of the other ways to summarize list information.

QUICK REFERENCE

TO REFRESH A PIVOTTABLE:

• CLICK THE REFRESH DATA BUTTON ON THE
  PIVOTTABLE TOOLBAR.

  OR...

• SELECT DATA → REFRESH DATA FROM THE MENU.

Formatting and Charting a PivotTable

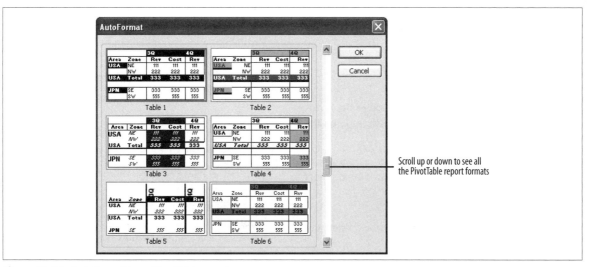

Figure 11-20. AutoFormatting a PivotTable report.

Scroll up or down to see all the PivotTable report formats

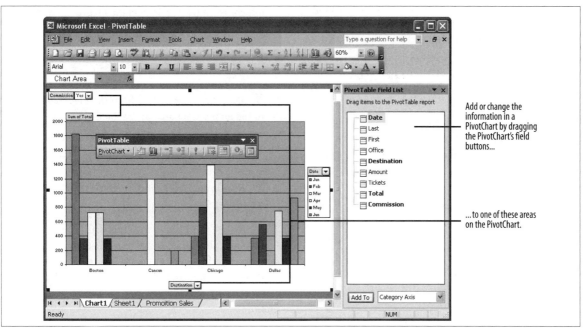

Figure 11-21. The completed PivotChart.

Add or change the information in a PivotChart by dragging the PivotChart's field buttons...

...to one of these areas on the PivotChart.

This lesson explains how you can quickly format a PivotTable report using the AutoFormat command and how to create a PivotChart—both new features that are introduced in Excel 2003.

First, let's discuss how to format your PivotTable with AutoFormat. AutoFormat is a built-in collection of formats such as font sizes, patterns, and alignments you can quickly apply to a PivotTable report. AutoFormat lets you

select from 20 different preset formats. It is a great feature if you want your PivotTables to look sharp and professional, but don't have the time to format them yourself.

Format Report button

Chart Wizard button
Other Ways to Insert a Chart:
• Select **Insert**→**Chart** from the menu.

1 Make sure the cell pointer is located in the Pivot-Table report and click the Format Report button on the PivotTable toolbar.

The AutoFormat dialog box appears, as shown in Figure 11-20. You can format your PivotTable report using a preset format.

2 Scroll down the AutoFormat dialog box, select the Table 2 format, and click OK.

The PivotTable is formatted with the preset Table 2 formatting settings.

Let's move on to this lesson's other topic; creating a PivotChart. A PivotChart is similar to an ordinary chart created in Excel, except that it plots a PivotTable's information. PivotCharts differ from ordinary Excel charts because they are dynamic, just like PivotTable reports. You can change a PivotChart's structure just like you would with a PivotTable.

3 Make sure the cell pointer is located in the Pivot-Table report and click the Chart Wizard button on the PivotTable toolbar.

Excel creates a chart from the PivotTable and places it on a new sheet tab, labeled Chart1. You can format and work with a PivotChart just like you would with a regular chart. Since there's so much information in our PivotTable, the PivotChart we just created looks cluttered. As with PivotTables, you can specify which items you want to appear in a PivotChart.

4 Click the Destination drop-down list located above the chart's legend, remove the checkmarks from all the destinations except Boston, Cancun, Chicago, and Dallas, and click OK.

Only the specified destinations are plotted on the PivotChart. Let's change the chart type to make our PivotChart easier to understand.

5 Select Chart → Chart Type from the menu.

The Chart Type dialog box appears.

6 Select a Clustered Column Chart from the Chart Sub-Type list and click OK.

The chart type is changed to a clustered column chart, as shown in Figure 11-21.

Just about everything you can also do to a PivotTable report you can do to a PivotChart. For example, you can easily add, change, remove, or rearrange what the PivotChart plots.

7 Drag the Sum of Total field (located in the upper left corner of the chart) from the PivotChart back to the PivotTable Field List to remove it.

Since the PivotChart has no data to plot, it displays the message "Drop Data Items Here."

8 Drag the Tickets field from the PivotTable toolbar to the empty Data area of the PivotChart.

The PivotChart now plots the total number of tickets sold to each destination.

9 Save your work and then close the PivotTable worksheet.

That's it—we're finished working with PivotTables and PivotCharts! PivotTables are the most powerful way to summarize information in a list, but they're not the only method you can use. The remainder of this chapter explores some of the other ways to summarize list information.

QUICK REFERENCE

TO FORMAT A PIVOTTABLE:

* MAKE SURE THE CELL POINTER IS LOCATED IN THE PIVOTTABLE REPORT AND CLICK THE FORMAT REPORT BUTTON ON THE PIVOTTABLE TOOLBAR. SELECT THE FORMATTING YOU WANT TO APPLY AND CLICK OK.

TO CREATE A PIVOTCHART:

* PLACE THE CELL POINTER ANYWHERE IN A PIVOTTABLE REPORT AND CLICK THE CHART WIZARD BUTTON ON THE PIVOTTABLE TOOLBAR. YOU WILL PROBABLY HAVE TO CHANGE THE CHART TYPE.

  OR...

* CREATE A PIVOTTABLE AND PIVOTCHART FROM SCRATCH. SEE THE INSTRUCTIONS FOR CREATING A PIVOTTABLE.

TO MODIFY A PIVOTCHART:

* MODIFY A PIVOTCHART THE SAME AS YOU WOULD A PIVOTTABLE: DRAG AND DROP FIELDS TO AND FROM THE PIVOTTABLE TOOLBAR AND THE PIVOTCHART.

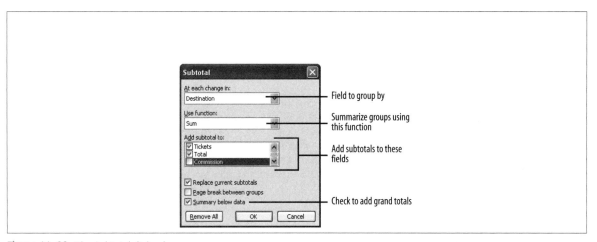

Figure 11-22. The Subtotal dialog box.

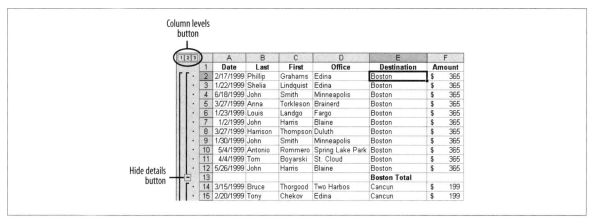

Figure 11-23. A subtotaled list, with all details displayed.

1 2 3		A	B	C	D	E	F
	1	Date	Last	First	Office	Destination	Amount
	13					**Boston Total**	
	23					**Cancun Total**	
	41					**Chicago Total**	
	58					**Dallas Total**	
	67					**Detroit Total**	
	86					**Duluth Total**	
	95					**Fargo Total**	
	105					**Houston Total**	
	112					**Lincoln Total**	
	119					**London Total**	
	136					**Los Angeles Total**	
	142					**Milwaukee Total**	
	166					**New York Total**	
	173					**Norfolk Total**	

Show details button

Figure 11-24. A collapsed subtotal list, with only the subtotal values displayed.

So far in this chapter, we've been summarizing information in a list using PivotTables. Another quick and easy way to group and summarize data is to use Excel's *subtotals* feature. Usually you create subtotals with the SUM function, but you can also create subtotals using functions such as COUNT, AVERAGE, MAX, and MIN.

1 Open the workbook named Lesson 11C.

You need to sort the list before you use the Subtotals command. You want to sort the list alphabetically by destination.

Sort Ascending button

2 Click any cell in the E column and click the Sort Ascending button on the Standard toolbar.

The list is sorted alphabetically by destination. Now that the list is sorted, you can use the Subtotals command.

Column Level buttons

3 Make sure the active cell is located within the list and select Data → Subtotals from the menu.

The Subtotal dialog box appears, as shown in Figure 11-22. You want to summarize the list based on the Destination field—the field you sorted in the previous step.

4 Select Destination from the At each change in list, then select Sum from the Use function list.

This will create subtotals every time the destination changes (which is why you had to sort the list based on destination back in Step 2). Next, you need to specify that you want to add subtotals to the Annual Trips and Annual Cost of Tickets fields.

5 In the Add subtotal to list, check the Tickets check box and the Total check box (you may have to scroll up or down to find them). Make sure the other check boxes in the list aren't checked.

This will add subtotals to the Tickets and Total columns.

6 Make sure the Replace current subtotals and Summary below data check boxes are checked.

Compare your Subtotal dialog box to the one in Figure 11-22.

7 Click OK.

The dialog box closes and Excel summarizes the list and calculates the subtotals for each time the destination field changes. Notice Excel displays the outline symbols to the left of the worksheet, as shown in Figure 11-23. We'll save outlining for another lesson. For now, try using the Outline buttons to hide the list details.

8 Click the 2 Column Level Symbol button.

Excel hides the third level of detail in the list (the employees) and now only displays the totals for each office.

9 Click the 3 Column Level Symbol button.

All the outline details are again visible. You can turn off the subtotaling now.

10 Make sure the active cell is located within the list and select Data → Subtotals from the menu, then click Remove All.

The subtotals and outlining are removed from the list. You can remove Subtotals from a workbook at any time.

11 Close the workbook without saving it.

Knowing how to use the Subtotals command will give you an edge on many other Excel users. Most users don't realize Excel can automatically add subtotals to their worksheets, and as a result they needlessly spend hours manually adding subtotals themselves.

QUICK REFERENCE

TO CALCULATE SUBTOTALS:

1. MAKE SURE THE LIST IS SORTED.

2. SELECT DATA → SUBTOTALS FROM THE MENU.

3. ENTER THE APPROPRIATE INFORMATION IN THE SUBTOTAL DIALOG BOX AND CLICK OK.

TO REMOVE SUBTOTALS:

• MAKE SURE THE ACTIVE CELL IS LOCATED WITHIN THE LIST, THEN SELECT DATA → SUBTOTALS FROM THE MENU AND CLICK REMOVE ALL.

Using Database Functions

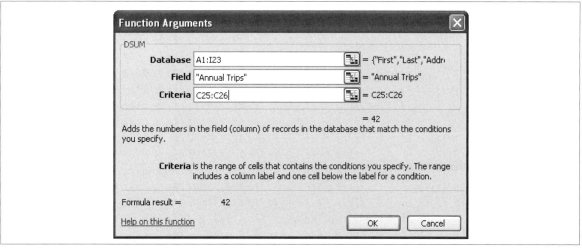

Figure 11-25. Using the Insert Function tool to create a DSUM formula.

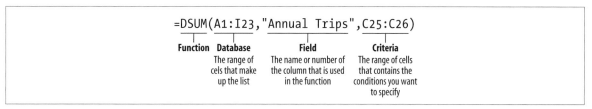

Figure 11-26. The syntax of the DSUM function.

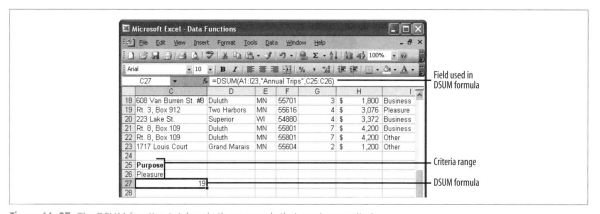

Figure 11-27. The DSUM function totals only those records that meet your criteria.

Excel's database functions perform calculations only for records that meet the criteria you specify. For example, you might want only to count tickets that were sold to Boston. All the database functions use the same basic syntax: =Function(*database, field, criteria*). These arguments (parts) of database functions include:

- **Database:** The cell range that makes up the list or database.

- **Field:** Indicates which column is used in the function. You can refer to fields by their column labels as long as you enclose them with double quotation marks, such as "Name". You can also refer to fields as a number that represents the position of the column in the list: 1 for the first column in the list, 2 for the second, and so on. Make sure you refer to their position in the list and not the column heading numbers!

• **Criteria:** A reference to the cell or cell range that specifies the criteria for the function.

This lesson explains how to use database functions by creating a formula with the simplest database function—the DSUM function. (See Figure 11-26 for the syntax of the DSUM function.)

1 Open the Lesson 11D workbook and save it as Data Functions.

Start by adding a meaningful label for the results of the DSUM formula.

2 Click cell C25 (scroll down if necessary), click the Bold button on the Formatting toolbar, type Purpose and press Enter.

Next, enter the criteria the DSUM function will use. (You'll see how the criteria works later when we actually create a DSUM formula.)

3 Type Business in cell C26 and press Enter.

We'll enter a DSUM formula in cell C27.

Insert Function button

4 Make sure the active cell is C27, then click the Insert Function button on the Formula bar.

The Insert Function dialog box appears.

5 Select Database from the Or Select a Category list, select DSUM from the Select a Function list, and click OK.

The Function Arguments dialog box appears, as shown in Figure 11-25. You're ready to start entering the DSUM formula to calculate the total for Annual Trips amounts for only those records that have "Business" in the Purpose column. The first argument in the DSUM function is to define the database—the cell range that makes up the list.

Collapse Dialog button

6 Click the Database text box and select the entire list—the cell range A1:I23 (you may have to use the Collapse dialog box button).

The second argument in the DSUM function is to define the Field—the column that is used in the function. You can enter the Field by typing the column label enclosed between double quotation marks, such as "Annual Trips" or as a number that represents the position of the column in the list: 1 for the first column, 2 for the second column, etc. For example, the column you want to total, Annual Trips, is the seventh column in the list, so you would type either 7 or "Annual Trips" for the Field argument.

7 Click the Field text box and type "Annual Trips".

The last argument in the DSUM function is the Criteria—the range of cells that contains the conditions you want to specify. You can use any range for the criteria argument, as long as it includes at least one column label and at least one cell below the column label for specifying a condition for the column.

8 Click the Criteria text box and select the cell range C25:C26.

The cell range C25:C26 contains both the column label, Purpose, and the criteria, Business.

9 Click OK to close the Function Arguments dialog box.

Excel displays the result of the DSUM function, 42, in cell C26. Try changing the criteria value in C26 to calculate the total number of annual flights for the records that contain "Pleasure" in the Purpose column.

10 Click cell C26, type Pleasure, and press Enter.

The DSUM value in cell C26 changes to 19; the total number of annual flights for the records that contain "Pleasure" (see Figure 11-27).

11 Save your work.

QUICK REFERENCE

TO USE THE DSUM FUNCTION IN A FORMULA:

- WRITE THE FORMULA USING THE SYNTAX =DSUM(DATABASE, FIELD, CRITERIA).

OR...

1. CLICK THE INSERT FUNCTION BUTTON ON THE STANDARD TOOLBAR TO OPEN THE FUNCTION ARGUMENTS DIALOG BOX.

2. SELECT DATABASE IN THE FUNCTION CATEGORY LIST, SELECT DSUM IN THE FUNCTION NAME LIST, AND CLICK OK.

3. ENTER THE REQUIRED ARGUMENTS FOR THE DSUM FUNCTION.

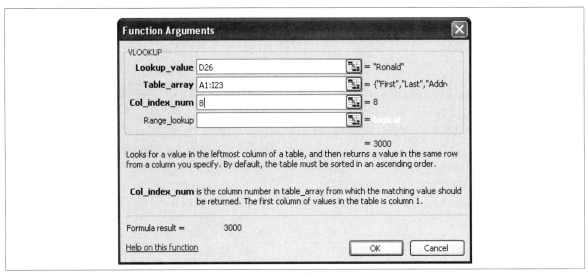

Figure 11-28. Using the Insert Function tool to create a VLOOKUP formula.

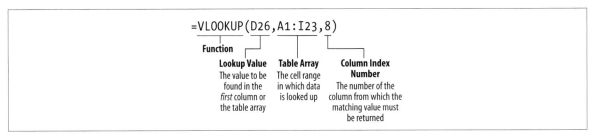

Figure 11-29. The syntax of the VLOOKUP function.

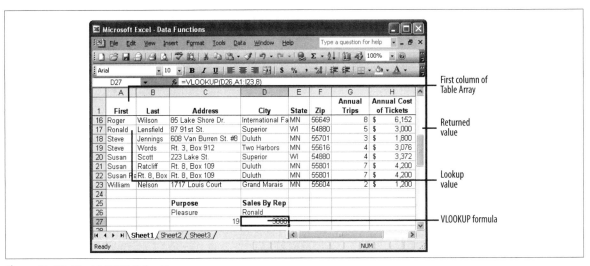

Figure 11-30. The VLOOKUP function.

The VLOOKUP function looks up information in a worksheet. The VLOOKUP searches vertically down the *leftmost* column of a cell range until it finds the value you specify. When it finds the specified value, it then looks across the row and returns the value in column you specify. The VLOOKUP function works a lot like looking up a number in a phonebook: first you look down the phonebook until you find the person's name, then you look across to retrieve the person's phone number.

Are you thoroughly confused yet? The VLOOKUP function is almost impossible to explain unless you've actually used it—and you'll use the VLOOKUP function in this lesson.

1 Click cell D25, click the Bold button on the Formatting toolbar, type Sales By Rep, and press Enter.

Next, enter the lookup value for the VLOOKUP function (you'll see how the lookup value works when we actually create the VLOOKUP formula).

2 Type Ronald in cell D26.

Before using the VLOOKUP function, you should sort the list by the column that contains the lookup value.

Sort Ascending button

3 Select any cell that contains data in the A column and click the Sort Ascending button on the Standard toolbar to sort the list.

We'll enter the VLOOKUP formula in cell D27.

Insert Function button

4 Click cell D27 and click the Insert Function button on the Formula bar.

The Insert Function dialog box appears.

5 Select Lookup and Reference from the Or Select a Category list, select VLOOKUP from the Select a Function list, and click OK.

The Function Arguments dialog box appears, as shown in Figure 11-28. You're ready to start entering

the VLOOKUP formula to lookup annual trip costs by the employee's first name. The first argument in the VLOOKUP function is to specify the value you want to look up in the first column of the cell range. Lookup values can be values, references, or labels. Cell D26 contains the value you want to look up—the client's first name. (See Figure 11-29 for the syntax of the VLOOKUP function.)

Collapse Dialog button

6 Click the Lookup_value box and click cell D26 (you may need to use the Collapse dialog box button).

The second argument in the VLOOKUP function is to define the Table Array—the cell range that contains the data you want to look up.

NOTE *Remember that when you define the Table Array, the VLOOKUP function looks up values from the first column of the specified cell range. So if you want to look up values by City instead of by First Name, make sure that the City column was the first column in the selected cell range.*

7 Click the Table_array box and select the entire list—the cell range A1:I23 (you may have to click the Collapse dialog box button).

The third argument in the VLOOKUP function is to specify the Column Index Number—the column number from which the matching value must be returned. For example, the column you want to lookup, Annual Cost of Tickets, is the eighth column in the list, so you would type 8 for the Column Index Number argument.

8 Click the Col_index_num box, type 8, and click OK.

Excel looks up the first value in the First column that matches the Lookup Value in cell D26, "Ronald" and displays the value in the eighth column of that row, 3000. Try changing the Lookup Value in D26 to look up the annual ticket cost for another name.

9 Click cell D26, type John, and press Enter.

The VLOOKUP value in cell D26 changes to 1686—the ticket cost for John Peters.

10 Save your work and close the Database Functions workbook.

The HLOOKUP function is similar to the VLOOKUP function, except it searches horizontal from left to right across the *top* row of a cell range until it finds the value you specify. When it finds the specified value it then looks down the column to find the specified value.

QUICK REFERENCE

TO USE THE VLOOKUP FUNCTION IN A FORMULA:

* WRITE THE FORMULA USING THE SYNTAX =VLOOKUP (LOOKUP_VALUE,TABLE_ARRAY, COL_INDEX_NUM)

OR...

1. CLICK THE PASTE FUNCTION BUTTON ON THE STANDARD TOOLBAR TO OPEN THE FUNCTION ARGUMENTS DIALOG BOX.

2. SELECT LOOKUP AND REFERENCE IN THE FUNCTION CATEGORY LIST, SELECT VLOOKUP IN THE FUNCTION NAME LIST, AND CLICK OK.

3. ENTER THE REQUIRED ARGUMENTS FOR THE VLOOKUP FUNCTION.

Grouping and Outlining a Worksheet

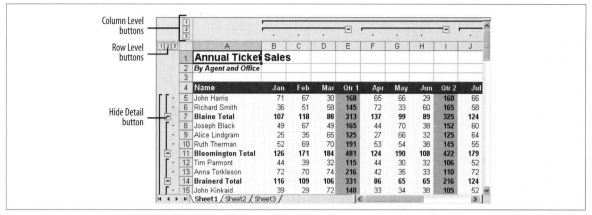

Figure 11-31. A worksheet displayed in Outline view.

Figure 11-32. Clicking the group Hide or Show Details button.

Many spreadsheets are created in a hierarchical style. For example, a worksheet might contain a column for each month, followed by a total column. By *outlining* your worksheets, you make them easier to understand and read. Instead of sifting through irrelevant information, you can collapse an outline to display each group's total or bottom line.

There are several ways to outline a workbook:

- **Using the Subtotals Feature:** The Data → Subtotals command calculates subtotal and grand total values for the labeled columns you select. Excel automatically inserts and labels the total rows and outlines the list. We covered creating and working with subtotals earlier in this chapter.

- **Using the Consolidate Feature:** You can consolidate several sheets selecting Data → Consolidate from the menu.

- **Using the Auto Outline Feature:** The Data → Group and Outline → Auto Outline command automatically outlines a selected range of cells or the entire worksheet, based on formulas and the direction of references.

- **Manually Creating an Outline:** You can group rows and columns manually by selecting them and selecting Data → Group and Outline → Group from the menu.

This lesson explains how to use the third and fourth methods and how to work with an outline.

1 Open the Lesson 11E workbook.

We'll start this lesson by manually grouping the rows for the Blaine office.

2 Select rows 5 and 6 and select Data → Group and Outline → Group from the menu.

Excel groups the selected rows in an outline. Notice the Hide Details button that appears to the left of the worksheet. Clicking a Hide Details button hides, or collapses, its group of records.

3 Click the Hide Details button to the left of the worksheet.

Excel hides the details, rows 5 and 6, for the Blaine office and changes the Hide Details button (▢) to a Show Details button (▢), indicating it contains hidden records. Clicking the Show Details button displays, or expands, its group of records.

Show Details button

4 **Click the** Show Details button **to the left of the worksheet.**

Excel displays the hidden records. It's just as easy to ungroup records as it is to group them.

5 **Select** rows 5 **and** 6 **and select** Data → Group and Outline → Ungroup **from the menu.**

Excel ungroups the records.

Before you manually create an outline by grouping dozens of records, you should see if Excel can automatically create the outline for you. Excel can automatically outline worksheets if they contain formulas that consistently point in the same directions. Excel can automatically group and outline this worksheet since it *does* contain formulas that all consistently point to the right (the quarterly subtotals) and down (the office subtotals).

6 **Click any cell in the worksheet to deselect rows 5 and 6, and then select** Data → Group and Outline → Auto Outline **from the menu.**

Excel analyzes the formulas in the worksheet and creates an outline, as shown in Figure 11-31. You can still expand and collapse each group in the outline by clicking the corresponding Show Detail or Hide buttons, but an easier way is to use the Column Level

buttons. The Column Level buttons display or hide a specific level in your worksheet. For example, if an outline has three levels, you can hide all the third levels by clicking the ③ button.

7 **Click the** Row Level 2 button.

Excel displays only the first two levels in the outline—the totals for each office. You can also hide and display columns the same way.

Column Level 2 button

8 **Click the** Column Level 2 button.

Excel collapses the outline so that only the quarterly and annual totals are displayed. To expand the outline, just click the symbol for the lowest row and column level. For example, if there are three levels, click the ③ button.

9 **Expand the outline by clicking the** Column Level 3 button **and the** Row Level 3 button.

It's easy to remove an outline from a worksheet:

10 **Select** Data → Group and Outline → Clear Outline **from the menu.**

The outline is removed from the worksheet.

11 **Exit Excel without saving your changes.**

QUICK REFERENCE

TO MANUALLY GROUP COLUMNS OR ROWS:

- SELECT THE COLUMNS OR ROWS YOU WANT TO GROUP AND SELECT DATA → GROUP AND OUTLINE → GROUP FROM THE MENU.

TO MANUALLY UNGROUP COLUMNS OR ROWS:

- SELECT THE GROUPED COLUMNS OR ROWS AND SELECT DATA → GROUP AND OUTLINE → UNGROUP FROM THE MENU.

TO OUTLINE A WORKSHEET AUTOMATICALLY:

- SELECT DATA → GROUP AND OUTLINE → AUTO OUTLINE FROM THE MENU.

TO REMOVE AN OUTLINE:

- SELECT DATA → GROUP AND OUTLINE → CLEAR OUTLINE FROM THE MENU.

TO HIDE/DISPLAY OUTLINE DETAILS:

- CLICK THE GROUP'S SHOW DETAILS BUTTON OR THE HIDE DETAILS BUTTON.

  OR...

- CLICK THE APPROPRIATE ROW LEVEL BUTTON OR COLUMN LEVEL BUTTON.

Chapter Eleven Review

Lesson Summary

Creating a PivotTable

A PivotTable summarizes list information dynamically—meaning, once you have created a PivotTable, you can rearrange or "pivot" it to view its data in different ways.

To Create a PivotTable: Make sure the cell pointer is located in the list and select Data → Pivot Table and PivotChart Report from the menu. Follow the on-screen instruction to create the PivotTable.

Specifying the Data a PivotTable Analyzes

To Specify PivotTable Data: Make sure the cell pointer is located in the PivotTable. Drag the field names you want to summarize to the appropriate section of the PivotTable diagram (Page, Column, Row, or Data).

Changing a PivotTable's Calculation

Make sure the cell pointer is located in the PivotTable and click the Field Settings button on the PivotTable toolbar. Select the calculation you want to use from the Summarize by list and click OK.

Selecting What Appears in a PivotTable

To Add a Page Field to a PivotTable: Make sure the cell pointer is located in the PivotTable and click the Pivot-Table Wizard button on the PivotTable toolbar. Drag the field name you want tot u se to filter the PivotTable to the PAGE section of the PivotTable diagram and click Finish.

To Filter a PivotTable's Summary Information: Select what you'd like to see on the PivotTable report from the Row heading, Column heading, or Page Field drop-down list.

Grouping Dates in a PivotTable

Select the row or column heading that contains the date or time value you want to group by and click the Group button on the PivotTable toolbar. Or, select any row or column heading that contains the date or time value you want to group by and select Data → Group and Outline → Group from the menu. Then specify the starting and ending dates and the interval you want to group the dates or time by, then click OK.

.

Updating a PivotTable

A PivotTable isn't automatically updated if you modify its source data. You can refresh a PivotTable by clicking the Refresh Data button on the PivotTable toolbar or selecting Data → Refresh Data from the menu.

Formatting and Charting a PivotTable

To Format a PivotTable: Make sure the cell pointer is located in the PivotTable report and click the Format Report button on the PivotTable toolbar. Select the formatting you want to apply and click OK.

To Create a PivotChart: Place the cell pointer anywhere in a PivotTable report and click the Chart Wizard button on the PivotTable toolbar. You will probably have to change the chart type.

To Modify a PivotChart: Modify a PivotChart the same as you would a PivotTable—drag and drop fields to and from the PivotTable toolbar and the PivotChart.

Creating Subtotals

To Calculate Subtotals: Sort the list, select Data → Subtotals from the menu, enter the appropriate information in the Subtotal dialog box, and click OK.

To Remove Subtotals: Make sure the active cell is located within the list, then select Data → Subtotals from the menu and click Remove All.

Using Database Functions

Database functions perform calculations only for records that meet the criteria you specify. The syntax for all database functions is =FUNCTION(Database, Field, Criteria).

Using Lookup Functions

The VLOOKUP function looks up information in a worksheet by searching vertically down the leftmost column of a cell range until it finds the value you specify and then across the row to find the value in column you specify.

The syntax for the VLOOKUP function is =VLOOKUP(lookup_value,table_array, col_index_num).

Grouping and Outlining a Worksheet

To Manually Group/Ungroup Columns or Rows: Select the columns or rows you want to group and select Data → Group and Outline → Group (or Ungroup) from the menu.

To Outline a Worksheet Automatically: Make sure the worksheet contains formulas that consistently point in the same directions, then select Data → Group and Outline → Auto Outline from the menu.

To Remove an Outline: Select Data → Group and Outline → Clear Outline from the menu.

You can view the details of a group by clicking its Show Details button (⊞) and hide the details by clicking its Hide Details button (⊟).

You can hide or display a specific level in an outline by clicking its Row Level (1 2 3) or Column Level button.

Quiz

1. Which of the following statements is NOT true?

   A. PivotTables summarize the information in a list.

   B. You can add a PivotTable as an embedded object on a worksheet, or on its own separate worksheet.

   C. The Data → Pivot Table Report command starts the PivotTable Wizard.

   D. You specify which fields you want to summarize in the PivotTable by dragging them to the appropriate areas of the PivotTable diagram.

2. You must create a new PivotTable if you want to summarize information from different fields. (True or False?)

3. Which of the following statements is NOT true?

   A. You can specify how dates should be grouped in a PivotTable by selecting the field that contains the date information, clicking the Group button on the PivotTable toolbar, and specifying how you want the information summarized (by days, months, quarters, or years).

   B. PivotTables are automatically updated whenever you change their source data.

   C. Adding a Page Field to a PivotTable lets you filter the information the PivotTable summarizes.

   D. You can modify the structure of a PivotTable by clicking the PivotTable Wizard button on the PivotTable toolbar.

4. You should sort a list before you group and summarize its information using the Subtotals command. (True or False?)

5. Which of the following statements is NOT true?

   A. The Subtotals command subtotals a column at each value change.

   B. The Subtotals command displays the worksheet in outline view.

   C. The Subtotals command summarizes the worksheet by creating a PivotTable.

   D. You can add Subtotals to a worksheet by selecting Data → Subtotals from the menu.

6. Excel's database functions perform calculations only for records that meet the criteria you specify. (True or False?)

7. Which of the following statements is NOT true?

   A. You should use the Insert Function command to help you enter complicated database functions.

   B. You can hide or display details in an outlined worksheet by clicking the Hide Details button or Show Details button, or by clicking the various Column Level or Row Level buttons.

   C. A worksheet must be sorted in order for Excel to automatically outline it.

   D. You can manually group rows and columns in a worksheet by selecting Data → Group and Outline → Group from the menu.

Homework

1. Open the Homework 11 workbook and save it as "PivotTable Practice."

2. Select any cell in the table then select Data → Pivot-Table Report from the menu.

3. Using the PivotTable Wizard, create a PivotTable report that summarizes the worksheet information like the following illustration:

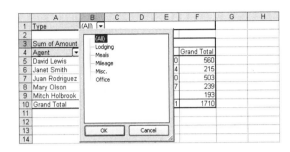

	A	B	C	D	E	F	G
1	Sum of Amount	Type					
2	Agent	Lodging	Meals	Mileage	Misc.	Office	Grand Total
3	David Lewis	58	276	59	44	123	560
4	Janet Smith	56	20	63	38	38	215
5	Juan Rodriguez	272	111	22	98		503
6	Mary Olson	63	46	68	62		239
7	Mitch Holbrook		94	25	24	50	193
8	Grand Total	449	547	237	266	211	1710

4. Modify the PivotTable's structure so that the column summarizes by Date instead of by Type.

5. Click the Date field and then click the Group button on the PivotTable toolbar. Group the dates by month.

6. Modify the PivotTable's structure by adding the Type field as the Page Field.

7. Use the Page Field to filter the information summarized in the PivotTable by the various Types of expenses.

8. Click the Sheet 1 sheet tab and sort the A column alphabetically.

9. Use the Data → Subtotals command to subtotal the worksheet.

10. Practice expanding and collapsing the worksheet while it's in Outline view.

Quiz Answers

1. C. The Data → PivotTable and PivotChart Report command starts the PivotTable and PivotChart Wizard.

2. False. It is incredibly easy to modify which fields a PivotTable summarizes. Just click the PivotTable Wizard button on the PivotTable toolbar and drag the fields you want to summarize to the appropriate areas of the PivotTable diagram.

3. B. PivotTables are NOT automatically updated when you change their source data. You must click the Refresh Data button on the PivotTable toolbar to update the PivotTable.

4. True. Always sort a list before using the Subtotals command.

5. C. The Subtotals command does not summarize information using a PivotTable—that's what the PivotTable command is for!

6. True. Database functions calculate only those records that match your criteria.

7. C. A worksheet must contain formulas that consistently point in the same direction to use the automatic outline feature. Sorting the worksheet doesn't make any difference.

CHAPTER 12

WHAT-IF ANALYSIS

CHAPTER OBJECTIVES:

Create a scenario

Create a scenario summary report

Create one and two-input data tables

Use Goal Seek

Set up complex what-if analysis with Solver

CHAPTER TASK: ANALYZE DIFFERENT WHAT-IF SITUATIONS

Prerequisites

- **Understand how to use menus, toolbars, dialog boxes, and shortcut keystrokes**
- **Understand how to select cell ranges**
- **Understand how to enter values, labels, and formulas into a cell**
- **Understand how to reference cells**

If you've ever used a worksheet to answer the question "What if?", you've already performed *what-if analysis*. For example, what would happen if your advertising budget for your department increased by 40%? If you were considering taking out a home mortgage based on your income, how much money could you borrow for a 20-year mortgage? How much money could you borrow for a 30-year mortgage?

Most people don't realize that Excel has numerous analysis features and instead perform what-if analysis the slow and hard way—by manually inputting different values into their worksheets, looking at the results, and then inputting another set of values. This method is fine for simple what-if scenarios, but doesn't work well for answering complex what-if questions.

In this chapter, you will learn how to create multiple what-if scenarios using Excel's Scenario Manager. You will create one-input and two-input data tables to report several different outcomes. You will also use Excel's Goal Seek and Solver to solve more complex what-if questions.

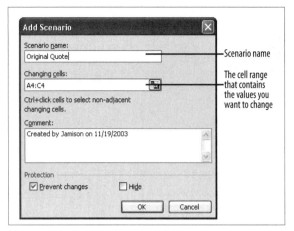

Figure 12-1. The Add Scenario dialog box.

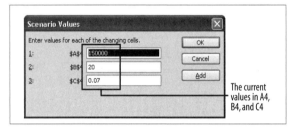

Figure 12-2. The Scenario Values dialog box.

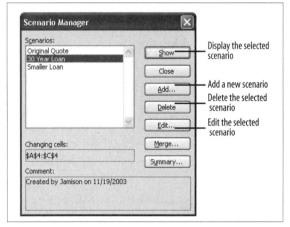

Figure 12-3. The Scenario Manager dialog box.

A *scenario* is a set of values you use in what-if analysis. Imagine you are considering taking out a home mortgage and have to determine what type of loan to take out. One scenario you are considering is a 30-year loan with a 7.5% interest rate. Another scenario is a 20-year loan with an 8.5% interest rate. Excel's *Scenario Manager* lets you create and store different scenarios in the same

worksheet. Once you have created a scenario, you can select it and display the worksheet using its values.

In this lesson, you will use the Scenario Manager to perform what-if analysis on a home mortgage. You will create three different scenarios to see how changing the amount and length of the loan will change your monthly payments.

1 **Start Microsoft Excel, open the workbook named** Lesson 12A, **and save it as** Mortgage What-If.

This workbook contains information for a mortgage. To help assist you with deciding what type of mortgage to take out, you will use Excel's Scenario Manager to create several scenarios with different loan amounts and terms. The first step in creating a Scenario is to select the cells that change.

2 **Select the cell range** A4:C4 **and select** Tools → Scenarios **from the menu.**

The Scenario Manager dialog box appears with the message "No Scenarios defined. Choose Add to add scenarios." You want to add a new scenario.

3 **Click** Add.

The Add Scenario dialog box appears, as shown in Figure 12-1. You must give your scenario a name and specify the scenario's changing cells, if necessary. The cell range A4:C4 appears in the changing cells text box because you selected those cells before you opened the Scenario Manager. First, create a scenario with the original values.

4 **Type** Original Quote **in the Scenario name box and click** OK.

The Scenario Values dialog box appears, as shown in Figure 12-2. with the existing values in the changing cells boxes. Since this is the original quote, you can save the scenario without changing the values.

5 **Click** OK.

The Scenario Values dialog box closes and you return to the Scenario Manager dialog box. Next, create a scenario with a longer loan length—30 years instead of 20.

6 Click Add, **type** 30 Year Loan **in the Scenario name box (as shown in Figure 12-3) and click** OK.

The Scenario Values dialog box appears. You need to change the values for this scenario.

7 Change the 20 **in the second changing cell box ($B$4) to** 30 **and click** Add.

Excel saves the 30 Year Loan scenario and you return to the Scenario Manager dialog box. Create another scenario with a smaller loan amount.

8 Type Smaller Loan **in the Scenario name box and click** OK.

The Scenario Values dialog box appears.

9 Change the 150000 **in the first changing cell box ($A$4) to** 125000 **and click** OK.

Excel saves the Smaller Loan scenario and returns you to the Scenario Manager dialog box. You're ready to test your scenarios.

10 Select the Smaller Loan **scenario from the Scenario list and click** Show.

The length of the loan changes to 20 years and the amount of the loan changes to $125,000.

NOTE *The Scenario Manager dialog box doesn't close, so you might need to move it out of the way so that you can see the cells.*

11 Select the 30 Year Loan **scenario from the Scenario list and click** Show.

Excel changes the length of the loan in B4 from 20 years to 30 years.

Notice the monthly payment decreases from $1,162.95 to $997.95, and the Interest paid increases from $129,107.62 to $209,263.35.

You're finished working with the Scenario Manager for now.

12 Click Close **to close the Scenario Manager and save your work.**

Great! You've learned how to use your first What-If Analysis feature.

Figure 12-4. The Create Names dialog box.

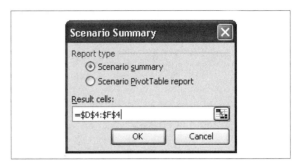

Figure 12-5. The Scenario Summary dialog box.

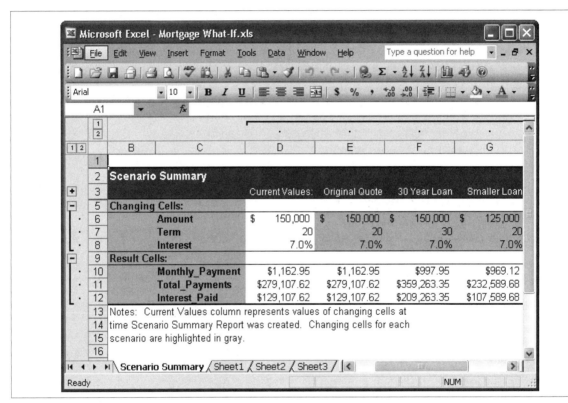

Figure 12-6. The Scenario Summary report.

If you've defined two or more scenarios, you can summarize them by creating a *scenario summary report*. A scenario summary report is a single compiled report that summarizes the results from several scenarios. It's usually much easier to read a single scenario summary report than switching between several different scenarios.

1 Select the cell range A3:F4 and select Insert → Name → Create **from the menu.**

The Create Names dialog box appears, as shown in Figure 12-4. The Create Names will automatically cre-

ate range names, based on the current selection. Naming the cells will make them easier to read when you create the scenario summary report.

2 Verify that the Top row **check box is checked and click** OK.

The Create Names dialog box closes and Excel automatically creates names for the selected cell range. You can verify that Excel created the correct names by clicking the Name box arrow.

3 Click the Name Box List arrow.

The column heading names should appear in the Name Box list.

4 Click anywhere in the worksheet window to close the Name Box list.

You're ready to create a Scenario Summary report.

5 Select Tools → Scenarios from the menu and click the Summary button.

The Scenario Summary dialog box appears, as shown in Figure 12-5. You can create two types of reports:

- **Scenario summary:** Creates a report that lists your scenarios with their input values and the resulting cells. Use this report only when your model has one set of changing cells provided by a single user.

- **Scenario PivotTable report:** Creates a PivotTable report that gives you an instant what-if analysis of your scenarios. Use this type of report when your model has multiple sets of changing cells provided by more than one user.

You will use the Scenario summary report, which is the default option.

6 Verify that the Scenario summary option is selected, double-click the Results cells text box, if necessary, then select the cell range D4:F4.

The Results Cells (Monthly Payment, Total Payment, and Interest Paid) are the cells that are affected by the Changing Cells (Amount, Term, and Interest).

7 Click OK.

The Scenario Summary dialog box closes, and Excel creates a scenario summary report on a new sheet in the workbook, as shown in Figure 12-6.

8 Save your work.

QUICK REFERENCE

TO CREATE A SCENARIO SUMMARY REPORT:

1. MAKE SURE YOU'VE DEFINED AT LEAST TWO SCENARIOS.

2. SELECT TOOLS → SCENARIOS FROM THE MENU.

3. SELECT THE TYPE OF REPORT (SCENARIO SUMMARY OR SCENARIO PIVOTTABLE).

4. SPECIFY WHICH CELLS YOU WANT TO INCLUDE IN THE REPORT.

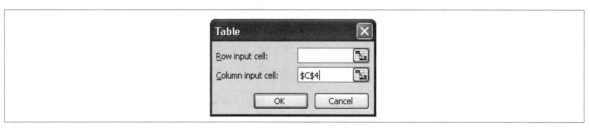

Figure 12-7. The Table dialog box.

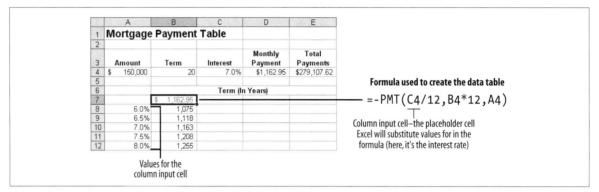

Formula used to create the data table

=-PMT(C4/12,B4*12,A4)

Column input cell–the placeholder cell
Excel will substitute values for in the
formula (here, it's the interest rate)

Figure 12-8. The completed one-input data table with monthly payments for each interest rate.

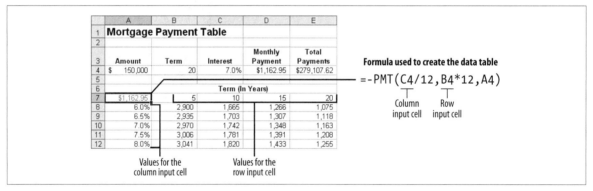

Formula used to create the data table

=-PMT(C4/12,B4*12,A4)

Column   Row
input cell   input cell

Figure 12-9. The completed two-input data table with monthly payments for each interest rate and each term.

(Not Used)	Formula
Input Value	Results
Input Value	Results
Input Value	Results

Structure of a One-Input Table

Formula	Input Value
Input Value	Results
Input Value	Results
Input Value	Results

Structure of a Two-Input Table

Another way to get answers to your what-if questions is by using a *data table*. A data table is a cell range that displays the results of a formula using different values. For example, you could create a data table to calculate loan payments for several interest rates and term lengths. There are two types of data tables:

- **One-Input Data Table:** Displays the results of a formula for multiple values of a *single* input cell. For example, if you have a formula that calculates a loan payment, you could create a one-input data table that shows payment amounts for different interest rates.

- **Two-Input Data Table:** Displays the results of a formula for multiple values of a *two* input cell. For example, if you have a formula that calculates a loan payment, you could create a two-input data table that shows payment amounts for different interest rates *and* different term lengths.

1 **Return to Sheet 1 in the 12A workbook. Click cell B7.**

The first step in creating a data table is to enter the formula the data table will use. Since you want to calculate the monthly payment of the loan based on different interest rates, you will use the same PMT formula you created in cell D4.

2 **Type** =-PMT(C4/12,B4*12,A4) **and press** Enter.

Excel will use this formula to calculate values in the data table.

The next step in creating your input data table is to enter the inputs (in your case, the interest rates) that you want to use into the data table. The cells in this workbook have already been formatted with the correct number formatting, so you can enter the data table inputs.

3 **Click cell** A8, **type** .06, **press** Enter, **type** .065, **press** Enter, **type** .07, **press** Enter, **type** .075, **press** Enter, **type** .08, **and press** Enter.

Since the data table formula includes a rate, or percentage, the values used in the formula must also be a percent.

4 **Select** A8:A12, **click the** Percent Style button, **and click the** Increase Decimal button **on the Formatting toolbar.**

You're ready to have Excel fill in your data table using the different interest rates you just entered in the A column.

5 **Select the cell range** A7:B12 **and select** Data → Table **from the menu.**

The Table dialog box appears, as shown in Figure 12-7. You must specify the location of the input cell in the Row Input Cell or Column Input Cell box. The input cell is the placeholder cell that is

referred to in the Table formula—in your case, the Interest rate, which is located in cell C4.

6 **Click the** Column Input Cell **box, click cell** C4 **(the placeholder for the interest rate in the table formula), and click** OK.

Excel fills the table with the results of the table formula with one result for each input value or interest rate.

7 **Click cell** B8.

Excel has added the formula {=TABLE(,C4)} to the cell. The C4 reference refers to the Input Cell for the formula—in this case, the interest rate.

You can also create data tables based on *two* input variables. For example, you can create a data table that uses the Interest Rate as one input variable (arranged in columns) and the Term as the other input variable (arranged in rows). The structure of a two-input data table is slightly different from that of a one-input data table—the formula has to be where the row and column that contain the input values intersect—in your case, A7 (see Figure 12-8). You can't change a table once it has been created, so you will first have to delete the current table.

8 **Select the cell range** B8:B12, **press** Delete **to delete the data table, and then move the formula in** B7 **to** A7.

Now you can enter the different terms as Column Input values.

9 **Click cell** B7 **and type** 5, Tab, 10, Tab, 15, Tab, 20, **and press** Enter.

Now select the data table range and open the Table dialog box.

10 **Select the cell range** A7:E12 **and select** Data → Table **from the menu.**

The Table dialog box appears. This time, you must specify two input cells. The Row Input Cell is placeholder cell that is referred to in the Table formula—in your case, the Term, which is located in cell B4. The Column Input Cell will be the Interest Rate, located in cell C4.

11 Click the Row Input Cell, click cell B4, click the Column Input Cell, click cell C4, and click OK.

Excel computes the table using the Term (B4) as the Row Input Cell and the Interest Rate (C4) as the Column Input cell. Compare your table to the one in Figure 12-9.

12 Save your work.

QUICK REFERENCE

TO CREATE A ONE-INPUT TABLE:

1. SET UP THE TABLE AREA. MAKE SURE YOU INCLUDE THE FORMULA IN THE TOP ROW, AND THE INPUT VALUES IN THE LEFT COLUMN.

2. SELECT THE TABLE RANGE AND SELECT DATA → TABLE FROM THE MENU.

3. SPECIFY THE WORKSHEET CELL YOU WANT TO USE AS THE INPUT VALUE AND CLICK OK.

TO CREATE A TWO-INPUT TABLE:

1. SETUP THE TABLE AREA. MAKE SURE YOU INCLUDE THE FORMULA IN THE UPPER-LEFT CELL AND THE VALUES FOR THE FIRST INPUT CELL IN THE LEFT COLUMN, AND THE VALUES FOR THE SECOND INPUT CELL IN THE TOP ROW.

2. SELECT THE TABLE RANGE AND SELECT DATA → TABLE FROM THE MENU.

3. SPECIFY THE WORKSHEET CELL YOU WANT TO USE FOR THE ROW INPUT CELL AND THE COLUMN INPUT CELL AND CLICK OK.

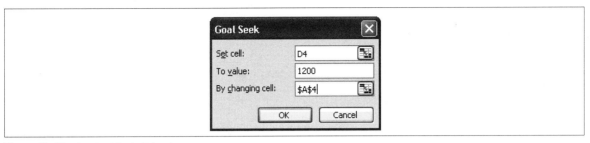

Figure 12-10. The Goal Seek dialog box.

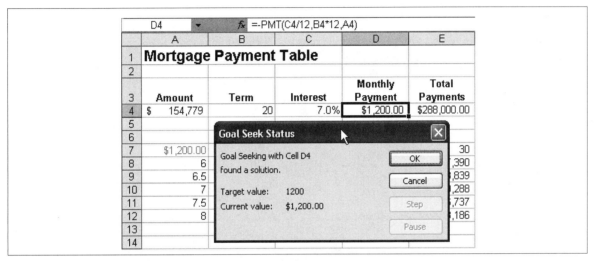

Figure 12-11. The Goal Seek Status dialog box displays the solution.

When you know the desired result of a single formula, but not the value the formula needs for the result, you can use the Goal Seek feature. For example, you can afford a $1,200 monthly payment, so how much of a loan can you take out? When goal seeking, Excel plugs in different values into a cell until it finds one that works.

1 Select cell D4.

You want to know what the maximum 20-year mortgage you can afford is if the interest rate is 7% and the maximum monthly payments you can make are $1,200. Cell D4, the Monthly Payment, is the formula cell for the Goal Seek command; you will change its value to find a specific goal. You don't necessarily have to select the formula cell before using the Goal Seek command, but it saves you a step later on.

2 Select Tools → Goal Seek from the menu.

The Goal Seek dialog box appears, as shown in Figure 12-10. To find any goal, you must specify three things:

- **Set cell:** The cell that contains the formula you want to find a solution for—in your case, the monthly payments value in cell D4.

- **To Value:** The target number you want to solve for—in your case, the maximum monthly payment you are able to make ($1,200).

- **By changing cell:** The cell that contains the value you want to change to solve for the target value—in your case, the mortgage amount in cell A4.

3 Verify that D4 appears in the Set cell box.

Remember that the set cell contains the formula you want to find a solution for—the monthly payments formula. In the next step you'll enter the goal: the maximum monthly payment you are able to make.

4 Click the To value **box and type** 1200.

The last step in using Goal Seek is specifying what cell will change in order to reach the solution: the mortgage amount.

5 Click the By changing cell **box and click cell** A4.

You're ready to use Goal Seek to find the maximum 20-year, 7% interest rate mortgage you can take out with monthly payments of $1,200.

6 Click OK.

The Goal Seek Status dialog box appears with the message "Goal Seeking with Cell D4 found a solution" and displays the solution in the worksheet window.

You can click OK to accept the new worksheet values found by Goal Seek, or click Cancel to return the original worksheet values. You decide to keep the values Goal Seek found.

7 Click OK.

The Goal Seek dialog box closes and changes the worksheet values.

8 **Save your work and close the current workbook.**

Super! You're almost done with the What-If Analysis chapter. Just one more lesson....

QUICK REFERENCE

TO USE GOAL SEEK:

1. OPEN OR CREATE A WORKBOOK THAT USES THE FORMULAS YOU WANT TO USE.

2. SELECT TOOLS → GOAL SEEK FROM THE MENU.

3. COMPLETE THE GOAL SEEK DIALOG BOX BY SPECIFYING WHICH FORMULA CELL TO CHANGE, THE VALUE TO CHANGE IT TO, AND THE CELL TO CHANGE.

4. CLICK OK.

5. CLICK OK TO REPLACE THE ORIGINAL VALUE OR CLICK CANCEL TO KEEP THE ORIGINAL VALUE.

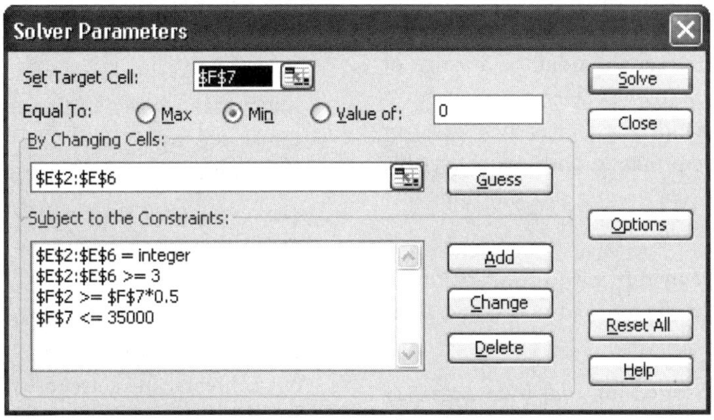

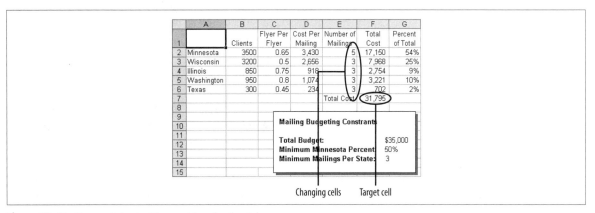

Figure 12-12. The Solver Parameters dialog box.

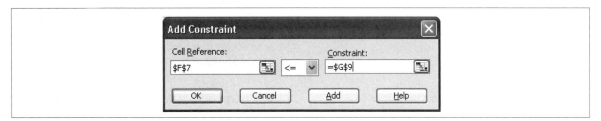

Figure 12-13. The worksheet with a problem for the Solver.

Figure 12-14. The Add Constraint dialog box.

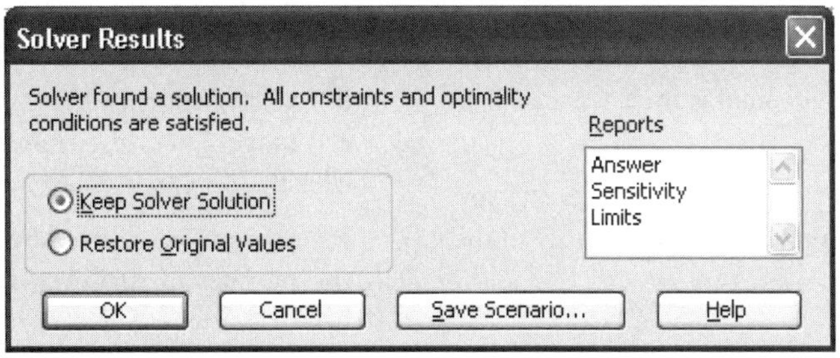

Figure 12-15. The Solver Results dialog box.

Goal Seek works great for problems that have a single variable and an exact target value, but not for complex problems that have several variables and/or a range of values. For these more complex problems, you need to use Excel's *Solver* command. The Solver can perform advanced what-if analysis problems with many variable cells. You can also specify *constraints*, or conditions that must be met to solve the problem.

If the Solver seems especially difficult to you, you're not alone. The Solver is one of the most advanced and complicated features in Excel.

TIP *The Solver is an optional add-in to Excel. If you can't find the Solver Command in your Tools menu, you can add it by selecting Tools → Add-Ins from the menu.*

1 Open the workbook named Lesson 12B and save it as Annual Mail.

This worksheet contains the problem with which you're faced (see Figure 12-13). Imagine you've been put in charge of a annual mailing campaign for existing clients in five states. Your boss has given you the following budget constraints:

- Your total budget is $35,000.
- You must spend at least 50% of the budget on Minnesota mailings.
- At least three mailings must go out in each state.

Based on this information, your job is to find out how many mailings you can send out to the clients in each state. Yikes! That's a tricky math problem! Luckily, you can use Excel's Solver to help you find the answer to this problem.

2 Select Tools → Solver from the menu.

The Solver Parameter dialog box appears, as shown in Figure 12-12. First, you need to specify the goal or target you want to solve. For this lesson, you want to minimize your total mailing cost—the value in cell F7.

3 Make sure the insertion point is the Set Target Cell box and click cell F7.

$F$7 appears in the Set Target Cell box. Next, you want Solver to set the target cell (the total cost) to the lowest value possible.

4 Click the Min option.

For other problems, you might want to find the highest possible value by selecting the Max option. Or you might want Solver to find a solution that makes the target cell equal to a certain value by selecting the Value option and entering the value.

Next, you need to specify which cells will change in order to reach the solution—the number of mailings per state.

5 Click the By Changing Cells box, clear any previous contents, and select cells E2:E6.

Now you're ready to specify the constraints Solver has to work with.

6 Click the Add button.

The Add Constraint dialog box appears, as shown in Figure 12-14. Start by adding the constraint that the total mailing cost cannot exceed the $35,000 budget.

7 Select cell F7 (the Total Cost cell), ensure that <= appears in the middle drop-down list, click the Constraint box, and type 35000.

Compare your Add Constraint dialog box with the one in Figure 12-14. The next constraint you need to add is that 50% of the total amount must be spent in Minnesota.

TIP *You have to be very precise when using the Solver. If you don't specify the proper constraint, Solver won't be able to find a solution to your problem (if there indeed is a solution) or else may return invalid data.*

8 Select cell F2 (Minnesota's Total Cost), select >=, click the Constraint box, click cell F7, and type *.5.

$F$7*.5 should be displayed in the constraint box. Next, add a constraint so at least three mailings must be sent in each state.

9 Click Add, click the Cell Reference box, select the cell range E2:E6 (the Number of Mailings), select >=, click the Constraint box, and type 3.

Finally, you need to add a constraint to specify that the number of mailings is restricted to whole numbers (otherwise, Solver will use numbers with decimal places).

10 Click Add, click the Cell Reference box, select the cell range E2:E6 (the Number of Mailings), and select int.

That's it! You've finished adding all the constraints.

11 Click OK.

The Add Constraint dialog box closes and you return to the Solver Parameter dialog box. Let's see if the Solver can find a solution for this perplexing problem.

12 Click Solve.

Excel analyzes the problem and plugs trial values into the variable cells, and tests the results. After a moment the Solver Results dialog box appears, indicating that Solver succeeded in finding a solution to how many mailings you can afford to send out to each state, while meeting all the constraints, as shown in Figure 12-15.

You have several choices here. You can keep the values from the Solver solutions, you can return the original values, or you can create one of three types of detailed reports on a separate worksheet that summarize Solver's answer.

13 Make sure the Keep Solver Solution option is selected and click OK.

The dialog box closes and the solution values appear in the worksheet. You've successfully found the best combination of mailings by state using Solver. The settings you entered in Solver will be saved with the workbook, so you can easily come back to them.

14 Save your work and exit Microsoft Excel.

QUICK REFERENCE

TO INSTALL SOLVER:

- SOLVER IS AN OPTIONAL EXCEL ADD-ON. IF YOU CAN'T FIND SOLVER UNDER THE TOOLS MENU, YOU CAN INSTALL IT BY SELECTING TOOLS → ADD INS FROM THE MENU, SELECTING THE SOLVER ADD-IN, AND CLICKING OK.

TO USE SOLVER:

1. OPEN OR CREATE A WORKBOOK THAT CONTAINS THE PROBLEM YOU WANT TO SOLVE, AND THEN SELECT TOOLS → SOLVER FROM THE MENU.

2. SPECIFY THE GOAL OR TARGET YOU WANT TO SOLVE FOR IN THE SET TARGET CELL BOX.

3. SPECIFY MAX, MIN, OR EQUAL TO, THEN SPECIFY THE CELLS THAT NEED TO CHANGE TO MEET YOUR GOAL IN THE BY CHANGING CELLS BOX.

4. ADD YOUR CONSTRAINTS BY CLICKING ADD AND THEN SPECIFYING THE CONSTRAINTS (REPEAT FOR AS MANY CONSTRAINTS AS YOU NEED).

5. CLICK SOLVE.

Lesson Summary

Defining a Scenario

A scenario is a set of values you use in what-if analysis, such as various interest rates, loan amounts, and terms for a mortgage. You can save and then easily display these values once you have saved them in a scenario.

To Create a Scenario: Create or open a worksheet that contains the results of one or more formulas. Select Tools → Scenarios from the menu and click the Add button to add a new scenario. Complete the Add Scenario dialog box, giving the scenario a name and identifying the "changing cells" (the cells that contain the values you want to change), and then click OK. Click the Add button and enter the name and changing cells for each additional scenario.

To View a Scenario: Select Tools → Scenarios from the menu, select the scenario from the list, and click Show.

Creating a Scenario Summary Report

A scenario summary report is a single compiled report that summarizes the results from several scenarios.

To Create a Scenario Summary Report: Make sure you've defined at least two scenarios and select Tools → Scenarios from the menu. Select the type of report you want (Scenario summary or Scenario PivotTable) and which cells you want to include in the report.

Using a One and Two-Input Data Table

A Data Table displays the results of a formula using different values. A One-Input Data Table displays the results of a formula for multiple values of a single input cell, while a Two-Input Data Table displays the results of a formula for multiple values of a two input cells.

To Create a One-Input Table: Type the list of values you want to substitute in the input cell down one column. Type the formula in the row above the first value and one cell to the left of the column of values. Select the substitute cell range and select Data → Table from the menu. Select the worksheet cell you want to use as the input value and click OK.

To Create a Two-Input Table: In a cell on the worksheet, enter the formula that refers to the two input cells. Type one list of input values in the same column, below the formula, and type the second list in the same row, to the right of the formula. Select the range of cells that contains the formula and both the row and column of values, and select Data → Table from the menu. Select the Row input cell and the Column input cell, and click OK.

Understanding Goal Seek

When you know what the result of a single formula should be but not the value the formula needs to determine the result, you can use the Goal Seek feature.

To Use Goal Seek: Open or create a workbook that uses the formulas you want to use and select Tools → Goal Seek from the menu. Complete the Goal Seek dialog box by specifying which formula cell to change, the value to change it to, and the cell to change.

Using Solver

Use Solver to find solutions to complex what-if problems that have multiple variables and a range of values.

Solver is an optional Excel add-on. If you can't find Solver under the Tools menu you can install it by selecting Tools → Add Ins from the menu, selecting the Solver Add-in, and clicking OK.

To Use Solver: Open or create a workbook that contains the problem you want to solve, and then select Tools → Solver from the menu. Specify the goal or target you want to solve for in the Set Target Cell box, then specify the Max, Min, or Equal to. Open and specify the cells that need to change to meet your goal in the By Changing Cells box. Add your constraints by clicking Add and then specifying the constraints (repeat for as many constraints as you need.) Click Solve when you've finished setting up the problem.

Quiz

1. Which of following is NOT one of Excel's What-If functions?

   A. Scenario Manager

   B. Solver

   C. Goal Seek

   D. Auto Outline

2. Which of the following statements is NOT true?

   A. The Scenario Manager lets you save several sets of values or scenarios to use in what-if analysis.

   B. You must specify the cells that change in a scenario.

   C. You must specify the target cell in a scenario.

   D. The Scenario Manager is located under Tools → Scenarios.

3. After carefully considering your budget, you decide the maximum monthly payment you can afford is $500 on a three-year loan. Based on this information, which feature would be the fastest and easiest way to determine how much of a loan you can take out?

   A. Goal Seek

   B. Solver

   C. Scenario Manager

   D. A Two-Input Data Table

4. Solver can find solutions to problems with multiple variables, constraints, and ranges of values. (True or False?)

5. Which of the following is NOT information you can specify using the Solver? (Select all that apply.)

   A. Target cell

   B. Changing cells

   C. Constraints

   D. Input cells

Homework

1. Open the Homework 12 workbook and save it as "What-If Practice."

2. Click the Car Loan sheet tab. Select the cell range B3:B5 (the changing cells) and select Tools → Scenarios from the menu.

3. Click Add and name the scenario "Original Loan Term." Save the scenario with the original values.

4. Click Add, and name the scenario "9 Percent, 36 Months." Save the scenario with a $25,000 loan amount, .09% interest rate, and 36 months.

5. Practice switching between the two scenarios by selecting Tools → Scenarios from the menu, selecting a scenario, and clicking View.

6. Create a Scenario Summary report for the worksheet.

7. Click cell B11, type =B7, and press Enter.

8. Setup a one-input data table as follows:

	A	B
11		$610.32
12	0.08	
13	0.08	
14	0.09	
15	0.09	

9. Select Data → Table from the menu and select cell B4 as the Column input cell. Your results should be:

	A	B
11		$610.32
12	0.08	604.47
13	0.08	610.32
14	0.09	616.21
15	0.09	622.13

10. Click cell B7 and select Tools → Goal Seek from the menu. Use Goal Seek to find the maximum car loan you can take out (cell B3) if you can afford an $800 monthly payment.

Extra Credit: Click the Solver sheet tab. Use Solver to find a solution to the specified problem. The target cells, changing cells, and constraints are all color-coded to make it a little easier for you.

Quiz Answers

1. D. The auto outline feature has nothing to do with what-if analysis.

2. C. Goal Seek and the Solver have target cells, but not scenarios.

3. A. Actually, you could use any of the other methods to eventually find the answer, but Goal Seek would be the fastest and easiest in this instance.

4. True.

5. D. Input Tables require Input cells, not Solver.

CHAPTER 13

ADVANCED TOPICS

CHAPTER OBJECTIVES:

Add, remove, and position toolbars

Create a custom toolbar

Create a custom AutoFill list

Password protect a workbook

Change Excel's default options

Find a file

View and change a file's properties

Share a workbook for group collaboration

Revise a shared workbook

CHAPTER TASK: LEARN HOW TO CUSTOMIZE MICROSOFT EXCEL

Prerequisites

- **Understand how to use menus, toolbars, dialog boxes, and shortcut keystrokes**
- **Understand how to select cell ranges**
- **Understand how to open and save a file**

You can customize Excel in a number of ways to meet your own individual needs and tastes. This chapter explains how you can tailor Excel to complement the way you work. You are already familiar with toolbars and how they make it easy to access frequently used commands. In this chapter, you will get to create your very own toolbar and add the commands you use the most frequently to it. This chapter also explains how to create your own custom AutoFill lists.

Another topic covered in this chapter is *workbook collaboration*. Like it or not, if you're part of the corporate world, someday you will have to create a workbook as part of a team. For example, you might create a workbook and then have your manager review it and make changes. Then you go back to the workbook, make the changes, and send it off to its final destination. The folks at Microsoft realized that people sometimes work together when they create workbooks, so they included several features that enable several users to collaborate to create and update workbooks. This chapter explains how you can *share* a workbook so that several users can work on it, and how you can track, review, and then accept or reject any changes made to the shared workbook.

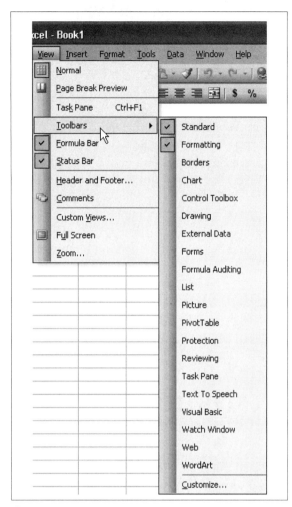

Figure 13-1. Selecting a toolbar to view.

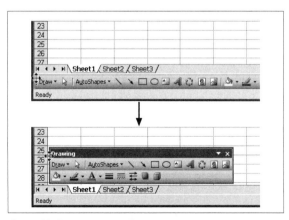

Figure 13-2. Moving a toolbar.

When you first start Excel, two toolbars—Standard and Formatting—appear by default. As you work with Excel, you may want to display other toolbars, such as the Drawing toolbar or the Chart toolbar, to help you accomplish your tasks. Before you know it, your screen is covered with more buttons than NASA's mission control room. This lesson explains how to remove all that clutter by moving Excel's toolbars to different positions on the screen or by removing them all together.

1 **Start the Microsoft Excel program and select** View → Toolbars **from the menu.**

A list of available toolbars appears, as shown in Figure 13-1. Notice that check marks appear next to the Standard and Formatting toolbars. This indicates the toolbars are already selected and appear on the Excel screen.

2 **Select** Formatting **from the toolbar menu.**

The Formatting toolbar disappears. You can hide a toolbar if you don't need to use any of its commands or if you need to make more room available on the screen to view a document.

3 **Select** View → Toolbars → Formatting **from the menu.**

The Formatting toolbar reappears. Another way to add and remove toolbars is to right-click anywhere on a toolbar or menu.

4 **Right-click either the Standard toolbar or the Formatting toolbar.**

A shortcut menu appears with the names of available toolbars.

5 **Click** Drawing **from the Toolbar shortcut menu.**

The Drawing toolbar appears along the bottom of the Excel screen (unless someone has previously moved it). You can view as many toolbars as you want; however, the more toolbars you display, the less of the document window you will be able to see.

6 Move the pointer to the move handle, ⫶, at the far left side of the Drawing toolbar. Click and drag the toolbar to the middle of the screen, then release the mouse button.

The Drawing toolbar is torn from the bottom of the screen and floats in the middle of the document window. Notice that a title bar appears above the Drawing toolbar. You can move a floating toolbar by clicking its title bar and dragging it to a new position. If you drag a floating toolbar to the edge of the program window, it becomes a docked toolbar.

7 Click the Drawing toolbar's title bar and drag the toolbar down until it docks with to the bottom of the screen.

The Drawing toolbar is reattached to the bottom of the Excel screen.

8 Right-click any of the toolbars and select Drawing from the Toolbar shortcut menu.

The Drawing toolbar disappears.

QUICK REFERENCE

TO VIEW OR HIDE A TOOLBAR:

- SELECT VIEW → TOOLBARS FROM THE MENU AND SELECT THE TOOLBAR YOU WANT TO DISPLAY OR HIDE.

  OR...

- RIGHT-CLICK ANY TOOLBAR OR MENU AND SELECT THE TOOLBAR YOU WANT TO DISPLAY OR HIDE FROM THE SHORTCUT MENU.

TO MOVE A TOOLBAR TO A NEW LOCATION:

- DRAG THE TOOLBAR BY ITS MOVE HANDLE (IF THE TOOLBAR IS DOCKED) OR TITLE BAR (IF THE TOOLBAR IS FLOATING) TO THE DESIRED LOCATION.

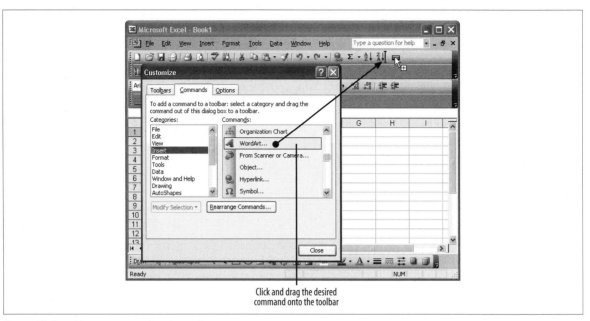

Figure 13-3. Adding a command to the toolbar.

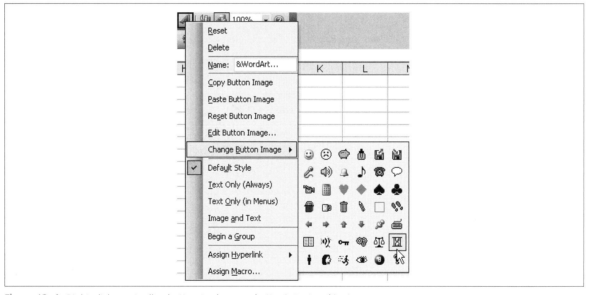

Figure 13-4. Right-click any toolbar button to change a button's text and/or image.

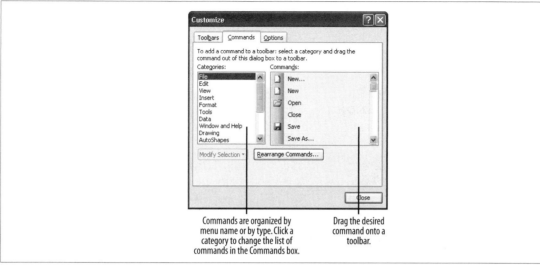

Figure 13-5. The Customize dialog box.

The purpose of Excel's toolbars is to provide buttons for the commands you use most frequently. If Excel's built-in toolbars don't contain enough of your frequently used commands, you can modify Excel's toolbars by adding or deleting their buttons. If that isn't enough, you can even create your own custom toolbar.

In this lesson, you will learn how to modify Excel's toolbars.

1 Select View → Toolbars → Customize from the menu.

The Customize dialog box appears, as shown in Figure 13-3. You can select toolbars you want to view or create a new custom toolbar in this dialog box.

2 Click the Commands tab.

The Commands tab appears in front of the Customize dialog box, as shown in Figure 13-5. Here you select the buttons and commands you want to appear on your toolbar. The commands are organized by categories just like Excel's menus.

3 In the Categories list, scroll to and click the Insert category.

Notice the Commands list is updated to display all the available commands in the "Insert" category.

4 In the Commands list, scroll to the WordArt button and drag it to the end of the Standard toolbar, as shown in Figure 13-3.

The WordArt button appears in the Standard toolbar.

It's easy to change the image or text that appear on any toolbar button. Here's how:

5 Right-click the WordArt button on the toolbar and select Change Button Image → 🔲 as shown in Figure 13-4.

You're finished modifying the toolbar!

6 Click Close to close the Customize dialog box.

Notice the 🔲 icon appears on the new WordArt button on the Standard toolbar. When you no longer need a toolbar button, you can remove it. Here's how:

7 Select View → Toolbars → Customize from the menu.

The Customize dialog box appears. To remove a button, simply drag it off the toolbar.

8 Click and drag the WordArt button (🔲) off the toolbar.

Move on to the next step and close the Customize dialog box.

9 Click Close to close the Customize dialog box.

Adding your frequently used commands to the toolbar is one of the most effective ways to make Microsoft Excel more enjoyable and faster to use.

QUICK REFERENCE

TO ADD A BUTTON TO A TOOLBAR:

• SELECT VIEW → TOOLBARS → CUSTOMIZE FROM THE MENU.

OR...

1. RIGHT-CLICK ANY TOOLBAR AND SELECT CUSTOMIZE FROM THE SHORTCUT MENU.

2. CLICK THE COMMANDS TAB.

3. SELECT THE COMMAND CATEGORY FROM THE CATEGORIES LIST, FIND THE DESIRED COMMAND IN THE COMMANDS LIST, AND DRAG THE COMMAND ONTO THE TOOLBAR.

TO CHANGE A BUTTON'S TEXT OR IMAGE:

• SELECT VIEW → TOOLBARS → CUSTOMIZE FROM THE MENU.

OR...

1. RIGHT-CLICK ANY TOOLBAR AND SELECT CUSTOMIZE FROM THE SHORTCUT MENU.

2. RIGHT-CLICK THE BUTTON AND MODIFY THE TEXT AND/OR IMAGE USING THE SHORTCUT MENU OPTIONS.

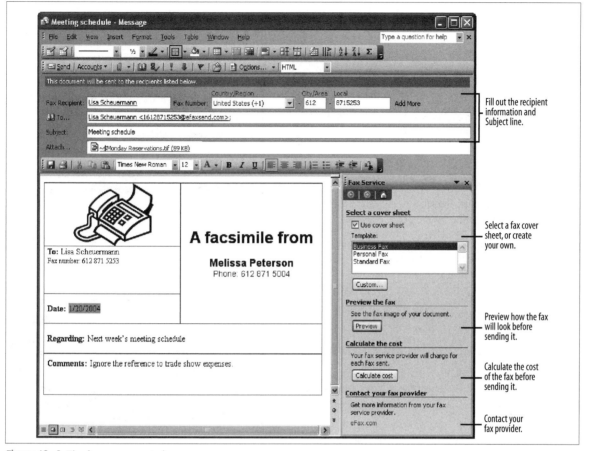

Figure 13-6. The fax message window.

A new feature in Excel 2003 is the ability to send faxes right from the program. Instead of scanning paper copies into a fax machine, Excel creates (.TIF) image files of the workbook and cover letter. These image files are then sent to the fax service provider in an e-mail. When the fax message is received, the fax service sends the image files through the telephone wires to the fax machine.

If none of that made sense, all you really need to know is that the new fax feature saves time and a lot of paper, and is incredibly easy to use.

NOTE *You must have Outlook and Word installed to use the fax service, and Outlook must be open to send your fax. If Outlook is not open and you click Send, the fax will be stored in your Outbox until the next time you open Outlook.*

1 Open the file you want to fax.

If you don't have the file open you can always attach it, just as you would attach a file to an e-mail message.

2 Select File → Send to → Recipient using Internet Fax Service from the menu.

An e-mail message window opens, as shown in Figure 13-6.

NOTE *You must sign up with a fax service provider to use the fax service. If you do not have a fax service provider installed on your computer, you will be prompted to sign up with a provider over the Internet. It's very easy to sign up; just follow the instructions to choose a provider and sign up for the fax service. Many providers offer a free 30-day trial in case you're trying to decide whether or not you want this service.*

Complete the information in the fax message window.

3 Enter the recipient's name and fax number at the top of the window.

You can send the same fax to multiple recipients by clicking the Add More button at the end of the row.

4 Type the fax subject in the Subject line.

Once you have entered the fax message information, fill out the cover letter.

5 Select the Business Fax cover sheet template in the Fax Service task pane.

The template appears. Replace the template text with information that applies to the fax being sent.

NOTE *The information you include on your cover sheet may require some extra thought if you are sending the fax to multiple recipients.*

Once you've completed the cover letter, check out other options in the Fax Service task pane.

6 Click the Preview button in the Fax Service task pane.

The FaxImage window appears with a preview of the pages in the fax.

You can also get an estimate of how much the fax is going to cost you from your fax service provider.

7 Click the Calculate Cost button in the task pane.

A browser window opens with an estimate of what your provider will charge you for sending the fax.

8 Close the browser window.

Once you're satisfied with how your fax is going to look, you're ready to send it.

9 Click the Send button in the fax message window.

The fax e-mail is sent, and the recipient will receive the fax in no time.

You should also receive an e-mail from your provider, telling you whether or not the fax was successful.

QUICK REFERENCE

TO USE THE FAX SERVICE:

• YOU MUST BE SIGNED UP WITH A FAX SERVICE PROVIDER.

  AND...

• YOU MUST HAVE WORD AND OUTLOOK 2003 INSTALLED ON YOUR COMPUTER.

TO SEND A FAX:

1. OPEN THE FILE YOU WANT TO FAX.

2. SELECT FILE → SEND TO → RECIPIENT USING INTERNET FAX SERVICE FROM THE MENU.

3. ENTER THE FAX INFORMATION: RECIPIENT NAME AND FAX NUMBER, AND A SUBJECT.

4. CHOOSE THE TYPE OF COVER SHEET YOU WANT TO USE IN THE FAX SERVICE TASK PANE AND FILL IT OUT.

5. CLICK THE SEND BUTTON.

TO PREVIEW THE FAX:

• CLICK THE PREVIEW BUTTON IN THE FAX SERVICE TASK PANE.

TO CALCULATE COST OF FAX:

• CLICK THE CALCULATE COST BUTTON IN THE FAX SERVICE TASK PANE.

TO FAX MULTIPLE FILES:

• CLICK THE ATTACH BUTTON IN THE FAX MESSAGE WINDOW AND ATTACH EACH FILE YOU WANT TO FAX.

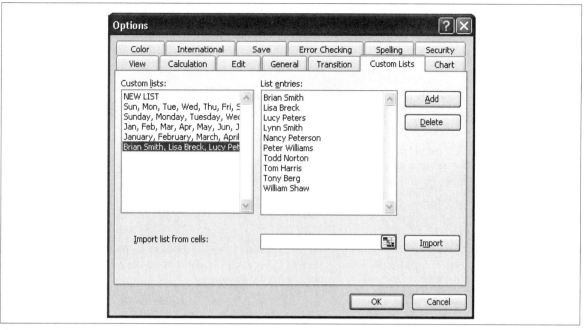

Figure 13-7. The Custom Lists tab of the Options dialog box.

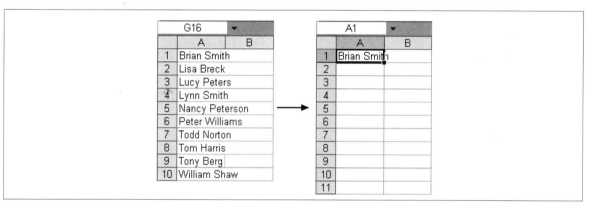

Figure 13-8. Using a custom AutoFill list.

You're already familiar with Excel's *AutoFill* feature. It's the nifty function that automatically enters a series of values. If you find yourself typing the same list of words frequently, you can save yourself a lot of time by creating a *custom AutoFill list*. Once you have done this, all you have to do is type the first entry of the list in a cell and use AutoFill to have Excel complete the rest of the list for you.

1 Click cell A1 and type Monday.

For a quick refresher, we'll use AutoFill to enter the remaining days of the week.

2 Position the pointer over the fill handle of cell A1, until it changes to a +, click and hold the mouse and drag the fill handle down to cell A7, then release the mouse button.

AutoFill completes the series, entering the days of the week in the selected cell range.

Fill handle

3 Close the current workbook (you don't need to save it) and open the workbook named Lesson 13A.

This workbook contains a list you need to type out regularly—the names of the employees in your office. To save time, you decide to add the names to an Auto-Fill list. To do this, you first need to select the information you want to define as an AutoFill list—in this case, the employee's names.

4 Select the cell range A1:A10.

Now that the names are selected, you can add them to a custom AutoFill list.

5 Select Tools → Options from the menu and click the Custom Lists tab.

The Custom Lists tab of the Options dialog box appears, as shown in Figure 13-7. Here you can view or delete the existing AutoFill lists, or add your own. Notice the Import list from cells text box contains the cell range you selected: A1:A10.

6 Click Import.

The list of employees is added to the Custom lists box, and its contents are displayed in the List entries box. Close the Options dialog box.

7 Click OK.

Test out your new AutoFill list.

Enter button

8 Click the Sheet2 tab, type Brian Smith in cell A1, as shown in Figure 13-8, and then click the Enter button on the Formula bar.

9 Position the pointer over the fill handle of cell A1, until it changes to a +, click and hold the mouse, drag the Fill handle down to cell A10, then release the mouse button.

Excel fills the selected range with the list of employees. Now that you know how to create your own custom AutoFill list, you need to delete it.

10 Select Tools → Options and then click the Custom Lists tab.

The Custom Lists tab of the Options dialog box reappears.

11 Select the list of employees in the Custom lists box and click Delete.

A dialog box appears, asking you to confirm the deletion of the custom list.

12 Click OK to confirm the deletion, then click OK again to close the dialog box.

13 Close the workbook without saving any changes.

QUICK REFERENCE

TO CREATE A CUSTOM AUTOFILL LIST:

1. SELECT THE CELL RANGE THAT CONTAINS THE INFORMATION YOU WANT TO INCLUDE IN YOUR CUSTOM AUTOFILL LIST.

2. SELECT TOOLS → OPTIONS FROM THE MENU AND CLICK THE CUSTOM LISTS TAB.

3. CLICK IMPORT AND CLICK OK.

TO USE A CUSTOM AUTOFILL LIST:

1. ENTER THE FIRST NAME FROM THE LIST IN A CELL.

2. SELECT THE CELL YOU USED IN STEP 1 AND CLICK AND DRAG THE FILL HANDLE TO COMPLETE THE SERIES IN THE CELLS YOU SELECT.

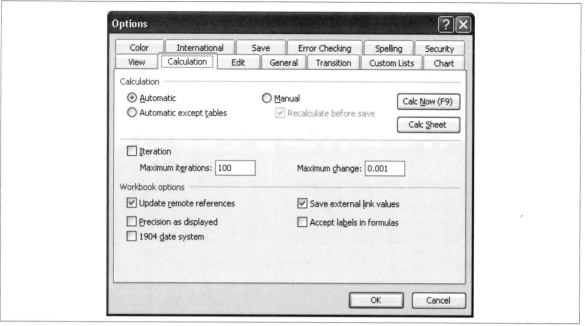

Figure 13-9. The Calculation tab of the Options dialog box.

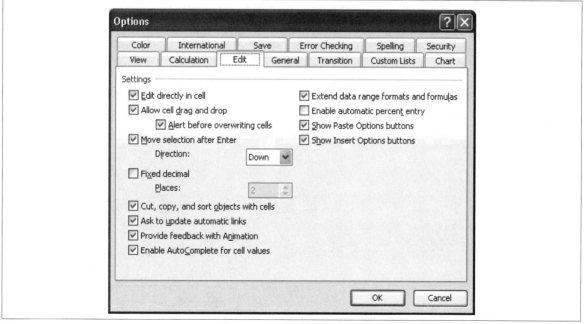

Figure 13-10. The Edit tab of the Options dialog box.

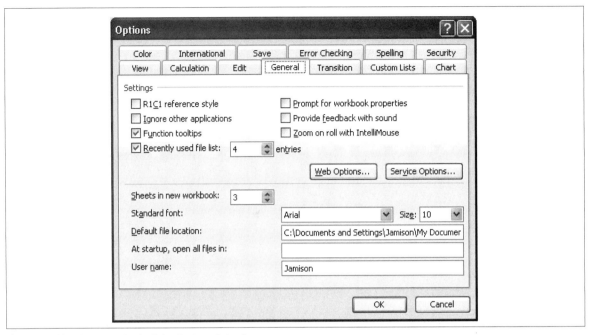

Figure 13-11. The General tab of the Options dialog box.

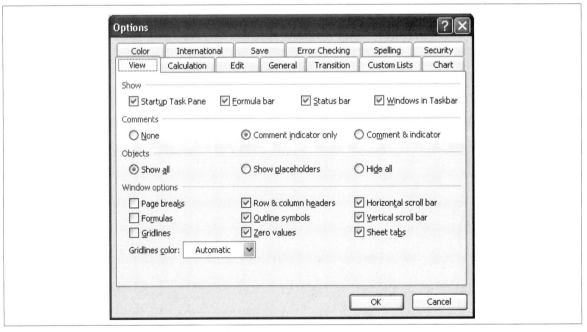

Figure 13-12. The View tab of the Options dialog box.

Microsoft spent a lot of time and research when it decided what the default settings for Excel should be. However, you may find that the default settings don't always fit your own needs. For example, you might want to change the default folder where Excel saves your work-

books from *C:\My Documents* to a drive and folder on the network.

This lesson isn't so much an exercise as it is a reference on how to customize Excel by changing its default settings.

1 Select Tools → Options from the menu.

The Options dialog box appears.

2 Refer to Table 13-1 and click each of the tabs shown in the table to familiarize yourself with the Options dialog box. Click OK when you're finished.

Table 13-1. The Options Dialog Box Tabs

Tab	Description
Calculation	Controls how Excel calculates the worksheet—automatically (the default setting) or manually.
Chart	Determines how Excel plots empty cells in a chart, and if chart tips—names and values—are displayed when you rest the pointer over a data marker.
Color	Allows you to edit any of the original 56 colors on the color palette to create custom colors.
Custom Lists	Allows you to view, add, and delete custom AutoFill lists.
Edit	Allows you to change Excel's editing features, such as whether you can directly edit a cell, where the cell pointer moves when you press Enter, and if you want to enable drag and drop or AutoComplete.
Error Checking	Controls Excel's new background error-checking features.
General	Allows you to change the default location where Excel looks for and saves files, the user name, how many sheets appear in a new workbook, and if the Properties dialog is displayed when saving a workbook.
International	Allows you to specify international options, such as the currency symbol used in numbers.
Save	Controls how often Excel automatically saves a workbook recovery file. If your computer hangs (stops responding) or you lose power unexpectedly, Excel opens the AutoRecover file the next time you start Excel.
Security	Allows you to password protect your workbooks. For example, you could specify that a user must enter a password to either open or modify a workbook.
Spelling	Allows you to specify which language you want to use to check the worksheet's spelling.
Transition	For users switching to Excel from Lotus 1-2-3. Allows Excel to accept Lotus 1-2-3 commands, navigation keys, and formulas.
View	Controls whether the Formula bar, status bar, comments, row and column headers, gridlines, and formulas are displayed.

QUICK REFERENCE

TO CHANGE EXCEL'S DEFAULT OPTIONS:

• SELECT TOOLS → OPTIONS FROM THE MENU, CLICK THE APPROPRIATE TABS, AND MAKE THE NECESSARY CHANGES.

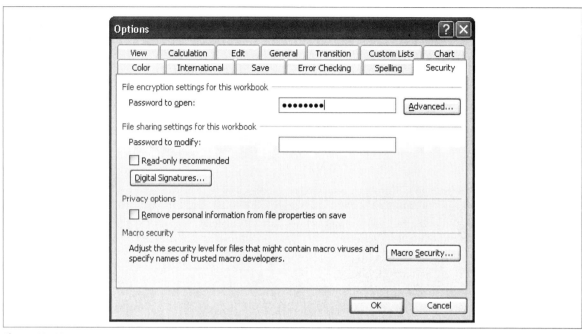

Figure 13-13. The Security tab of the Options dialog box.

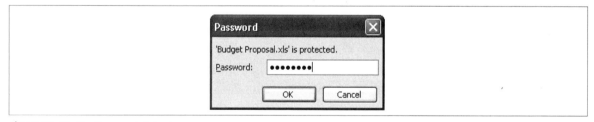

Figure 13-14. The Password dialog box.

If a workbook contains sensitive data you don't want anyone else to see or modify, you can password protect the workbook, restricting the workbook access to only yourself or those people that know the password. You can assign passwords so that users must enter a password to either open and/or modify a workbook. This lesson will show you how to add a password to a workbook, how to open a password-protected workbook, and how to remove a password if you decide a workbook no longer needs to be password protected.

1 Open the workbook named Lesson 13B and save it as Budget Proposal.

Here's how to password protect a workbook.

2 Select Tools → Options from the menu and click the Security tab.

The Options dialog box appears, as shown in Figure 13-13. Here you can assign passwords to your workbook, requiring users to enter a password to either open or modify the workbook. Notice there are two text boxes where you can enter a password:

- **Password to open:** Adding a password here will require that a user enter the assigned password in order to open the workbook.

- **Password to modify:** Adding a password here will require that a user enter the assigned password in order to modify the workbook.

3 In the Password to open **text box, type** flower.

Notice the text you type appears as a string of ●●●●●●●●'s. This is so someone can't look over your shoulder and see your password.

4 Click OK.

The Confirm Password dialog box appears. You must reenter your password, "flower," once more, just in case you mistyped the first time.

5 Type flower, **then click** OK.

Now you need to save your workbook.

6 Click the Save button **on the Standard toolbar.**

Excel saves the Budget Proposal workbook.

7 Close the workbook.

8 Select File → 1 Budget Proposal **from the recent files list from the menu.**

The Password dialog box appears, as shown in Figure 13-14. You must enter the correct password, "flower," in order to open the workbook. Try entering an incorrect password to see what happens.

9 Type pencil **and then click** OK.

The Incorrect Password dialog appears. You cannot open a password-protected workbook without entering the correct password. A dialog box appears informing you that you have typed an incorrect password.

10 Click OK to close the Incorrect Password dialog box.

11 Select File → 1 Budget Proposal **from the recent files list in the menu.**

The Password dialog box appears. This time enter the correct password.

12 Type flower **and then click** OK.

The Budget Proposal opens.

Removing password protection from a workbook is just as easy as adding it.

13 Select Tools → Options **from the menu and click the** Security tab.

The options dialog box appears.

14 Delete the ●●●●●●●● **in the Password to open text box, and then click** OK.

15 Click the Save button **on the Standard toolbar.**

Excel saves the workbook without any password protection.

QUICK REFERENCE

TO PASSWORD PROTECT A WORKBOOK:

1. SELECT TOOLS → OPTIONS FROM THE MENU AND CLICK THE SECURITY TAB.

2. TYPE A PASSWORD IN EITHER THE PASSWORD TO OPEN OR PASSWORD TO MODIFY TEXT BOX AND CLICK OK.

TO REMOVE PASSWORD PROTECTION FROM A WORKBOOK:

• REPEAT THE ABOVE STEPS, ONLY DELETE THE PASSWORD FROM EITHER THE PASSWORD TO OPEN OR PASSWORD TO MODIFY TEXT BOX AND CLICK OK.

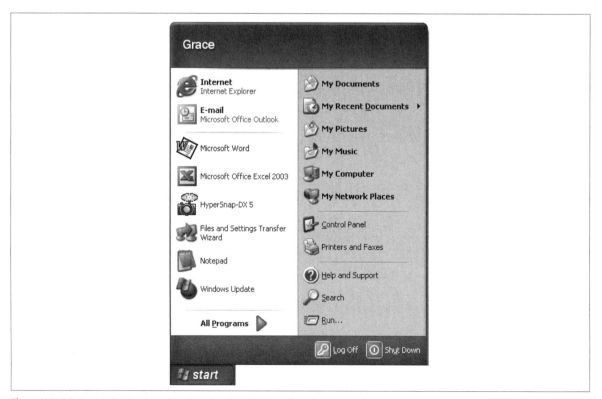

Figure 13-15. The File Properties dialog box.

Figure 13-16. Search for Excel workbooks using the Windows Search command.

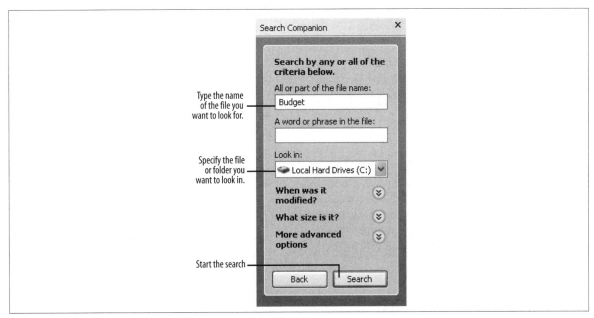

Type the name of the file you want to look for.

Specify the file or folder you want to look in.

Start the search

Figure 13-17. The Search by Criteria dialog box.

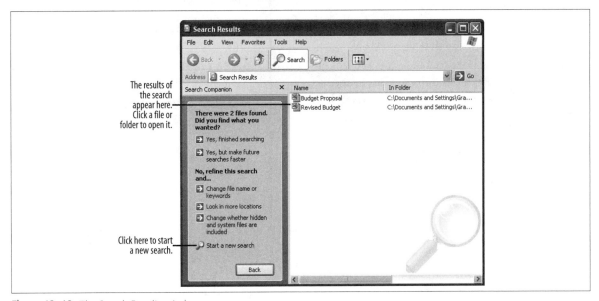

The results of the search appear here. Click a file or folder to open it.

Click here to start a new search.

Figure 13-18. The Search Results window.

We'll cover two related topics in this lesson. The first topic is File Properties. Information about the size of a workbook, when it was created, when it was last modified, and who created it, can all be found with the File → Properties command. The File Properties dialog box also has custom fields, such as Subject and Category, so you can add your own information to your workbooks.

The second topic covered in this lesson is how to find a file. It is just as easy to misplace and lose a file in your computer as it is to misplace your car keys—maybe easier! Luckily, Excel comes with a great Find feature that can track down your lost files. Find can search for a file, even if you can't remember its exact name or location.

1 Verify that the Budget Proposal **workbook is open,** then select File → Properties **from the menu and click the** General tab.

The General tab of the Properties dialog box appears. The General tab of the Properties dialog box tracks general information about the file, such as its size, its location, when the file was created, and when it was last accessed or modified.

2 Click the Summary tab.

The Summary tab of the Properties dialog box. as shown in Figure 13-15, lets you enter your own information to describe and summarize the file, such as the author, subject, keywords, and category. You can use the information in the Summary tab to help you search for files.

3 Click the Keywords **box, type** 1999 Budget Proposal, **and click** OK.

Excel saves the summary information and closes the Properties dialog box.

4 Save your changes and close the workbook.

Okay, let's move on to how to find a file. Actually, the Find feature is part of Windows and can be used to find any type of file—not just those created in Microsoft Excel.

Start button

5 Click the Windows Start button **and select** Search **(see Figure 13-16).**

The Search Results window appears.

NOTE *If you are using an earlier version of Windows, click Start → Find → Files and folders, type Budget in the Named box, and click Find Now. Double-click the Budget Proposal file in the Search Results list to open the workbook.*

6 Click the All files and folders **arrow.**

This opens the Search by Criteria dialog box, as shown in Figure 13-17.

7 Type Budget **in the** All or part of the file name **box.**

This will search for any file that contains the word "budget," such as "1999 Budget Proposal" and "Budget Report." So, if you know only part of the file name, you can enter the part of the file name that you know.

8 Using the Look in **drop-down menu, navigate to your Practice folder or disk, then click** Search.

A list of files that match the criteria you entered in the "All or part of the file name" box appears in the window (see Figure 13-18).

9 Double-click the Budget Proposal **file.**

The Budget Proposal workbook opens in Microsoft Excel.

QUICK REFERENCE

TO VIEW A WORKBOOK'S PROPERTIES:

- SELECT FILE → PROPERTIES FROM THE MENU.

TO FIND A WORKBOOK:

1. CLICK THE WINDOWS START BUTTON AND SELECT FIND → FILES OR FOLDERS FROM THE START MENU.

2. ENTER THE SEARCH CONDITIONS AND WHERE TO LOOK ON THE APPROPRIATE TABS: NAME & LOCATION, DATE, AND ADVANCED).

3. CLICK FIND NOW TO START SEARCHING FOR THE FILE(S).

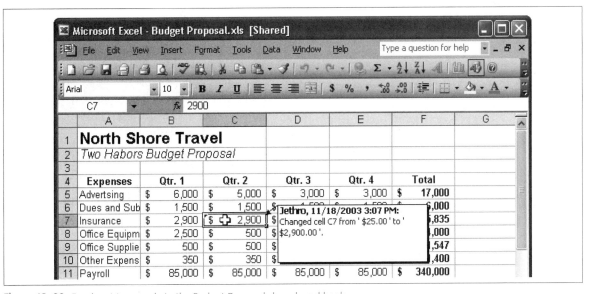

Figure 13-19. The Highlight Changes dialog box.

Figure 13-20. Excel revisions made in the Budget Proposal shared workbook.

You can share your Excel workbook files with other people, so that you can work on the data collaboratively. *Sharing* a workbook has several benefits:

- Several people can use the same shared workbook simultaneously.
- Excel keeps track of any changes made to a shared workbook, when they were made, and who made them.
- You can review and accept or reject any changes made to a shared workbook.

This lesson explains how you can share a workbook when you need to collaborate on a project with other people.

1 Make sure the Budget Proposal **workbook is open and select** Tools → Track Changes → Highlight Changes **from the menu.**

The Highlight Changes dialog box appears, as shown in Figure 13-19.

2 Check the Track changes while editing **check box.**

Checking this check box does two things. First, it shares the workbook, so other users can use it simultaneously. Second, it tracks any changes made to the workbook.

3 Click OK.

A dialog box may appear, informing you that Excel must save the workbook in order to share it.

4 Click OK.

Excel saves and shares the Budget Proposal workbook. Notice that "[Shared]" appears after the workbook name in Excel's title bar, indicating that you are working on a shared workbook.

That's all there is to sharing a workbook. If you're on a network, multiple users can now open and edit the workbook at the same time (normally, only one person can open and edit the same file at a time). Now that the workbook is shared, you or other users can track any changes made to the workbook. The remainder of this lesson and the next lesson will show how you can track changes in a shared workbook.

You decide to break up the insurance payment of $5,800 into payments spanning two quarters instead of one. Move on to the next step to make the revisions.

Change Indicator

5 Select cell B7, type 2900, press Tab to move to cell C7, type 2900, and press Enter.

Excel highlights the revisions you made in cell B7 and C7 with tiny blue triangles in the upper left-hand corners of the modified cells, as shown in Figure 13-20. You can review your changes later and accept or reject them.

6 Move the cell pointer over the revised cell B7.

A note appears by the cell listing the revisions made to it.

7 Click the Save button on the Standard toolbar to save your changes to the shared workbook.

You can also make copies of the workbook that you can distribute to reviewers. When you make a copy of a shared workbook, you can later compare, or *merge*, the copied workbook to the original to review any changes that have been made to the copy. Here's how you can create a copy of a shared workbook:

8 Select File → Save As from the menu.

The Save As dialog box appears. Save a copy of the shared workbook with a different name.

NOTE   *When you make copies of a shared workbook, make sure you give the copies a different name than the original.*

9 Type Revised Budget in the "File name" text box and click OK.

The "Budget Proposal" workbook is saved with the new name, "Revised Budget," and the original workbook, "Budget Proposal," closes. Now that you're working with a copy of the original workbook (the Revised Budget file), make some revisions to the workbook. You will get a chance to accept or reject the changes in the next lesson.

10 Click cell B5, type 6000, press Tab to move to cell C5, type 6000, and press Enter.

Remember—now you're working with the copied workbook "Revised Budget" and not the original "Budget Proposal" workbook. Excel highlights your changes in cell C5.

11 Click cell A10, type Misc Expenses, and press Enter.

You're finished making revisions to the Revised Budget workbook, so save your changes and close the workbook.

12 Save your changes and then close the Revised Budget workbook.

QUICK REFERENCE

TO SHARE A WORKBOOK:

1. SELECT TOOLS → TRACK CHANGES → HIGHLIGHT CHANGES FROM THE MENU.

2. CHECK THE TRACK CHANGES WHILE EDITING CHECK BOX.

3. MAKE SURE YOU SAVE THE WORKBOOK WHERE IT IS ACCESSIBLE TO OTHER USERS (I.E., A SHARED FOLDER ON A NETWORK DRIVE).

TO VIEW CHANGES MADE TO A CELL:

• POSITION THE MOUSE POINTER OVER THE MARKED CHANGED CELL AND WAIT A FEW SECONDS.

TO MAKE A COPY OF A SHARED WORKBOOK:

• CREATE A COPY OF THE SHARED WORKBOOK BY SELECTING FILE → SAVE AS AND SAVING IT WITH A DIFFERENT NAME. THEN YOU CAN DISTRIBUTE THESE COPIES TO OTHER USERS AND LATER COMPARE OR "MERGE" THEM WITH THE ORIGINAL TO REVIEW ANY CHANGES MADE.

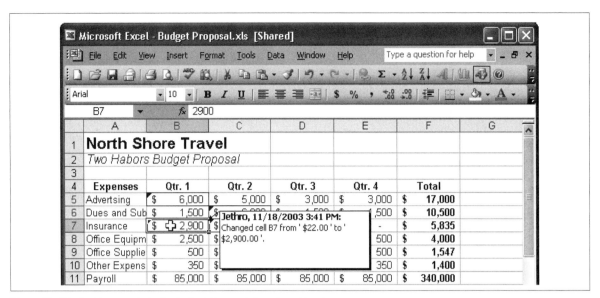

Figure 13-21. Revisions made in the Budget Proposal shared workbook.

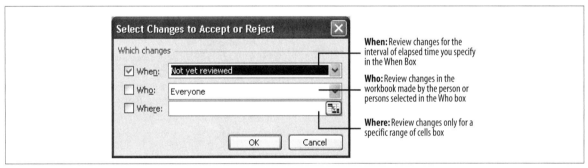

Figure 13-22. Selecting changes that have not yet been reviewed in the Select Changes to Accept or Reject dialog box.

Figure 13-23. The Accept or Reject Changes dialog box.

Once a shared workbook has been revised, you can review the changes and decide if you want to accept the changes and make them part of the workbook or reject them. Revising workbooks using Excel's revision features can save a lot of time, because you merely have to accept

the changes to incorporate them into your workbook instead of manually typing the changes yourself.

You can also compare, or *merge*, copies made of a shared workbook, and review, accept, and/or reject any changes made.

1 Open the workbook named Budget Proposal.

Budget Proposal is the shared workbook you created in the previous lesson. Display the revisions you made in the previous lesson.

2 Select Tools → Track changes → Highlight changes from the menu.

The Track Changes dialog box appears.

3 Verify that the When box is checked, then click the When drop-down list, select All, and click OK.

Excel highlights the revisions you made in cells B7 and C7.

Now that you have the original shared workbook open, you can merge it with the copied workbook, Revised Budget, to review any revisions made to the copy.

4 Select Tools → Compare and Merge Workbooks from the menu.

The Select Files to Merge Into Current Workbook dialog box appears. Here you must select the copy of the shared workbook that you want to compare or merge with the original.

5 Select the Revised Budget workbook and click OK. Click OK if you are prompted to save the shared workbook.

Excel merges the revisions made into the Revised Budget workbook with the original Budget Proposal workbook, as shown in Figure 13-21.

6 Move the cell pointer over the revised cell B7.

A note appears by the cell with the revisions made to it.

7 To review all the revisions made to a shared workbook and either accept or reject them, select Tools → Track Changes → Accept or Reject Changes from the menu.

The Select Changes to Accept or Reject dialog box appears, as shown in Figure 13-22.

8 Make sure the When check box is selected, and that "Not yet reviewed" appears in the When list box, then click OK.

The Accept or Reject Changes dialog box appears with the first of five changes made to the workbook—changed cell B7 from $5,800.00 to $2,900.00. Accept this change.

9 Click Accept to accept the first change, and Accept again to accept the second change in the workbook—changed cell C7 from $5,800.00 to $2,900.00.

After accepting the first two changes made to the workbook, the third change appears—changed cell B5 from $5,000 to $6,000. You decide to reject this change.

10 Click Reject to reject the third change, and Reject again to reject the fourth change in the workbook—changed cell C5 from $5,000.00 to $6,000.00.

You decide to accept the fifth change made to the shared workbook—changed cell A10 from "Other Expenses" to "Misc. Expenses".

11 Click Accept to accept the fifth change made to the shared workbook.

The Accept or Reject Changes dialog box closes, and the revisions you accepted are made to the workbook.

12 Save the Budget Proposal workbook.

QUICK REFERENCE

TO HIGHLIGHT CHANGES IN A SHARED WORKBOOK:

1. SELECT TOOLS → TRACK CHANGES → HIGHLIGHT CHANGES FROM THE MENU.

2. SELECT WHICH CHANGES YOU WANT TO REVIEW (USUALLY NOT YET REVIEWED IN THE WHEN COMBO BOX) AND CLICK OK.

TO VIEW CHANGES MADE TO A CELL:

• POSITION THE MOUSE POINTER OVER THE MARKED CHANGED CELL AND WAIT A FEW SECONDS.

TO ACCEPT AND/OR REJECT REVISIONS:

1. SELECT TOOLS → TRACK CHANGES → ACCEPT OR REJECT CHANGES FROM THE MENU.

2. SELECT WHICH CHANGES YOU WANT TO REVIEW (USUALLY NOT YET REVIEWED IN THE WHEN COMBO BOX) AND CLICK OK.

3. CLICK EITHER THE ACCEPT CHANGE BUTTON OR THE REJECT CHANGE BUTTON.

TO MERGE SHARED WORKBOOKS:

1. SELECT TOOLS → MERGE WORKBOOKS FROM THE MENU AND SELECT THE FILE YOU WISH TO MERGE WITH THE OPEN WORKBOOK.

2. SEE THE INSTRUCTION ON HOW TO ACCEPT AND/OR REJECT REVISIONS.

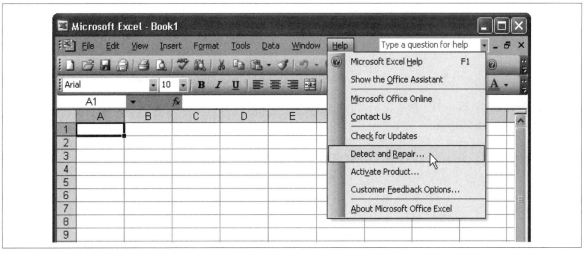

Figure 13-24. Selecting Detect and Repair from the Help menu.

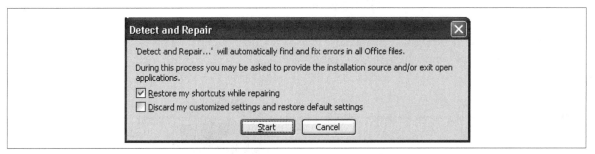

Figure 13-25. The Detect and Repair dialog box.

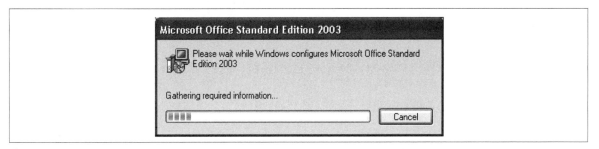

Figure 13-26. Detect and Repair finds and repairs any errors it finds in the Microsoft Office applications.

It's a sad fact of life. The more complicated programs get, the more there is that can go wrong with them. Programs sometimes become corrupted and have to be reinstalled to make them work right again. Fortunately for you and your network administrator, Microsoft has made this process relatively painless with the *Detect and Repair* feature. Detect and Repair searches for corrupted files and incorrect settings in any Microsoft Office applications and then finds and reinstalls the appropriate files.

Should your installation of Microsoft Excel become corrupted or buggy, this lesson explains how you can use Detect and Repair to fix the problem.

1 Make sure the Office 2003 CD is inserted in your computer's CD-ROM drive or is available through the network.

If you are connected to a large corporate network, hopefully your friendly network administrator will have made the Office 2003 files available to everyone on the network so that you can use the Detect and Repair feature. The only way you can find out if the Office 2003 installation files are available is to run Detect and Repair.

2 Select Help → Detect and Repair from the menu, as shown in Figure 13-24.

The Detect and Repair dialog box appears as shown in Figure 13-25. Here we go…

3 Click Start.

If Detect and Repair finds the Office 2003 installation files, it begins looking for and repairing any problems it finds with any Office programs (see Figure 13-26). This might be a good time for you to take a coffee break as Detect and Repair takes a long time to fix everything.

Detect and Repair not only fixes problems with Microsoft Excel, but with all your Microsoft Office 2003 applications as well, such as Microsoft Word and Microsoft PowerPoint.

QUICK REFERENCE

TO USE DETECT AND REPAIR:

• SELECT HELP → DETECT AND REPAIR FROM THE MENU.

Lesson Summary

Hiding, Displaying, and Moving Toolbars

To View or Hide a Toolbar: Select View → Toolbars from the menu and select the toolbar you want to display or hide, or right-click any toolbar or menu and select the toolbar you want to display or hide from the shortcut menu.

To Move a Toolbar to a New Location: Drag the toolbar by its move handle (if the toolbar is docked) or title bar (if the toolbar is floating) to the desired location.

Customizing Excel's Toolbars

To Add a Button to a Toolbar: Select View → Toolbars → Customize from the menu and click the Commands tab. Select the command category from the Categories list, then find the desired command in the Commands list and drag the command to the toolbar.

To Remove a Button from a Toolbar: Select View → Toolbars → Customize from the menu and drag the button off the toolbar.

Sending Faxes

To Use the Fax Service: You must be signed up with a fax service provider, and you must have Word and Outlook 2003 installed on your computer.

To Send a Fax: Open the file you want to fax and select File → Send to → Recipient using Internet Fax Service from the menu. Enter the fax information (recipient name, fax number, and a subject). Choose the type of cover sheet you want to use in the Fax Service task pane and fill it out. Click the Send button.

To Preview the Fax: Click the Preview button in the Fax Service task pane.

To Calculate the Cost of the Fax: Click the Calculate Cost button in the Fax Service task pane.

To Fax Multiple Files: Click the Attach button in the fax message window and attach each file you want to fax.

Creating a Custom AutoFill List

To Create a Custom AutoFill List: Select the cell range that contains the information you want to include in your custom AutoFill list, select Tools → Options from the menu, click the Custom Lists tab, and click Import.

To Use a Custom AutoFill List: Enter the first name from the list in a cell, select that cell, and then click and drag the Fill handle to complete the series in the cells you select.

Changing Excel's Options

You can change Excel's default options by selecting Tools → Options from the menu.

Password Protecting a Workbook

To Password Protect a Workbook: Select Tools → Options from the menu and click the Security tab. Type a password in either the Password to open or Password to modify text box and click OK.

To Remove Password Protection from a Workbook: Repeat the above steps, but delete the password from either the Password to open or Password to modify text box and click OK.

File Properties and Finding a File

You can view a file's properties (when it was created, by whom, etc.) by selecting File → Properties from the menu.

To Find a Workbook: Click the Start button and select Search from the Start menu. Click on the All files or folders button. Enter all or part of the file name, key words, or phrases that might appear in the file or a location. Click Search to start searching for the file(s).

Sharing a Workbook and Tracking Changes

Sharing a workbook allows several users to open and work on it at the same time. It allows you to track, review, and accept or reject any changes made to the workbook.

To Share a Workbook: Select Tools → Track Changes → Highlight Changes from the menu and click the Track changes while editing check box.

If the track changes option is selected, modified cells are highlighted. To view the changes made to a cell, position the mouse pointer over the cell and wait several seconds.

You can save copies of a shared workbook by saving the shared workbook with a different name using File → Save

As. You can then distribute these copies to other users and later compare or "merge" them with the original to review any changes made to them.

Merging and Revising a Shared Workbook

To Highlight Changes in a Shared Workbook: Select Tools → Track changes → Highlight changes from the menu, select which changes you want to review (usually Not yet reviewed in the When list box) and click OK.

To Accept and/or Reject Revisions: Select Tools → Track Changes → Accept or Reject Changes from the

menu, select which changes you want to review (usually Not yet reviewed in the When combo box), and click OK. Click either the Accept Change button, or the Reject Change button.

To Merge Shared Workbooks: Select Tools → Merge Workbooks from the menu and select the file you wish to merge with the open workbook.

Using Detect and Repair

To Use Detect and Repair: Select Help → Detect and Repair from the menu.

Quiz

1. Which of the following statements is NOT true?

    A. You can change the position of a toolbar by dragging it by its move handle (if it's docked) or title bar (if it's floating).

    B. You can display a toolbar by selecting View → Toolbars and selecting the toolbar you want to display from the list.

    C. You can display a toolbar by clicking the Toolbar button on the Standard toolbar and selecting the toolbar you wan to display from the list.

    D. Toolbars attach or "dock" to the sides of the program window.

2. Which of the following statements is NOT true?

    A. You can customize a toolbar by right-clicking any toolbar or menu and selecting Customize from the shortcut menu.

    B. You can customize a toolbar by selecting View → Toolbars → Customize from the menu.

    C. Once the Customize dialog box is open you can add buttons to a toolbar by double-clicking on the toolbar where you want to insert the button.

    D. Once the Customize dialog box is open you can add buttons to a toolbar by dragging them from the Commands list onto the toolbar.

3. You can modify Excel's built-in toolbars, and you can create your own toolbars. (True or False?)

4. To password protect a worksheet, select Tools → Protection and enter the password. (True or False?)

5. Which of the following statements is NOT true?

    A. You can find a workbook by clicking the Windows Start button, selecting Search, clicking the "All files or folders" button, entering any part of the workbook's name in the "All or part of the file name" box in the Search by Criteria dialog box, and clicking Search.

    B. Selecting File → Properties from the menu displays statistics on a file, such as its size and when it was last saved.

    C. Selecting File → Options from the menu opens the Options dialog box, which contains the default settings for Excel.

    D. You can create your own custom AutoFill lists.

6. Which of the following is NOT an advantage of working with a shared workbook?

    A. Several users can open and work on the workbook simultaneously.

    B. Excel can create a report summarizing all the changes made to the workbook.

    C. You can track, review, accept and/or reject any changes made to the workbook.

    D. You can create a copy of the workbook, distribute it to other users, and then later compare, or merge, the copy with the original to review any changes.

7. How can you track changes made by other users to a workbook?

A. Select File → Save As from the menu and select Multi-User workbook from the "Save as type" list.

B. Select Tools → Track Changes → Highlight Changes from the menu.

C. Have other users place a Post-It® Note on their monitors by the cells they change.

D. There's no way of doing this in Microsoft Excel.

Homework

1. Create a new blank workbook.

2. Select Tools → Customize from the menu and click New to create a new toolbar. Name the toolbar "My Commands."

3. Click the Commands tab, browse through the various Categories and Commands, and drag the commands you think you will use frequently onto the new My Commands toolbar.

4. Delete the My Commands toolbar when you're finished (click the Toolbars tab, select the My Commands toolbar, and click Delete).

5. Type some text and numbers into the blank workbook, save it as "Confidential." Password protect the workbook so that users must enter the password "leaf" to open the workbook.

6. Select Tools → Track Changes → Highlight Changes from the menu.

7. Modify the text and numbers you entered in the workbook—notice how Excel tracks the changes you make.

8. Review the changes you made by selecting Tools → Track Changes → Accept or Reject Changes.

Quiz Answers

1. C. There isn't a toolbar button in Excel.

2. C. Once the Customize dialog box is open, you can add buttons to a toolbar by dragging commands from the Commands list to the desired location on the toolbar—not by double-clicking.

3. True. You can modify Excel's existing toolbars and you can create your own custom toolbars.

4. False. Select File → Save As from the menu and click the Options button to password protect a workbook.

5. C. Select Tools → Options from the menu to open the Options dialog box.

6. B. Although you can track any changes made to a shared workbook, there isn't any way of creating a report that summarizes the changes.

7. B. Select Tools → Track Changes → Highlight Changes from the menu to track changes made to a workbook.

INDEX

R

RADIANS function, 267
RAND function, 267
RANDBETWEEN function, 268
ranges of cells
    adding together, 35
    deselecting/selecting, 33
RATE function, 270
recording macros, 310–311
records, 280
    adding to lists
        using Data Form dialog box, 284
        using Insert row, 284
    copying filtered records, 300–301
    deleting, 288
    filtering lists
        with Advanced Filters, 297–299
        with AutoFilter feature, 292, 295
        with Top 10 option, 295
    searching for
        using Data Form dialog box, 286
        using Find command, 286–287
    sorting, 290–291
    ungrouping, 402
recovering workbooks, 98–100
Redo button, 82
#REF! (cell reference not valid), 265
referencing cells in formulas, 37
Refresh Current Page button (Web toolbar), 353
Refresh Data button (PivotTable toolbar), 387
Refresh Data dialog box, 365

relative cell references, 72–74
REM statements, 321
remarks, adding to Visual Basic code, 321
Rename command, 92
renaming worksheets, 199
Repeat command (Ctrl + Y), 82
Replace All option, 146
Replace dialog box, 86–87
    using with records, 287
Replace Format dialog box, 146
Replace option, 146
Research Task Pane, 5
Reset Window Position button, 229
resizing
    charts, 157–158
    graphics, 341
    lists, 280
right mouse button, bringing up shortcut menus
        with, 19
right-aligning text in cells, 119
right-arrow scroll button, 28
right-clicking objects, 19
rotating
    3-D charts, 179
    text in cells, 144
ROUND function, 268
ROUNDDOWN function, 268
ROUNDUP function, 268
Row Height dialog box, 116–117
rows
    adjusting height of, 115–117
    charting by rows, 168
    deleting, 79
    grouping manually, 401
    hiding, 226
    inserting, 79
    using labels in formulas, 253
    printing labels for, on every page, 219

S

Save As dialog box, 25, 90–92
Save dialog box, 23
Save tab in Options dialog box, 435
saving
    files in different formats, 344–345
    worksheets as interactive Web pages, 360–361
    worksheets as non-interactive Web pages, 356–358
scaling size of worksheets, 221
scatter charts, 169
Scenario Manager, 408
scenario summary reports, creating, 410
Scenario Values dialog box, 408
scenarios
    creating, 408
    viewing, 409
Screen Tips, 14

About CustomGuide, Inc.

CustomGuide, Inc. (*http://www.customguide.com*) is a leading provider of training materials and e-learning for organizations; their client list includes Harvard, Yale, and Oxford universities. CustomGuide was founded by a small group of instructors who were dissatisfied by the dry and technical nature of computer training materials available to trainers and educators. They decided to write their own series of courseware that would be fun and user-friendly; and best of all, they would license it in electronic format so instructors could print only the topics they needed for a class or training session. Later, they found themselves unhappy with the e-learning industry and decided to create a new series of online, interactive training that matched their courseware. Today employees, students, and instructors at more than 2,000 organizations worldwide use CustomGuide courseware to help teach and learn about computers.

CustomGuide Staff and Contributors

Jonathan High	President
Daniel High	Vice President of Sales and Marketing
Melissa Peterson	Senior Writer/Editor
Kitty Rogers	Writer/Editor
Kelly Waldrop	Writer/Editor
Steve Meinz	Writer/Editor
Stan Keathly	Senior Developer
Jeffery High	Developer
Chris Kannnenman	Developer
Jeremy Weaver	Senior Programmer
Luke Davidson	Programmer
Lisa Price	Director of Business Development
Soda Rajsombath	Office Manager and Sales Representative
Stan Guimont	Senior Sales Representative
Megan Diemand	Sales Representative
Hallie Stork	Sales Representative
Sarah Saeger	Sales Support
Julie Geisler	Narrator

Colophon

Our look is the result of reader comments, our own experimentation, and feedback from distribution channels. Distinctive covers complement our distinctive approach to technical topics, breathing personality and life into potentially dry subjects.

Mary Brady was the production editor and the proofreader for *Excel 2003 Personal Trainer*. The cover image is an original illustration by Lou Brooks. Marlowe Shaeffer and Claire Cloutier provided quality control. Judy Hoer wrote the index.

The cover image of the comic book hero is an original illustration by Lou Brooks. The art of illustrator Lou Brooks has appeared on the covers of *Time* and *Newsweek* eight times, and his logo design for the game Monopoly is used throughout the world to this day. His work has also appeared in just about every major publication, and it has been animated for MTV, Nickelodeon, and HBO.

Emma Colby designed and produced the cover of this book with Adobe InDesign CS and Photoshop CS. The typefaces used on the cover are Base Twelve, designed by Zuzana Licko and issued by Emigre, Inc., and JY Comic Pro, issued by AGFA Monotype.

Melanie Wang designed the interior layout. David Futato designed the CD label. This book was converted by Andrew Savikas and Joe Wizda to FrameMaker 5.5.6 with a format conversion tool created by Erik Ray, Jason McIntosh, Neil Walls, and Mike Sierra that uses Perl and XML technologies. The typefaces are Minion, designed by Robert Slimbach and issued by Adobe Systems; Base Twelve and Base Nine; JY Comic Pro; and TheSansMono Condensed, designed by Luc(as) de Groot and issued by LucasFonts.

The technical illustrations that appear in the book were produced by Robert Romano and Jessamyn Read using Macromedia FreeHand MX and Adobe Photoshop CS.

Also Available

Windows XP Personal Trainer

By CustomGuide, Inc.
ISBN 0-596-00862-7, Includes CD-Rom
456 pages, $29.95

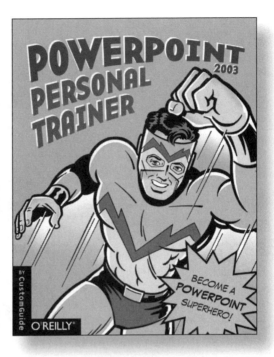

PowerPoint 2003 Personal Trainer

By CustomGuide, Inc.
ISBN 0-596-00855-4, Includes CD-Rom
336 pages, $29.95

Coming Winter 2005

Access 2003 Personal Trainer, *ISBN 0-596-00937-2, $29.95*
Outlook 2003 Personal Trainer, *ISBN 0-596-00935-6, $29.95*
Word 2003 Personal Trainer, *ISBN 0-596-00936-4, $29.95*

Windows XP Home Edition:
The Missing Manual,
2nd Edition

By David Pogue
ISBN 0-596-00897-X
600 pages, $24.95

Windows XP Pro:
The Missing Manual,
2nd Edition

By Craig Zacker, Linda Zacker
& David Pogue
ISBN 0-596-00898-8
680 pages, $29.95

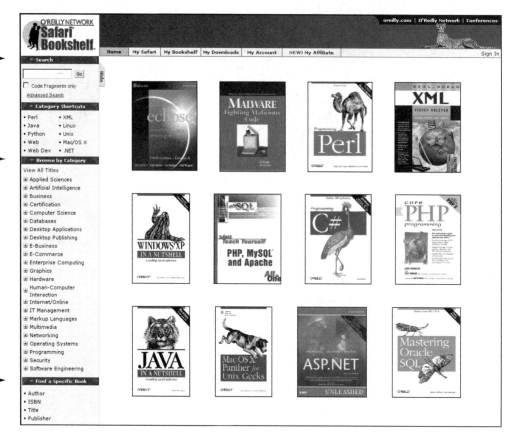

Related Titles Available from O'Reilly

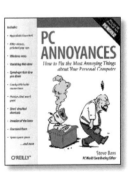

Windows Users

Access Cookbook, *2nd Edition*

Access Database Design & Programming,
3rd Edition

Excel Hacks

Excel Pocket Guide

Outlook 2000 in a Nutshell

Outlook Pocket Guide

PC Annoyances

Windows XP Annoyances

Windows XP Hacks

Windows XP Home Edition:
The Missing Manual

Windows XP in a Nutshell

Windows XP Pocket Guide

Windows XP Power User

Windows XP Pro:
The Missing Manual

Windows XP Unwired

Word Hacks

Word Pocket Guide, *2nd Edition*

Keep in touch with O'Reilly

1. Download examples from our books

To find example files for a book, go to:

www.oreilly.com/catalog

select the book, and follow the "Examples" link.

2. Register your O'Reilly books

Register your book at *register.oreilly.com*

Why register your books?
Once you've registered your O'Reilly books you can:

- Win O'Reilly books, T-shirts or discount coupons in our monthly drawing.
- Get special offers available only to registered O'Reilly customers.
- Get catalogs announcing new books (US and UK only).
- Get email notification of new editions of the O'Reilly books you own.

3. Join our email lists

Sign up to get topic-specific email announcements of new books and conferences, special offers, and O'Reilly Network technology newsletters at:

elists.oreilly.com

It's easy to customize your free elists subscription so you'll get exactly the O'Reilly news you want.

4. Get the latest news, tips, and tools

www.oreilly.com

- "Top 100 Sites on the Web"—PC Magazine
- CIO Magazine's Web Business 50 Awards

Our web site contains a library of comprehensive product information (including book excerpts and tables of contents), downloadable software, background articles, interviews with technology leaders, links to relevant sites, book cover art, and more.

5. Work for O'Reilly

Check out our web site for current employment opportunities:

jobs.oreilly.com

6. Contact us

O'Reilly & Associates
1005 Gravenstein Hwy North
Sebastopol, CA 95472 USA

TEL: 707-827-7000 or 800-998-9938
      (6am to 5pm PST)

FAX: 707-829-0104

order@oreilly.com
For answers to problems regarding your order or our products. To place a book order online, visit:

www.oreilly.com/order_new

catalog@oreilly.com
To request a copy of our latest catalog.

booktech@oreilly.com
For book content technical questions or corrections.

corporate@oreilly.com
For educational, library, government, and corporate sales.

proposals@oreilly.com
To submit new book proposals to our editors and product managers.

international@oreilly.com
For information about our international distributors or translation queries. For a list of our distributors outside of North America check out:

international.oreilly.com/distributors.html

adoption@oreilly.com
For information about academic use of O'Reilly books, visit:

academic.oreilly.com

O'REILLY®

Our books are available at most retail and online bookstores.
To order direct: 1-800-998-9938 • order@oreilly.com • www.oreilly.com
Online editions of most O'Reilly titles are available by subscription at *safari.oreilly.com*